The Rule of St Basil in Latin and English

The Rule of St Basil
in Latin and English

A Revised Critical Edition

Translated by
Anna M. Silvas

A Michael Glazier Book

LITURGICAL PRESS
Collegeville, Minnesota

www.litpress.org

A Michael Glazier Book published by Liturgical Press

Cover design by Jodi Hendrickson. Cover image: Wikipedia.

The Latin text of the *Regula Basilii* is keyed from *Basili Regula—A Rufino Latine Versa*, ed. Klaus Zelzer, *Corpus Scriptorum Ecclesiasticorum Latinorum*, vol. 86 (Vienna: Hoelder-Pichler-Tempsky, 1986). Used by permission of the Austrian Academy of Sciences.

Scripture has been translated by the author directly from Rufinus's text.

1	2	3	4	5	6	7	8	9

Library of Congress Cataloging-in-Publication Data

Basil, Saint, Bishop of Caesarea, approximately 329–379.
    The Rule of St Basil in Latin and English : a revised critical edition / Anna M. Silvas.
        pages   cm
    "A Michael Glazier book."
    Includes bibliographical references.
    ISBN 978-0-8146-8212-8 — ISBN 978-0-8146-8237-1 (e-book)
        1. Basil, Saint, Bishop of Caesarea, approximately 329–379. Regula.
    2. Orthodox Eastern monasticism and religious orders—Rules.   I. Silvas, Anna, translator.   II. Title.   III. Title: Rule of Basil.

BX386.2.L3   2013
255'.81—dc23
                                                              2012050879

In memory of Sven Lundström (1914–2007),
eminent Swedish Latinist and scholar

Contents

Acknowledgments   ix

Introduction   1

Regula Basilii   44

The Rule of Basil   45

APPENDIX 1:
Comparative Table of Recensions   291

APPENDIX 2:
Three Extra Pieces from the *Questions of the Brothers*   299

APPENDIX 3:
Index of Scriptural Citations and Allusions in the *Regula Basilii*   303

Bibliography   309

Acknowledgments

It is a glad duty of gratitude to acknowledge here those whose help has been instrumental in the furtherance of this book: first of all my university, the University of New England, and the Australian Research Council for funding the research project of which this book is part outcome; the Österreichische Akademie der Wissenshaften, holder of the copyright of Zelzer's critical edition of the *Regula Basili*, for their gracious permission to make use of the Latin text; Klaus Zelzer himself for his expression of good will; the family of the late Sven Lundström, both for their good will and for their permission to reproduce the stemma diagram from Lundström's book; Greg Horsley, Peter Flood, Heiko Daniel, and other academic colleagues whose personal support has been invaluable; Hans Christoffersen and the staff of Liturgical Press for their prompt and professional care in publication. Many thanks to you all.

Anna M Silvas
The University of New England
NSW Australia
Ash Wednesday, 13 February 2013

The site of Basil's ascetic retreat (AD 358–362) and earlier of Naucratius' and Chrysaphius' retreat (c. 351–356) as reconnoitred, identified, and photographed by the author on 17 March 2006. The view is to the south southwest. It is situated in mountainous gorge country, just after the confluence of the Rivers Lycus and Iris, heading north to the Black Sea. Here is a small sloping plane, cut off on all sides except for narrow access by foot at the top of the ridge above. The river Iris (very turbulent in the early spring) surrounds it almost on three sides. Annisa (Uluköy), the family villa where Emmelia and Macrina lived, is about eight kilometers distant, on the other side of the ridge, in the direction of the top right hand. See the report, Anna M. Silvas, "In Quest of Basil's Retreat: An Expedition to Ancient Pontus," *Antichthon* 41 (2007): 73–95.

Introduction

The idea of the present volume came partly from *RB 1980*.[1] In that volume the editors and commentators availed themselves of the critical Latin text already established by Jean Neufville for the *Sources Chrétiennes* series, volumes 181–186 (1971–72), endeavouring to distil and convey academic scholarship to a less specialized audience.

The subject of this book is itself one of the major sources of the *Rule of Benedict* (RB), namely, the 'Rule of our Holy Father Basil' recommended to zealous monks in RB 73.4. The *Regula Basilii* (RBas) is St Basil the Great's *Small Asketikon* as translated into Latin by Rufinus of Aquileia in AD 397.

The choice of a Latin text for the RBas, however, was a little more problematic than that faced by the editors of *RB 1980*. The first and only truly critical edition is *Basili Regula—A Rufino Latine Versa*.[2] Two new tranches of critical awareness, however, suggest an updating of Zelzer's text. First is the study of the transmission of the *Regula Basilii* by Sven Lundström, tentatively at first in his review of Zelzer's edition published in *Gnomon* 60 (Munich 1988), 587–90, and then very forensically indeed in a monograph, *Die Überlieferung der lateinischen Basiliusregel*.[3]

Second, there is the study of the Syriac translation of the *Small Asketikon*, the title of which is ܕܐܚ̈ܐ ܫܘ̈ܐܠܐ, *Quaestiones Fratrum* ('QF') = *Questions of the Brothers*. In fact, the present author has examined the QF from the manuscripts and is concurrently publishing its first critical edition.

---

[1] *RB 1980: The Rule of Saint Benedict in Latin and English with Notes*, ed. Timothy Fry, et al. (Collegeville, MN: Liturgical Press, 1981).

[2] *Basili Regula—A Rufino Latine Versa*, ed. Klaus Zelzer, CSEL 86 (Vienna: Hölder-Pichler-Tempsky, 1986).

[3] *Die Überlieferung der lateinischen Basiliusregel*, Acta Universitatis Upsaliensis, *Studia Latina Upsaliensia* 21 (Uppsala: Academia Upsaliensis, 1989).

The present volume will therefore present an updated version of Zelzer's Latin text, emended in the light of Lundström's advice and as generally confirmed by the Syriac text, together with an annotated English translation. It is in effect a new Latin edition, but assuming and entirely referring back to the work accomplished by Zelzer. Philological specialists will certainly need to continue to use Zelzer. The notes to the Latin text here largely concern justifications of changes to Zelzer's Latin text, and two cases in which Lundström's emendments have not been admitted.

The primary interest of this volume is in the *Regula Basilii* as a text in its own right, and not merely as a tool of access to a lost Greek original, however important a goal that may be. The aim of the author has been to mediate somewhat between the rigours of academic research on the one hand and the interests of an intelligent non-specialist readership on the other hand. Ultimately the hope is that when the Syriac edition and translation is published even readers without all the languages may be able to make their own comparisons, up to a point.

Before proceeding to textual matters, let us first consider the origin of the *Small Asketikon* itself. It begins with a person, Basil of Caesarea, and on the familial, ecclesiastical, theological, and historical ground that informed his vocation in the Christian church.

Basil of Caesarea

Basil of Caesarea (AD 329–378), called 'the Great' by later generations, was very possibly the first non-martyr accorded the cult of a saint in the Christian tradition.[4] He was the second child and eldest son of a tenaciously Christian and aristocratic family of Pontus in Eastern Anatolia, south of the Black Sea. His mother, Emmelia, came from a family in Cappadocia to the south. His father, Basil Senior, was a rhetorician and advocate in the city of Neocaesarea, metropolis of Pontus Polemoniacus. Sts Emmelia and Basil the elder are recognized with a feast day in the Greek church. Amid contemporary efforts to promote Christian family life and the possibilities of married holiness, the retrieval of this husband and wife team from the early church for wider recognition in the church Catholic would seem an obvious recourse.

---

[4] To judge from the timing and intent of St Gregory of Nyssa's encomium on his brother, *In Basilium Fratrem*, in *Gregorii Nysseni Opera* 10.1, 109–34, written in 381. Gregory's aim was to promote January 1 as his brother's memorial day. He proposed that his exceptional holiness of life merited this formal recognition by arguing that Basil's life and virtues were in every way the equal of those of the prophets and martyrs.

As eminent as the younger Basil became, he was but one of several remarkable siblings. The firstborn was St Macrina the Younger, the spearhead in the family of zeal for the ascetic life and the subject of one of the greatest biographies of the patristic era, written by her brother Gregory. The third-born child and second son of the family was Naucratius, the first to follow his sister's example in a life of ascetic retirement from the world. The third son was no less than St Gregory of Nyssa, who became a great speculative theologian and church father in his own right. Another daughter, Theosebia, was highly praised by Gregory Nazianzen as her brother's companion and a leader among Christian women. Finally, the last-born, St Peter II of Sebasteia, was a monastic father in his own right who became metropolitan of Sebasteia in Armenia Minor.

The Christian antecedents of the family too are notable. Basil's paternal grandmother was St Macrina the Elder. She and her husband had suffered confiscation and outlaw status for seven years during the last savage persecution of Christians in the Roman east by Maximin Daia in the early fourth century. This Macrina was a great champion of the traditions of the church of Neocaesarea, which had been founded by St Gregory Thaumaurgus (ca. 213–ca. 270), disciple and panegyrist of the seminal Christian thinker of Alexandria, Origen (ca. 185–253). A moderate, not uncritical Origenism was part of the family's Christian intellectual culture. On the other side of the family, Basil's maternal great-grandfather had died a Christian martyr in the Decian persecutions in the mid-third century.[5] The memory of martyrs and confessors of the faith ran deep in this family.

During the 330s and 340s, while resident in Neocaesarea, Basil's family came to know and befriend a controversial figure, Eustathius of Sebasteia (ca. 300–379), leader of an unsettling ascetic movement then making its influence felt across northern Anatolia from Constantinople to Armenia. The exaggerations and disorders of this movement were the object of censures in a spate of church councils. Eustathius himself seems to have taken note and modified his approach, as he continued his association with the family throughout the 350s and 360s.

Having begun the higher curriculum with his own father (who died ca. 345) as teacher, Basil went on to pursue the best classical Greek

---

[5] Most of these details can be found in Gregory Nazianzen's Oration 43, his eulogy on Basil, which in its expanded and published form became a lengthy biography. See Leo P. McCauley, et al., trans., "On St. Basil the Great," 27–99 in *Funeral Orations by Saint Gregory Nazianzen and Saint Ambrose,* Fathers of the Church 22 (Washington, DC: CUA Press, 1953, repr. with corrections 1968). Basil's family history is in chapters 5–8, pp. 30–35.

education then available, first at Caesarea in Cappadocia, then in Constantinople (349), followed by some five years in Athens under such masters as Himerios and Prohairesios.[6] There his dearest companion was Gregory of Nazianzus from Cappadocia, who also went on to gain lasting renown as a Christian orator, being acclaimed as 'the Theologian' and studied as a model of Greek style for many centuries to come.

In 356 Basil suddenly returned from Athens, very possibly in response to a family tragedy. His brother Naucratius had been living an ascetic life for some five years in a hidden retreat he had discovered by the river Iris in the mountain gorge country, about 8 kilometers from the family villa at Annisa. But early in the spring of that year Naucratius, while fishing in the river, died in a sudden onrush of waters. Basil spent a term teaching rhetoric in Caesarea of Cappadocia, but on his return home to Annisa in Pontus, his elder sister Macrina brusquely challenged him concerning his earlier intention of pursuing the ascetic life, a life of maximum dedication to the Christian ideal, including the choice of celibacy. Most of these details we learn from Gregory of Nyssa's *Life of Macrina*, where he says memorably of Macrina and Basil:

> He was at that time excessively puffed up with the thought of his own eloquence and was disdainful of local dignities, since in his own inflated opinion he surpassed all the leading luminaries. She, however, took him in hand and drew him with such speed towards the goal of philosophy that he withdrew from the worldly show and despised the applause to be gained through eloquence, and went over of his own accord to the life where one toils even with one's own hands, providing for himself through perfect renunciation a life that would lead without impediment to virtue.[7]

Thus, thanks to his sister's intervention, Basil did not continue to pursue the same way of life as his father, that of the Christian profes-

---

[6] For an excellent study of Basil's intellectual formation and his attitude to Greek *paideia*, see Philip Rousseau, *Basil of Caesarea* (Berkeley: University of California Press, 1994), 27–60. Basil synthesises his own ideas on the use of classical Hellenism in the education of Christian youths in his *Pros tous Neous*, written for the benefit of nephews. It became a great favourite in the Renaissance, being taken as a classic statement of Christian humanism. For text and translation see Roy J. Deferrari, trans., *Saint Basil—The Letters*, 4 vols., LCL (Cambridge, MA.: Harvard University Press, 1926, 1928, 1930, 1934), 365–435. For analysis see Ann Moffat, "The Occasion of St Basil's *Address to Young Men*," *Antichthon* 6 (1972): 74–86.

[7] Anna M. Silvas, trans., *Macrina the Younger, Philosopher of God* (Turnhout: Brepols, 2007), 117. See also Pierre Maraval, ed. and trans., *Grégoire de Nysse: La Vie de Sainte Macrine*, SC 178 (Paris: Cerf, 1971), with this passage on p. 162.

sional man and landed aristocrat. In the year 358 he committed himself to 'philosophy', i.e., the celibate, dedicated ascetic life, in what was evidently the same retreat Naucratius had vacated by his death.

In the 360s and 370s Basil gained a large and lasting influence in the churches of central and eastern Anatolia and Syria. In terms of the universal church his greatest work was to give coherence and leadership to what is called the Neo-Nicene movement. The Christian churches had been tormented for much of the fourth century by the Arian controversy. In a nutshell, Arianism was the attempt to recalibrate *the name of the Father and the Son and the Holy Spirit* of Matthew 28:19 to a sophisticated Neo-Platonist emanationism. In this view only the Father was truly God, while the *Logos,* or the Son emanating from the Father, was a created entity, however lofty, while the Spirit too was created, but on the next rung down from the *Logos.* In essence, the bar between the uncreated and the created was set between the Father on the one hand and all else on the other, the Logos and the Spirit included. At stake was Christian identity: was Christian faith and doctrine commensurable with the latest and best in philosophical thinking, or was there something in its genius inalienably deriving from other sources and irreducible to the spirit of the times?

Beginning in the late 360s, in league with such leaders as Meletius of Antioch and Eusebius of Samosata, Basil forged a theological alliance based on a clarification of the terms οὐσία (substance, essence, related to nature) and ὑπόστασις (individual subsistence, related to person). Earlier the semantics of these terms had been somewhat confused. This had led not a few church leaders to be suspicious of the definition of the Nicene Council in 325 that the Son is ὁμοούσιος ('consubstantial', or 'of the same essence') with the Father, if this could be taken to mean *identity of subsistence* or *person* with the Father. Once the distinction between three divine *hypostases* was soundly articulated it became easier to argue the legitimacy and the authority of the Nicene definition. Despite the intimidations of the Arian Emperor Valens, the Neo-Nicene initiative gathered momentum under Basil's captaincy throughout the 370s till it eventually triumphed under a new and staunchly Nicene Emperor, Theodosius I, in the Council of Constantinople in 381.[8] This council reaffirmed the

---

[8] It commenced with Basil's friend, Gregory of Nazianzus, who was then the bishop-designate of Constantinople. He had been instrumental in rallying the Neo-Nicene orthodox in the imperial city. For a general survey of the Arian controversy culminating at this council, see Henry Chadwick, *The Early Church,* rev. ed. (London: Penguin, 1993), 133–51, and Jean Daniélou and Henri Marrou, *The Christian Centuries: The First Six Hundred Years* (London: Darton Longman and Todd, 1964), 255–68. For a more

central Christian intuition, that the divine absolute is both inalienably *one*, and also mysteriously and inalienably *three*, and hence personal, and hence a communion of love, with immense consequences for one's understanding of the constitution of the universe and of the human being. The reaffirmation of orthodox Christian belief insisted that the bar between the uncreated and the created lay between the *Father, the Son, and the Holy Spirit* on the one hand, and all else, from angels to rocks, on the other.

Scarcely less important than Basil's labours in theological exposition and church politics was his role as a leader of ascetic reform and a father of monks. Indeed, it was the mainspring of his theological and ecclesial vocation, for at the heart of all his activity Basil was always the ascetic and man of prayer. There was something awesome in his single-minded seeking of God. At the beginning of his commitment to the ascetic life in the late 350s he had become deeply depressed at the terrible mess of the contemporary church.[9] He conceived a solution: the promotion of small communities in which could be realized a full and uncompromised dedication to the Christian vocation, the life of obedience to *all* the commandments. The experience of the years was to teach him that true doctrine always needed to be accompanied by true *praxis*, and *praxis* by true doctrine, that one without the other tilted toward a failure of the Christian life, and the failure of the church.[10]

Showing an outstanding capacity for leadership, Basil addressed himself to the rather unruly and idiosyncratic ascetic movement of northern Anatolia, which till then had looked to the leadership of Eustathius of Sebasteia. It is my contention, argued in several places, that Macrina and her direction of the community at Annisa in the late 350s and early 360s was a determinative influence in the early maturing of Basil's conception of the Christian ascetic community. Basil was never Macrina's spiritual father. Rather, in more than one sense she was his spiritual mother, as indeed she was the spiritual mother of her own mother. All the other

---

detailed study of the later phase and the pivotal role of the Cappadocian Fathers, see Thomas A. Kopecek, *A History of Neo-Arianism* (Cambridge, MA: Harvard University Press, 1979).

[9] He tells of his dismay at the contemporary chaos in the church, his conclusions about the cause of it, and what to do about it in *De Iudicio Dei*, PG 31.653–676. See the translation by W. K. Lowther Clarke, *The Ascetic Works of St Basil* (London: SPCK, 1925), 77–89.

[10] The corollary with Socrates/Plato was that the dialectical quest for truth on the intellectual plane could not be validly engaged without an accompanying commitment to the quest for virtue on the moral plane.

siblings looked up to Basil as their 'father', but not his elder sister. While Basil was away in Cappadocia from ca. 362–363 Peter, the youngest of the siblings, reached a 'vowable' age of about 17 years. In taking this step Peter resolved not to depart to the secluded retreat in the mountain gorge country, but to stay at the Annisa villa. In this way the family household reached its final transformation into a dedicated ascetic community, comprising a house of virgins, a house for dedicated men or monks, a house for children, and a house for guests, with a common 'house of prayer'. When Basil returned north in 363, this final 'monastic' transformation of Annisa is what confronted him.

Thus between the years 358 and 363 Basil's ascetic thinking underwent a considerable shift from the earlier freelance life of male ascetics to a comprehensively communitarian conception of the Christian ascetic life. During his mission in Pontus, 363–365, he preached and taught a well-ordered cenobitic (from κοίνος βίος, 'common life') monasticism, inserted into, exemplary for, and at the service of the wider church.[11] This conception of Christian community went hand in glove with the theology of communion and order in the Holy Trinity. The divine summons of the human person to communion was reflected in the very constitution of humanity, made in God's image as a social being. This call to communion was realized and refracted in the church at large and in each local community, and in a very concrete fashion in the Christian ascetic community. Thus Basil's ascetic and moral teaching was based on a well-thought-through anthropology and pedagogy, an understanding of what human beings were created to be and how they might be best helped to achieve their ultimate calling. One of the strongest arguments in Christian literature against the solitary life is found in the *Small Asketikon* 3.35. Meditating the scene portrayed in John 13:5, Basil targets the ascetic individualist with the immortal words: 'Whose feet will you wash? For whom will you perform the duties of care?'

Basil worked for the reform of the ascetic movement by means of his preaching tours through the 360s and 370s. The corpus of his ascetic writings, above all his *Asketikon*, is the fruit of this mission.[12] This work

---

[11] See my book, *The Asketikon of St Basil the Great* (Oxford: Oxford University Press, 2005). Chapter 4, "The Emergence of Monasticism in Fourth-Century Anatolia," 51–101, traces in detail the development of Basil's thinking and practice of the Christian monastic life.

[12] The textual transmission of Basil's ascetic works is an exceedingly complex and ramified affair involving analyses of manuscripts in Greek, Latin, Syriac, Armenian, Arabic, Georgian, and Slavonic, et al. It has received magisterial attention by Paul J.

originated during conferences in which the ascetics would ask Basil how they might live the Gospel life with greater accuracy under this aspect or that. Their questions and Basil's replies were taken down by tachygraphers and eventually worked up as a single book. Basil himself describes the procedure in his Letter 223, addressed to Eustathius in about 375, by which time a serious falling out over doctrinal issues had taken place between them. He asks Eustathius:

> Ask yourself: how often did you come to look in on us at the abode by the river Iris (ποσάκις ἐμάς ἐπεσκέψω ἐπὶ τῆς μονῆς τῆς ἐπι τῷ ῎Ιριδι ποταμῷ), when, moreover, our most divinely beloved brother Gregory was present with me, achieving the same purpose in life as myself? . . . And how many days did we spend in the village on the opposite side, at my mother's (πόσας δε ἡμέρας ἐπὶ τῆς ἀντίπεραν κώμης, παρὰ τῇ μητρί μου), where we lived as friends among friends, with conversation astir among us day and night? . . . And all the time were your tachygraphers not present with me as I dictated matters against the heresy? Were the most faithful of your disciples not in my presence the whole time? While visiting the brotherhoods (ἀδελφότητας) and spending whole nights with them in the prayers, always speaking and hearing things concerning God without contention, did I not furnish precise proofs of my own mind?[13]

The first edition, the *Small Asketikon*, represents the matured conception of the Christian community Basil had developed between his own first beginnings as an ascetic in ca. 357/358 and his second, permanent return to Caesarea in 365, as priest and assistant to Bishop Eusebius. It seems very likely that he finished editing the work in about 366 and sent it back to Pontus as a legacy to those he had left behind.

Basil continued to make pastoral visits to ascetic communities during the late 360s and throughout his years as Bishop of Caesarea (370–378). Further question and answer sessions were recorded and incorporated into the text. Thus the *Asketikon* was a 'work in progress' as long as Basil lived and was able to devote strength to visiting and encouraging the ascetic communities. By the time he died in September 378 the revised form of the *Asketikon*, called the *Great Asketikon*, had expanded to more than twice the size of the original edition and was itself already extant

---

Fedwick. See especially his *Bibliotheca Basiliana Universalis* 3: *Ascetica*, CCSG (Turnhout: Brepols, 1997). Analyses of the *Asketikon* transmission occupies pp. 1–698.

[13] Basil, "Letter 223," in *Correspondance*, vol. 3, ed. and trans. Yves Courtonne, 2d ed. (Paris: Les Belles Lettres, 2003), 14; English in Deferrari, *Letters* 3, 302–5.

in two or three versions. A major reordering of the *Great Asketikon* along thematic lines—the 'Pontic Recension'—may have been carried out as early as Basil's last visit to Annisa in 376. It is my contention that Peter, Basil's youngest brother and both priest and male superior there, may have had a significant role as the editor of this 'Pontic Recension' under his brother's eye.

Rufinus of Aquileia

Basil's influence as a monastic father also left its mark in the life of the Western church. His great mediator to the west was Rufinus of Aquileia (ca. 354–411).[14] From about 370 to 397 Rufinus was a member of a Latin monastery on the Mount of Olives in Jerusalem. It had been founded by Antonia Melania (St Melania the Elder). The structure of Melania's monastery seems to have been very like the conception of the *adelphotes* in Basil's *Asketikon*: separate houses for women, for men, for guests, etc., all using a common church and all conceived as part of the one Christian ascetic community. In about the year 378 Rufinus journeyed north to Syria on a book–hunting expedition. He visited Antioch and even reached as far as Edessa, the heartland of Syriac-speaking Christianity. Since Basil himself had visited upper Syria, and certainly Samosata, Rufinus only missed him in these regions by a few years.[15] It is very tempting to think that during this journey Rufinus may have acquired his copy of the Greek *Small Asketikon* and that he and Melania used it thereafter in the governance of their community.[16] However, it must be said that the Greek text used by the Syriac translator shows such distinctive features, to be discussed below, that it does not seem to have been quite the same version

---

[14] On the life and chronology of Rufinus see Francis X. Murphy, *Rufinus of Aquileia (345–411): His Life and Works*, (Washington, DC: CUA Press, 1945), and Giorio Fedalto, "Rufino di Concordia. Elementi di una biografia," *Antichità Altoadriatiche* 39 (1992): 19–44. Useful summary studies are E. C. Brooks, "The Translation Techniques of Rufinus of Aquileia (343–411)," *Studia Patristica* 18 (1982): 357–64, and Monica Wagner, *Rufinus the Translator*, (Washington, DC: CUA Press, 1945), especially chapter 3, "Adaptation Procedures," 29–64.

[15] According to Benoît Gain, Basil visited Samosata more than once: *L'Église de Cappadoce au IVe Siècle d'après la correspondance de Basile de Césarée 330–379*, OCA 225 (Rome: Pontifical Oriental Institute, 1985); Appendix 2: "Voyages de Basile," 393–96. In his letter 145 to Eusebius, written in 373, Basil speaks of his "returning from Syria."

[16] For a study of Rufinus's role as an intermediary see my "Edessa to Cassino: the Passage of Basil's *Asketikon* to the West," *Vigiliae Christianae* 56 (2002): 247–59. In that article I argued for a Syrian source of Rufinus's copy. Now I would be more cautious about such an assertion.

as used by Rufinus. Alternatively, Melania and Rufinus may have acquired their copy during its postal progress down to the monks in Egypt.[17] Basil himself had contact with monks on the Mount of Olives in the 370s, and this relationship may have gone back to the late 360s.[18] So here too is another possible point of access to the *Small Asketikon* in Palestine, and the most direct, from Basil himself. Alas, the Origenist controversy, sparked by Epiphanius of Salamis and fanned by Theophilus of Alexandria and Jerome of Bethlehem, caused fierce controversy in the church in Palestine in the 390s. The local church became too hot to contain both Jerome and Rufinus, and in 397 the latter returned to the west.

When Rufinus disembarked, probably in Puteoli or Naples, and was on his way up the *Via Appia* to Rome, he was very pleased to accept hospitality in a monastery at 'Pinetum', which appears to have been somewhere near Terracina on the Tyrrhenian coast. As Rufinus relates in his own prefatory letter, the superior there, Ursacius, after hearing Rufinus wax lyrical about Basil as a monastic father, begged him to translate for his monks this work of so renowned a Greek father. By acceding to this request Rufinus launched his career as a Latin translator of the Greek fathers that filled the remainder of his days. In his prefatory letter Rufinus refers to the document as the *Institutiones Basilii* (the 'Institutes of Basil'), though it soon became known as the *Regula Basilii* or Rule of Basil.

Rufinus expressed the hope that Basil's rule might become the standard for the monks of the West. It did not quite work out that way. Instead, this Latin Rule became part of a canon of monastic writings circulating

---

[17] A fragment of the Greek *Small Asketikon* from Egypt, preserved in the Ashmolean Museum Oxford, was recognized by Sever J. Voicu, "P. Antin. 111, un testimone ignorato delle *Eratopokriseis brevius tractatae* di Basilio," *Basil of Caesarea: Christian, Humanist, Ascetic*, ed. Paul Jonathan Fedwick (Toronto: PIMS, 1981), 565–70. Significantly, this fragment includes the equivalent of RBas 117 and 118, which do not appear in the QF, clearly implying a Greek text closer to that which lay before Rufinus. Fedwick, *BBV* 3, 3, also lists two other fragmentary traces of the Greek *Small Asketikon*, one originally from the Great Lavra, Mount Athos; the other from St Catherine's Monastery, Sinai.

[18] Basil certainly had connections with monks on the Mount of Olives in the 370s. The earliest letters from around 370/371 suggest the familiarity is already well-established, i.e., going back into the 360s. See Letter 258 to Epiphanius (a masterpiece of courteous irony), Deferrari, *Letters* 4, 38–39, and Letter 259, ibid., 46–49. See also the note on pp. 206–7. Basil's intermediaries with the monks on the Mount of Olives were Palladius and Innocent. This Palladius may have been the one who wrote to Athanasius (PG 26, 1167) bidding him counsel the monks in Caesarea to cease opposing Basil—apparently over Basil's "economy" in discussing the divinity of the Holy Spirit.

in southern Italy in the fifth and sixth centuries. Thus it was available in that time and in that region when the author of the sixth-century *Rule of Benedict* made use of it as one of his major sources. So it was not the *Rule of Basil*, but the *Rule of Benedict* that in the Carolingian era was made the canonical standard of Western monasticism. At the very end of the RB zealous monks, eager for something more, are sent to 'the rule of our Holy Father Basil'.[19] The discourse of the RB inherited much of the language and thought-world of Egyptian monasticism, particularly through the influence of the so-called 'Rule of the Master' and of St John Cassian's *Institutes* and *Conferences*. This desert tradition laid stress on individual endeavour and austere asceticism. It tended to esteem the anchorite or hermit as the ultimate ideal of the monk.

The influence of Basil, however, together with that of Augustine and others, acted on the author of the RB to qualify this anchoretically inspired heritage with a doctrine of the primacy of communion and of mutual love as the way of life of Christians, and of the necessity of a well-tested good order and a certain sense of moderation, all under the protection of a common obedience. Some of the most famous 'Benedictine' tags of the RB prove on closer inspection to derive from Basil.[20] When RB 1.12, in discussing four types of monks, describes cenobites— monks who live in a well-ordered community under a superior—as without doubt 'the strongest (or should we understand 'bravest'?) kind of monks', it very much conveys the mind of Basil, who spends his longest chapter, RBas 2, arguing just that.

The *Regula Basilii* as a document

Modern critical investigation of the text of the *Regula Basilii* begins with Jean Gribomont's major work, *Histoire du Texte des Ascétiques de Saint Basile*.[21] Up to that time it was generally assumed that the Latin version of the *Asketikon* had been Rufinus's heavy-handed précis of the much longer extant Greek version.[22] Acknowledging the prior work of

---

[19] RB 73.5. An accessible edition, in both Latin and English with copious historical studies and notes, is *RB 1980* (see above).

[20] E.g., the Benedictine stress on the reverent handling of all material things, based on RB 31.10: *He will regard all utensils and the goods of the monastery as sacred vessels of the altar.* This essentially derives from the *Small Asketikon / Regula Basili* 103.

[21] Jean Gribomont, *Histoire du Texte des Ascétiques de Saint Basile* (Louvain: Muséon, 1953).

[22] An example of the older view: "What he, Rufinus, actually did was to combine the two sets of questions and answers (the 55 *regulae fusius* and the 313 *brevius tractatae*)

Ferdinand Laun,[23] Gribomont confirmed and demonstrated extensively the existence of the *Asketikon* in two versions: an earlier and shorter one called the *Small Asketikon*, and a later revised and much augmented version, the *Great Asketikon*. The integral Greek text of the *Small Asketikon* has not survived,[24] though of course much of it remains embedded in Basil's later revisions.

Gribomont highlighted the information supplied by the Scholiast.[25] This erudite editor of Basil's *Great Asketikon* in the late fifth or early sixth century told of a shorter earlier version of Basil's *Asketikon* and how a subsequent longer version came to be produced. Finally, Gribomont furnished conclusive proof of the prior existence of the *Small Asketikon* with a study of the content of the Syriac translation, which is based on essentially the same shorter text as Rufinus's translation. Gribomont concludes: 'In the collection of these Questions, Rufinus and the Syriac translator knew one and the same shorter text, the existence of which was attested in the sixth century by the Vulgate Scholiast. The prior existence of this recension, affirmed by the Scholiast, deserves to be admitted'.[26]

Study of the transmission of Basil's *ascetica* and other writings culminated in what today must be considered the first port of call for all investigators in this field. This is Paul J. Fedwick's multi-volume *Bibliotheca Basiliana Vniversalis*, especially, in our case, volume 3: *Ascetica*. Analysis of the textual transmission of Basil's *Asketikon* in its several versions and editions, and the libraries preserving the manuscripts, covers nearly six hundred pages, 1–585. The *Small Asketikon* (Fedwick's 'Asketikon 1') is surveyed on pp. 1–86; within those pages the report on Rufinus's Latin translation ('Asketikon 1r') is found on pp. 4–43, and that on the Syriac version ('Asketikon 1s') on pp. 43–46.

---

that made up the Rules of Basil into 203 questions and answers, rearranging the order, combining several of the originally separate sections, and rather freely translating the whole." Murphy, *Rufinus of Aquileia*, 91.

[23] Ferdinand Laun, "Die beiden Regeln des Basilius, ihre Echtheit und Entstehung," *Zeitschrift für Kirchengeschichte* 44 (1925): 1–61, acknowledged by Gribomont, *Histoire du Texte*, 1, 2, 193 n. 1, 207, 237 n. 2, 252–53.

[24] Except for three fragments, noted in Fedwick, *BBV* 3: *Ascetica*, 2–4.

[25] On the Scholiast see Gribomont, *Histoire*, 151–57, and Anna M. Silvas, *The Asketikon of St Basil the Great* (Oxford: Oxford University Press, 2005), 4–8. He was the *Endredaktor* of what Gribomont calls the Vulgate recension of the *Great Asketikon*, later designated "Asketikon 3" by Fedwick (on whom more below), and what I prefer to call the Pontic Recension.

[26] Gribomont, *Histoire*, 238 (present author's translation).

Towards a critical text of the *Regula Basilii*

We now narrow our focus to 'Asketikon 1r', the *Regula Basilii*. But first we should clarify the spelling of the Latin title. It long puzzled me just what the genitive of Basil's name in Latin, 'Basilius', ought to be. Zelzer renders it as 'Basili'. But then, the genitive of 'Gregorius' is posted as 'Gregorii' in the title *Gregorii Nysseni Opera*. Finally, I questioned Professor Benoît Gain about it, and record gratefully the following advice:

> 1. According to a strict philology, the genitive is in –i; for that of nouns (i.e., substantives) in –ius, it is in –i until the era of Augustus. For adjectives, the transformation seems to have taken place somewhat earlier: already in Lucretius, there is *patrii* in I.832, and several other examples. From then on manuscripts present a genitive in –ii, even the oldest manuscript of the *Regula Basilii*, namely Sessorianus 55, from the second half of the sixth century (see the apparatus in K. Zelzer, p. 3).
>
> 2. Zelzer has adopted the orthography of the classical era, the 'Ciceronian' so to speak. It is a learned affectation. Perhaps he took example from the writings of Ambrose? I do not know, it would have to be verified from the critical editions of St Ambrose, which I do not have to hand. Perhaps, even without doubt, not one example of 'Basili' as the latinised form of the Greek name of a man (*Basileios* in Greek), and hence of our Basil, has been preserved from the fourth century.
>
> In conclusion, in order to avoid shafts from Zelzer, you could justify the orthography *Basilii* by saying that you have adopted the orthography in use at the time of Rufinus, which is not the classical orthography.
>
> What I have been able to say is after verification from Alfred Ernout, *Morphologie historique du latin*, 3ᵉ édition revue et corrigée, Paris, 1953, pp. 28–29. In France, that is the Bible of the student of Latin.[27]

In this book 'Basilii' it shall be then, and hence: *Regula Basilii*. A brief sketch of the course of its appearance in editions[28] will show us the long trail of the centuries that lead towards a truly critical edition.

We begin with the twelfth century, which saw the last flourishing of 'the Benedictine Centuries' under such leaders as Bl Peter the Venerable,

---

[27] Author's translation from French.
[28] See the survey in Gribomont, *Histoire,* 323–32, and the comprehensive gazette of editions in Fedwick, *BBV* 3, 521–85.

St Bernard of Clairvaux, and St Hildegard of Bingen. Early in the following century, in November 1215, the fourth Lateran, the 'Great Council'
as it was called, was held under Pope Innocent III. In its thirteenth canon
a brave attempt was made to curb the proliferation of new religious
orders or congregations, a phenomenon destined for a long career in the
western church.[29] Though these are not mentioned individually, henceforth there were to be only four monastic rules accepted in practice: the
Rule of Benedict, the Rule of Basil (the RBas)[30], the Rule of Augustine[31],
and the Rule of Francis, approved by Pope Innocent in principle as re-
cently as 1209.[32]

---

[29] Concilium Lateranense IV, Capitulum XIII: *Ne nimia religionum diversitas gravem
in ecclesia Dei confusionem inducat, firmiter prohibemus, ne quis de cetero novam religionem
inveniat: sed quicumque voluerit ad religionem converti, unam de approbatis assumat. Similiter qui voluerit religiosam domum fundare de novo, regulam & institutionem accipiat de
religionibus approbatis.* . . . . Latin text from Giovan Domenico Mansi , ed., *Sacrorum
Conciliorum nova et amplissima collectio*, vol. 22, cols. 1002–3 (Paris: Hubert Welter, 1901;
repr. 1960): "Lest too great a variety lead to confusion in the Church of God, we firmly
forbid that anyone henceforth found a new religious order: but if anyone wants to
be converted to a religious life let him take on one of (its forms already) approved.
Likewise whoever wants to found a new religious house, let him accept a rule and
constitution from the religious orders that are approved."

[30] The estrangement of Eastern and Western Christendom had lately been reinforced
by the notorious 1204 sack of Constantinople by the Fourth Crusade. Thus Eastern
monks who looked to Basil as their father (or really, preeminent among their fathers)
and were in communion with Rome would have been reduced at this time to those
of the monastery of Grottaferrata near Rome and monasteries of Sicily and southern
Italy, all heirs to the cenobitic reforms of St Theodore Studite. The idea of an "Order
of St Basil the Great" or congregations based on the Rule of Basil are post-Tridentine
developments.

[31] The sanction of this brief Rule reflects the status of the premier father in the
Western church. Its earliest appearance was in the collections of Rules in the pre-
Carolingian era. RM and RB quote it. The RA first came into its own in the post-
Carolingian period, being associated not with monasteries but with clerics in
community (canons). It first began to be used as a monastic rule proper by a variety
of institutes, including the Premonstratensians and the Knights Templar, in the twelfth
century. Its use escalated after the Great Council. The most important of the new
orders to adopt it was the Order of Preachers or Dominicans, because their constitutions came to be a model for the constitutions of other orders, even of the Franciscans
and Carmelites, who had their own primitive rules. See Raymond Canning and
Tarcisius Jan Van Bavel, *The Rule of Augustine* (London: Darton Longman and Todd,
1984), 3–6.

[32] St Francis's "Rule" had been approved in germ by Innocent in 1209 but was still
in the process of articulation until Francis's last years. The Rule of Albert received
initial approval by Honorius III in 1226, since it had been composed at Acre by the
Latin Patriarch of Jerusalem between 1206 and 1214. See Joachim Smet, "Carmelites,"
New Catholic Encyclopedia, vol. 3 (Washington, DC: CUA Press, 1967), 118. The Rule

The first appearance of the RBas in print reflects this canonical legis-
lation.[33] On 13 April 1500 a collection of the Rules of Benedict, Basil,
Augustine, and Francis, compiled by Jean François Brixianus, a Benedictine monk of the Congregation of St Justina of Padua, was published
at Venice by Jean Émeric de Spire. The manuscripts used were not indicated, nor had they been identified to the time of Fedwick's *BBV* 3. This
first edition was subsequently republished at Rouen in 1510, Paris in
1514 and 1519, and Cologne in 1575. The same text was borrowed un-
changed, although with chapters divided differently, in an edition of
Sancti Basili Opera, published at Paris by Josse Bade and republished at
Paris in 1523, Cologne in 1523 and 1531, Zurich in 1588, and Geneva in
1619 and 1669.

The Cistercian scholar François Bivar (Franciscus Bivarius) was the
first editor of the RBas to pay some critical attention to his sources. He
prepared a new edition using H, and noted variants from a manuscript
(not identified but very like Brixianus's text) he attributed to Smaragdus.
However, he died prematurely in 1634 so that his text did not appear till
1662, when it was published at Lyons by his confrère Thomas Gomez.

In 1661 Vitale Mascardus published at Rome the *Codex Regularum* of
St Benedict of Aniane in an edition prepared by Lucas Holste. As the basis
of his text Holste used a copy of a Cologne manuscript (*Hist. Archiv.* W. f.
231) made in 1643 for Fabio Chigi, papal nuncio in Cologne at the time.[34]
The Cologne manuscript itself was copied from a Trier manuscript, M.
This edition of the *Codex Regularum* was republished in Paris in 1663 and
in Augsburg in 1759. It was also the version used by Migne in 1851,
Patrologia Latina vol. 103, cols. 423–702. The RBas is found in cols. 483–
554; introductory material, including Rufinus's preface, is in cols. 483–86,
the text beginning in col. 487. Compared with M, Holste's edition showed
faulty readings, regrettable omissions, and a text left unintelligible in
places. But even the text of Benedict of Aniane (M) shows that the latter
had been collating, emending, and editing on his own account in the
eighth century,[35] for M itself was far from representative of the RBas text.
Zelzer says that 'this version of the text (M) was known to Benedict from

---

of Clare, drawing in part on those of Francis and Benedict, was approved at the urgent
insistence of the saint just before her death in 1253.

[33] See Gribomont, *Histoire*, 100–2.

[34] Chigi was Pope Alexander VII by the time of this printing in Rome and was
known for his fostering of scholarship and archival science.

[35] Gribomont, *Histoire*, 102, adduces the text-critical work of A. Boon, whose study
of the Rule of Pachomius is in the same collection.

his south-west Gallic home. That helps explain the Holste text, which ultimately goes back to M and which text version deviates strongly from the general transmission, as a consequence of the exceptional form of the south-Gallic/Spanish transmission'.[36]

Gribomont[37] made a couple of textual 'soundings': first, of the opening of Rufinus's preface, second, of RBas 8. He used S, L, C, D, two eleventh-century Monte Cassino manuscripts (#16, 17), the Venice edition of 1500, Bivar, and Holste. His judgement of Holste was: 'Holste's, nevertheless, is the best of the three editions . . . his text contains several literary improvements . . . with other late witnesses, he adapts his biblical text to that of the Vulgate . . . but is in general faithful'.[38] Zelzer in the meantime more thoroughly researched the matter and found he could not support Gribomont's relatively favourable assessment of Holste's edition.[39]

Zelzer's edition of the *Regula Basilii*

The first comprehensively critical edition of the *Regula Basilii* was published in 1986, i.e., Klaus Zelzer, *Basili Regula—A Rufino Latine Versa*.[40] Zelzer explains in his preface that his work was part of a long-term project to publish critical editions of the Latin monastic rules. His volume is the third in a series, following Rudolph Hanslik's edition of the *Rule of St Benedict* and Adalbert de Vogüé and Ferdinand Villegas's edition of the *Rule of Eugippius*.

In the account of his editorial work (pp. xxviii–xxix) Zelzer furnishes a list of sixty-five codices containing the text of the RBas. They date from the sixth to the fifteenth centuries. He appends a list of five codices mentioned in catalogues of manuscripts of the ninth and tenth centuries but that are now lost. For his edition Zelzer examined twenty of them and chose fourteen, ranging from the sixth to the eleventh centuries, for collation. The following is a list of his selection with abbreviated notes,[41] together with a note on the Holste edition.

---

[36] Klaus Zelzer, "Zur Überlieferung der Lateinischen Fassung der Basiliusregel," in idem, Überlieferungsgeschicht*liche Untersuchungen,* ed. Franz Paschke (Berlin: Akademie-Verlag, 1981), 634.

[37] Gribomont, *Histoire,* 103–5.

[38] Author's translation from French.

[39] Zelzer, "Zur Überlieferung," 635 n. 1.

[40] See n. 2 above.

[41] Zelzer's notes on the text may be found on pp. xvii–xxvii. See also Gribomont's notes, *Histoire,* 96–102, and Fedwick's notes, *BBV* 3, 15–33.

Codices and Edition collated by Zelzer

Of the following codices, only B and C, and in a qualified sense T, contain only the RBas. All other manuscripts consist of collections of monastic rules and other ascetical writings of interest to monks, of which the RBas is but one, albeit an important one.

B

Codex Mediolensis Ambrosius C. 26 sup. (Milan, Ambrosian Library), seventh century; in Anglo-Saxon majuscule script (and orthography) very like script from the monastery of Bobbio; corrected by later hands.

C

Codex Leninopolitanus F. v. I. 2,[42] formerly 'Corbeiensis', end of seventh, beginning of eighth century; uncial and semiuncial script very like script from Corbie abbey ca. 700; Merovingian orthography; together with E and S often preserves more the sparer, most authentic text.

E

Codex Parisiensis Bibl. Nat. lat. 12634 (Paris), late sixth century; in southern Italian uncial script. Passed through the abbeys of Corbie and S. Germain-des-Prés, whence to the National Library. This interesting and very old codex originally came from the same locale (Compania) and is almost contemporary with the composition of the RB, bearing witness to the same field of monastic reading as that underlying the RB. De Vogüé has plausibly connected the codex with Eugippius of Lucullanum, whose library was also the source of a transmission of Rufinus's translations.[43] Folios 9r-77v contain a collection of excerpts from the rules of Augustine, the Four Fathers, the Master, Basil, Pachomius, the works of Novatian, the Conferences and Institutes of Cassian, and Jerome's Letter 125. The ensemble is edited by de Vogüé and Ferdinand Villegas under the name *Regula Eugippi*.[44] It contains seventeen chapters of the RBas. Together with C and S, E it tends to preserve a sparer, more authentic text.

F

Fragmenta codicis Aurelianensis 192 (169) (Orléans), ff. 2–3, sixth/seventh century; in southern Gallic script; once of the abbey of St Benoît-sur-Loire, Fleury; mutilated condition; an inept later hand has 'corrected' with mistakes, e.g., 8.25 *vagos* (accusative) to *vagus*.

---

[42] I do not know whether the manuscript has been renamed following the reversion of Leningrad to its former name, St Petersburg, or returned to the manuscript's former name, "Corbeiensis."

[43] See Zelzer, "Zur Überlieferung," 5.

[44] It was published as volume 87 in the CSEL series, immediately following the *Regula Basili*.

G

Codex Sangallensis 926 (Sankt Gallen), pp. 2–226, ninth century; in Carolingian minuscule; written without doubt at the abbey; its collection of documents stems ultimately from Lerins and very close to LW, even deriving from a single copy (Zelzer 1980, 634); represents the most 'amplified' or augmented text.

H

Codex Londiniensis Musei Britannici Add. 30055 (London), ff. 142–194, tenth century; a collection of monastic rules, beautifully executed in Visigothic script with Visigothic orthography; it once belonged to the monastery of St Peter in Cardeña, diocese of Burgos, and was known as *Codex Caradignensis*, whence Dom Bivar borrowed it for his edition. It includes texts from the Iberian Fathers.

J

Codex Rotomagensis 728 (Rouen), ff. 1–50, tenth century. Once of the monastery of Jumièges; the order of chapters (which Zelzer gives) is in considerable disarray; Merovingian orthography.

L

Codex Lambacensis XXXI (Lambach), ff. 1–72, beginning of ninth century; a collection of Rules and monastic writings in Carolingian script very like that of the monastery of Münsterschwarzach; heavily corrected by later hands; composed of two parts, joined, it is thought, in the twelfth century. The earlier part is an extensive collection of monastic rules and writings deriving ultimately from Lerins and representing the most 'amplified' or augmented text of the RBas.

M

Codex Monacensis Bibl. Nat. Lat. 28118 (Munich), ninth century. Codex Regularum S. Benedicti Anianensis—St Benedict of Aniane's collection of monastic rules and of a dating contemporary with him. It is a huge collection, beginning with the RB; once of St Maximinus of Trier, written before the year 821 in the same monastery in which Codex Z was written, perhaps Indae (Kornelimünster). Transmitted from copy to copy, it is the ultimate source of Holste's printed edition. Zelzer (1980 p. 632) tested M against concurrences of the two oldest Italian manuscripts, E and S, and found that of all the codices containing the RBas, M had the widest divergence.

P

Codex Parisiensis Bibl. Nat. Lat. 12238 (Paris), ff.1–72, beginning of ninth century; once of St Germain-des-Prés; in southern Gallic script.

S

Codex Romanus Bibl. Nat Sessorianus 55 (Rome), second half of sixth
century. S, along with E, is the oldest surviving witness to the text. In
northern Italian semiuncial script; it was renovated in the eighth/ninth
century at the monastery of Nonantola (near Modena); folios 68 and 69
are in a pre-Carolingian minuscule; folios 169–176 are a palimpsest over
the natural history of Pliny the elder (at folio 177 RBas begins). Together
with C and E, S tends to preserve the sparer, most authentic text.

T

Codex Turonensis 615 (Tours), ninth century. This codex, containing only
the RBas, is the first part of a codex of monastic rules from the monastery
of Marmoutiers and was divided into three in Toulouse at the beginning
of the eighteenth century; Visigothic orthography.

W

Codex Guelferbytanus 4127 (Wolfenbüttel), ff. 81–118^v, eighth/ninth
century. Title in the first folio: *Codex of the monastery of the holy apostles Peter
and Paul in Wissenburg* (where it was written); its collection of writings
derives ultimately from Lerins; represents the most 'amplified' or augmented text.

Z

Codex Aurelianensis 233 (203) (Orléans), beginning of the ninth century.
Concordia Regularum S. Benedicti Anianensi, i.e., St Benedict of Aniane's
collection of monastic rules; once of the monastery of Fleury; see M; written before 821.

Hol.

Benedicti Aniansis Codex Regularum, ed. Lucas Holste, Paris, 1663; first
published at Rome by Vitale Mascardus, 1661; this printed edition of the
Codex Regularum was reproduced by Migne in 1851, PL 103, cols. 423-702.
The RBas is found in cols. 483-554, introductory material including Rufinus's
Preface, cols. 483-486, the text, col. 487-702. Though Zelzer adduces Holste's
text in the apparatus he by no means investigated its sources or methods,
but simply states that Holste culled his text from the transmission in codices
of the rules of Benedict of Aniane and in other texts available to him in Rome,
and glossed it with his own additions as was the custom at that time.

The early dissemination of the Regula Basilii

Zelzer's account of the textual transmission[45] may be fittingly supplied
here. He begins with a sketch of the pattern of dissemination.

---

[45] Largely from pp. x–xvi.

The most ancient witnesses, the codices **E** and **S** on the one hand and the codices **G**, **L**, and **W** on the other, show that Rufinus's Latin translation was already well used in the sixth century both in Italy and in the monasteries of Lerins. GLW, copied in the eighth and ninth centuries in various German locations, contain not only the RBas but other monastic texts whose authors were very popular during the fifth and sixth centuries in the monastery of Lerins and were held in high repute in southern Gaul. From this it is clear that their text of the RBas derived from a source in the monastery of Lerins. This text in many places and their own index of chapters already differ in the earliest centuries from the text in the Italian and certain other Gallic codices, whose principal codices are **CES**. That is, even before **CES** were written the text had already been widely disseminated in the monasteries of Italy and Gaul and been adapted by the monks of Lerins to their own purpose.

The period from the sixth to the eighth centuries was the era of the 'mixed rules'. The RBas was used in many monasteries of Italy and Gaul as one of a growing library of monastic rules and monastic literature, e.g., the Rules of Basil, of Pachomius, of Columbanus, of the Master, of Benedict, and others. Sometimes this body of monastic writings was synthesised by local abbots into a rule for their particular time and place. This is exactly the historical milieu in which the Rule of Benedict was originally composed.

The codices **HO**[46]**T** show that another form of the text was disseminated through the region of Visigothic Spain. Very like it was the text used by Benedict of Aniane in the compilation of his Codex and his *Concordia Regularum*, attested in the codices **MZ**. From these two latter codices it is evident that though Benedict of Aniane primarily derived his text of the RBas from the Visigothic tradition, he also accepted readings from the tradition of Lerins; whether he himself conflated the Visigothic and southern Franco-Gallic traditions or found some such 'contaminated' transmission among the monks is uncertain.

Thus the codices of the *Regula Basilii* from the sixth to the tenth centuries do not offer a very consistent text, but show several different strands of transmission. Since both the **Italian** and **Gallic** codices, of which **CES** are the most ancient, differ among themselves in several places and do not lack errors and corruptions, and the codices that followed the **Lerins (GLW)** and **Spanish Visigothic (HOT, MZ)** transmissions not only cohere among themselves in adding certain corrupt readings of their own but also accord in different ways with other wit-

---

[46] Not used in Zelzer's collation.

nesses or show a discrepancy from them, it appears that already in the earliest centuries the Latin text of the RBas was corrupted, altered, intermixed, and corrected (by copyists and proofreaders) in various ways.

Zelzer's critical material summarized above does not pursue the dissemination of the RBas beyond Italy, Gaul, Germany, and Spain. I am indebted to Fr. Mark Savage of Pluscarden Abbey for bringing to my notice the likelihood that St Columba (521–597) also knew and used the RBas. The early Gaelic poem *Amra Choluimb Chille* ('The Elegy of Colum Cille') extols this great church father of Ireland and Scotland, 'the Apostle of the Picts'. Written shortly after Columba's death by the Irish poet nicknamed Dallán Forgaill, it declares 'Ar-bert Bassil bráthu / ar-gair gnímu de adbsib airbrib aidblib' ('He applied the judgments of Basil / who forbids acts of boasting by great hosts').[47] Columba also seems to have known Cassian.[48]

1. ERRORS IN THE EARLIEST COPIES

*1. There are some places in all or most codices which demonstrate that **even the oldest copies, or the text either of the translator himself or of those who transmitted it in the first decades, are not without several faults, errors, omissions, and corruptions,** e.g., Pref. 2 *saeculo dedit* (where a lacuna might be suspected?); 4:11 *qui*; 7:14 *nec*; 8:13 *dum/ cum* (omitted through correction PW); 9:12 *elementi* (corrected by Benedict of Aniane); 36:4[49] *eius* (for *Iesu*); 46:3 *non* (through translator's error?); 49:3 *si in opere . . . contendamus;* 99:2 *dat/det*; 122:7 *et quidem* (for *equidem*); 171:3 *et quia* (for *ex qua*); 172:4 *pro* omitted (through haplography); 178:3 *replere illius* (for *replebimus*); 184:7 *audit autem* (for *audita autem* through haplography).

2. WHERE C(E)S ARE PREFERABLE

*2. However, it is clear from several places that **the most ancient codices C(E)S more often preserve the authentic text,** where:

> ***2.1** their text accords with the Greek text of the *Great Asketikon*, to which it is most probable that the lost Greek text of the *Little Asketikon* had been very close, e.g., 2:82 *speculam quandam* CS; 3:38 *et alt.* CES, P, GLW; 5:9 *est*

---

[47] In Thomas Owen Clancy and Cilbert Márkus, eds. and trans., *Iona: the Earliest Poetry of a Celtic Monastery* (Edinburgh: Edinburgh University Press, 1995), 107.
[48] See Clancy and Márkus, *Iona*, 109.
[49] A correction of Zelzer's 36:3.

vobis CS; 6:2 *sancta doctrinae* S; 13:1 *Iothor* Cac.S; 29:1 *hoc contrarium est illi testimonio* CES, JP; 34:2 *faciebat* CS; 55:2 *voluntates* CS; 78:1 *zelus tuus* CS, P; 80:1 *ille me misit* S; 99:2 *suscipiet* ES; 101:2 *ingressibus* CS; 120:3 *oboeditis* S; 122:7 *cum furatus est linguam auream* ES, J, *ira Domini* CES, J; 122:8 *equidem* ES; 123:6 *libertatem* CS, J; 132 Quest. *illa* S, J; 139:3 *ait* CS, PT; 155:1 *praecipua sunt* CS; 162:1 *audientiam* CS, P.[50]

*2.2 their text lacks those words which when added to the Latin version make it more easily intelligible, or lacks those words added to passages of Sacred Scripture that extend it more fully (from which places it is clear that **the Lerins tradition is more contaminated with certain additions than are the other traditions**),[51] e.g., Prol.5 *manifestare* GLW, M, Hol.; *sermonis* GLW, M, Hol.; Prol.11 *spatium* GLW, Hol.; 2:7 *a Deo* GLW, Hol.; 14:3 *nostri Iesu Christi* (for *Dei Sui*) GLW; 42:4 *vias eius discas et* GLW, PMZ, Hol.; 43:1 *debet* GLW, JMZ, Hol.; 52:3 *et non egerunt paenitentiam* GLW, H.; 55:3 *et requiem temporibus meis* GLW, Hol.; 112:5 *vel voluntate . . . Dei moderetur* GLW, MZ, Hol.; 164:3 *vel a maioribus* GLW, HJMPT, Hol.; 172:3 *similiter et peram* GLW, M, Hol.; 173:1[52] *possitis* GLW, HM, Hol.; 173:3 *et non ipsis praesumus sed* GLW, HM, Hol.

*2.3 their text preserves the errors of either the Greek text of Scripture or of Rufinus the translator, e.g., 8:2 *in sanctitate* CS; 74:1 *audientes* CS, JP, GL.

*2.4 Such examples demonstrate that even those places for the adjudication of which neither the Greek text nor any other criterion avail may be determined by the testimony of the codices **C(E)S**. Thus of the highest importance are those places in which the oldest codices, ES, not corresponding completely between themselves, agree with Corbeiensis, i.e., **C**, e.g., 3:3 *usibus*; 3:5, 6 (quite often) *ne . . . quidem*.

3. Where C(E)S do not offer the best text

*3. However, from certain places it is clear that these codices **C(E)S** are not without errors, corruptions, and variant readings where:

*3.1 their text is plainly corrupt: 3:19 †*proditur*† ES alone;

*3.2 the vowels *e/i*, *o/u* and the labials *b/v* are confused, e.g., 12:1 *loquitur* for *loquetur*, cf. 125:2; 3:8 *visitavit* for *visitabit*; 44 Quest. *observavimus* for *observabimus*; 69:1 *quid debet ad* for *qui devitat*; 86 Quest. *qui in opere* for *qui nuper*;

---

[50] These are cases where more weight attaches to the witness of a minority of codices (CES) *and* that of the *Great Asketikon* than to the witness of the majority of codices.

[51] The principle of *lectio difficilior*.

[52] I correct Zelzer's "173: Quest."

*3.3 their readings disagree with the text of other codices when these accord with the Greek: when versions are found, in codices C(E)S and others, of passages of Sacred Scripture disagreeing with the authentic text of Scripture they may be taken, as we said above, for the genuine versions of Rufinus. These versions of Scripture, having arisen from errors either of the text itself or of the translator, were afterwards corrected in a number of other codices according to the authentic text of Scripture. However, we do suspect that certain places of the Rule itself which disagree with the text of certain other codices that are themselves in accord with the Greek are readings proper to the codices C(E)S rather than genuine readings of Rufinus (e.g., 22:2 *germinabunt* CS, P) since it is manifestly unlikely that the Latin text of the RBas copied from the codices C(E)S would have been corrected afterward according to the Greek text.

4. Where GLW are preferable

*4. Thus it is clear that **in a few places codices GLW,** either alone or with other codices—excepting CES—**preserved the authentic text from the Greek**, e.g., 2:67 *ergo per primum completur et secundum;* 79:1 *si;* 88:2 *ab apostolo;* but in many places they offer a poorer text, affected of course by the Lerins transmission, whether through alterations or additions, or exhibiting in passages of Scripture needing translation a Vulgate version, as we call it, for the use of Rufinus the translator.

Moreover, we may regret that codex Floriacensis (**F** Fragmenta codicis Aurelianensis 6/7c.) One suspects that though it does not lack faults and corruptions it might have added something to contribute to the determining of the text, but unfortunately it has come down to us in little fragments.

5. The importance of the Greek text

*5. The testimony of the Greek text of the *Great Asketikon* is of special importance when it alone indicates to us what the Latin version, corrupted by errors of the translator or of the later copyists, means to convey; e.g., **49:3, where the Latin text is manifestly corrupt**; 69:4, where Rufinus has defectively put *vel . . . vel* for ἢ . . . ἤ; 79:2ff., where the Latin text is scarcely intelligible; 99:2, where it is apparent that the meaning of the question/heading appears to have been contaminated with the addition of the word *misericordiae;* 178:3, where we find *replere illius* defectively for *replebimus*.

All the same, the Greek text is not everywhere of the same importance, since the text of the *Great Asketikon* is not the same as that of the *Small*

Asketikon as translated by Rufinus, now lost, nor did Rufinus himself always translate his Greek text word for word.

6. PROBLEMS WITH VERSIONS OF SCRIPTURE

*6. The wording of sacred scripture used by Basil is far more difficult to decide than the rest of his Latin translation, since not only was the Greek text of Scripture itself already marked by diverse readings, but also the Latin text of Scripture was transmitted in several versions, whether of the Old Latin or of the Vulgate. Not only that, but often the copyists wrote down not only readings of the Vulgate instead of the Old Latin readings but even readings retained in their memory instead of those found in any copy, e.g., 8:9 *instabunt* HJMTZ, Hol.; 16:1 *corripe* GLW, P; 16:3 *ecclesiam non* B, GLW, P; 18:2 *sed timorem* HJMT, Hol.; 26:4 *erue* GLW, P, Hol.; 26:5 *membrorum tuorum* GLW, HJM(T)Z, Hol.; 82:8 *ad imitandum* B, GLW, HMTZ, Hol.; 114:3 *talenta* GLW, M, Hol.; 118:2 *reliquimus* GLW; 156:7 *dilectione* GLW, HMT, Hol.

Lundström's review of Zelzer's edition

In 1978 Sven Lundström, a specialist in Latin textual criticism at the University of Lund, published a lengthy book review of Zelzer's edition. He suitably commends Zelzer's achievement, because by means of it we are acquainted with the readings of the important manuscripts. He praises the critical apparatus, which he says is seldom or never incorrect, and the full and very reliable Index Verborum. He regards Zelzer's text in most cases as correct.

The major fault he would find with Zelzer's approach, however, is that he insufficiently investigated the stemma, i.e., the systematic pattern of descent and relationship between the manuscripts. To work that out, he says, one must look for passages where obviously impossible readings are transmitted in more than one manuscript, and must then work out errors relating to the linking and division of words. So he briefly sketches the probable stemma, using sigla for sub-archetypes:

- class α consisting of S and C.

- class β consisting of sub-classes γ (i.e., P and W, LG) and δ (i.e., B and TH, MZ and J).

Copyists and proofreaders, of course, carried out their own corrections and conjectures, and sometimes consulted some other manuscript apart from their primary exemplar. This is where the stemma can be useful in discerning the crossed lines of influence, or 'contamination', to use Lundström's term.

In a section of smaller font-size he proceeds to gives a few instances of what he means. Most cases show that Zelzer's judgment has been faulty due to the lack of a clear sense of the stemma.[53] They are usually of such slight consequence that they rarely impact on translation. Even from the few examples Lundström gives in this review it was clear that he himself had worked in intimate detail with the Latin manuscripts.

Lundström's monograph

The full extent of Lundström's familiarity with the interrelationship of the manuscripts was revealed in a monograph he published in the following year: *Die Überlieferung der lateinischen Basiliusregel.*[54] Lundström verifies his discernment of the stemma by very many examples and his judgment, so well attested, deserves consultation.

After a brief introduction in which he recapitulates his book review, Lundström divides his work into three sections:

1. The Filiation: the genealogical descent of the manuscript transmission.

2. Contamination: when copyists and proofreaders consulted other manuscripts or versions of Scripture in addition to their primary exemplar, thereby mingling the lines of descent, and also when they conjectured and editorialized, sometimes very thoughtfully, over problematic words or passages.

3. The Archetype: highlighting the fact that there were errors and omissions even at the earliest stage of the transmission.

Lundström's diagram of the stemma on p. 9, showing the lines of filiation and contamination, is reproduced here with permission.

In summarizing *Die Überlieferung* below, only those examples will be mentioned in each case that represent departures from Zelzer's editorial decisions.

---

[53] The opening of 79.1 is greatly varied in the MSS, and Zelzer decided to reconstruct it as "*si possibile est*," in keeping with the available Greek, εἰ δυνατόν ἐστι. This seems a reasonable choice. Lundström, however (L[1] 589), considers that Rufinus originally wrote "*sane*," which is not so close to the available Greek text.

[54] See n. 3 above.

On p. 82 Lundström supplies an index or 'Stellenregister' (List of Passages), subtitled 'Abweichungen von Zelzer und Querverweise' (Departures from Zelzer and cross-references). Eighty-five items are listed, a few of them containing two, and in one case (122.7) three wordings under consideration. A few passages where Zelzer is corrected (or in the case of 122.5 potentially corrected) are not listed: 11.35, 11.39, 61.3, 87.Q, 122.5.

The subtitle of this Stellenregister is somewhat puzzling on two counts: (1) Many more passages in the RBas are examined in the monograph than find a place in this list and (2) of the passages listed, more than a third, about thirty, are instances where Zelzer's editorial choice is confirmed, not corrected. For example, on p. 41, Lundström: 'in 10,1 Zelzer rightly chose the reading *qui*'. Thus the accuracy of Zelzer's edition is better than might appear from a first glance at this list, because even if Zelzer did not give a formal account of the stemma he worked with an implicit understanding of it. All the same, we are greatly in Lundström's debt for the range of emendations he expertly demonstrates. The following, then, is Lundström's summary list of references to the RBas, to which I have added a few references to passages where Zelzer is corrected that do not appear on the list. These are marked by an asterisk.

Praef.2, Prol.13, 2.Q, 2.2, 2.25f., 2.29, 2.70, 2.71, 2.76, 2.97, 3.18, 3.19, 3.31, 3.32, 5.3, 8.11, 9.22, 10.1, 10.6f., 11.8, 11.16, 11.25, 11.35*, 11.39*, 14.1, 29.3, 34.3, 37.1, 40.2, 45.3, 49.3f., 61.4, 63.3, 64.1, 67.Q, 68.Q, 70.2, 74.1, 77.2, 79.1, 79.2, 82.3, 87.Q*, 83.1, 87.4, 88.Q, 92.2, 96.1, 101.2, 113.1, 114.Q, 121.2, 121.6, 122.7, 122.8, 123.Q, 123.11, 123.12, 126.6, 127.8f., 130.3, 130.4, 137.4, 139.2, 139.3, 140.3, 145.1, 156.5, 164.Q, 171.1, 173.3, 173.4, 175.Q, 175.5, 184.Q, 184.3, 186.1, 190.Q, 195.9, 196.Q, 196.4, 198.2, 199.1, 202.1, 202.2f., 202.7.

In the Latin text all cases in which I have followed Lundström's advice and emended Zelzer's text are footnoted.

I. *Errors*

I. A. Errors in α (= S and C) (pp. 10–13)

Identifiable errors in the earliest manuscripts highlight the fact that sounder readings may be preserved in later manuscripts. Examples: 92.2, where five words are omitted through haplography. Zelzer was also mistaken to have followed α rather than β in 2.2, 82.3, and 101.2.

STEMMA CODICUM

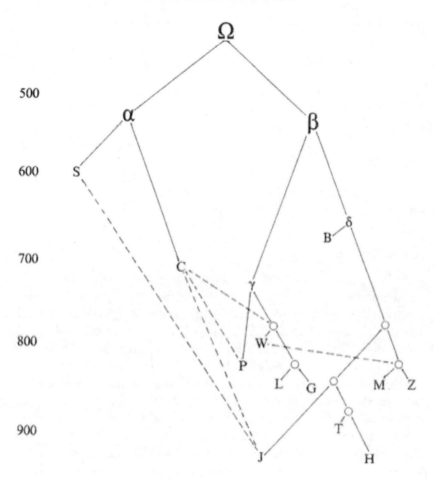

I. B. Errors in β (= P, WLG, B, TH, J, MZ) (pp. 13–18)

Here Lundström examines some ten cases in which Zelzer rightly rejected a mistaken reading from β. Then he says there are four cases in which Zelzer incorrectly followed β instead of α. They are: 108.1, 5.3, 198.2, 156.5. It is difficult to see what Lundström's issue with Zelzer's rendition of 5.3 is, except over-punctuation. It may be that the *quam* of α was preferable to the *quantum* of β, but Lundström maintains that *quantum* was Rufinus's text, just as Zelzer has it. The issue reappears in

198.2 where, according to Lundström, Rufinus wrote *quam fieri potest rationabiliter* instead of the *quantum fieri potest rationabiliter* of Zelzer's text. But there is no textual support, and the argument seems opaque.

I. C. Errors (Variants) in γ (= P and WLG) (pp. 18–19)

Here Zelzer has rightly treated many readings peculiar to P and WLG as errors or faulty variants. Lundström advocates no departures from Zelzer's edition in this category.

I. D. Errors (Variants) in δ (= B and THJ, MZ) (pp. 19–21)

Zelzer has correctly discerned the errors in this class. Lundström has no departures from his text to recommend.

II. *Contamination*

As Lundström notes,[55] theoretically a proofreader could by means of contamination pick up both correct and incorrect readings. His intention is always, of course, to improve the text, but naturally he will err from time to time and retain a false reading in place of a correct reading. In the working out of the stemma, faulty readings played a great role. The correct readings are not really reliable indicators, since a proofreader can rectify a mistake in his source document through his own conjecture or through the use of another manuscript and thereby obscure the character of the manuscript in question. The issue here is how some manuscripts are dependent on certain other manuscripts through contamination. Here indeed the errors are important, because by and large a proofreader scarcely replaces correct readings of his source document with obviously false readings he finds in another manuscript.

II. A. From C to P (pp. 22–30)

Lundström argues a correction at 2.Q, where he says both sub-archetypes α and β probably had *ait* rather than *ais*. P borrowed C's idiosyncratic conjecture *asseris*. Corrections likewise occur at 63.3, 68.Q, 130.4, 110.1, 122.7 (*e[t]quidem*), 122.8, 123.Q, 164.Q, 173.3–4, 108.1 (two cases), 190.Q, 195.9.

---

[55] L^2 22.

II. B. FROM C TO J (pp. 30–32)

In this category Lundström corrects Zelzer's text only at 45.3.

II. C. FROM C TO WLG (pp. 32–43)

Here Lundström corrects Zelzer's text at 3.31, 2.25, 79.1, 121.2.

II. D. FROM W TO MZ (pp. 43–48)

Lundström commends Zelzer (p. 44) for eradicating the errors in MZ that had been imported into Holste. The only correction is at 139.2 (*incident/incedunt*).

II. E. FROM S TO J (pp. 48–54)

Lundström corrects Zelzer's text at 3.18, 113.1, 130.2, 130.3, and 137.4. At 122.7 *Nam Achar ille cum furatus est linguam auream*, Lundström confirms Zelzer's choice of *linguam* over the *regulam* of most manuscripts, but is undecided between the *furatus est* of EJS and Zelzer's text and the subjunctive *furatus esset* of the other manuscripts.

II. F. NOT FROM S TO P (pp. 54–58)

In this section it is demonstrated how P often shows the same errors as S, but not through contamination. It had access to the α transmission through S. Lundström corrects Zelzer's text only at Prol. 13.

II. G. NOT FROM WLG TO J

J has adopted readings from C (Chapter II B), and certainly also from S (Chapter II E). There are certain agreements between J and W. One can easily gain the impression thereby that J is also dependent on WLG. In this section Lundström shows how this is not so. There are no corrections of Zelzer's text.

III. *The Archetype*

By the 'archetype' Lundström refers to a state of the text before its separation into α and β streams, though sometimes he also refers to an archetype of the sub-classes. 'Archetype' therefore does not strictly refer to Rufinus's text as far as it can be established. He begins by commending Zelzer's corrections of many errors that had already appeared in the archetype. Here he corrects Zelzer's text at 40.2.

III. A. Omissions (pp. 63–78)

This section examines the instances of lacunae in the ms. text, most often in the archetype, and their bearing on a correct estimate of the text. Zelzer's text receives corrections at Praef. 2, 2.71, 3.19, 11.8, 11.16, 11.25, 49.3, 61.3 (not in the list on p. 82), 61.4, 79.1, 83.1, 87.Q (not in the list on p. 82), 87.4, 126.6, 175.Q, and 184.3.

Lundström paid special attention to passages obelized or put between cruces by Zelzer as corrupt or irredeemably problematic, and he has provided solutions in every case. At Praef.2 he commends Zelzer for resisting Manlius Simonetti's emendment and for suspecting a lacuna, which he now supplies. At 3.19, †*proditur*†, Zelzer had rightly indicated a corruption. Lundström goes further and restores the original word. At 49.3 Lundström wonderfully elucidates, as incomprehensible except through the Greek, a difficult Latin passage Zelzer had also placed between cruces. At 79.2 the wording of Zelzer's text is correct, but Lundström finds that his cruces, marking it as a corrupt text, are needless. He elucidates the meaning through a change of punctuation.

No doubt the most sweeping display of Lundström's expertise is his detailed analysis and reconstruction of the transmission at 11.8.

III. B. Miscellaneous errors (pp. 78–81)

These discuss passages at 74.1, 3.32, 61.3 and 4, and 140.3.

Rufinus's Approach to Translation

When investigating the RBas 'backwards' rather than 'forwards', i.e., as a witness to the lost Greek text of the *Small Asketikon*, a careful estimate of Rufinus's translation techniques and of Basil's editorial techniques in the *Great Asketikon* is absolutely essential. The present author has published an extensive study of these issues.[56] Here a selective summary is

---

[56] Anna M. Silvas, *The Asketikon of St Basil the Great* (see n. 5 above), chap. 5: "Rufinus, Witness of the *Small Asketikon*," 102–29, and chap. 6: "Basil and the *Great Asketikon*," 130–45.

in order, so that the reader may be implicitly aware of Rufinus's rhetorical style and approach to translation.

Rufinus's tendency to paraphrase, gloss his text, interpolate material into it, and abbreviate or omit sections, has often been noted[57] and deplored.[58] He candidly explains his approach to translation in the prefaces to several works and is consistent in carrying out his intentions. The following statement from the preface to his translation of Gregory of Nyssa's *Life of Gregory Thaumaturgus* may be taken as characteristic:

> When experienced teachers of the Sacred Scriptures try to convey something from the Greek language for Latin ears, they take care not to translate word for word, but sense for sense. And well they might. For if Latin discourse intended to imitate the Greek idiom, it would quite choke both the rhythm of speech and the sense of meaning. And this is also true for us in translating the life of Gregory Thaumaturgus from Attic speech. In recasting what the holy Gregory of Nyssa composed in a foreign, that is, in the Greek tongue, we have made many additions and many omissions, as the most suitable meaning required, attending to the sense while fittingly accommodating Latin readers.[59]

In short, Rufinus sought to refashion his Greek source as a Latin work in its own right. In this more or less broad approach to translation he was following an established convention of both pre-Christian and Christian

---

[57] Useful summary studies are Brooks, "Translation Techniques," and Wagner, *Rufinus the Translator*, esp. chap. 3 (see n. 14 above).

[58] J. E. Oulton, "Rufinus's Translation of the Church History of Eusebius," *Journal of Theological Studies* 30 (1929): 150–74, deplores Rufinus's approach: "But even when no temptation lay upon him, Rufinus transgressed the bounds of freedom which every translator must be expected to observe. It is not merely that he eschews the bald literalism of Aquila or the Latin translator of Irenaeus: he is continually taking unjustifiable liberties with his original. He omits, abbreviates, transposes, expands according to taste: and perhaps his favourite method is to produce a kind of paraphrase which gives the general sense."

[59] *Sanctarum scripturarum doctores egregii, cum de graeca lingua latinis auribus tradere aliquid statuerunt, non verbum verbo, sed sensum sensui reddere curaverunt. Et merito. Nam si latinus sermo graeco idiomati respondere voluerit, et euphoniae subtilitatem et rationis sensum penitus suffocat. Et nos beati Gregorii Thaumaturgi vitam ex loquela attica transferentes, imitando eam quam sanctus Gregorius Nyssenus pontifex in peregrina, hoc est in graeca lingua composuit, plurimis additis, plurimis ademptis, ut ratio utillima postulabat, sensum attendentes latinis viris compediose curavimus ministrare.* For the text, see Stephen Mitchell, "The Life and Lives of Gregory Thaumaturgus," 99–138 in Jan Willem Drijvers and John W. Watt, eds., *Portraits of Spiritual Authority: Religious Power in Early Christianity, Byzantium and the Christian Orient* (Leiden: Brill, 1999), at 132.

translators. The topic of translation theory was well canvassed by Jerome in his Letter 57. In fact, Rufinus invoked Jerome himself as an exemplar of the approach he wished to follow.[60]

In assessing the character of Rufinus' translation, one must of course be constantly reading the RBas against the Greek text of the *Great Asketikon.* Although much of the *Small Asketikon* is more or less embedded in the expanded Asketikon, the extant Greek text does not necessarily preserve the Greek text Rufinus had before him. One has to be constantly alert also to Basil's editorial techniques, which on occasion involve deleting text, refining the expression of text, interpolating text, and eliding earlier text altogether with a much expanded treatment.

With those provisos understood, we can now present a selective summary of Rufinus's translation techniques, with a few examples in each category.

Preserving text loss from the Greek.

Nothing is more welcome than when Rufinus preserves those small personal interjections, 'I think', 'it seems to me', etc., that Basil later edited out. Such interjections preserve the original oral delivery. For example, RBas 199.1 has 'It seems to me more honourable and religious', against the declaration in the Greek: 'It is more seemly and pious'.

A particularly striking example occurs at RBas 2.18: 'The utterly ineffable love of God—as I at any rate experience it—which can be more easily experienced than spoken of, is a certain inexplicable light'. This personal, testamentary phrase has been lost from the later Greek.

With access to the Syriac text, it is now possible to test some of these cases. At times the RBas preserves the earlier form of text which is embedded in a partial and scattered form in the later Greek text. Here the state of the earlier text seems to have served Basil as a springboard to revise and expand his teaching, sometimes very considerably. It usually affects only the nuances and not the substance of his doctrine. Examples occur at RBas 1.5 (LR 1), RBas 6.4–11 (LR 10.1), RB 7.3, 5–10, 11–13 (LR 15).

---

[60] Much to Jerome's annoyance! Cf. Rufinus's preface to the Περὶ Ἀρχῶν (NPNF, ser. 2, vol. 3, 427–28) and his *Apologia* against Jerome (PL 21, cols. 541–624, NPNF ser. 2, vol. 3, Book 1, chap. 14, 441; chap. 16, 442; chap. 19, 445; Book 2, chap. 8, 463, and especially chap. 27a, 472), where he comments on Jerome's Letter 57, insisting that he was only following the task set by Jerome himself and imitating his approach to translation—the same Jerome who had previously expressed his contempt of *verbatim* translations and had himself inserted explanatory phrases into his translated text.

This last example concerns the upbringing of the young in the brotherhood and the age at which profession ought to be considered valid. In his revised edition Basil completely abrogated his earlier text and gave the topic a far more extended treatment. The QF version of the text falters, whether through misunderstanding on the part of the translator or perhaps through reflecting local practice. It appears to say that profession is to be considered valid from the time a child reaches the age of reason, or the ability to discern good and evil. This is definitely not St Basil's thought. Here the RBas, rather than the QF, certainly preserves Basil's earlier version.

Pleonasm

Rufinus frequently expands his original text with words or even phrases of explanation or interpretation. There are innumerable instances. Here is just one example, from RBas 123.Q. Rufinus's putative glosses are in brackets. A translation of the present state of the Greek text follows for comparison:

> 'Why is it that sometimes upon the soul, (even) without much effort, spontaneously as it were, a (kind of) sorrowing (of heart) falls upon it and a compunction (from the fear of God), while at other times, so great a listlessness (or negligence) holds down (the soul) that even though (a man) forces himself, he cannot assume any (sorrow or) compunction (of heart)?

> SR 16.Q: 'Why is it that sometimes the soul feels compunction without much effort, a sorrow coming upon it spontaneously as it were, while at other times, it is so unconcerned that even if it forces itself, it cannot induce any compunction?'

For further comparison, this is how it looks in a translation of the Syriac:

> QF 109.Q: Why is it that sometimes, even without our making an effort, a sorrow falls upon our soul without toil, while at other times even when we wish to experience this sorrow, and even constrain ourselves, we cannot?

As can be seen, Rufinus has not actually changed the meaning of the text in any way, but he has expressed it rather fulsomely.

One of Rufinus's commonest forms of pleonasm is his use of 'doublets', as I called them in my earlier study, i.e., hendiadys, expressing one idea with two terms. No doubt Rufinus is very aware of the multiple nuances of some Greek words and strives to convey that richness of nuance by using two slightly different synonyms. But often this duplication of words is redundant. The Latin text is studded with samples of this device.

For example, RBas 1.Q ends with 'he could make a beginning anywhere on the circle (or crown)'. 'Circle' has received a perfectly needless synonym.

In the following case there is a double translation of the Greek term, and then Rufinus supplements it with the original Greek term anyway:

> RBas 170.Q: 'What is (worthy or) holy (which the Greeks call ὅσιον), and what is just?'

It is a refreshing change occasionally to find instances in which Basil himself uses hendiadys, perhaps due to later editorial revision, and Rufinus uses only one term.

Idiomatic and literary enhancement

Here we can only briefly suggest the rich field of Rufinus's efforts to enhance his text. He was constantly on the lookout for ways of ensuring the rhetorical quality of his text and of 'naturalizing' it as a Latin literary work. As we have seen, he frequently expresses more fully in a Latin idiom what is expressed tersely or elliptically in the Greek. Where he can, he renders expressions more sharply or vividly. He is so conversant in both languages that he knows well how to use an *idiomatic equivalent*. He personalizes impersonal constructions, often by using the first person plural.

The following are some examples of negotiations of vocabulary in which Rufinus can be seen to change the nuance slightly: πάθος is commonly translated as *vitium*, e.g., RBas 67.Q (SR 117); Θεόπνευστος (literally 'God-breathed') as *sanctum*, e.g., RBas 1.6 (LR 1), where Θεοπνεύστοις Γραφαῖς is translated *sanctis scripturis*; ἀδελφότης is not translated *fraternitas* but *fratres*, prefixed with a preposition as in *ad fratres* in RBas 196Q (SR 94.Q), 192.Q (SR 105.Q); τῇ ἀδελφότητι appears as *inter fratres* in RBas 25.3 (SR 159). Εὐλάβης, i.e., 'pious' and 'piety', is commonly translated as *religiosus*, e.g., SR 171 (RBas 116), χρεία as *usus*, as in RBas 95.4 (SR

168), κρίμα as *sentencia* (very commonly) and as *iudicium* in RBas 100.1, 2 (SR 169), γνησίως as *ex corde*, as in RBas 23.12 (SR 16), RBas 27.Q (SR 8), etc. In (RBas 159.1) he uses an idiomatic equivalent for the qualifying adverb τάχα in SR 55 as a qualifying *puto*, 'I think'.

Many examples of Rufinus's enhancements may be found in RBas 2. RBas 2.73 (LR 4) improves on the style of the Greek, infusing some Latin elegance with a play on words between *pondus* = 'weight' and *gravioris* = 'heavier'. RBas 2.77 (LR 5) recasts the original more elegantly, person- alising it by using a cohortative mood and expanding a single adjective, ἀνεξάλειπτον, into a clause. In RBas 2.99 (LR 6) the more dynamic Greek verb περιγένεσθαι, 'to prevail against former habits', appears twice, so Rufinus employs *variatio* and creates a doublet with a shift of verbal nuance: *reflectat et revocet*, 'to reexamine and recall oneself from former bad [added] habits'. In the following sample the original text is artfully rearranged and expanded to add emphasis and rhetorical effect.

> RBas 2.109-110: 'Then by reason of (the obstacles and) the tumults and preoccupations with which the common life (of human beings) is usually filled, the soul is unable to preserve that which is (greater and) more precious (than anything else), the memory of God. (With this memory repulsed and shut out from the soul) it not only . . .'
>
> LR 6.2: 'Then by reason of the tumults and preoccupations with which the common life is usually filled, the soul is unable to preserve the more precious memory of God, it not only . . .'

We can compare the Syriac translator, who also takes a liberal approach:

> QF 2.109: 'Yet again, through the tumult and the hindrance at work in that mingled way of life, he will be defrauded of the memory of God, which memory should above all be constant in our disposition'.

These three headings barely introduce the reader to the many issues involved in Rufinus's approach to translation.

Consulting the Syriac

The present author has worked on a critical edition of the Syriac *Quaes- tiones Fratrum*, concurrently with updating the critical edition of the *Regula Basilii*. Some background information on the QF for the reader of the RBas is in order.

The liberal approach to translation, the pre-Peshitta rendering of scriptural citations, the archaic orthography of the best readings, and the peculiar character and interests of the translator all suggest that the Syriac translation of Basil's *Small Asketikon* took place very early, certainly in the fourth century, perhaps even in Basil's lifetime. It is an intrguing possibility that Eusebius of Samosata might have been the mediator of this seminal work of monastic wisdom in Greek to the Syriac-speaking world. Eusebius was an older contemporary of Basil who appears to have come to friendship with Basil during the consolidation of the Neo-Nicene front in the late 360s. He travelled all the way from Samosata on the Euphrates to be one of Basil's co-consecrators as bishop in September of 370. From the evidence of eighteen or more surviving letters from Basil, he seems to have been Basil's closest confidante and friend during his last years. When Basil occasionally mentions his discussion of theological terms with a Syriac speaker, one can well imagine it might have been with the bishop of Samosata.[61] Eusebius did not survive his friend for long. He died a martyr at the hand of an Arian assassin on his return to Samosata after exile, within a year of Basil's death.

The Syriac text has been collated from the five following manuscripts, denoted by their *sigla*, A to E:

A. British Library, Additional 14544; parchment, 5th–6th centuries.

B. British Library, Additional 14545; parchment, 5th–6th centuries.

C. Biblioteca Apostolica Vaticana (Vatican Library), sir. 122; parchment, completed 769.

D. Vatican Library, sir. 126; paper, completed 1226.

E. Ambrosian Library, Milan, Fragments 10/34, no. 38, 10 folios 155–164, parchment, 8th–9th centuries.

Very briefly, two major items of bibliography concerned with the QF are:

---

[61] On Basil's contacts with Syriac-speaking Christians, see David G. K. Taylor, "Les Pères cappadociens dans la tradition syriaque," 43–61 in Andrea B. Schmidt and Dominique Gonnet, eds., *Les Pères grecs dans la tradition syriaque*, Études Syriaques 4 (Paris: Geuther, 2007); idem, "Basil of Caesarea's Contacts with Syriac-speaking Christians," *Studia Patristica* 32 (1997): 213–19; and the introduction to Taylor's *The Syriac Versions of the De Spiritu Sancto by Basil of Caesarea*, 2 vols. CSCO 576, 577 (Leuven: Peeters, 1999).

1. Gribomont, *Histoire du Texte des Ascétiques de Saint Basile*, 'La version syriaque', 108–48, especially at 108–14. Marred by a few typographical errors, and by the fact that Gribomont took a poor view of the QF, being only interested in it as a witness to the lost Greek text, this monument of philological enquiry nevertheless remains a touchstone for all study of the QF.

2. Fedwick, *Bibliotheca Basiliana Universalis* 3: *Ascetica*, 'A Comparative Table Between *Ask 1r, Ask 1s and Ask 4*', 9–15; 'iii. The Syriac Version: *Ask 1s*', 43–46.

The Syriac translator only gradually became more liberal in his approach as he progressed through Basil's *Asketikon*. He is quite capable of translating with a fair degree of verbatim accuracy, and he begins in this vein. Only in QF 1.4 do we detect the translator recasting his text somewhat and alluding to rather than actually citing a scriptural passage. The glosses initially are of words and brief phrases, the kind of thing Rufinus himself does. Even in QF 2, philosophically the most sophisticated segment of the Asketikon, the translator steers generally close to the text. Then the glosses begin to lengthen, an entire sentence or two typically being added to the end of an answer. This can be particularly well seen in QF 106, which is an almost verbatim translation to which a lengthy invented passage has been added at the end. Rufinus never went nearly as far as this. It seems that about halfway through the QF the Syriac translator's sense of liberty suddenly escalated. Perhaps QF 69.2 represents the turning point. The translation remains quite close to the text for a few lines. Then we see the translator really beginning to take leave of his text, adding further scriptural texts and paraphrasing and amplifying so completely as to be making up his own text. Other examples are QF 79 and QF 149. From then on he departs ever more freely from his text by recasting it and adding sizeable passages of his own invention. Basil's text has become a springboard for his own reflection and teaching. It is precisely because we have such material that is verifiably of his own invention that we can build up a picture of the Syriac translator's distinctive interests and character, 'profile' his personality, so to speak.

It remains for us here to investigate to what extent Lundström's emendments of the Latin text can be supported or verified from the Syriac translation. The principle to bear in mind is that we are not seeking confirmation of the Greek text but of the *Latin* text, which on occasion may reflect a different text from the Greek or the Syriac. Hence if the Syriac does not have Lundström's emendment of the Latin it may be because it preserves a text closer to the Greek, which is not our concern here. In other cases where the Syriac is liberally paraphrasing or inventing it is impossible to confirm or disconfirm. We now revisit our list of notable passages above, eliminating those for which there is no parallel in the Syriac. ~~Strikethrough~~ is used for cases where Lundström and Zelzer agree; – signifies 'not applicable or unverifiable', x 'disconfirms', and ✓ 'confirms'.

Praef.2, –Prol.13, –2.Q, x2.2, ✓2.25f., ~~2.29~~, ~~2.70~~, –2.71, ✓2.76, ~~2.97~~, –3.18, –3.19, –3.31, –3.32, ~~5.3~~, ✓8.11, ~~9.22~~, ~~10.1~~, –10.6f., ✓11.8, x11.16, –11.25, –11.35*, –11.39*, ~~14.1~~, ~~29.3~~, ~~34.3~~, ~~37.1~~, ✓40.2, ✓45.3, ✓49.3f., –61.3*, x61.4, x63.3, ~~64.1~~, ~~67.Q~~, ✓68.Q, ~~70.2~~, ✓74.1, ~~77.2~~, ✓79.1, ✓79.2, –82.3, ✓83.1, –87.Q*, –87.4, ~~88.Q~~, ~~92.2~~, ~~96.1~~, –101.2, –121.2, –121.6, ✓122.7, –122.8, –123.Q, ~~123.11~~, ~~123.12~~, ✓126.6, ~~127.8f.~~, ✓130.3, x130.4, –137.4, ~~139.2~~, ✓139.2(2nd), ~~139.3~~, –140.3, ~~145.1~~, –156.5, –164.Q, ~~171.1~~, –173.3, –173.4, –184.Q, ✓184.3, ~~186.1~~, ✓190.Q, x195.9, –196.Q, ✓196.4, ~~198.2~~, –199.1, ~~202.1~~, ~~202.2f.~~, ~~202.7.~~

Some comment on the disconfirmations are in order.

In 2.2 both QF and the α text of RBas, chosen by Zelzer, lack the word 'whole' in the standard scriptural phrase: *the whole law and the prophets.* The fact that both the QF and RBas α lack a normalised scriptural citation favours the retaining of Zelzer's reading. On this argument the oldest Latin ms., S, would preserve not an archetype error, as Lundström argues, but Rufinus's original text, and all later manuscripts, including the Greek of the *Great Asketikon,* represent various instances of normalisation. 'Ipsa' gives the impression of being Rufinus's own attempt to add a certain rhetorical punch, in the absence of a form of 'whole'. So here we do not adopt Lundström's emendation.

RBas 61.4 happens to be a case where the Syriac parallel, QF 62.4, is translating quite verbatim. With ܐܠܐ ܕܡܬܬܙܝܥ it uses a passive form of the verb 'to move' ('and is not moved') which, in a reflexive sense, appears in the phrase *vel movendo* in the majority Latin text. With not the faintest possibility of 'contamination', and the chance of coincidence being too much to ask, this surely is an endorsement of Zelzer's reading against Lundström's emendation. Here too there is enough independent evidence to maintain Zelzer's reading.

The lack of '*et*' in Zelzer's text of RBas 63.3 is paralleled by its absence from QF 64.3. The Syriac translator is usually exceedingly liberal in using ܐܦ (too/also/even), so its lack here points to an archaic form of text.

QF translates: 'as the Apostle says' or 'in accordance with what the Apostle says', which is probably closer to the original Greek exemplar. But in this case the overriding principle is our concern with the integrity of the *Latin* text, and the appearance of '*et*' as part of the introductory phrase '*maxime cum et*' ('especially when the Apostle too says') suggests a certain exercise of rhetorical emphasis coming from Rufinus himself. We retain Lundström's emendation of Zelzer.

In RBas 130.4 there is another issue of '*et*'. Here QF 117.4 parallels the Latin with an earlier use of '*et*' in the sentence, but, as in Zelzer's choice, lacks the second instance. The case turns on the very slim hazards of introducing a scriptural citation. The Syriac introduces it with ܕ ('that'), and not ܘ ('and'), which is the Greek usage in Scripture and in the *Great Asketikon*. We might have some modest case for maintaining Zelzer's text, but it is tenuous, and Lundström's emendation stands.

In RBas 195.9, in a citation of Isaiah 5:14, Lundström corrects Zelzer's plural *uvas* with the singular *uva*, following the singular σταφυλήν of the Septuagint text. QF 178.9, on the other hand, uses the plural ܥܢ̈ܒܐ, and this is supported by the plural marker, *seyame*, which appears in all available mss., including the oldest (from the late fifth/early sixth centuries). At issue of course is the notorious ambiguity of both the Greek and the Latin words. Each has one term encompassing a singular meaning, 'grape', and a collective meaning, 'cluster of grapes'. As to number these words could fall either way in translation. Lundström's marshalling of evidence is sound. He even quotes Rufinus elsewhere citing the same scriptural passage using a singular noun, so Lundström's emendation here stands.

To turn now to the cases of confirmation: what a testimony it is to Lundström's expertise as a Latinist and a text critic that so many of his emendments are corroborated by the Syriac text, of which he knew nothing. It may be worthwhile pausing over a few of the more interesting cases.

RBas 45.3 concerns the gospel phrase *the evil man (malus homo) brings forth evil things from the evil store of his heart* (Matt 12:35). Following three mss., Zelzer jettisoned *homo*, mistaking it for a Vulgate normalisation. But the Greek text has ὁ πονηρὸς ἄνθρωπος, so that Lundström restored *malus homo* with most Latin mss. QF 45.3 confirms the emendment with ܒܪ ܢܫܐ.

In RBas 49.3 the linchpin of a very technical elucidation of the confused Latin text is Lundström's restoration of ‹usu› *eorum quae desideramus* as the object of *perfrui*. QF 50.3 bears this out with the use of a noun, ܒܘܝܐܐ ('satisfaction'/'consolation') 'of the things desired'.

RBas 74.1 is confirmed simply and elegantly. In a passage cited from the parable, '*And seeing this,* it says, *his fellow servants told their master'*, Zelzer has *audientes*, i.e. 'hearing', corrected by Lundström to *videntes*, 'seeing'. The Syriac confirms this with ܘܟܕ ܚܙܘ 'and when they saw. . . .'

In RBas 139.3 is a very fine linguistic point, deciding between *incident* ('will fall into') and *incedunt* ('tread/step upon'), two different verbs, each of which can fit the context. Lundström validated *incident* as the better reading. QF 125.2 backs this up with ܡܬܛܒܥܐ ('sinking'/'subsiding'), with a shared sense of 'going down into'.

RBas 184.Q confirms, although it concerns a fine nuance, *devocare* versus *revocare*. The restored Latin has *in irritum devocare quod male fuerat definitum*, 'that he call off as invalid what was wickedly decided'. QF 184.Q runs ܗܘ ܡܪܡ ܕܒܝܫ ܐܬܬܚܡ ܗܘܐ ܠܡܫܒܩܘ 'that he leave off what was wickedly determined'.

In RBas 190.Q Lundström validates the inclusion of a word *quasi*. At issue are not only the variants of the Latin text but also weighty variants in the Greek mss. of the *Great Asketikon* and in the printed editions. Amidst this maze of variants in three languages, QF 175.Q lends support to Lundström's emendation with its use of the adverb ܐܝܟܢܐ at precisely this point.

There are many other ways in which comparison with the Syriac text can bring light to the understanding of the Latin text, and I have noted some of these cases in the English translation. I will discuss just one here, concerning the use of the noun ἀδελφότης ('brotherhood') to denote the dedicated ascetic community, i.e., what we would call a monastery.

There is a certain 'anti-monastic' reading of Basil's *Small Asketikon*, which I have discussed before.[62] Gribomont was its protagonist, and Fedwick followed his cue.[63] An anti-institutional animus seems to inspire it, something that possibly owes more to a certain *Zeitgeist* of the 1960s and 1970s than to evidence of the texts. Misconstruing Basil's use of

---

[62] See Silvas, *Asketikon of St Basil the Great*, 23 n. 11; 29 nn. 19, 20. My analysis of the ascetic doctrine in the *Small Asketikon* is found in chapter 2, "The Ascetic Community in the Two Versions of Basil's Asketikon," 19–37. My account of the ascetic development of Basil's family and in his own life and doctrine is found in chapter 4, "The Emergence of Christian Monasticism in Fourth Century Anatolia," 51–101.

[63] See Paul J. Fedwick, *The Church and the Charisma of Leadership in Basil of Caesarea* (Toronto: Pontifical Institute of Mediaeval Studies, 1979). This is a book, which, with a very idiosyncratic hermeneutic, sweepingly misconstrues the character of Basil's auditors and of his doctrine in the *Small Asketikon*.

generically Christian terminology in his ascetic writings, the idea is that
in the *Small Asketikon* Basil is tentatively offering 'advice' to casual groups
of freelance Christian enthusiasts living in the world, who can take it or
leave it as they please. The evidence of dedicated, disciplined communities of ascetics withdrawn from the common life of the world, living in
voluntary poverty and a God-oriented common obedience only occurs
in the *Great Asketikon*, they think. *Not.*

Gribomont, for example, several times avers in print that ἀδελφότης
as the title for a dedicated ascetic community occurs only in the *Great
Asketikon.*[64] Already in a comparison of the RBas and the Greek of the
Great Asketikon it was possible to infer that Rufinus had paraphrased
instances where the Greek uses the noun for *brotherhood* by using a form
of 'brothers' instead. Comparison with the QF now confirms such an
inference, and it is a puzzle why Gribomont, who knew the Syriac text
very well, missed it. In RBas 6.9 (the only case in which Rufinus actually
uses *fraternitas*), 194.Q, 196.Q and 4, we find the Syriac using the substantive ܐܚܘܬܐ ('brotherhood') where the Greek also uses the substantive
ἀδελφότης, but where Rufinus for his part uses a form of *fratres*. RBas 6.9
is particularly valuable, since at this point in the *Great Asketikon* Basil
considerably editorializes and expands his text, and the relevant passage
from the *Small Asketikon* has vanished. Here the Latin has *corpori fraternitatis* and the Syriac has ܐܚܘܬܐܕ ܓܘܫܡܐ, which is exactly the same
phrase, verbatim: 'in(to) the body of the brotherhood'.

Variant recensions of the Greek *Small Asketikon*

In a comparison of the QF to the RBas and the *Great Asketikon*, many
cases of a Syriac/Greek alliance against the Latin are to be found. Not all
of these are due to Rufinus's method of translation. Some examples are:

> QF 112.5 omits Matt 6:31, but in agreement with the Greek presents
> it immediately following in QF 113.Q as part of the question; QF
> 13.1, a good section of sentence is attested in both Syr/Gk, but not
> in RBas 11.39. In QF 18.5, Gk/Syr show up an odd passage at the
> very end of RBas 16.5, as if he is translating a scribal error in his

[64] See, for example, Gribomont, "Le renoncement au monde dans l'idéal ascétique
de s. Basile," *Irénikon* 31 (1958): 282–307, at 299, and idem, "Saint Basile," in *Théologie
de la vie monastique, Études sur la tradition patristique*, Faculté de Théologie S.J. de
Lyon-Fouvière (Paris: Aubier, 1961), 99–113, at 106.

Greek text; QF 19.2 uses Prov 13:13 with the Gk, whereas RBas 17.2 uses Sir 19:1, QF 112.5 omits Matt 6:31 but in agreement with the Greek presents it immediately following in QF 113.Q as part of the question.

An accumulation of such instances gives an impression that there may have been some differences in the actual Greek text that lay before the two translators. Might there have been at least two recensions of the *Small Asketikon*, as early as the period, 365–370?

One historical hypothesis is that the Greek text behind the RBas reached Palestine very early, possibly as part of Basil's correspondence with monks on the Mount of Olives there. This might be as early as 366. The text of the *Small Asketikon* that lies behind the QF would then represent the editorial progress of a very few years, say by 368–369, and it was this slightly revised version, with three extra pieces, that perhaps Eusebius of Samosata took back with him late in 370 after his presence at Basil's ordination as bishop.

And yet, as soon as one frames this hypothesis one is left with a conundrum. If the RBas has behind it an earlier Greek text, why does it preserve some seventeen questions/answers that do not appear in the QF? Since most of the missing items in the QF are all in a single bloc (RBas 106–118), one wonders whether something very simple and pragmatic could be the explanation: if a quire of a codex slipped its threads, say, as it was being carted about over long distances.

And whence the three questions/answers that appear only in the QF? The following hypothesis suggests itself. We know clearly enough the process from oral delivery to edited written text. The tachygraphers took down notes during the visits of the renowned monastic father to various ascetic communities, in Pontus to begin with, then also in Cappadocia. There was a systematic 'in-gathering' of these notes, or fair copies made from these notes, which became the basis of editorial work by Basil himself. Perhaps these *extravagantes* have their origin in some tachygraphers' notes, from one particular community for example, that somehow missed the general muster but were preserved and surfaced later, perhaps towards the end of the 360s in the text of a slightly amended *Small Asketikon*.

Abbreviations

RBas: *Regula Basilii,* Rufinus's Latin translation of Basil's *Small Asketikon.*

L¹: Sven Lundström, review of Zelzer's edition of the RBas, published in *Gnomon* 60 (Munich 1988): 587–90.

L²: Sven Lundström, *Die Überlieferung der lateinischen Basiliusregel,* Acta Universitatis Upsaliensis, *Studia Latina Upsaliensia* 21 (Uppsala: Academia Upsaliensis, 1989).

SR: *Shorter Rules* of the *Great Asketikon,* Pontic/Vulgate recension (Fedwick's 'Ask 4'), *Regulae Brevius Tractatae,* PG 31 cols. 1079-1506.

LR: *Longer Rules* of the *Great Asketikon,* Pontic/Vulgate recension (Fedwick's 'Ask 4'), *Regulae Fusius Tractatae,* PG 31 cols. 889-1052.

QF: *Quaestiones Fratrum/Questions of the Brothers,* the Syriac translation of Basil's *Small Asketikon.*

Zelz.:   Klaus Zelzer, *Basili Regula—A Rufino Latine Versa,* Corpus Scriptorum Ecclesiasticorum Latinorum 86 (Vienna: Hölder-Pichler-Tempsky, 1986).

Regula Basilii

This is keyed from the critical edition edited by Klaus Zelzer,[1] February 2007. Justifications for emendations to the Latin text are found in the footnotes. Paragraphing is reconsidered and matched with my English translation.

Praefatio[2]

1 Satis libenter, carissime frater Ursaci, adventantes de partibus orientis et desiderantes iam fratrum consueta consortia monasterium tuum ingressi sumus, quod superpositum angusto arenosi tramitis dorso hinc atque hinc passivi et incerti maris unda circumluit; **2** rara tantummodo latentes locos eminus arguit pinus,[3] ex qua et Pineti clarum nomen saeculo decidit.[4]

3 Et inde maxime delectati sumus, quod non, ut aliquibus mos est, vel de locis vel de opibus orientis sollicite percontatus es, **4** sed quaenam ibi observatio servorum dei haberetur, quae animi virtus, quae instituta servarentur in monasteriis perquisisti.

---

[1] *Basili Regula—A Rufino Latine Versa* (Vienna: Hoelder-Pichler-Tempsky, 1986).

[2] See also the critical edition of this preface by Manlius Simonetti: "Tyranni Rufini Prologus in Regulam Sancti Basilii," 239–41 in *Tyranni Rufini Opera*, CCSL 20 (Turnhout: Brepols, 1961).

[3] *Rara . . . pinus*: the cadence of the hexameter will be noted.

[4] *De‹ci›dit*, restored L² 64–65; †*saeculo dedit*† Zelz., with a note that a lacuna is suspected, which Lundström has now supplied. Zelzer rightly rejected Simonetti's conjecture *saeculum*, maintaining the *saeculo* of all MSS except "solo" in GL. Rufinus expresses to Ursacius a courteous analogy: as a cone drops from a pine to the ground, so the name of Pinetum has dropped down to the world.

The Rule of Basil

Preface

Letter of Rufinus To Ursacius of Pinetum

1 Most dear brother Ursacius, when we had arrived from eastern parts and we were already longing again for the accustomed fellowship of brothers, how gladly we entered that monastery of yours, sited there above the narrow ridge of a sandy causeway, washed about on this side and that by the waves of the shifting and uncertain sea. **2** Only a scattering of pines marked out the hidden places at a distance,[1] from which the famous name of Pinetum has dropped down to the world.[2]

3 But we were especially delighted in this, that you did not, as is the way with others, press inquiries about the places or riches of the East. **4** Instead, you asked eagerly about the observance of the servants of God there, their character of mind, and the institutes kept in their monasteries.

---

[1] W. K. L. Clarke, *The Ascetic Works of Saint Basil* (London: SPCK, 1925), 28–29 n. 1, puzzles over a monastery situated *above* (*superpositum*) the ridge and the places *lying hidden* (*latentes*). He provides three diagrams of possible geographic arrangements.

[2] The location of Pinetum has been matter of some debate. Earlier opinion, e.g., Clarke, *Ascetic Works*, 28, placed it on the upper Adriatic coast near Ravenna, evidently because Jordanis in his *History of the Goths* spoke of an ancient pine forest called *Pinetum* as one of the three parts of Ravenna. Later opinion has settled for a site at or near Terracina on the Tyrrhenian coast, some eighty kilometers south of Rome. Francis X. Murphy, *Rufinus of Aquileia* (Washington, DC: CUA Press, 1945), 90, says in favour of the Terracina location: "I believe the notice of Paulinus of Nola (Letter 47) mentioning the fact that Cerealis would have to go out of his way on the journey between Nola and Rome to see Rufinus, then staying at Pinetum, is decisive; especially when taken in conjunction with Rufinus's answer in his *Praef. ad De bened. patriarcharum* II,2." The usual route to Rome from Nola lay inland through Capua and up the Via Latina, which followed the Liri/Sacco valley.

5 Ad haec ego ne quid tibi minus digne, non dico quam geritur sed quam geri debet, exponerem, **6** sancti Basilii Cappadociae episcopi, viri fide et operibus et omni sanctitate satis clari, instituta monachorum, quae inter-rogantibus se monachis velut sancti cuiusdam iuris responsa statuit, protuli. **7** Cuius cum definitiones ac sententias mirareris, magnopere poposcisti ut hoc opus verterem in Latinum, **8** pollicens mihi quod per universa occiduae partis monasteria si haec sancti et spiritualis viri sancta et spiritalia innotescerent instituta, **9** omnis ille servorum dei profectus qui ex huiuscemodi institutionibus nasceretur, mihi quoque ex eorum vel meritis vel orationibus aliquid gratiae vel mercedis afferret.

10 Exhibui ergo ut potui ministerium meum: imple et tu et omnes qui legitis et observatis gratiam, ut et agentes et orantes sic quemadmodum statuta haec continent, mei quoque memores sitis. **11** Tui sane sit officii etiam aliis monasteriis exemplaria praebere, ut secundum instar Cap-padociae omnia monasteria eisdem et non diversis vel institutis vel observationibus vivant.

5 To your request I reply—but that what I expound for you may not be unworthy, I say, not of myself, but of the dignity of the subject—**6** I bring forth from the holy Basil, bishop of Cappadocia, a man greatly renowned for faith and works and for every mark of holiness, his Institutes for Monks, which he handed down as a kind of sacred case-law[3] to monks who questioned him. **7** For when you were admiring his definitions and expressions, you begged me urgently to translate this work into Latin, **8** promising me that if these holy and spiritual institutes of a holy and spiritual man were to become known through all the monasteries of the west, **9** the great progress that would accrue to the servants of God from precepts like these would, through their merits and prayers, bring me some grace or reward.

10 I have exerted myself, therefore, to the best of my ability: do you fulfil your part then, and may all you who read this also observe the favour, and remember me as you act and pray in accordance with the content of these statutes. **11** Make it your task to provide copies also for other monasteries, so that, after the likeness of Cappadocia, all the monasteries may live not by different, but by the same institutes and observances.[4]

---

[3] The analogy appears to be Roman civil law, in which interpretations of already existing statutory law were made by authorised jurists on a case-by-case basis. This is not such an inaccurate idea of Basil's approach, which is to look on Scripture as the "God-breathed" testimony of the Lord's commandments to be used, quite literally, strictly, and in detail, Christian ascetics, as the rule of life for Christian ascetics and on his own role as merely a dispenser of the scriptural word, understood with the sensibility of the faith of the church and lived in the testimony of the Holy Spirit. Thus Rufinus, in looking to Basil himself and his "Rule" as a statutory source of authority, and even in using the term "monks," reflects a certain institutionalizing of monastic life and the canonizing of the holy orthodox "fathers" as guarantors in their own person of authentic Christian doctrine.

[4] Here most manuscripts mark the transition to the text of Basil with a discretionary formula variously put, e.g., "The Preface of the Rule of holy Basil the Bishop finishes. The chapters begin . . ." C; "It finishes. The book of holy Basil the Bishop on the Institute of monks begins . . ." G; "The Rule of holy Basil the Bishop on the Institute of monks begins . . ." H; "Here begins the teaching of the holy Basil Bishop of Cappadocia to monks . . ." M; "The Preface finishes; here begins the Institute for monks, dispensed by the holy Basil to seniors who questioned him . . ." P; "The Prologue finishes. Here begin the sayings of holy Basil the Bishop . . ." S.

Prologue

(Zelzer 5–7, QF Prologue, **1–11** SR Prologue [PG 31.1080], **12–20** LR Prologue [900–1])

1 Humanum genus diligens deus et *docens hominum scientiam* his quidem quibus docendi contulit gratiam praecipit per apostolum *permane*re in doctrina, **2** his vero qui aedificari divinis institutionibus indigent per Moysen protestatur dicens *Interroga patrem tuum et annuntiabit tibi, presbyteros tuos et dicent tibi.*

3 Propter quod necesse est nos quidem quibus ministerium verbi creditum est, in omni tempore paratos esse et promptos ad instructionem perfectionemque animarum, **4** et quaedam quidem in communi ecclesiae auditorio simul omnibus de praeceptis domini contestari, quaedam vero secretius perfectioribus quibusque disserere, **5** et inquirere atque interrogare volentibus de fide et veritatem evangelii domini nostri Iesu Christi et de conversatione perfecta copiam nostri facultatemque praebere, **6** quo possit ex his *perfectus* effici et consummatus *homo dei.*

Prologue

1 God who loves the human race[5] and *who teaches man knowledge* (Ps 94:10), through the Apostle commands those on whom he has bestowed the gift of teaching, to *persevere in teaching* (1 Tim 4:16; Rom 12:7), **2** while through Moses he also exhorts those who are in need of being built up by the divine instructions, saying *Ask your father and he will declare it to you, your elders[6] and they will tell you* (Deut 32:7).

3 Wherefore, we to whom *the ministry of the word* (Acts 6:4) is entrusted[7] must at all times be prepared and eager for the instruction and perfecting of souls,[8] **4** now bearing witness to all in the common hearing of the church concerning the commandments of the Lord,[9] now making ourselves available in private to the best of our ability to any of the more perfect[10] **5** who wish to enquire and ask questions concerning the faith and the truth of the gospel of our Lord Jesus Christ and the perfect way of life[11]—**6** through which the *man of God* might be made *perfect* and complete (2 Tim 3:17).

---

[5] SR Prol. PG 31.1080A: Ὁ φιλάνθρωπος θεός.

[6] 1080A: πρεσβυτέρους σου. This hints that Basil is ordained to the presbyterate.

[7] The "charism of the word," tested and approved, i.e., empirically verified, is pivotal to Basil's conception of discerning leadership in the community. See also RBas 17, 32.2, 33.2, 35, 45.2.

[8] 1080A: πρὸς τὸν καταρτισμον τῶν ψυχῶν.

[9] "Concerning . . . Lord" appears only in Colb. (Fedwick's "Ask 6") here.

[10] *Perfectioribus quibusque . . . .* Rufinus has either taken προσιόντων for some form of "the advanced" or has inserted "*perfectioribus*" here as a gloss to specify the class of Basil's addressees, i.e., the more zealous Christians and ascetics. Jean Gribomont ("Obéissance et Évangile selon Saint Basile le Grand," *Supplément de la Vie Spirituelle* 21 (1952): 192–215, n. 21) considers that Rufinus has interpreted to the more evolved mentality of his own time. Yet the concept of being more or less "perfect/complete" in the Christian life was very much part of Basil's thought. His ascetic and anthropological vocabulary is studded with the words τελέω, τέλειος, i.e., "perfection" and its field. For him Christian "perfection" involves a progress towards maturity and completeness; it is fostered by instruction and diligence and can be skilfully monitored, e.g., LR 2.2 (RBas 2.7-10), LR 3.1, 59-63; it implies assiduous effort towards the goal of piety, imitation of a pattern or a correspondence to a template, e. g., LR 5 (RBas 2.82–93). In fact, Basil himself uses the term "the more perfect," e. g., τελειοτέροις, in LR 10.1, LR 15.1 (and note), LR 15.2 (twice), LR 4. Basil's teaching on perfection is very clear in *Homily on Ps 44* (PG 29.388A) where he describes its attainment as a gradual process. "This psalm seems to be one adapted to the perfecting (τελειωτικός τις ὢν) of human nature, one that lends help towards gaining the end (τέλος) set before those who have chosen to live according to virtue. For there is need of the teaching this psalm provides, if those making progress (προκόπτουσι) are to be perfected (τελειωθῆναι)."

[11] SR Prol. 1080A: τὰ τε πρὸς ὑγείαν τῆς πίστεως καὶ ἀλήθειαν τῆς κατὰ τὸ Εὐαγγέλιον τοῦ Κυρίου ἡμῶν Ἰησοῦ Χριστοῦ πολιτείας—concerning the soundness of faith and

7 Vobis autem convenit nullum tempus vacuum praeterire, quominus ad ea quae communiter cum omni ecclesia discitis, etiam secretius de eminentioribus et perfectioribus inquiratis, **8** ut omne aevum vitae vestrae in inquirendo de melioribus et in percontando de utilioribus transigatis.

9 Quoniam ergo et in hoc nos congregavit deus, et paululum quid a molestiis turbarum silentii agimus et quietis, **10** neque in aliud opus animum demus neque residuum temporis somno rursus et remissioni corporeae mancipemus, **11** sed in inquisitione et sollicitudine meliorum noctis hoc quod superest exigamus, adimplentes illud quod dictum est per beatum David quia *In lege eius meditabitur die ac nocte.*

12 Si quid ergo unusquisque vestrum deesse sibi ad scientiam putat, ad communem id proferat inquisitionem, **13** facilius enim pluribus simul conferentibus, si quid illud difficile vel obtectum videtur esse,[5] clarescit, deo sine dubio inveniendi gratiam quaerentibus largiente.

---

[5] *Videtur esse*, SPJ, Hol., in the sub-archetype of β, confirmed L² 56; *esse videtur* WLG; *videtur* Zelz., following CH.

7 It befits you for your part not to allow any time to pass by idly, so that in addition to what you learn in common with the whole church you also inquire in private concerning the higher and more perfect things **8** and so conduct the whole span of your life enquiring what are the better things and searching out what is more useful.

9 Since God has brought us together here and we enjoy some small silence and quiet from the disturbances of the crowds, **10** let us not give our mind to any other task, or devote the remaining time to sleeping again and the repose of the body **11** but spend what is left of the night[12] in enquiry and concern for the better things, fulfilling what was said by the blessed David: *On his Law he shall meditate by day and by night* (Ps 1:2).

12 So then, whatever knowledge each of you thinks he is lacking, let him bring it forward for common investigation, **13** for if something appears to be difficult or obscure it is more easily clarified when the many look into the matter together, since God without doubt bestows the grace of *finding* upon those who *seek* (Matt 7:7).

---

the truth of the way of life according to the Gospel of our Lord Jesus Christ. Rufinus may have reordered the sequence somewhat; even so, there is a new stress in the later Greek text on "soundness" of faith. A similar reediting of the intent occurs a few lines later in LR Preface (RBas Prol. 14). In either the Latin or Greek version the indirect interrogative clause comes down to two elements: doctrine and way of life. The necessary link of sound doctrine and moral endeavour is also argued in SR 20. In Letter 294 (Def IV, 206–9) from the late 370s, after the rupture with Eustathius, Basil addresses a community formerly under Eustathian influence seeking reform along his lines: "neither a strict way of life by itself is of benefit, except it be illumined by faith in God, nor can an orthodox confession, bereft of good works, commend you to the Lord, but both of these must go together, that *the man of God may be perfect.*" On Letter 294 see Susanna Elm, *Virgins of God: The Making of Asceticism in Late Antiquity* (Oxford and New York: Oxford University Press, 1994), 214–15. Basil likewise stresses the complete interdependence of prayer and an effective moral life.

[12] This reveals something of the original setting of the *Small Asketikon*: Basil has attended, if not presided at, a vigil in common with other Christians, for the Sunday liturgy maybe, or for one of the "synods" or local festivals (cf. LR 40 and note), or for a gathering of superiors of communities that Basil advises in LR 54. When the service is over, a smaller group of the devout gather round Basil to question him and hear his teaching till dawn. The location is certainly in Pontus. Basil describes such occasions in Letter 223 Def III, 302–5, quoted in the introduction. This *modus operandi* continued in Cappadocia. In *Homily on Ps 114* (PG 29.484–93), *Way* 351–59, dating from the 370s when Basil was bishop, his addressees have kept vigil at a sanctuary of the martyrs from midnight to midday, waiting for him to arrive. The lack of the usual commotion that Basil so deplores at these "synods" (LR 40), his hearers' piety and their affection for him all indicate that they are the devout faithful and ascetics.

14 Sicut ergo nobis necessitas imminet et *vae mihi erit si non evangelizem,* ita etiam vobis, si ab interrogatione et inquisitione cessetis vel remissiores ac resolutiores ad ea implenda quae recta inventa fuerint exsistatis, simile discrimen impendit. **15** Propterea enim et dominus dixit quia *Sermo quem locutus sum* vobis, *ille iudicabit* vos *in novissimo die,* **16** Et iterum *Servus qui ignoravit voluntatem domini et fecit digna plagis, vapulabit paucis, qui autem cognovit* et fecit contra voluntatem domini, *vapulabit plurimum.*

17 Oremus ergo misericordiam domini, ut et nobis verbi inculpabile tribuat ministerium et vobis fructuosum doctrinae concedat eventum, **18** tamquam ergo scientes quoniam stabunt ante faciem vestram verba haec ante tribunal Christi, *Arguam* enim *te,* inquit, *et statuam ea ante faciem tuam;* **19** ita et intendite animum vigilanter ad haec quae dicuntur, et ad opus dignum quae audistis festinanter adducite, **20** quia *nescimus qua die* vel *qua hora dominus* noster *veniat.*

14 Now if *necessity is laid upon us* and *woe upon me if I do not preach the Gospel* (1 Cor 9:16), so a like judgment hangs over you, if you cease from your investigation and inquiry, or show yourselves too indifferent and careless in carrying out what you have discovered to be right.[13] **15** For this is why the Lord said: *The word I have spoken to you, this shall judge you on the last day* (John 12:48), **16** and again: *the servant who did not know the will of his master yet has done what is worthy of blows, shall be beaten with few, he however who knew it and yet did what was contrary to the will of his master, shall be beaten with many* (Luke 12:47-48).

17 Let us beseech the mercy of the Lord therefore, that he may both grant to us a blameless *ministry of the word* and award to you a fruitful outcome of the teaching. **18** And since you know that these words shall rise up before you at the judgment seat of Christ: for *I will rebuke you*, he says, *and present* these things *before your face* (Ps 49:21), **19** so then, attend vigilantly to what is being said and apply yourselves without delay to the noble work which you have heard, **20** *for* we *know not the day nor the hour when* our *Lord shall come* (Matt 24:42).

---

[13] LR Prol. 4. 900B completes the sentence: or show yourselves indifferent and careless (ἀτόνως ["lacking tension"] καὶ ἐκλελυμένως) in keeping what is handed down and in fulfilling it in deeds. Basil expects that a certain holy tension, an *anxiety for the things of the Lord* (1 Cor 7:32, 34) will mark the true disciple. This matures as that perpetual "stretching forward" of Phil 13:13 to which Basil refers in RBas 82.5 and especially 151.1, which Gregory of Nyssa will develop in his mystical theology of *epekstasis*.

Interrogatio I

(Zelzer 8–9, QF 1, **1–6** LR 1[PG 31.905–908])

Interrogatio: Quoniam dedit nobis sermo tuus potestatem ut interroge-
mus, primo omnium doceri quaesumus, si ordo aliquis est et consequentia in mandatis dei, ut aliud quidem sit primum et aliud secundum et
sic per ordinem cetera, an omnia mandata ita sibi invicem cohaerent et
sunt aequalia, ut unde voluerit quis possit initium sumere tamquam in
modum circuli vel coronae.

Responsio: 1 Interrogatio vestra antiqua est et olim proposita in evangelio in eo, cum accedens ad dominum quidam legis doctor ait *Magister,
quod est mandatum primum in lege?* **2** et dominus respondit *Diliges dominum
deum tuum ex toto corde tuo et ex tota anima tua* et ex totis viribus tuis; *hoc
est primum et magnum mandatum.* **3** *Secundum vero simile huic, Diliges
proximum tuum tamquam te ipsum.*

4 Ipse ergo dominus ordinem mandatis imposuit *primum* dicens *et magnum* esse *mandatum deum ex toto corde et ex tota mente dilig*ere, **5** *secundum
vero* ordine et consequentia et quod illi esset *simile* per virtutem, immo
quod illud expleret et quod penderet ex primo, *diligere proximum sicut
se ipsum.* **6** Sed et de aliis similiter in sanctis scripturis invenies, et ser-
vatur, ut ego arbitror, in omnibus mandatis ordo quidam et consequentia
praeceptorum.

Question 1

Q: Since your discourse[14] has given us authority to ask questions, first of all we seek to learn if there is any order and sequence in the commandments of God, such that one would be first, another second, and so for the others in their order; or whether all the commandments are so intimately linked to one another and of equal value that one could make a beginning anywhere he pleases, as in the manner of a circle or crown.

R: 1 Your question is an old one and was put long ago in the gospel, the one where a teacher of the law came up to the Lord and said: *Master, what is the first commandment in the law?* **2** And the Lord replied: *You shall love the Lord your God with all your heart and with all your soul and with all your strength. This is the first and the great commandment.* **3** *The second however is like it: You shall love your neighbour as your very self* (Matt 22:36-39; Mark 12:28-31).

4 So the Lord himself imposed an order among the commandments, saying that *the first and the great commandment* is to *love God with the whole heart and with the whole mind,* **5** *the second however* in order and sequence and which is *like it* in virtue—inasmuch as it fulfills and depends on the first—is to *love your neighbour as your very self.* **6** and also from other similar passages in the holy Scriptures, a certain order and sequence of precepts is observed, as I myself observe, among all the commandments.

---

[14] Ὁ λόγος, lit. "the word," also "speech," "address," etc. The Latin *sermo,* and QF ܡܠܬܐ, have the same basic meaning and range of nuances as the Greek. It refers to Basil's introductory invitation or perhaps to the scriptural "word" of Deut 32:7 cited by Basil in RBas Prol. 2 and later displaced in the *Great Asketikon* to SR Preface.

Interrogatio II

(Zelzer 9–25. QF 2, **1–57** LR 2 [PG 31.907–916], **58–69** LR 3 [915–917], **70–73** LR 4 [919–920], 74–93 LR 5 [919–924]; **94–112** LR 6 [925–928])

I: Quoniam igitur de caritate dei primum ait[6] esse mandatum, inde nobis primum omnium dissere; nam quia oportet diligi audivimus, quomodo tamen hoc possit impleri desideramus addiscere.

R: 1 Optimum sumpsistis sermonis exordium et proposito nostro valde conveniens; deo itaque iuvante nos ut dicitis faciemus.

2 Sciendum ante omnia est quod mandatum istud unum quidem videtur, sed omnium in se mandatorum virtutem complectitur et constringit ipso domino dicente quia *In his duobus mandatis ipsa lex*[7] *pendet et prophetae.* **3** Nec tamen nos per singula discutere aggredimur ordinem mandatorum—alioquin videbimur totum opus introducere in parte—**4** sed quantum ad propositum sufficit et praesens ratio postulat inquirimus, illud ante omnia designantes quod omnium mandatorum quae a deo accepimus, virtutes in nobis ipsis insitas gerimus; **5** quo scilicet neque difficultas nobis sit tamquam novum aliquid et alienum a nobis expetatur, **6** neque rursum elationis dari nobis aliqua videatur occasio, si putemus nos plus aliquid offerre deo quam ab ipso in natura nostrae creationis accepimus.

---

[6] *Ait* S, confirmed L² 23; *agit* H; *ais* ("you say") Zelz. following J, L, F; *asseris* CP.

[7] *Ipsa lex*, S, and ܪܕܘܬܐ (the Law/Torah) QF 2.2; *omnis ipsa lex* Zelz. following S and *omnis ipsa lex* F; *omnis lex* (*the whole law*) WLG, HJ, P, Lundström, which is the normal scriptural text. According to Lundström, L² 11, *ipsa lex* was an archetype error in α. However, now that we know that the Syriac (5th/6th century mss.) also lacks the standard phrase, the case for the anomalous reading of the oldest ms. of the RBas is strengthened.

Question 2

Q: Since therefore he says that the first commandment concerns love for God, so then, speak to us first of all about this. For we have heard that he ought to be loved;[15] what we want to learn, however, is how this can be fulfilled.

R: 1. 1 You have taken up the very best introduction to the talk and one most suited to our goal. So, with God's help, let us do as you have said.

2 It needs to be understood before all else that this commandment[16] seems to be one, yet it embraces and binds together in itself the virtue of all commandments, for the Lord himself says: *On these two commandments hang the law itself and the prophets* (Matt 22:40). **3** We shall not however approach the order of the commandments by discussing them one by one—otherwise we shall seem to introduce the whole work with details—**4** but make enquiry as it accords with our goal and the present course requires it, noting before all else that we carry implanted within ourselves the capacities[17] of all the commandments that we have received from God. **5** Hence it is neither a difficulty to us, as if something novel or alien to us were being required of us—**6** nor again does any cause for elation appear to be given us, that we should think that we are offering to God something more than we received from him in the nature of our creation.

---

[15] LR 2 PG 31.908C: ὅτι μὲν φὰρ χρὴ ἀγαπᾶν (that it is necessary to love); QF: "this love that is towards God." The passive infinitive diligi (to be loved) was corrected to the active diligere in Hol. Grib. 141 notes the agreement of Rufinus and the Syriac against the Greek in the form of the question and the opening of Basil's response. Hence RBas probably retains the original.

[16] LR 2 PG 31.908D: κατόρθωμα, virtous act, action rightly done; the word κατορθόω and its field figure very prominently in Basil's ascetical vocabulary. His teaching is utterly free of every gnostic tendency, indeed, the greatest possible antidote to it, being governed by the Johannine teaching that love for God is in the obediential moral act (John 14:15): "This is knowledge (γνῶσις) of God: the keeping of God's commandments," *Homily on the Martyr Mamas*, PG 31.597A. Both RBas and QF have "commandment" instead of κατόρθωμα.

[17] LR 2 909A: τὰς δυνάμεις, powers/faculties, QF: ܚܝܠܐ with the same range of meaning.

7 Quoniam quidem ea quae nobis insita sunt si recte et competenter moveamus in opus, hoc est secundum virtutem vivere; si vero naturae beneficia corrumpamus, hoc est in malitiam vergere. **8** Est ergo mali ista definitio: non recte uti motibus animi a deo nobis insitis; et rursum virtutis ista definitio: recte uti, id est secundum mandatum dei et secundum conscientiam animi, motibus a deo nobis insitis.

9 Cum ergo haec ita se habeant, idem hoc invenimus etiam de caritate constare. **10** Mandatum accepimus diligere deum: dilectionis virtutem in ipsa statim prima conditione a deo anima sibi insitam gerit; **11** in quo nec extrinsecus testimoniis indigemus, unusquisque enim in semet ipso et ex semet ipso horum quae dicimus sumit indicia. **12** Omnis homo desiderat omne quod bonum est, et affectu quodam naturali constringimur ad omne quod bonum putamus; **13** sed et erga consanguineos et carnis proximos nullo docente in amore constringimur, his quoque quorum beneficia accipimus omni affectu et officiis copulamur.

14 Et quid aliud tam bonum habetur quam deus? Immo quid aliud bonum nisi solus deus? **15** Qui decor, qui splendor, quae pulchritudo quam naturaliter diligere provocamur, usquam talis qualis in deo est et esse credenda est? **16** Quae usquam talis gratia, quae amoris flamma quae animae secreta et interiora succendat, sicut amor dei inflammare debet mentis arcana, **17** praecipue si sit ab omni pollutione purgata, si sit munda anima et quae vero affectu dicat quoniam *Vulnerata caritatis ego sum*?

18 Ineffabilem prorsus ego sentio amorem dei et qui sentiri magis quam dici possit, inenerrabilis quaedam lux est; etiam si fulgura, si coruscum adhibeat vel comparet sermo, non patietur auditus. **19** Si luciferi fulgores, si lunae splendores, si ipsum solis lumen assumas, ad comparationem gloriae illius, obscura sunt omnia et multo taetriora quam si caeca nox et obscuritate profundae caliginis mersa limpidissimo meridiani solis lumini comparetur.

7 Now if we put into effect rightly and fittingly those things which have been implanted in us, this is to live according to virtue. If on the other hand we corrupt the endowments of nature, this to turn towards vice. **8** Here, then, is a definition of vice: to make evil use of the movements of the soul implanted in us by God, and again this is the definition of virtue: to use rightly the movements of the soul implanted in us by God, that is, in accordance with the commandment of God and in accordance with the conscience of the mind.

9 These things being so, we find the same case also with love. **10** We have received the commandment to love God: the soul bears the capacity to love implanted within itself by God at its first constitution. **11** Of this we need no proof from without, for each may discover the traces of what we say within himself and from himself. **12** Every human being desires all that is good, and we are drawn by a kind of natural disposition towards all that we think to be good.[18] **13** Indeed, without being taught, we are drawn in love towards blood relatives and those closest to us in the flesh, while we are attached with our whole affection and good services to those from whom we receive benefits.

14 But what greater good can we have than God? Indeed, *what other good is there but God alone*/cf. Matt 19:17)? **15** What loveliness, what splendour, what beauty which we are naturally moved to love is of such a kind as is in God and more claims our confidence? **16** What grace is so great, what flame of love which sets alight the secret and inward places of the soul is like to that love of God which ought to inflame the hidden places of the mind, **17** especially if it is cleansed of all defilement, if it is a pure soul which with true affection says: *I am wounded by love* (Song 2:5)?

18 The utterly ineffable love of God—as I at any rate experience it—which can be more easily experienced than spoken of, is a certain inexplicable light. Even if speech should cite or compare a lightning flash or a dazzling brilliance, still, the hearing cannot take it in. **19** Invoke if you will the rays of the morning star, the splendours of the moon, or the light of the sun itself—in comparison with that glory they are all more obscure and murkier by far than an ink-black night and the gloom of a dense fog compared with the flawlessly clear light of the noon-day sun.

---

[18] LR 2 909B: For we are by nature enamoured of the beautiful (τῶν καλῶν). The Greek term includes both the "beautiful" and the "good," hence Rufinus's legitimate translation. The erotic register is more obvious in the Greek text, which then adds a proviso: even if what exactly is the beautiful appears differently from one to another, εἰ καὶ ὅτι μάλιστα ἄλλῳ ἄλλο φαίνεται καλόν. QF has ܫܘܐ ܪܓܝܐ ܓܝ ܕܝ, "we are desirous of the beautiful, *shaphirto* having a valence similar to that of the Greek.

20 Decor iste corporeis oculis non videtur, anima sola et mente conspicitur; **21** qui decor si cuius forte sanctorum mentem animumque perstrinxit, flagrantissimum in eis amoris sui stimulum defixit. **22** Propterea denique velut amoris cuiusdam ignibus tabescentes et praesentem vitam perhorrescentes dicebant aliqui ex eis *Quando veniam et prarebo ante conspectum dei?* **23** et iterum dicebat istius ardoris ignibus flagrans *Sitivit anima mea ad deum vivum,* **24** et insatiabiliter habens erga eius desiderium orabat *ut vide*ret *voluntatem domini* et protegeretur in templo sancto eius; ita ergo naturaliter et concupiscimus quae bona sunt et amamus.

25 Nihil autem ut discimus tam summum bonum est quam deus, et ideo debitum quoddam exsolvimus hanc quam ab eo expetimur[8] caritatem; **26** quae utique si denegetur et minime exsolvatur, irae nos inexcusabili obnoxios facit. **27** Et quid dico irae obnoxios? Quae enim poterit esse maior ira, quae ultio gravior, quam hoc ipsum si accidat nobis alienos effici a caritate dei?

28 Quodsi parentibus inest naturalis affectus erga eos quos genuerunt, et non solum hoc in hominibus verum etiam in mutis animalibus invenitur, **29** videte ne inveniamur vel pecudibus hebetiores vel feris beluis immaniores, si nullo erga genitorem constringamur affectu. **30** Quem etiamsi qualis et quantus sit scire non possumus, ex hoc tamen solo quod ex ipso sumus venerari et diligere parentis debemus affectu atque indesinenter erga eius pendere memoriam, sicut erga genetrices suas parvuli faciunt, **31** sed et multo amplius multoque promptius, quanto et immensorum nos beneficiorum obnoxius scimus. **32** Quod et ipsum commune nobis esse puto etiam cum ceteris animalibus, meminerunt namque etiam illa si quid eis quis contulerit boni. **33** Si mihi non credis audi prophetam dicentem *Cognovit bos possessorem suum et asinus praesepe domini sui,* **34** absit autem de nobis dici ea quae sequuntur quia *Israel me non cognovit et populus me non intellexit.*

---

[8] *Expetimur* CJW, confirmed L[1] 590; *expetimus* ("we expect") Zelz. with all other MSS.

20 Such loveliness is not seen by bodily eyes; it is perceived[19] only by the soul and the mind. **21** If perchance this loveliness has grazed[20] the mind and heart of the saints, it left embedded in them a most fiery sting of yearning for it, **22** till at length, as if languishing in the fires of such love and shuddering at this present life, such as these would say: *When shall I come and appear before the face of God?* (Ps 41:2), **23** and again, one who is burning in the flames of this ardour would say: *My soul has thirsted for the living God* (Ps 41:1), **24** and being insatiable in his desire, would pray *that he might see the delight of the Lord and find shelter in his holy temple* (Ps 26:4). So therefore we naturally long for and love the good.[21]

25 But if, as we have said, there is no good, however sublime, to be compared with God, therefore the debt that we pay, that which is required of us by him, is love; **26** which if we deny or pay niggardly leaves us without excuse and liable to wrath. **27** And what do I mean by "liable to wrath"? What wrath could be greater, what punishment more grievous than if it should befall us to become strangers to the love of God?

28 If offspring have a natural affection towards those who begot them—and this is found not only among human beings but even among dumb animals—**29** see that we are not found more doltish than cattle or more unnatural than wild beasts, if we are not urged by any affection towards the one who gave us life. **30** For even though we cannot know just what he is or the measure of his greatness, still from the mere fact that we come from him we ought to revere and love him with the affection we have for parents, and cleave to the memory of him unceasingly, as little children do towards their mothers, **31** and this all the more unreservedly and promptly inasmuch as we know that the benefits for which we are indebted are immeasurable. **32** And this I think is common not only to us, but also to the other animals, for if someone bestows some good on them, they do remember it. **33** If you do not believe me, then listen to the prophet who says: *The ox knows its owner and the ass its master's stall*, **34** and far be it that what follows is said of us: *But Israel has not known me, nor has my people understood* (Isa 1:3).

---

[19] The majority Greek text has καταληπτὸν. However, Voss., Colb., and Reg prim. (*Ask* 3) have θεωρητόν, "visible," as does QF: ܪܘܚܐ. This must be the original sense.

[20] LR 2 909C: illumined, as also in QF.

[21] LR 2 912A: Οὕτω μὲν οὖν φυσικῶς ἐπιθυμητικοὶ τῶν καλῶν οἱ ἄνθρωποι, so then human beings are by nature enamoured of the beautiful.

35 Quodsi etiam eos qui beneficii aliquid contulerint nullo docente diligimus et omni studio quantum fieri potest referre gratiam nitimur, **36** quomodo sufficiemus gratiam referre beneficiis dei, quae tanta sunt ut effugiant numerum, et talia ut sufficiat unum aliquod ex omnibus per totam vitam nostram efficere nos obnoxios largitori? **37** Nam omitto cetera omnia—quae quidem et ipsa magna sunt et praeclara, verum a maioribus et melioribus velut stellae quaedam splendentioribus solis radiis obteguntur—, **38** quoniam quidem nec tempus nobis est amplius dilatare sermonem, ut possimus etiam de minimis divina erga nos enumerare beneficia.

39 Sileamus igitur cotidianos solis ortus et unius lampadis fulgore illuminatum universum mundum, **40** sileamus lunae circuitus, aeris permutationes vicissitudinesque, imbres ex nubibus, flumina fontesque de terra, latitudines atque altitudines maris, **41** universitatem terrae ac nativitates eius animantium quae in aquis gignuntur et quae coalescent vel oriuntur in terris, nostris ministeriis vel usibus deputata.

35 Even if we, without any to teach us, love those benefactors who have favoured us in some way, and strive with all zeal to repay our gratitude as far as we can, **36** how shall we ever be able to repay our gratitude for the gifts of God, which are so many as to surpass number, and so great and of such a kind that just one among them all obliges us to give thanks to our benefactor for our entire life? **37** For I leave aside all other benefits—which are themselves magnificent and splendid—yet are outshone by the greater and the better as are the stars by the more resplendent rays of the sun—**38** since there is no leisure for us to enlarge on them more fully, even if we could enumerate the divine benefits to us in lesser things.

3. 39 So then, let us pass over in silence the daily risings of the sun and the whole world illumined by the brilliance of a single torch. **40** Let us pass over in silence the orbits of the moon, the changing patterns and vicissitudes of the atmosphere, showers from the clouds, streams and springs from the earth, the expanses and depths of the sea, **41** the whole of the earth and the living beings that are born of it, those which teem in the sea and those which are established and flourish on the land, all that is assigned to the service and use of our life.

42 Haec ergo omnia et cetera innumerabilia praetermitto, hoc solum quod ne volenti quidem praeterire possibile est, silere non possumus, **43** et quamvis reticere non sit possibile, multo tamen impossibilius est, ut dignum est et ut competit, proloqui: **44** hoc, inquam, quantum est, quod scientiam sui donavit homini deus et rationabile animal fecit esse in terris et ineffabilis paradisi abuti voluptate ac decore concessit. **45** Quemque serpentis arte deceptum et in peccatum lapsum ac per peccatum in mortem quoque devolutum lapsum ac per peccatum in mortem quoque devolutum nequaquam despexit, **46** sed legem in adiutorium dedit, praefecit angelos, destinavit prophetas, conatus malitiae comminationum severitate compescuit, **47** bonorum desideria munificentissimis repromissionibus provocavit, et finem utriusque viae in multis imaginibus praesignavit.

42 These things therefore and countless others I leave aside. There is however one thing only, which even if someone could leave it aside who wanted to, we cannot pass over in silence, **43** and though it is impossible to hold back, it is however much more impossible to utter anything worthy and befitting. **44** This one thing so great of which I speak is that God[22] gave to man knowledge of himself and made him a rational animal on the earth and provided for his enjoyment the delight and loveliness of ineffable paradise. **45** And when he was deceived by the craft of the serpent and fell into sin and through sin fell headlong into death, he by no means despised him, **46** but gave him the Law for a help, set angels over him, sent prophets, checked the impulses of vice by the severity of threats, **47** stirred desires for the good by the most lavish promises, and declared beforehand the end of either course in many images.

---

[22] The text of RBas and QF are in complete accord here, whereas LR 2.3 913B inserts at this point: *"made man in his image and likeness* (cf. Gen 1:26-27) and . . . ."* There are resonances of liturgical texts throughout this section. See also RBas 134. Embedded in RBas 2.44-50 are the following verbatim or near verbatim echoes of the *Anaphora of St. Basil*, from the section between the Sanctus and the institution narrative which relates the economy of creation and salvation: *God* [*made*] *man in his image* . . . *delight* [*in the inconceivable beauties*] *of paradise* . . . *beguiled by the serpent* . . . *he did not turn away* . . . *gave him the Law for a help, set angels over him* . . . *sent prophets* . . . [quoting Phil 2:6-7] *he did not deem equality with God as something to be grasped, rather he divested himself, accepting the form of a slave.*

Since most of these liturgical echoes are already present in the *Small Asketikon* it is clear that, during his mission among the ascetics of Pontus in 363–65, Basil was already using an earlier, shorter form of anaphora in the liturgy (of Antiochene provenance). The fact that in the *Great Asketikon* the allusion to Gen 1:27 is replaced with an express citation of Gen 1:26 hints at stages of accretion in the texts of both the *Asketikon* and the anaphora in Basil's lifetime. According to Gregory Nazianzen, *Oration* 43.34, Basil's activities as a presbyter under Eusebius in the late 360s included "formulation of prayers, regulations for good order in the sanctuary." See Augustine Holmes, *A Life Pleasing to God: The Spirituality of the Rules of St. Basil* (Kalamazoo: Cistercian Publications, 2000), 82–84, and esp. nn. 13 and 88. See also Louis Bouyer, *Eucharist: Theology and Spirituality of the Eucharistic Prayer* (Notre Dame, IN: University of Notre Dame Press, 1968), esp. 292–96. Bouyer shows in graphic form three different strata in the composition of the Anaphora of St. Basil.

48 Verum cum post haec omnia in malis nostris et incredulitatibus duraremus, non est aversus nec dereliquit nos pii domini bonitas, neque cum beneficiis eius essemus ingrati avertere potuimus et excludere misericordiam eius a nobis, **49** sed revocamur a morte et iterum vivificamur per dominum nostrum Iesum Christum **50** *qui cum in forma dei esset non rapinam arbitratus est esse se aequalem deo, sed semet ipsum exinanivit formam servi accipiens.* **51** Et *infirmitates nostras accepit et aegritudines nostras portavit* et pro nobis *vulneratus est* ut *livore* illius *sanar*emur. **52** *et a maledicto nos redemit factus pro nobis maledictum,* et *morte turpissima condemn*atus est ut nos revocaret ad vitam. **53** Nec sufficit vivificare nos mortuos sed et divinitatis suae participium tribuit et munus aeternitatis indulget, **54** et supra omne quod vel petere vel intellegere possumus, credentibus vel diligentibus se praeparat *quod oculus non vidit nec auris audivit nec in cor hominis ascendit.*

55 *Quid* ergo *retribuem*us *domino pro omnibus quae retribuit* nobis? Verum ille ita benignus et clemens est ut ne retributionem quidem reposcat, sed sufficit ei ut pro his omnibus quae largitus est diligatur. **56** Quis ergo tam irremediabiliter ingratus est ut post tanta et talia beneficia non diligat largitorem?

57 Et de caritate quidem dei ista sufficiant: propositum namque est, ut superius diximus, non omnia dicere—impossibile enim est—sed breviter et succincte commemorare ea quae amorem deis inserere animae et suscitare sufficient.

58 Consequens iam nunc est etiam de eo mandato quod ordine et virtute secundum diximus, explicare. **59** Et quidem quoniam lex eas virtutes quae animae a creatore insitae sunt, elimet et excolat, iam in superioribus diximus. **60** Quia ergo praecipimur diligere proximum sicut nos ipsos, videamus si etiam inest nobis virtus et facultas ad huius quoque mandati expletionem.

48 Yet when after all these things were hardened in our vices and our disbelief,[23] even then the generosity of a faithful Lord did not turn away from us or forsake us, and we, notwithstanding our ingratitude for all his benefits, were unable to deflect or shut out his mercy towards us, **49** but were recalled from death and restored to life again through our Lord Jesus Christ **50** who, *though he was in the form of God, he did not deem that he was equal to God as something to be grasped, but emptied himself, taking the form of a slave* (Phil 2:6-7) **51** *And he took on our infirmities and bore our sicknesses and was wounded* for us, *that by his bruises we might be made whole* (Isa 53:4-5, 11), **52** *and he redeemed us from the curse, having become a curse for us* (Gal 3:13) *and was condemned to a most shameful death* (Wis 2:2) that he might recall us to life. **53** And it was not enough to give life to us who were dead, he even bestowed *a participation in his divinity* (cf. 2 Pet 1:4) and lavished on us the gift of eternity, **54** and he prepared for those who believe and love, beyond all that we could seek or understand *what eye has not seen nor ear has heard, nor has it entered into the heart of man* (1 Cor 2:9).

55 *What return,* therefore, *shall we make to the Lord for all that he has given to us* (Ps 115:12)? Yet he is so generous and tender that he seeks no recompense, but is enough for him, that for all that he has bestowed he should be loved. **56** Who then is so incurably ungrateful as not to love his benefactor for benefits so great and of such a kind?

57 Let that suffice, then, concerning love for God, for it is not our purpose, as we said above, to say everything—for that is impossible—but briefly and succinctly to call to mind those things which may suffice to instil and to stir up love for God in the soul.

58 It follows now to explain that commandment which we said is the second in order and power. **59** We have already said above that the law cultivates and nurtures those powers which are implanted in the soul by the Creator. **60** Since we are charged *to love our neighbour as our very self* (Matt 22:39), let us see whether there is also in us the power and the capacity to fulfil this commandment.

---

[23] LR 2.3 913C and QF: disobedience.

61 Et quis ignorat quoniam humanum animal et communicabile homo est et non agreste aliquod ac ferum; **62** nihil enim tam proprium est naturae nostrae quam alterum alterius indigere et requirere invicem ac diligere quod requiret. **63** Quia ergo dominus harum in nobis virtutum semina seminavit, sine dubio horum etiam fructus requiret et testimonium nostrae erga se dilectionis dilectionem accipiet proximorum. **64** *In hoc* enim, inquit, *scient omnes quia mei discipuli estis, si invicem diligatis.* **65** Et ita in omnibus duo ista mandata coniungit, ut etiam misericordiae opera quae in proximum fiunt transferat in semet ipsum: *Esurivi* enim, inquit, *et dedistis mihi manducare.* **66** Et reliqua quae in proximum gesta sunt se dicit esse perpessum, cum dicit quia *Cum fecistis uni ex minimis istis fratribus meis, mihi fecistis.*

67 Ergo per primum completur et secundum, per secundum vero ascenditur et reditur ad primum, ut qui diligit dominum sine dubio diligat et proximum: **68** ait enim dominus *Qui diligit me mandata mea custodit, hoc est* autem, inquit, *mandatum meum ut invicem diligatis.* **69** Ita qui diligit proximum explet in deum caritatem, quia ipse in se recipit quicquid confertur in proximum.

70 Et quidem in his qui initia habent ad timorem dei et ad primos aditus religionis accedunt, prima institutio est utilior[9] per timorem, secundum sententiam sapientissimi Salomonis dicentis *Initium sapientiae timor domini.*

71 Vos vero qui iam parvuli in Christo esse desistis[10] nec ultra lacte indigetis, cibos solidos ex dogmatum firmitate perquirite ad nutriendum et pascendum interiorem hominem, **72** quo per eminentiora quaeque mandata perveniat ad perfectum et *in omni* quae in Christo est *veritatem* firmetur. **73** Observandum sane est ne forte copiosioris gratiae pondus causa nobis gravioris condemnationis exsistat, si ingrati inveniamur muneribus largitoris.

---

[9] *Utilior* Zelz. With α and most β MSS, confirmed L[2] 43, 45; *utilius* MW.

[10] *Desistis* S, W, L before correction, THJM, confirmed L[2] 64; other varieties in MSS; *desi‹i›stis* Zelz. following Holste's conjecture.

61 Who does not know that man is a domesticated and sociable animal, not one savage and wild?[24] **62** Nothing is more characteristic of our nature than that each has need of the other, and seeks out the other and loves what he seeks. **63** Since the Lord sowed the seeds of these virtues in us, without doubt he also seeks fruit from them, and as the testimony of our love for him, he accepts our love for our neighbours. **64** For *By this*, he says, *all shall know that you are my disciples, if you love one another* (John 13:35). **65** And he has so joined together these two commandments in every way that the works of mercy which are done for our neighbour he refers to himself. For *I was hungry*, he says, *and you gave me to eat* (Matt 25:35), **66** And he says of the other things done for our neighbour that he is the one receiving them, since he says *When you did this to one of the least of these brothers of mine, you did it to me* (Matt 25:40).

67 Therefore by means of the first the second also is completed, but by means of the second there is an ascent and a return to the first, so that if anyone loves the Lord he without doubt also loves his neighbour, **68** for *Whoever loves me*, says the Lord, *keeps my commandments* (John 14:15). But *this*, he says, *is my commandment, that you love one another* (John 15:12). **69** Thus whoever loves his neighbour completes his love for God, since it is he who receives to himself whatever is bestowed on the neighbour.

70 For those who are receiving their initiation into the fear of God and approaching their first entrance to piety, an elementary instruction through fear is more useful, according to the counsel of Solomon the most wise who said: *The fear of the Lord is the beginning of wisdom* (Prov 1:7).

71 But you who by now have ceased to be *little children in Christ* (cf. 1 Cor 3:1-2) and have no further need of *milk*, require the *solid food* (cf. Heb 5:12) that comes from the firmness of doctrines in order to feed and nourish *the inner man* (Eph 3:16). **72** by which, through the more leading commandments, you may at last reach maturity (cf. Eph 4:13) and be confirmed in *the whole truth* (John 16:13) which is in Christ. **73** We must surely be on our guard lest the weight of a more copious grace becomes for us a cause of heavier judgment,[25] should we be found ungrateful for the gifts of our benefactor.

---

[24] LR 3.1 917A: ὅτι ἥμερον καὶ κοινωνικὸν ζῷον ὁ ἄνθρωπος, καὶ οὐχὶ μοναστικόν, οὐδὲ ἄγριον. For Basil's "monastic" (="solitary"), Rufinus has substituted a synonym for "wild."

[25] LR 4 920A: ἡ περιουσία τῶν δωρεῶν τοῦ θεοῦ βαρυτέρας [sic] αἰτία ὑμῖν κατακρίσεως. Rufinus infuses Latin elegance with a play on words between *"pondus"* = "weight" and *"gravioris"* = "heavier."

74 Illud autem ante omnia considerandum est, quia neque aliud ullum mandatum neque hoc quod de caritate dei et proximi praecipitur implere quis poterit, si per varias et diversas occupationes animus oberret; **75** sed neque artificium ullum vel ullius industriae disciplinam adipisci possibile est eos qui frequenter ex aliis ad alia referuntur.

76 Omni ergo custodia oportet nos servare cor nostrum, ne forte desiderium dei mala desideria et sordidae cogitationes depellant a[11] nostris animis ac detrudant, **77** sed e contrario assidua recordatione et memoria dei formam quodammodo eius ac figuram animae nostrae signaculis infigamus quae nullis queat interturbationibus aboleri. **78** Sic enim et desiderium nobis divinae caritatis accedit, dum frequens eius memoria mentem atque animos illustrat, et ad opus mandatorum dei erigimur ac suscitamur, **79** et ex ipsis rursus caritatis operibus vel conservatur in nobis dei caritas vel augetur.

80 Et hoc puto ostendere volentem dominum dicere, aliquando quidem *Si diligitis me mandata mea servate,* **81** aliquando autem *Si* facitis quae ego dico vobis permanetis *in caritate mea, sicut ego servavi mandata patris mei et maneo in caritate eius.*

82 Ex quibus edocet nos prospectum operis nostri debere ex sua voluntate pendere, ut tamquam speculam quandam ipsum habentes et semper ad ipsum respicientes opus nostrum fixo ad ipsum cordis oculo dirigamus.

83 Sicut enim artificia quae in hac vita sunt prospectum quendam animi gerunt, et ita secundum hoc quod animo conceperint etiam in opere utuntur manuum ministerio, **84** sic et in hoc nostro opere unus manet nobis iste prospectus atque unus terminus fixus est quo deo placere debeamus; secundum hunc ergo prospectum opus dirigamus mandatorum. **85** Impossibile namque est aliter constare posse operis nostri formam, nisi voluntas eius qui iniunxit opus in memoria semper habeatur, **86** ut eius voluntate servata et labore operis ac diligentia competenter expleta semper iungamur deo, dum semper eius memores sumus.

---

[11] *A nostris* J by correct conjecture, confirmed L² 66; *e* S; omitted by Zelz. with all other MSS.

74 It needs to be considered before all else that no-one can succeed in keeping any commandment at all, neither the one that charges us concerning love for God, nor the one concerning love for one's neighbour, if the mind is wandering off among varied and scattered occupations, **75** for it is impossible that those who are constantly fluctuating between one thing and another should attain any craft or the discipline of any skill.

76 We ought therefore to guard our heart with all watchfulness lest it happen that base desires and sullied thoughts cast out and displace from our minds the desire for God. **77** On the contrary, by the diligent recollection and memory of God, let us so deeply fix his form and figure as it were in our soul like a seal, that no disquietudes may cause it to be lost. **78** For in this way desire for the divine love comes upon us when the memory of him constantly illumines our mind and dispositions, and we are roused and stirred to the work of the commandments of God, **79** and conversely, by these works of love the love of God is safeguarded in us and increased.

80 And the Lord wants to show this, I think, when on one occasion he says: *If you love me, keep my commandments* (John 14:15), **81** while elsewhere he says: *If you* do what I tell you, *you abide in my love, just as I have kept my Father's commandments and abide in his love* (John 15:10).

82 From this he teaches us that the goal of our work ought to hinge on his will, as though we had a kind of mirror to which we continually look back and, by keeping the eye of our heart upon it, direct our work.

83 Just as the crafts of this life set before the mind a certain goal and work through the ministry of the hand in accordance with this goal engendered in the mind, **84** so also in our work only one purpose remains for us and one goal is fixed: that we should please God. Let us, therefore, direct the work of the commandments toward this goal. **85** For it is impossible otherwise to give definite form to our work unless we hold him continually in memory who enjoined the work, **86** so that, by keeping his will and fulfilling it exactly through the labour and diligence of our work, we shall always be joined to God while we are ever mindful of him.

87 Sicut enim verbi causa faber securem faciens aut falcem meminit semper eius qui opus iniunxit, et retinet in corde suo cuius magnitudinis vel qualitatis vel formae iniunxerit fieri securem, **88** et illud semper intendens quod sibi meminit a domino operis iniunctum ad hoc dirigit manuum ministerium, ut forma operis cum eius qui iniunxit animis ac voluntate conveniat—**89** si autem obliviscatur, quid vel quale sit quod sibi fuerat imperatum, sine dubio alius aliquid quam iniunctum fuerat faciet—**90** ita et Christianus omnem conatum et omne studium in actibus suis adhibere debet, **91** ut secundum voluntatem dei qui opus iniunxit, suum quoque dirigat opus, ut et actus sui ornentur et possit eius qui praecepit voluntas impleri. **92** Tunc etiam illud compleri potest quod scriptum est *Sive manducates sive bibitis sive aliud quid facitis, omnia in gloriam dei facite.* **93** Si vero declinet a regula et corrumpat observantiam mandati, ex hoc ipso arguitur quod sit immemor dei.

94 Plurimum autem prodest ad conservandum memoriam dei etiam secretius et semotius habitare, nam permixtum vivere cum his qui neglegentius agunt circa timorem dei et contemptum habent mandatorum eius, plurimum nocet; **95** sicut et Salomonis sermo testatur dicens *Cum homine iracundo ne habitaveris, ne forte discas vias eius et accipias laqueos animae tuae,* **96** et iterum quod dicit *Exite de medio eorum et separamini, dicit dominus,* ad hoc ipsum respicit.

97 Igitur ut neque per oculos neque per aures recipiamus[12] illecebras ad peccandum, et paulatim longo usu inhaereamus consuetudini pessimae, et rursum ut possimus orationi vacare, oportet primo secretius habitare; **98** hoc enim modo et praecedentes consuetudines excidimus in quibus contra mandatum dei agebamus. **99** Non enim parvus labor est ut se aliquis a priori non bona consuetudine reflectat ac revocet, quoniam quidem mos longo tempore confirmatus vim quodammodo obtinet naturae; **100** oportet ergo nos primo omnium negare nos ipsos et tollere crucem Christi et sic eum sequi.

---

[12] *Recipiamus* Zelz. following C, P, WLG, confirmed L² 25; *respiciamus* HJMST, an archetype error.

87 Just as, for example, a smith making an axe or a scythe constantly remembers him who ordered the work and retains in his heart the size and kind and shape in which he ordered the axe to be made, **88** and, ever intending that which he remembers in himself was enjoined by the master of the work, directs the service of his hands to this end, that the form of the work might accord with the mind and will of him who ordered it—**89** but who, if he forgets what and of what kind it is that was commanded him, will without doubt make something else or something of a kind different to that which was ordered him, **90** so also the Christian ought to exert every effort and every diligence in his activities, **91** so that he directs his own work according to the will of God who enjoined the work, with the result that his own actions are finished well and he is able to fulfil the will of him who gave the charge. **92** Then he is also able to fulfil what is written: *Whether you eat or drink, or whatever you do, do all for the glory of God* (1 Cor 10:31). **93** But if he strays from the rule and corrupts his observance of the commandment, by this very fact his forgetfulness of God is demonstrated.

94 It is of the greatest help in preserving the memory of God to dwell in retirement and seclusion.[26] For to live mixing with those who act without a care for the fear of God and who show contempt towards his commandments is greatly harmful, **95** as the word of Solomon bears witness saying: *Do not dwell with a wrathful man, lest you learn his ways and acquire snares for your soul* (Prov 22:24), **96** and again the saying: *Come out from their midst and be separated, says the Lord* (2 Cor 6:17) makes the same point.

97 That we may not therefore admit inducements to sin through the eyes or the ears and so, little by little, through long habit, become settled in a most wretched way of life, and again that we might be able to give time to prayer, we ought first of all seek a retired dwelling. **98** For by this means we cut out former habits, in which we behaved contrary to the commandment of God. **99** And this is no mean struggle, to reexamine and recall oneself from a former unworthy way of life, because behaviour strengthened by length of time acquires, as it were, the force of nature. **100** Therefore we ought before all else to *deny ourselves and take up the cross* of Christ, and so *follow him* (Matt 16:24).

---

[26] LR 6 925A: Retirement to a secluded dwelling also contributes to the soul's undistraction (τό ἀμετέοριστον τῇ ψυχῇ). QF also has "when his soul is undistracted."

101 Negamus autem nos hoc modo, si per omnia praeteritae consuetudines obliti voluntates proprias abnegemus et ita non solum a hominibus non recte agentibus, verum etiam a nostris ipsis inordinatis et incompositis moribus secedamus; **102** alioquin ut in eadem quis consuetudines atque in priori conversatione permanens emendare se possit et corrigere difficillimum est, immo ut verius dicam, penitus impossibile. **103** Sed ad hoc ipsum ut *tollat* quis *crucem suam et sequatur* Christum, plurimum impedit societas et permixtio eorum qui vitam dissimilem vivunt. **104** Nam paratum esse ad mortem pro Christo et *mortificare membra quae sunt super terram* et pro nomine Christi libenter ferre omne discrimen, hoc est *tollere crucem suam;* **105** ad quod grande videmus impedimentum posse nobis oboriri ab his qui dissimiles sunt vel vita vel moribus.

106 Et ad cetera alia quae multa sunt accedit etiam hoc, ut respiciens anima ad multitudinem nequiter viventium primo quidem occupetur et impediatur **107** ne suorum malorum capiat intellectum et possit vel purgare per paenitentiam quae deliquit vel causas culpae recidere emendatione vitiorum; **108** in comparatione etenim pessimorum aliquid se iam magni aestimat perfecisse.

109 Tum deinde impedimentis et interturbationibus atque occupationibus quas communis hominum vita habere solet, illud quod maius omnium est et pretiosius, memoriam dei, non potest custodire; **110** qua[13] depulsa ab animis et exclusa non solum omni laetitia et gaudio caret divino et delectationis domini sustinet detrimenta **111** et dulcedinem divini non sentit eloquii ut dicat *Quam dulcia faucibus meis eloquia tua, super mel et favum ori meo,* **112** sed et in neglectum et oblivionem pervenit iudiciorum dei et in contemptus consuetudinem decidit; quo maius malum et perniciosius pati nihil potest.

---

[13] Zelz. with β MSS, confirmed L[1] 589; *quae* CS, an archetype error.

101 Now we deny ourselves in this way if, forgetting everything to do with our former habits, we renounce our own will and so secede not only from people who do not act uprightly but also from our own disordered and unbridled ways. **102** Otherwise, to emend and correct oneself while continuing in the same habits and former way of life is very difficult or, to speak more truly,[27] completely impossible. **103** Indeed, to associate and mingle with those who live by a different life greatly hinders this saying, that *one take up one's cross and follow* Christ (Matt 16:24). **104** For to be *ready to die for Christ* (cf. Luke 22:23) and to *mortify one's members that are upon the earth* (Col 3:5) and to willingly bear every *danger* for the name of Christ (cf. Rom 8:35-37)—this is to *take up one's cross* (Matt 16:24). **105** And we observe what a great hindrance can arise for us from those who are of dissimilar life and conduct.

106 In addition to many other obstacles it even happens that a soul, as it looks about the multitude of those living iniquitously, is in the first place preoccupied and hindered **107** from gaining an understanding of its own ills, and so from being able through repentance to purge its own failings and cut back the causes of sin by the emendment of vices. **108** And it even happens that by comparing itself with those who are worse, it reckons that it has already made great progress.

109 Second, by reason of the hindrances and tumults and preoccupations with which the common life of human beings is usually filled, the soul is unable to safeguard that which is greater and more precious than anything else: the memory of God. **110** With this repulsed and shut out from the soul, it not only suffers the loss of all gladness and divine joy and of delight in the Lord **111** and does not feel the sweetness of his word to say *Sweeter to my throat are your words than honey and honeycomb to my mouth* (Ps 18:10), **112** but it even arrives at neglect and forgetfulness of the judgments of God and sinks into the habit of contempt. A greater or more ruinous evil than this it is not possible to suffer.

---

[27] LR 6 925C has a negative here that is missing in RBas 2.102: ἵνα μὴ λέγω ὅτι παντελῶς ἀνεπίδεκτον (if I do not say completely impossible). QF also preserves this negative: in other words, it might just be possible with immense difficulty. Basil, as bishop, certainly had to make his way in the midst of customary indifference. Rufinus may have misconstrued ἀδιαφόρῳ συνηθείᾳ as referring to one's own formerly indifferent habits (already referred to), but to judge from the Greek and the Syriac, it refers rather to the way of life in the world at large.

Interrogatio III
(Zelzer 25–32, QF 3, LR 7 [PG 31.927–934])

I: Quia ostendit nobis sermo tuus periculosum esse cum his qui mandata dei contemnunt vitam ducere, nunc discere cupimus, si oporteat eum qui ab huiuscemodi consortiis discesserit semotum esse et solum, an vero cum fratribus eiusdem propositi et eiusdem animi vitam suam sociare.

R: In multis utile esse video vitam communem ducere cum his qui eiusdem voluntatis sunt ac propositi,

2 primo quod etiam ad usus corporales victusque ministerium unusquisque nostrum solus sibi non sufficit, et ideo pro his quae ad ministerium vitae nostrae necessaria sunt invicem opera nostra egemus. **3** sicut pes hominis in alio quidem suis viribus utitur, in alio vero indiget alienis et sine adiumento ceterorum membrorum nec explere opus suum nec sufficere suis usibus potest, **4** ita etiam vita solitaria mihi pati videtur, cum neque quod ei inest utile esse possit neque acquiri quod deest. **5** Praeter hoc autem ne ratio quidem caritatis unumquemque permittit quod suum est quaerere dicente apostolo *Caritas non quaerit quae sua sunt.*

6 Deinde sed ne culpas quidem suas unusquisque ac vitia facile dinoscit, cum qui arguat nemo sit, **7** et facile huiusmodi homini accidere potest illud quod scriptum est *Vae soli, quia si cediderit non est alius qui erigat eum.* **8** Sed et mandata a pluribus quidem facilius adimplentur, ab uno vero dum unum videtur impleri aliud impeditur: ut puta quomodo solus quis visitabit infirmum aut quomodo suscipiet peregrinum?

9 Si vero omnes *corpus sumus Christi, singuli autem alterutrum membra,* per consonantiam velut in unius corporis compagem in spiritu sancto aptari et coniungi debemus ad invicem. **10** Quodsi unusquisque nostrum solitariam eligat vitam, scilicet non tali aliqua causa vel ratione quae deo sit placita vel quae ad communem ceterorum pertineat dispensationem, sed propriae voluntati et passioni satisfaciens, **11** quomodo possumus discissi et divisi adimplere et integram assignare membrorum ad se invicem consonantiam? **12** Iste enim talis neque *cum gaudentibus gaude*t neque *cum flentibus fle*t, quoniam quidem separatus et divisus a ceteris ne cognoscere quidem necessitates poterit proximorum.

Question 3

Q: Since your discourse[28] has shown us the danger of living among those who hold the commandments of God in contempt, we now want to learn whether it is better for one who has withdrawn from such society to live privately by himself[29] or to associate his life with brothers of the same goal and of the same mind?

R: 1 I observe that to lead a life in common with those of the same will and purpose is of advantage in many ways.[30]

2 First, even in regard to bodily needs and the provision of sustenance not one of us suffices for himself alone, and so for those things which are necessary for the provision of our life we need our tasks to be for one another. **3** Just as the foot of a man has use of its own powers, yet has need of others, and without the aid of the other limbs could neither fulfil its own task nor suffice with its own powers, **4** so also this is what happens, it seems to me, in the solitary life, since what it has cannot be of use and what it lacks it cannot obtain. **5** Besides, the very character of love does not allow an individual to seek his own interests, for the Apostle says: *Love seeks not its own* (1 Cor 13:4).

6 Second, the individual does not easily recognize his own faults and vices since there is no one to reprove him **7** and it can easily happen to such a man as it is written: *Woe to one alone, for if he falls there is none else to raise him up* (Eccl 4:10). **8** Moreover, the commandments are more easily fulfilled by the many, but by someone alone, when one commandment appears to have been fulfilled, another is hindered. For how do you think that one alone shall *visit the sick* or else *welcome the stranger*? (Matt 25:36, 35)

9 But if *we* all *are the body* of *Christ and each members of the other* (Rom 12:5) then we ought to be fitted and joined together through our harmony into the compact of one body in the Holy Spirit. **10** But if each of us chooses the solitary life, that is, for no cause or principle that is pleasing to God or that pertains to that common dispensation of others, but to satisfy one's own will and passion—**11** how could we, thus split off and divided, fulfil and apply that harmonious relation of the members towards each another? **12** For such a one will neither *rejoice with the joyful* or *weep with those who weep* (cf. Rom 12:15), because he is separated and divided from others, and shall be unable to know the needs of his neighbours.

---

[28] LR 7.Q 928B: ὁ λόγος, QF ܪ̈ܠܬܐ. See note to RBas 1.Q.

[29] LR 7.Q 928C: καθ᾽ ἑαυτὸν, referring to the "philosophic" life.

[30] RBas 3 constitutes one of the most persuasive arguments for community life over solitary life ever mounted in Christian literature.

13 Tum deinde nec sufficere potest unus ad suscipienda omnia dona spiritus sancti, quia secundum uniusquiusque mensuram fidei et donorum spiritalium distributio celebratur, **14** quo id quod per partes unicuique distributum est, rursum tamquam membra ad aedificationem unius corporis coeat et conspiret. **15** *Alii* enim *datur sermo sapientiae, alii sermo scientiae, alli fides, alli prophetia, alli gratia sanitatum* et cetera, quae singula utique non tam pro se unusquisque quam pro aliis suscipit ab spiritu sancto. **16** Et ideo necesse est uniusquiusque gratiam quam susceperit ab spiritu dei in commune prodesse. **17** Accidit ergo ut is qui semotus vivit et separatus unamquamcumque suscipiat gratiam, et hanc ipsam inutilem facit dum nihil per eam operatur sed defodit eam in semet ipso: **18** quod cuius et quanti sit periculi nostis omnes qui legistis[14] evangelium. **19** Si autem ceteris communicat gratiam, perfruitur et ea ipsa proprie quam ipse suscepit—et multiplicatur in eo dum communicatur et ceteris—et ipse nihilominus prod‹uc›itur[15] gratia reliquorum.

20 Habet autem et alia quam plurima bona communis vita ista sanctorum, quae non est nunc possibile omnia dinumerare, **21** interim ut diximus ad conservanda sancti spiritus dona commodior est multo quam si degamus in solitudine. **22** Sed et adversus insidias inimici quae extrinsecus inferuntur, multo cautior est et utilior societas plurimorum, **23** ut facilius suscitetur somno, si quis forte *obdormi*erit somnum illum qui ducit ad *mortem.* **24** Sed et delinquenti delictum suum facilius apparebit cum a pluribus vel arguitur vel notatur, secundum quod et apostolus dixit *Sufficit ei qui eiusmodi est obiurgatio haec quae fit a pluribus.*

25 Sed et in oratione non parvum emolumentum a pluribus nascitur cum consensu et unanimitate orantibus, ut ex multorum personis per gratiam quae in nobis est deo gratiae referantur.

26 Sed et interim periculo proxima est vita solitaria: primo quidem illi periculo subiacet, quod certe gravissimum est, in quo ipse sibi placet et neminem habens qui possit probare opus ipsius videbitur sibi a summam perfectionem venisse.

---

[14] *Legistis* (perfect tense reflecting οἱ ἀνεγνωκότες) JS, confirmed L² 49-50; *legitis* (present tense): Zelz. following C, β.

[15] *Prod‹uc›itur* restored L² 65, consulting the Greek καρποῦται; †*proditur*† ('benefited') Zelz. with ES, but marking it as a corruption and suggesting that a passive form of the verb *prodesse* may have originally been here; *proficiet* C, WLG; *fruitur* HJMTZ; *perfruitur* P.

13 Then too, one alone cannot suffice to receive all the gifts of the Holy Spirit, since the distribution of the Spirit is given *according to the proportion of each one's faith* (cf. Rom 12:6), **14** so that what is distributed to each in part comes together again and acts together as do limbs to the building up of the one body. **15** For *to one is given the word of wisdom, to another the word of knowledge, to another faith, to another prophecy, to another the gifts of healings* (1 Cor 12:8) and so on, each of which the individual receives from the Holy Spirit not so much for himself as for others. **16** It is therefore necessary that the grace which each receives from the Spirit of God is brought forth in common. **17** It therefore happens that one who lives secluded and separate[31] may perhaps receive one gift, and this very gift he renders useless since he accomplishes nothing with it, but buries it in himself. **18** The one whose danger this was—and how great a danger!—all you who have read the gospel know (cf. Matt 25:18-25). **19** If however he shares his gift with others he both enjoys what he himself has received and it is multiplied in him by sharing it with others, and he is no less advanced by the gift of others.

3. **20** Besides, the life of the saints in common has many other advantages, which cannot all be enumerated now. **21** For the present, as we have said, it is far more conducive to fostering the gifts of the Holy Spirit than if we spent our life in solitude, **22** and much safer and more helpful for warding off the ambushes of the enemy which are brought in from without. **23** Hence one will be roused more easily from sleep, should it happen that anyone *falls asleep* in that slumber which leads to *death* (cf. Ps 12:4). **24** And his offence will be more readily brought home to an offender when it is reprimanded and censured by the many in accordance with what the Apostle said: *For such a one let the punishment wrought by the many suffice* (2 Cor 2:6).

25 Moreover, in prayer no small gain is generated by the many when they pray with one mind and heart, so that from many persons, through the grace which is in us, thanks are rendered to God.[32]

26 But meanwhile the solitary life is in immediate danger. First, it lies fast by that danger which is certainly of the utmost gravity: in that he pleases himself, and, having no-one able to test his work, he will appear to himself to have arrived at the highest perfection.

---

[31] This is Rufinus's rendering of καθ᾽ ἑαυτὸν ζῶν.

[32] The presence of this passage, which has dropped out in the longer Greek text, in the *Small Asketikon* is supported by the QF in a somewhat glossed and amplified form. The passage teaches that greater power is engendered when the many pray together.

27 Tum deinde sine ullo exercitio degens neque quid sibi vitii abundet neque quid virtutus desit agnoscit, **28** neque discretionem habere poterit in operum qualitate, pro eo quod operandi materia omnis exclusa sit. **29** In quo enim humilitatem suam probabit neminem habens cui se humilem debeat exhibere, in quo misericordiam demonstrabit totius consortii et societas alienus? **30** Ad patientiam vero quomodo semet ipsum exercebit nullum habens qui videatur eius voluntatibus obviare? **31** Si quis autem dicat sufficere sibi scripturae doctrinam et apostolica praecepta ad emendationem morum[16] vitamque formandam, **32** simile mihi aliquid facere videtur eis qui semper fabrile artificium discunt, numquam tamen fabrefaciunt[17] opus, **33** vel his qui structorum artem semper docentur, numquam tamen aedificandae domui operam dabunt.

34 Ecce enim et dominus non aestimavit sufficere solam verbi doctrinam, sed et opere ipso voluit nobis trader humilitatis exemplum,[18] cum *praecinc*tus *linte*o *lavit pedes discipulorum* suorum. **35** Tu ergo cuius pedes lavabis? Quem curabis officiis? Cuius inferior aut ultimus eris cum solus vivas? **36** Sed et illud quod dicitur *Bonum et iucundum habitare fratres in unum*, quod *unguent*o pontificale *de capite in barbam descend*enti sanctus spiritus comparavit, quod in solitaria habitatione complebitur?

37 Stadium namque est quodam, in quo per virtutis exercitium proficitur, in quo meditatio divinorum mandatorum effulget amplius et clarescit, et communis inter se unanimorum fratrum habitatio? **38** habens in se illam similitudinem et exemplum quod in actibus apostolorum refert de sanctis scriptura divina dicens quia **39** *Omnes crede*ntes *erant* in unum *et habebant omnia communia.*

---

[16] *Morum*, P, THJMZ Hol., confirmed L² 37 matching the Gk: πρὸς τὴν κατόρθωσιν τῶν ἠθῶν; omitted by Zelz. following SC, WLG.

[17] *Fabrefaciunt* restored L¹ 589; *fabrifaciunt* Zelz., following the MSS, an archetype error, L¹ 589.

[18] *-plum* GJL, Gk, Syr.; *-pla* CEHMPSTZ, Zelz; *-lo* W.

27 The second is this, that spending his life without any training, he recognizes neither what vice flourishes in him nor what virtue is lacking, **28** nor will he be able to discern the character of his work, because he is stripped of all material with which to work. **4. 29** For in what way shall he put his humility to the test if he has no-one before whom he must show himself humble? In what way shall he show mercy who is estranged from all communion and society? **30** How indeed shall he exercise himself in patience, if he has no-one who appears to thwart his wishes? **31** But if anyone says that for the amendment of conduct and the guidance of his life the teaching of Scripture and the apostolic precepts are sufficient for him, **32** then he seems to me to make himself like those who are ever learning the technique of a craft, yet never put their craft into practice, **33** or like those who are always learning the art of building yet never give themselves to the task of the building of a house.

34 For behold, the Lord too did not deem the mere teaching of the word sufficient, but wished to deliver to us an example of humility in very deed, when he, *having girded himself with a linen cloth, washed the feet of his disciples* (John 13:5). **35** Whose feet then will you wash? For whom will you perform the duties of care? In comparison with whom shall you be lower or even the *last* (Mark 9:35), if you live by yourself? **36** Yes, and that saying: *A good and delightful thing it is when brothers dwell in unity,* which the Holy Spirit compares to the high-priestly *anointing flowing down from the head upon the beard* (Ps 132:1-2), how shall this be accomplished by dwelling alone?

37 For here is a kind of stadium in which progress is made through the exercise of virtue; in which meditation of the divine commandments shines out more fully and becomes bright—*that common dwelling of brothers in unity* among themselves (Ps 132:1), **38** which possesses in itself the likeness and example of the saints which the divine Scripture records in the Acts of the Apostles, where it says: **39** *All the believers were of one mind and held all things in common* (Acts 2:44).

Interrogatio IIII

(Zelzer 32–34, QF 4, LR 8 [PG 31.933–942])

I: Si oportet primo renuntiare omnibus et ita venire ad hanc vitam vel conversationem quae secundum deum est?

R: 1 Domino et Salvatore nostro Iesu Christo dicente *Si quis* venit a me, *abneget se ipsum et tollat crucem suam et sequatur me,* **2** et iterum *Qui non renuntiaverit omnibus quae possidet, non potest meus esse discipulus,* **3** qui ad hoc venit ut dominum sequatur, etiam se ipsum negat et tollit crucem suam; certum est autem quia et ante iam diabolo renuntiavit et operibus eius. **4** Quod tamen non ab his qui in profectu vitae sunt vel qui iam ad perfectionem tendunt, sed ab his qui prima confessione initiantur fieri solet.

5 In hoc autem renuntiat, sicut superius diximus, etiam ipse sibi homo, id est priori consuetudini suae vel vitae, **6** renuntiat autem etiam moribus suis vel delectationibus saeculi huius, sed et consanguinitati corporali, illi maxime quae impedire eius propositum potest. **7** Et parentes quidem eos qui se *in Christo Iesu per evangelium genu*erunt, magis putabit, fratres autem eos qui eundem *adoptionis spiritum* susceperunt; possessiones vero omnes simul a se ducit alienas. **8** Et ut breviter dicam, hic cui pro Christo omnis *mundus crucifixus est et* ipse *mundo,* quomodo potest servus effici cogitationum et sollicitudinum mundi, cum dominus iubeat etiam animam ipsam negandam esse pro se? **9** Perfecta itaque abrenuntiatio in eo est, ut passionibus penitus careat dum adhuc in corpore est, **10** sed haec incipit agere ab his primo quae extrinsecus sunt, id est a possessionibus vel inani gloria et si qua sunt alia similia, ut ab his primo efficiatur alienus.

11 Et hoc est quod nos docuerunt apostoli Iacobus et Iohannes relinquentes patrem suum Zebedaeum et navem ipsam in qua erant, **12** sed et Matthaeus relinquens vectigal et surgens ac sequens dominum, qui non solum lucra reliquerat vectigalium, sed et periculum contempserat **13** quod utique poterat evenire a principibus saeculi, pro eo quod vectigalium rationes imperfectas atque incompositas reliquisset. **14** Ita autem cupiditate sequendi dominum ductus est, ut in nullo prorsus huius vitae respectum vel cogitationem sibimet reservaverit.

Question 4

Q: Is it necessary first to renounce everything and so come to this life and way[33] according to God?

R: 1. 1 Since our Lord Jesus Christ says: *If anyone comes to me, let him deny himself and take up his cross and follow me* (Matt 16:24), **2** and again, *Whoever does not renounce all that he possesses, cannot be my disciple* (Luke 14:33), **3** whoever comes for this purpose, that he might follow the Lord, let him also *deny himself and take up his cross*; for surely, he has already renounced beforehand the devil and his works. **4** This, after all, is what is normally done, not by those who have made progress in the life—by those, that is, already striving toward perfection—but by those being initiated in their first confession.

5 But at this point let a man renounce, as we said above, even his own self, that is, his former habits and way of life, **6** and let him also renounce his own ways and the delights of this world—yes and even the bodily kinship of blood and the things which can especially hinder his purpose. **7** Accordingly, such a one will deem as his parents those who *begot him in Christ Jesus through the Gospel* (cf. 1 Cor 4:15), and as his brothers those who have received the same *spirit of adoption* (Rom 8:15), while all possessions he will regard as alien to him. **8** If I may put it briefly, how could one to whom for Christ's sake *the whole world is crucified and himself to the world* (cf. Gal 6:14) be enslaved to the thoughts and *the cares of the world* (Matt 13:22), when the Lord bade that for his sake he should deny even *his own self* (Luke 14:26)? **9** And so perfect renunciation consists in this, to be utterly free of passions while still in the body. **10** But one begins to do this first by the renunciation of external things, that is, of possessions and empty glory and other things of this kind, so that one becomes a stranger to them from the outset.

11 And this is what the apostles James and John taught when they left their own father Zebedee and the very boat they were in (cf. Matt 4:21-22), **12** and Matthew too by leaving the tax office and rising up and following the Lord (cf. Matt 9:9). He not only left behind the profit from tax-gathering, but also disregarded the danger **13** that might come upon him from the princes of this world for having left his tax-gathering accounts unfinished and in disarray. **14** He however was so led by a longing to follow the Lord that he did not retain a concern for anything whatever to do with this life or a thought for himself.

---

[33] *Hanc vitam vel conversationem*—So Rufinus renders πολιτεία, i.e., the concrete *praxis* of life in community.

15 Quia autem neque ad affectus parentum, si adversantur dominicis praeceptis, neque ad ullam aliquam humanam delectationem oporteat aliquem respicere et per hoc a eo quod proposuit impediri, dominus nos edocet dicens **16** *Si quis ergo venit ad me et non odit patrem suum et matrem suam et uxorem et filios et fratres et sorores, insuper et animam suam, non potest meus esse discipulus.* **17** Quo est simile illi quod dixit, ut deneget quis *se ipsum.*

Interrogatio V
(Zelzer 35–36, QF 5, LR 9 [PG 31.941–944])

I: Si oportet eum qui servis dei sociari vult relinquere indifferenter propinquis suis portionem facultatum suarum?

R: **1** Domino dicente *Vende omnia bona tua et da pauperibus et habebis thesaurum in caelis et veni sequere me,* et iterum *Vendite omnia quae habetis et date elemosynam,* **2** arbitror quod is qui accedit ad ei servitium non debeat contemnere et utlibet relinquere ea quae sibi competunt, **3** sed temptet omnia, si fieri potest cum summa diligentia, assumpta tamquam ea quae iam domino consecrata sunt, quantum[19] fieri potest rationabiliter dispensare, sciens quia non est absque periculo in opere dei agere neglegenter.

4 Si vero propinqui eius vel parentes contra fidem veniant, debet rursum meminisse domini dicentis quia **5** *Non est qui reliquerit domum aut fratres aut patrem aut matrem au uxorem aut filios aut agros propter me et propter evangelium, qui non accipiat centuplum in praesente tempore et in futuro saeculo vitam aeternam.* **6** Verumtamen oportet eum his qui sibi quae sua sunt denegant et resistunt et de fide faciunt, protestari et denuntiare **7** quia sacrilegii crimen incurrunt secundum mandatum domini dicentis quia *Si peccat in te frater tuus vade et argue eum* et reliqua.

---

[19] *Quantam* Zelz., most MSS, confirmed L² 16-17 ; *quam* CS.

2. 15 Moreover, that one must look neither to the affection of parents, if they oppose themselves to the Lord's precepts, nor to any human delight if he is hindered thereby from what he has proposed to do, the Lord teaches us, saying: **16** *And therefore if anyone comes to me and does not hate his father and mother and wife and children and brothers and sisters and yes, even his own soul, he cannot be my disciple* (Luke 14:26), **17** which is like that which he said: *let a man deny himself* (Matt 16:24).

Question 5

Q: Should one who wishes to join himself to the servants of God relinquish his property to his relatives indifferently?

R: 1 Since the Lord says: *Sell your possessions and give to the poor and you shall have treasure in heaven, and come follow me* (Matt 19:21), and again: *Sell all that you have and give alms* (Luke 12:23), **2** I consider that one who is coming to the service of God ought not to esteem lightly and give up the things that belong to him as he pleases, **3** but should as far as possible assess all things with the utmost diligence, since henceforth they are consecrated to the Lord, and should dispose of them reasonably[34] as far as it can be done, aware that not without peril does one *carry out the work of God negligently* (Jer 48:10).

4 But if his relatives or even his parents should come out against the faith, then he should remember what the Lord says: **5** *There is no one who has left house or brothers or father or mother or wife or children or fields for my sake and for the sake of the gospel, who shall not receive a hundredfold in this present time and in the world to come eternal life* (Mark 10:29-30 + Luke 13:26). **6** He must however protest to and denounce those who deny what belongs to him, and resist and take action on behalf of the faith, **7** since they incur a sin of sacrilege (cf. Rom 2:22), according to the commandment of the Lord who says *If your brother sins against you, go and show him his fault* and so on (Matt 18:15).

---

[34] LR 9.1 941B: μετὰ πάσης εὐλαβείας, "with all piety"; QF: "with the uprightness of the fear of the Lord." In the Syriac, "fear of the Lord" is always used to translate the Greek words for "piety": *eulabeia* and *eusebeia*.

8 Iudicio vero experiri de his apud iudices saeculi abnuit religionis auctoritas per id quod dixit apostolus *Audet aliquis vestrum negotium habens adversus alium iudicari apud iniustos et non apud sanctos,* **9** et rursum quia *Iam quidem omnino delictum est vobis quia iudicia habetis inter vos.*

Interrogatio VI
(Zelzer 36–38, QF 6, LR 10 [PG 31.943–948])

I: Si oportet omnes qui veniunt ad nos suscipere aut cum probatione, et qualis ista debet esse probatio?

R: 1 Cum dei clementia omnes vocet per illam praedicationem qua dicit *Venite a me omnes qui laboratis et onerati estis et ego reficiam vos,* non est sine discrimine abicere quempiam venientem ad nos.

2 Verumtamen neque immundis ut aiunt pedibus indulgendum est introire quempiam in sancta doctrinae,[20] **3** sed sicut dominus noster Iesus Christus iuvenem illum qui ad se venerat interrogavit de priori vita sua, et cum audisset quia recte transacta est, quod deerat ei praecepit adimplere et ita demum iussit eum sequi se, **4** ita ergo etiam nos oportet inquirere de praeterita vita et conversatione, ne forte simulata quis mente et fallaci animo accedat ad nos. **5** Quod ita demum dinoscitur si facile omnem laborem corporis qui iniungitur ferat et ad castigatiorem vitam pronius inclinatur, **6** vel si etiam delictum aliquod suum cum interrogatus fuerit nequaquam pronuntiare confunditur et medelam delicti quae adhibita fuerit gratanter assumit **7** et si ad omnem humilitatem absque ulla verecundia inclinatur ac vilioribus et abiectioribus artificiis si ita ratio poposcerit tradi se non accipit aspernanter. **8** Cum ergo ex his singulis documentis fuerit comprobatus quia firma mente et stabili consilio ac prompto animo sit, tunc suscipi eum decet.

---

[20] LR 10.1 944C: τῆς σεμνότητος ἐπιβαίνειν τῶν διδαγμάτων "to tread upon the hallowed ground of the teachings"; QF: trample upon the sobriety/reverence of the teaching. *Sancta doctrinae* in S only is closer to the Greek text; *sancta doctrina* CH; *sanctae doctrinae* T; *sanctam doctrinam* (the easiest reading, "enter upon the sacred doctrine/teaching") GJLMPWZ Hol. *2.1.

8 But the sanction of piety[35] forbids us to bring these matters to trial before the secular judges through that saying of the Apostle: *Does any of you, having a grievance against another dare to go to court before the unrighteous instead of before the saints?* (1 Cor 6:1), **9** and again: *it is already an utter defeat for you, that you have litigation among yourselves at all* (1 Cor 6:7).[36]

Question 6

Q: Ought we accept all who come to us, or only after testing and of what kind should that testing be?

R: 1 Since the loving-kindness of God invites everyone by that proclamation which says: *Come to me all you who labour and are burdened and I will refresh you* (Matt 11:28), it is not without hazard[37] that we send away anyone who comes to us.

2 Nonetheless, no one should be permitted to enter upon the holy ground of the teachings with unwashed feet, as they say (cf. John 13:8). **3** Instead, just as our Lord Jesus Christ questioned the young man who came to him concerning his former life and, when he had heard that it was conducted uprightly, bade him complete what was still lacking and only then ordered him to follow him (cf. Matt 19:16-21), **4** so therefore we too should enquire concerning their former habits and manner of life, in case it happens that someone comes to us with a duplicitous mind and a false motive. **5** Thus let it be discerned at length whether he readily carries out every bodily labour enjoined on him and inclines himself assiduously to a more disciplined life **6** or if he is questioned about some shortcoming of his, whether he is not at all put out to declare it, and when a remedy for his fault is assigned, whether he accepts it agreeably, **7** and whether with all humility, without any embarrassment he inclines himself to the more menial and lowlier tasks, if reason so requires, and will not permit himself to submit disdainfully. **8** When, therefore, he has been shown by each of these proofs to be of firm mind and stable purpose and prompt disposition, it is fitting then that he be received.

---

[35] Ὁ τῆς θεοσεβείας λόγος, which Garnier translates as *"sermo pietatis"*; QF: "the word/principle of the fear of God."

[36] The omission of this second passage from 1 Corinthians 6 in the Greek text bears the mark of Basil's editorial work. Such a text too pointedly discountenanced *all* litigation, and he is just about to revise his earlier position and detail the circumstances in which he thinks piety might, in fact, condone involvement in public litigation.

[37] LR 10.1 944C: without a risk / danger (ἀκίνδυνον), QF: ܐܦ ܩܝ̈ܢܕܘܢܘܣ there is a danger if. . . .

9 prius autem quam corpori fraternitatis inseratur oportet ei iniungi quaedam laboriosa et quae videantur opprobrio haberi a saecularibus, **10** et observare oportet, si libenter haec et libere ac fiducialiter expleat nec confusionem eorum graviter ferat **11** vel etiam si in labore impiger inveniatur et promptus.

Interrogatio VII
(Zelzer 38–40, QF 7, **1–10** LR 15 [PG 31.951–958] ; **14–15** LR 14 [PG 31.949–952])

I: Ex qua aetate oportet nosmet ipsos offerre deo, vel virginitatis professionem quando oportet firmam ac stabilem iudicari?

R: 1 Dicente domino *Sinite infantes venire ad me,* et apostolo Paulo collaudante eum qui *ab infantia sacras litteras* didicisset, et rursum praecipiente *edu*cari *filios in doctrina et correptione domini,* **2** omne tempus a prima aetate opportunum quidem esse ducimus ad suscipiendum in eruditione et timore domini; **3** firma tamen tunc erit professio virginitatis, ex quo adulta iam aetas esse coeperit et ea quae solet nuptiis apta deputari ac perfecta.

9 But before he is grafted into the body of the brotherhood[38] he ought to have enjoined on him certain arduous tasks which are seen to be held in opprobrium by the worldly[39] **10** and one ought to observe whether he freely and generously and faithfully fulfils them and does not despond at the unpleasantness of them, **11** and even if he is found energetic and prompt in carrying them out.

Question 7

Q: From what age should we offer ourselves to God,[40] and when should the profession of virginity[41] be judged firm and stable?

R: 1. 1 Since the Lord says: *Let the little children come to me* (Mark 10:14) and the apostle Paul praises him *who from infancy* had learned *the sacred letters* (2 Tim 3:15), and again instructs that *children be brought up in the teaching and discipline of the Lord* (Eph 6:4), **2** we deem that any time, from the earliest age, is suitable for receiving them to the instruction and fear of the Lord. **3** The profession of virginity, however, will only be firm from the time that adult age begins, or that age which is usually considered appropriate and ripe for marriage.[42]

---

[38] *Fraternitatis* testifies to an original ἀδελφότητος; exactly confirmed in QF: ܪܚܐܘܪܟܐ ܪܬܩ ܐܒ. Cf. RB 61.6 *sociari corpori monasterii.*

[39] Cf. RB 58:7: *si sollicitus est . . . ad opprobria.* The context is identical: the testing of applicants; see Jean Gribomont, "The Commentaries of Adalbert de Vogüé and the Great Monastic Tradition," *ABR* 36 (1985): 229–62, at 256 #6, and Adalbert de Vogüé, "Twenty-five Years of Benedictine Hermeneutics—an Examination of Conscience," *ABR* 36 (1985): 402–52, at 410 n. 25.

[40] LR 15.Q (PG 31.952A): allow them to dedicate themselves to God. LR 15 very considerably expanded the text of the first version, so that it became a small treatise on pedagogy.

[41] LR 15.Q PG 31.952A: τὴν τῆς παρθενίας ὁμολογίαν; QF: ܪܚܐܠܐܕ܈ܐ ܪܚܘ.ܐܐܕ. LR 15 shows that Basil was the first to institute a formal monastic profession. See also Letter 199.18–19 (Def III, 105–11), where he is clearly introducing the idea of an irrevocable public vow for both men and women as something of a new principle, possible only because the church is "advancing." Note his cautious interjections: "it seems to me," "I think that," etc. See also Letter 217.60 (Def III, 251).

[42] RBas 7:3 is probably the most remarkable of the original passages preserved in the RBas. The QF, on the other hand, seems to time a valid profession to the age of reason, i.e., childhood: "But the proof that the profession of virginity is henceforth valid is from when it has reached that measure of age that can venture upon good and evil, and so let them be received." A passage inserted here in the later Greek version mentions the case of orphans, perhaps hinting at the year of the great famine, 369–370.

4 Oportet tamen infantes voluntate et consensu parentum, immo ab ipsis parentibus oblatos sub testimonio plurimorum suscipi, ut omnis occasio maledicti gratia excludatur hominum pessimorum.

5 Adhiberi autem eis oportet summam diligentiam, quo possint ad omne virtutis exercitium probabiliter institui, tam in verbo quam in intellectu et opere; **6** quicquid enim in tenero quis et parvo inseruerit, firmius et tenacius in posterum conservabit. **7** Iniungenda est ergo infantum cura his qui ante omnia in virtute patientiae documenta sui probabiliter prae-buerunt, qui possint pro merito delicti et aetatis singulis quibusque etiam correptionis adhibere mensuram, **8** et qui servent eos primo omnium a sermonibus otiosis et ab iracundia atque incitamentis gulae et cunctis indecentibus atque inordinatis motibus. **9** Si vero cum aetatis augmento nullus in eis deprehenditur profectus industriae sed vaga mens et animus cassus ac tumens etiam post instituta probabilia infructuosus perman-serit, **10** huiuscemodi abici oportet, et maxime cum iuvenilis fervor rudem lacessit aetatem.

11 Eorum vero qui aetate iam robusta accedunt ad servitium dei oportet inquirere, ut diximus, qualitatem vitae praeteritae, **12** et sufficere etiam hoc ipsum, si satis instanter hoc expetunt et si verum et ardens deside-rium est eorum erga opus dei. **13** Huiuscemodi vero fieri documenta ab his oportet qui valde prudenter de his discutere poterunt et probare. **14** Cum autem fuerint suscepti, si forte propositum suum transgressi fuerint, tunc videri eos oportet tamquam eos qui in deum deliquerint, quo teste confessionis suae pactum professi sunt. **15** Et *Si peccaverit,* inquit, *homo in hominem,* orabunt pro ipso ad dominum, *si autem in deum peccaverit quis orabit pro eo?*

4 Little children,[43] however, ought to be received with the will and consent of their parents, and indeed brought by the parents themselves and received before many witnesses, in order that every occasion for blame from those of ill-will be excluded.

5 Moreover, the greatest diligence should be applied to them, that they may be credibly grounded in every exercise of virtue, in word as much as in understanding and in deed. **6** For whatever one practises at a young and tender age he will preserve more firmly and tenaciously afterwards. **7** Therefore the care of little children should be assigned to those who above all have credibly afforded proofs of their exercise of patience,[44] who are able to apply to them the measure of discipline as the fault and the age of each one deserves **8** and are able to keep them first of all from indolent talk and from angry outbursts and from greedy impulses and from all unseemly and disorderly gestures. **9** But if any is discovered among them who has not steadily acquired diligence as he advanced in age, but who instead, with a wandering mind and a casual and inflated attitude continues unfruitful even after the tests of instruction, **10** such a one ought to be put out, especially when youthful excitability provokes immature age.

11 Of those who come to the service of God already at a robust age, inquiry ought to be made, as we have said, into the character of their previous life **12** and even this much may suffice: if they but seek this earnestly and if their desire for the work of God is true and ardent.[45] **13** But the approval of such cases should be made by those who are capable of sifting and testing these things with great prudence. **14** Once they have been received, however, if perchance they transgress their resolve,[46] then they ought to be regarded as those who have acted perversely against God, before whom as witness they professed the covenant of their confession.[47] **15** *If a man sins against a man,* it says, *they shall pray for him to God, but if he sins against God, who shall pray for him?* (1 Sam 2:25).

---

[43] Perhaps this does indeed include babies and toddlers. Certainly Macrina rescued babies abandoned by the roadside during the great famine.

[44] This sentence can be partially detected in the much expanded text at LR 15.2 953B: Let someone of mature years be put in charge of them, more experienced than the others, one who gives evidence of patience (καὶ μαρτυρίαν ἔχων ἐπὶ μακροθυμίᾳ).

[45] See RB 58.7: *si revera Deum quaerit, si sollicitus est ad opus Dei*; De Vogüé, "Twenty-five Years," 410 n. 25, cf. RBas 3.28.

[46] LR 14 949C: τὴν ὁμολογίαν ἀθετήσαντα. Ἀθετήσαντα ("annul," "retract," "set aside") is the exact negation of κατέθετο ("pledge," "undertake").

[47] LR 14 949C: τὴν ὁμολογίαν τῶν συνθηκῶν κατέθετο. In this text ἡ συνθήκη begins to acquire its later Greek meaning of "monastic vow." The present text in the *Small Asketikon* shows that some kind of a vow for monks was already operative in communities by the mid 360s.

Interrogatio VIII
(Zelzer 41–46, QF 8, **1–25** LR 16 [PG 31.957–962]; **26–36** LR 17 [PG 31.961–966])

I: Si oportet eum qui se piae ac religiosae vitae dederit etiam *continentia*m observare?

R: 1 Quia in omnibus necessaria sit continentia manifestum est primo omnium ex eo quod apostolus Paulus inter *fructus spiritus* sancti etiam *continentia*m nominat, **2** tum deinde etiam immaculatum ministerium per hanc servari posse designat cum dicit *In laboribus in vigiliis in ieiuniis in sanctitate,* **3** et iterum alibi *In labore et fatigatione, in vigiliis multis, in fame et siti, in ieiuniis frequenter,* et iterum *Omnis qui in agone contendit ab omnibus continens est,* **4** et rursum *Macero corpus meum et servituti subicio,* quod utique non aliter quam per continentiam videtur impleri.

5 Et iuventutis tumor ac fervor aetatis velut freno quodam restringi et reprimi per solam continentiam potest, *non* enim *expediunt stulto deliciae* secundum Salomonem. **6** *Et carnis curam,* inquit apostolus, *ne feceritis in concupiscentiis,* et iterum, *Quae in deliciis est vivens mortua est.* **7** Sed et exemplum illud divitis in deliciis viventis necessariam nobis ostendit esse continentiam, ne forte et nos audiamus quo audivit et dives quia *Consecutus es bona in vita tua.*

8 Quomodo autem incontinentia periculosa sit etiam apostolus edocet, cum eam proprie illis adscribit quos recedere a deo dicit; **9** ait enim *In novissimis diebus erunt tempora periculosa, erunt* enim *homines se ipsos amantes,* et cum plura malitiae genera enumerasset ad ultimum posuit Com-*messores incontinentes immites.* **10** Sed et *Esau* malorum suorum quasi fomitem quendam habuit incontinentiam, *qui* pro uno cibo *vendidit primitiva sua;* sed et prima illa praevaricatio non aliunde homini nisi per incontinentiam accidit.

Question 8

Q: Is it necessary that one who would give himself to the life of piety and religion also practise *self-control* (cf. Gal 5:22)?

R: 1.1 That in all things self-control is necessary is clear, first, from the fact that the apostle Paul counts *self-control* among the *fruits of the Holy Spirit* (Gal 5:22-23), **2** and second, he indicates that it is by this means that his *ministry is preserved without blame* (cf. 2 Cor 6:3), when he says: *In labours and in vigils, in fasts and in purity* (cf. 2 Cor 6:4-6), **3** and again, *In labour and fatigue, in many vigils, in hunger and thirst, in fasts often* (2 Cor 11:27), and again: *Everyone who contends in the struggle is self-controlled in all things* (1 Cor 9:25), **4** and again: *I treat my body rigorously and bring it into subjection* (1 Cor 9:27), which indeed does not appear to be accomplished in any other way except by self-control.

5 For only through self-control can the ferment of youth and the excitability of that age be restrained and checked as with a bridle, for *soft living is no help to the fool* (Prov 19:10), according to Solomon. **6** *And make no provision for the flesh,* says the Apostle, *in its cravings* (Rom 13:14), and again: *she who is given over to pleasures is dead even while she lives* (1 Tim 5:6). **7** Yes, and the example of the rich man who lived amidst delicacies shows us that self-control is necessary, lest we too hear what the rich man heard: *You received your good things during your life* (Luke 16:25).

2.8 Moreover, the Apostle teaches what a perilous thing is self-indulgence when he describes it as a mark of those whom he says withdraw from God, **9** for he says: *In the last days there shall be perilous times,* for *men will be lovers of self* (2 Tim 3:1-2), and, having listed many kinds of malice, he ends with *the calumniators,*[48] *the intemperate, the ungentle* (2 Tim 3:3). **10** And Esau too had intemperance as the tinder of his woes, when he *sold his birthright* for a single meal (Gen 25:33; Heb 12:16); yes, and that primal disobedience happened to man from no other source than through self-indulgence (cf. Gen 3:6).

---

[48] LR 16.2 957C διάβολοι, "accusers," "slanderers," QF: ܪ̈ܐܕܠܒܘܛܐ, "slanderers."

11 Omnis vero sanctorum vita atque ipsius domini in carne positi praesentia, quae nobis alia nisi continentiae proponit exempla?[21] **12** Moyses quidem continuato quadraginta dierum ieiunio adstitisse indefessus dicitur deo et meruisse legis auxilium humano generi deferre. **13** Helias quoque visione dei tunc dicitur dignus effectus cum et ipse simili spatio temporum a cibo se continuisse perscribitur. **14** Sed et Daniel et trium puerorum meritum apud deum, quod de omnibus inimicis suis et de ipso tyranno triumphum ceperunt, non aliunde nisi per continentiam venit. **15** Iohannis autem omnis vita continentia fuit, ab hac etiam dominus manifestationis suae initia prima patefecit.

16 Continentiam autem dicimus, non quod a cibo abstinendum sit, hoc enim est violenter vitam dissolvere, **17** sed eam qua vitae usus non superfluus, sed necessarius constat, cum refugimus quo suave est et explemus ea quae sola corporit necessitas poscit.

18 Et ut breviter dicam: omnia quae per passibilem concupiscentiam requiruntur, ab his abstinere virtus est continentiae. **19** Et ideo ergo non solum erga cibi libidinem continentiae virtus agnoscitur, sed cum ab omnibus in quibus delectamur quidem, sed in anima laedimur, abstinemus.

20 Verus ergo continens nec gloriam humanam desiderat, sed a vitiis se continet et ab ira et a tristitia et ab omnibus quae occupatas tenere consueverunt ineruditas animas et incautas. **21** Paene autem in omnibus mandatis dei hoc invenimus quod unum alteri cohaeret et separatum aliud ab alio compleri impossibile est. **22** Id tamen praecipue in hac ipsa continentia deprehenditur, quoniam quidem humilis ille iudicatur qui se a superbia continet, **23** et ille renuntiat omnibus facultatibus et secundum evangelium vendit omnia sua et dividit, qui sine dubio continet se a pecuniae desiderio, **24** sed et mansuetus ille erit qui iram continet et cohibet furorem. **25** Quid vero iam vagos oculi visus et auris auditus et linguae intemperantiam aliud quam continentia moderatur et cohibet?

---

[21] *Exempla* Zelz., most MSS, confirmed L² 32-33; *documenta et praecepta* C, F, WLG.

11 Indeed, the whole life of the saints and of the Lord himself while placed here in the flesh, what else do they put before us than examples of self-control? **12** Moses is said to have persevered without slackening in continual fasting and prayer before God for forty days and to have merited to hand down to the human race the aid of the Law (cf. Deut 25:33). **13** Elijah too is said to have been counted worthy of the vision of God when he himself continued for a like space of time abstaining from food (cf. 1 Kgs 19:8). **14** And the merit of Daniel and the three youths before God, when they gained the victory over all their enemies and over the tyrant himself, it came from no other source than self-control (cf. Dan 1:6-16; 3:24-28). **15** Why, John's entire way of life was self-control (cf. Matt 3:4). And it was by this means that the Lord too disclosed the first beginnings of his manifestation (Matt 4:2).

16 Yet by self-control we do not mean complete abstinence from food—this would indeed be the violent dissolution of life—**17** but that self-control which is consistent with the necessary but not superfluous[49] sustenance of life, when we avoid what is gratifying and fulfil solely what necessity requires for the body.

18 In sum then: abstinence from all that is demanded by passionate desire is the virtue of self-control. **19** And so virtue therefore is disclosed not only in regard to the pleasure of food, but also when we abstain from all those things in which we may take delight but by which we are wounded in soul.

20 Accordingly, anyone who is truly self-controlled does not desire human glory, but restrains himself from vices such as wrath and despondency and all those obsessions which untaught and incautious souls are wont to cling to.

21 One might go so far as to say that among all the commandments of God we find that the one is so linked with the other that it is impossible to accomplish one in isolation from another. **22** This is found to be especially the case with self-control itself, in that the humble person is judged to be one who has restrained himself from pride **23** and one who has renounced all his property and, according to the Gospel, sold all his possessions and distributed them to all (cf. Matt 19:21) is without doubt one who has restrained himself from the desire of money. **24** and the meek too will be one who has mastered his wrath and checked his rage. **25** And the wandering looks of the eye, the listening of the ear and the looseness of the tongue—what else but self-control can subdue and check them?

---

[49] *Superfluus*; cf RB 55.11; 61.6 (*superfluus*) and 36.4; 61.2 (*superfluitate*); see RBas 9.16 and Gribomont, "Commentaries," 237 #9.

26 Sed et intemperatos risus continentia coercet, sicut incontinentiae signum est inordinatis et incompositis motibus agere in risu, cum utique subridendo tantummodo laetitiam mentis oporteat indicari, **27** indecorum autem sit crepitantem cum sonitu elevare risum, quod certum est per incontinentiam mentis accidere solere etiam invitis. **28** Quae res gravitatem et constantiam animi emollire ac resolvere solet, unde et Salomon *Risui* inquit *dixi amentiam*, **29** et *Sicut vox spinarum sub olla ita risus stultorum*, et iterum *Stultus in risu exaltat vocem suam, vir autem sapiens vix tacite subridebit.* **30** Ostendit autem et dominus in semet ipso necessarias quidem carnis se habuisse passiones, id est quae virtutis testimonium ferrent, velut laborem et fletum ac tristitiam; **31** nusquam autem invenitur etiam risu usus quantum ad historiam pertinet evangelii, sed et deflere magis invenitur eos qui rident dicens *Vae vobis qui nunc ridetis quia flebitis.*

32 Nec sane seducere nos debet similitude nominis risus, mos namque est scripturae interdum laetitiam animae et affectum quendam laetiorem risum nominare, **33** sicut ibi *Sara Risum* inquit *mihi fecit deus*, et iterum *Beati qui flent* nunc quia *ride*bunt, **34** et in Iob quo dictum est *Os* autem veracium *replebitur risu*; haec enim omnia nomina pro gaudio animae accipiuntur. **35** Qui ergo liber est ab omni passione et nihil per incitamenta libidinum gerit, sed continenter et sobrie adversum omne quod potest laedere nititur, **36** hic perfecte continens dicitur, qui et sine dubio per hoc alienus invenitur ab omni genere peccati. **37** Libido namque est totius mali muscipula et per hanc omnes decipimur ad peccatum, per quam qui non resolvitur neque inclinatur ab ea, omne ex se peccati pessimum germen excidit.

26 Yes, and self-control also curbs immoderate laughter, just as a mark of intemperance is the kind of laughter that is accompanied by disorderly and unruly gestures. Since the cheerfulness of the mind need only be indicated by smiling, **27** it is unseemly to lift up a cackling laughter in a loud din, which is certainly wont to happen, even involuntarily, through intemperance of mind. **28** Such laughter usually softens and undermines gravity and constancy of mind, whence Solomon says:[50] *Of laughter I have said it is madness* (Eccl 2:2) and, *as the crackle of thorns under the cooking pot so is the laughter of fools* (Eccl 7:6), **29** and again, *The fool raises his voice in laughter, but the wise man will scarcely smile discreetly* (Sir 21:20). **30** The Lord, too, showed that he had in himself passions of the flesh, that is, those which tend to evidence of virtue, such as weariness and tears and grief. **31** But never is he found to have used laughter, so far as the gospel narrative touches on it. We find there instead that those who laugh shall lament even more when he says: *Woe to you who laugh now, for you shall weep* (Luke 6:25).

32 The ambiguity of "laughter" ought not at all deceive us, for it is often the custom of Scripture to call gladness of soul and a certain more cheerful emotion "laughter" **33** as in: *Sarah said, God has made laughter for me* (Gen 21:6) and again: *Blessed those who weep now for they shall laugh* (cf. Luke 6:21), **34** and in Job it is said: *the truthful mouth shall be filled with laughter* (Job 8:21). All these are terms used for the joy of the soul. **35** Therefore one who is superior to every passion and does nothing through the goads of pleasure, but with self-control and sobriety strives against all that can do harm, **36** this is called perfectly self-controlled—and such a one is thereby without a doubt a stranger to every kind of sin. **37** For pleasure is the rat-trap of all evil and through it we are all beguiled into sin. Therefore, anyone who is not undermined or waylaid by it, cuts out from himself every vile germ of sin.

---

[50] LR 17.1 961B corrects this to Ecclesiastes and then introduces Solomon before Sir 21:23. The RBas reading is confirmed by the *Ask* 4 reading: "Whence Solomon . . . smile quietly," which Garnier omitted, following *Ask* 3. Basil evidently corrected the ascription of scriptural authors in a later Pontic revision that did not find its way into the Caesarean text. RB 7.59 also quotes Sir 21:23 in the context of laughter.

Interrogatio VIIII
(Zelzer 46–49, QF 9, LR 19 [PG 31.967–970])

I: Quae est mensura *continentiae*?

R: 1 Quantum exspectat ad vitia vel passiones, penitus abstinere nec umquam superari, **2** quantum autem ad cibos, prout usus deposcit vel aetas vel labor vel robur corporis vel incommoditas eius, ita etiam modus et qualitas temperabitur cibi. **3** Neque enim possibile est omnes fratres unum ordinem vel modum ac regulam custodire, hi vero qui sani sunt possunt omnes eandem mensuram tenere in abstinentia. **4** Immutari autem oportet per singulos in quibus causa aliqua diversitatis exsistit, providentia ac provisione eorum quibus dispensandi haec cura permissa est.

5 Neque enim per singula sermone complecti possumus, sed ea tantummodo comprehendimus quae ad communem vel generalem pertinent institutionem. **6** Solacia vero incommodorum in cibis vel eorum qui iam fessi sunt ex opere continentiae sive aliis quibuslibet laboribus quos pro religione pertulerunt, hi qui praesunt secundum quod res et ratio deposcit adhibebunt.

7 Neque ergo tempus reficiendi omnibus idem statui potest neque modus cibi neque qualitas, sed prospectus iste unus sit omnibus, ut non usque ad satietatem persistamus in edendo. **8** Repleri enim ventrem et gravari ex cibo valde inutile est etiam corpori ad omne opus, tum deinde quia et gravatur in somnum et quia etiam laedi ex his facile potest.

Question 9

Q: What is the measure of *self-control*? (Gal 5:22)

R: 1 As far as the vices and passions are concerned, he expects complete abstinence, and never to yield. **2** The extent in regard to food, however: the measure and kind of food shall be proportoned as age and occupation and bodily strength and debility require. **3** For it is impossible that all the brothers[51] should observe the one order or measure or rule, though all those who are healthy can maintain the same measure of abstinence. **4** This however ought to be adapted in individual cases where there is some cause for variation, by the prudence and supervision of those entrusted with the responsibility of this distribution.

5 We cannot of course encompass each individual case in this instruction, but include only what pertains to a common and general framework. **6** Whether there are invalids needing to be built up with food, or those who are fatigued from the work of self-control, or from whatever other tasks they have carried out in the service of piety, let those who preside[52] administer as need and reason require.

7 Since, then, it is therefore impossible to establish the same time for meals for all, or the measure or quality of food, let there be one goal for all: that we do not continue in our eating to satiety.[53] **8** For to fill the stomach and to weigh it down with food renders even the body less useful for any task, since it is then inclined to sleep and more easily susceptible to harm.

---

[51] QF: ܪܚܡܘܬ ܟܠܗ "all the brotherhood"; 968A: τοὺς ἐν τῇ γυμνασίᾳ τῆς εὐσεβείας ("all in the gymnasium/training ground of piety"). This phrase, which is *not* in the RBas or QF, nevertheless shares a common sensibility with RB Prol 45: "*dominici schola servitii*"—"the school of the Lord's service."

[52] *Hi qui praesunt*; 968B οἱ ἐφεστῶτες; the Greek participial form might be translated by a conventional English "superiors," but since there is no express title as a noun in the RBas or the *Great Asketikon*, Rufinus's cue will be followed and a nominal phrase will be maintained even in English.

[53] RBas is closer to a variant of the text in LR 19.1 968B: τὸ μὴ ἀναμένειν τὸν κόρον (not to continue to satiety). Reg. prim., Voss. QF confirms the reading.

9 Sed ne suavia quidem quaeque in fine ciborum sectanda sunt, sed sufficit usum explere vivendi refutata luxuria; **10** si enim libidini serviamus nihil aliud est quam *deum facere ventrem* nostrum. **11** Quoniam quidem corpus humanum semper exolescit et defluit idcirco et repleri indiget ac reformari, propter quod et naturale est cibi desiderium, **12** id quod secundum rectam rationem usus ipse ad reparationem deposcit eorum quae exinanita fuerint et absumpta tam aridi quam etiam humidi alimenti.

13 Si quid ergo illud est quod potest vel brevius vel facilius explere hanc necessitatem corporis in cibis, id potius eligendum est. **14** Sed et dominus hoc, opinor, ostendit cum esurientes refecit *in deserto,* qui cum utique posset maiore miraculo copiosiores eis cibos parare nihil horum fecit **15** sed simplicem eis exhibuit victum, et secundum Iohannem quidem *panes hordeaceos et pisc*iculos apponit.

16 De potu vero ne mentio quidem ulla fit, ex quo illud sine dubio designatur, quod omnibus sufficiens esse possit aquae usus et pernecessarius, **17** nisi forte aliquis per infirmitatem corporis laedi ex hoc videatur, cui sine dubio secundum consilium apostoli Pauli a Timotheum scribentis cavendum est quod nocet. **18** Sed et quaecumque manifestam inferunt noxam corpori devitanda sunt, absurdum enim videtur propter substantiam corporis cibos sumere et rursus per ipsos cibos corpori inferre perniciem et inutile illud reddere ad ministerium mandatorum.

9 Indeed, pleasurable tastes must not be followed as the goal of food—the need that serves life is sufficient, with indulgence being shunned. **10** For if we serve pleasure, it is nothing other than to *make a god of our belly* (cf. Phil 3:19). **11** For since our human body is constantly being depleted and dehydrated, and needs replenishment and refreshment, because of which the appetite for food is natural, **12** therefore the use of food in accord with right reason calls for the replenishment of what has been depleted and the intake of nourishment both solid and liquid.

13 Therefore, whatever in the way of food can fulfil this need of the body quickly and easily should by preference be chosen. **14** And the Lord himself I think showed this, when he refreshed those who *were hungry in the wilderness* (cf. Matt 14:13, 15). Though he could certainly have extended the miracle in the desert and prepared for them a more lavish repast he did nothing of the sort, **15** but furnished for them a simple fare, and served, according to John, *barley bread and small fish* (John 6:9).

16 Of drink he made no mention at all, from which it may no doubt be inferred that the use of water could suffice[54] for all as most necessary **17**—unless perhaps someone appears to be harmed by it because of bodily infirmity, for whom without doubt is the advice the apostle Paul wrote to Timothy to *avoid what is harmful* (cf. 1 Tim 5:23). **18** But whatever manifestly brings harm to the body should be avoided anyway, for it seems absurd to take food for the sustenance of the body and then again by means of this very food to inflict harm on the body and render it useless for service of the commandments.

---

[54] LR 19.2 969A: ἀρκοῦντος ταῖς χρείαις. On "sufficiency," see RBas 8.17 / LR 16.2. Gribomont ("Commentaries," 237 #8), citing vol. VI, 919 of de Vogüé's *The Rule of St. Benedict*, says: "de Vogüé very properly notes that Benedict is influenced by the Basilian tendency to eliminate not only private property but also all superfluity. Monks, he thinks, ought not surpass a certain measure. His favorite word is *sufficit*." This verb appears variously three times in a single chapter of the RB, i.e., RB 55.4, 10, 15, and eight times elsewhere in the RB. But it occurs even more frequently in the RBas, 28 times in various forms, e. g., RBas 11.12, 31.

19 Oportet tamen omni modo illis uti cibis qui et facilius et vilius comparantur, uti ne occasione abstinentiae inveniamur pretiosiora quaeque et difficiliora sectari, **20** dum suavitate condimentorum viles natura cibos in summum et delicatum saporem conamur extollere. **21** Sed si quid est quod in unaquaque provincia facilius et vilius comparatur et quod in usu omnium communiter habetur, hoc ad usus nostros oportet assumi, **22** ea tantummodo inferentes quae ad vitam pernecessaria sunt, id est oleum et alia huiuscemodi, vel si qua etiam ad infirmantium solacia adhibebuntur.[22]

Interrogatio X
(Zelzer 50–51, QF 10, LR 21 [PG 31.975–976])

I: Quomodo oportet observare nos circa *cathedras* et *accubit*a, cum tempus poposcerit?

R: 1 Quoniam praeceptum domini habemus qui[23] nos in omnibus instituit ad humilatem, **2** in quo etiam de hoc pronuntiat, ut si ad convivium eamus discumbendi *locum novissimum* requiramus et non occupemus locum priorem, **3** illud nos scire oportet quia, ubi omnes eodem prospectu ac proposito convenimus, maxime si in multis et in maioribus humilitatis nostrae documenta iam dedimus, cupere quidem praevenire unumquemque inferiorem locum secundum mandatum domini condecens est.

---

[22] *Solacia adhibebuntur* Zelz. following SC, WLG, confirmed L² 40; *solamen adhibetur* β.

[23] *Qui* Zelz. following C, W, J, confirmed L² 41; *quod* HMTZ Hol.; *quo* S, B LG, P.

19 We ought in every way to use food which is easily and cheaply obtained, so that we are never found running after expensive and extravagant items on a pretext of abstinence **20** while we strive to raise our ordinary, natural food with a flavour of seasonings to a lofty and delicate savour. **21** We ought rather to choose for our own use whatever is easily and cheaply obtained in each locality[55] and available for common use, **22** and bring in from a distance only those things which are really necessary for life, such as oil and the like, or if something is to be used for the relief of the sick.

Question 10

Q: When the time[56] requires it, what should we observe concerning *places of seating* and *reclining* (Matt 23:6; cf. Luke 14:7-8)?

R: 1 Since we have a charge from the Lord who directs us to humility in all things, **2** in which he even declares that when we take our seat at a dinner[57] we should seek *the lowest place* and not occupy a higher place (Luke 14:8-10), **3** we ought to realize that when we who have the same purpose and goal all come together, especially if we are giving proof of our humility among the many or the great, it is fitting that each desire to take in advance the lower place, according to the Lord's command.[58]

---

[55] LR 19.2 969B: τὸ ἐν ἑκάστῃ χώρᾳ εὔλητρον καὶ εὐτελὲς τοῖς πολλοῖς εἰς χρῆσιν ἕτοιμον. Cf. RB 55.7, 10 in the context of clothing: *sed quales inveniri possunt in provincia qua degunt, aut quod vilius comparari possit*. Most commentators consider this a direct verbal dependence on the RBas. See Gribomont, "Commentaries," 257 #8, 9; J. T. Lienhard, "St. Basil's 'Asceticon Parvum' and the *Regula Benedicti*," *Studia Monastica* 22 (1980): 231–42, at 236.

[56] LR 21 976B: Reg. prim. Adds: τῶν ἀρίστων ἢ δείπνων, "of lunch or dinner." Basil in his response speaks only of τοῖς ἀρίστοις, the midday meal. QF: the time of the meal. Both terms may be later additions, ἢ δείπνων certainly so. The noonday meal mentioned in *An Ascetic Discourse* I, 4 (PG 31, 869–82, at 877c) (Wagner 213, Clarke 137) shows the practice of a community under Basil's guidance soon after his death.

[57] τοῖς ἀρίστοις, the ordinary term for the midday meal. RBas 10.1, *convivium*, is closer in meaning to the gospel text: *wedding banquet*.

[58] RBas 10.1-3 expresses the same ideas as the Greek text but with a very different arrangement, using third person. Zelzer's reading in RBas 10.3 follows the *lectio difficilior* of most manuscripts: "*dedimus*"; however "*debemus*," the reading from the 7th c. manuscript M, before correction, is closer to the obligatory sense of the Greek impersonal construction ἐπιβάλλον.

4 Sed rursum, si res a contentionem veniat de hoc et unus alium detrudere velut de loco inferiori conetur, valde est improbabile, **5** causa enim ex hoc perturbationis et inquietudinis nascitur si incipiat nemo alteri cedere, et si pro hoc certamina moveantur simile erit tamquam si de primatibus contendatur.

6 Propter quod oportet, etiam, in hoc consideratius pervidere vel[24] ‹sequi›[25], quid uniquique nostrum competat, vel certe indulgere ei cui ‹suscipiendi› cura commissa[26] est,[27] **7** et in ceteris et in recumbendo ordinem custodire et obtemperare ei ut impleatur in nobis illud quod dictum est *omnia* vestra *honeste et secundum ordinem fiant.*

Interrogatio XI

(Zelzer 51–58, QF 11.1-31 / 12.32-38 / 13.39-41, **1–31** LR 22 [PG 31.977–982]; **32–41** LR 23 [PG 31.981–982])

I: Quis est dignus vel decens habitus Christiani?

R: 1 Quoniam sermo in superioribus humilitatem necessariam docuit, ita ut qui vult religiose ac pie vivere in omnibus et simplicitatem et vilitatem requirat, id est ea quae parvo sumptu acquiruntur, **2** id observandum puto in corporalibus usibus, per quod occasiones nobis maiorum occupationum minimae fiant; hoc ergo etiam in observatione indumentorum custodiendum puto.

---

[24] *Vel* B, S, HJP, MTZ Hol., confirmed L² 71; omitted Zelz. with C, WLG.

[25] *Sequi* restored L² 71.

[26] *Commissa* β, JMPTZ Hol., confirmed L² 71; omitted α.

[27] *Vel . . . commissa est* restored L² 70–72. The Greek text, LR 21 976C: διόπερ χρὴ καὶ ἐνταῦθα τὸ πρέπον ἡμῖν περιεσκεμμένως γνωρίζοντας καὶ σπουδάζοντας ("Wherefore we ought prudently to recognize and observe what is fitting for us in this matter") ἐπιτρέπειν τῷ ὑποδεχομένῳ καὶ τὴν τῆς κλίσεως τάξιν ("and assuredly leave it to him who has the responsibility of seating"). According to Lundström, "Rufinus translated γνωρίζοντας καὶ σπουδάζοντας by *pervidere vel sequi.* A copyist then omitted *sequi* before *quid* as a false doublet, because he could not accept that the word here, in the sense of 'look to something' (direct one's gaze) was, by way of exception, linked to an interrogative clause (together with *pervidere*). Then *vel* was deleted as unintelligible."

4 But on the other hand, if the matter comes into contention over this and one tries to displace the other even if from a lower place, it is most unacceptable, **5** for an occasion of turbulence and disquiet arises from this, and if no-one begins to yield to the other,[59] and if they are stirred to fight over it, they will be just like those who fight over the first seats.

6 Wherefore we ought carefully to consider and follow what is fitting for each of us in this matter, and assuredly yield to him who is entrusted with the responsibility of hospitality, **7** and also keep order and comply with him in other matters as well as the order of seating, that the saying may be fulfilled in us, *let all* you do *be done decently and in order* (cf. 1 Cor 14:40).[60]

Question 11

Q: What is the worthy and befitting habit[61] for a Christian?[62]

R: 1 Since the word above has shown the necessity of humility, such that whoever wishes to live in religion and piety should seek simplicity and cheapness in all things, that is, those things which are obtained at modest cost, **2** the same I think is to be observed in regard to bodily needs so that occasions for us to busy ourselves overmuch are reduced to a minimum.

---

[59] LR 21 976C: On the other hand, to behave contentiously over this is unacceptable as destructive of good order (τῆς εὐταξίας) and a cause of disturbance. The all-important Basilian principle of *good order* is already well in place in the *Small Asketikon*.

[60] LR 21 976CD adds in conclusion: and we shall not show by our stubborn and vehement opposition that we are practising abasement to impress the many or to win popular favour. We shall express humility better through our amenability. For contentiousness is a greater sign of pride than is taking the first place, if we have accepted it when bidden to do so.

[61] LR 22 977A: τὸ πρέπον ἔνδυμα τῷ Χριστιανῷ. Garnier translates: *vestimentum conveniat Christiano*. ἔνδυμα was also used for the habit of a consecrated virgin and for the garment worn by the newly baptized.

[62] For Basil one garment is the principle; see also SR 70, 90, 168, 210 and note, Letters 2 (Def I, 20–21); 150 (Def I, 366–69); and 223 (Def III, 296–97)—this last shows how impressed the young Basil was by the mean clothing of the Eustathians. The *Life of Macrina* also notes her poverty in death: The deaconess Lampadion replied to her brother Gregory: "Cupboards? What cupboards? You have all that she stored up before you. There is her cloak, there her head-covering, there the worn sandals for her feet. This is her wealth, these are her riches. There is nothing stored up in secret places apart from what you see . . ." Anna M. Silvas, *Macrina the Younger: Philosopher of God* (Turnhout: Brepols, 2008), 138. Basil's approach to clothing is strictly practical, frugal, and scriptural in argument; compare the tendency to sacralise the monastic habit found in Pachomius's monastery at Tabbenisi, *Lausiac History* 32, and Cassian, *Institutes* II, 2–7.

3 Si enim studium nobis habendum est omnium esse minimos et *omnium novissimos*, certum est quia et indumentis omnium novissimos nos deputare debemus. **4** Nam si hi qui gloriam sibi ex indumentorum splendore conquirunt, satis agunt quomodo pretiosis et magnificis vestibus videantur induti, **5** ita consequens est eum qui de ultimis et novissimis, id est per nimiam humilitatem placere studet, eligere debere hoc in quo *omnium* ultimus et *novissimus* appareat, **6** sicut ille qui e contrario de summis et pretiosis videri clarus et nobilis gestit.

7 Si enim in publica cena arguuntur Corinthii, quod per suam abundantiam *confundunt eos qui non habent*, **8** certum est, quia et in hoc simplici et communi omnium indumento‹rum numero›, qui[28] ad communem habitum vel usum pertinet, si alter altero differat habitus[29] vel pretiosior inveniatur, ex ipsa comparatione confundimus non habentes.[30]

9 Sufficienter quoque etiam apostolus huiuscemodi usibus brevi sermone regulam posuit dicens *Habentes autem victum et vestitum his contenti sumus*, **10** ostendens indumento solo quo contegamur indigere nos, et non varietate aliqua vestigis et ornamento eius ac decore iactari; **11** quae utique postmodum introducta sunt humanae vitae artifices luxuriae ingenio conquisita. **12** Sed et primus ille indumenti usus haec eadem indicat, cum dicitur *deus* fecisse primis hominibus *pellicias tunicas*, sufficiebat enim ad confusionem contegendam huiuscemodi indumenti usus.

---

[28] *Qui* S, C, B before correction, H, J, W before correction, confirmed L² 74–75; *quod* Zelz. following P, W after correction, LG.

[29] *Habitus* S, C before correction, B after correction, H, J, WG, P, MTZ, confirmed L² 74; *habitu* Zelz. following S, B before correction, C after correction, L.

[30] 11.8 is masterfully restored by Lundström with detailed demonstration, L² 73–76, especially p. 75: "The readings *qui* [rather than quod] and *habitus* [rather than habitum] were therefore correct." *Qui* is the relative for *numero*, as is ὁ of χρήσει. LR 22 977B: οὕτω δηλονότι καὶ ἐν τῇ κοινῇ καὶ προφανεῖ τῶν ἐνδυμάτων χρήσει ὁ ὑπὲρ τούς πολλοὺς σχηματισμὸς οἰόνει διὰ τῆς συγκρίσεως καταισχύνει τὸν πένητα. As can be seen, Rufinus here was periphrastic and expansive in his translation.

3 If we ought to have a zeal for being the least and *the last of all*, we should certainly reckon ourselves *the last of all* in dress too (cf. Mark 9:35). **4** For if those who pursue glory for themselves through the splendour of their vesture go to great lengths to be seen decked in costly and magnificent robes, **5** so, accordingly, one who strives for *the least* and *the last*, that is, to acquit himself of the uttermost humility, should prefer that in which he will appear the least and *the last of all* (cf. Mark 9:35), **6** even as one who wishes to look noble and illustrious presents himself in the very best and most costly.

7 For if the Corinthians at their public feast were reproved because through their extravagance they *put to shame those who have nothing* (cf. 1 Cor 11:22), **8** it is established by this simple and common type of clothing for all, which is proper to a common habit or usage, that if one habit differs from another or is found more costly, we put to shame those who have nothing by the very contrast.

9 The Apostle also sufficiently set the rule of what we should observe in this matter in a brief word, saying: *If we have food and clothing, with these we are content* (1 Tim 6:8), **10** showing us that we only need clothing to cover us, and not to be decked in some sort or variety of clothing with its ornament and decoration. **11** Such things in any case were introduced to our human life afterward, through skilled contrivance in the arts of luxury. **12** The very first use of clothing however shows us the same thing, when it is said that *God made for* the first human beings *tunics of skins* (Gen 3:21). For the use of such clothing was sufficient for the covering of their modesty.

13 Verum quoniam nobis prospectus est indumentis etiam calefieri et foveri, necessarium videtur ut ad utrumque usus ipse temperetur, **14** quo et operiri nuditas videatur et vel vis frigoris vel omne quod extrinsecus laedit arceri. **15** Sed quoniam in his ipsis, alia quidem sunt meliora alia inferiora, consequens est ea deligere quae nobis usum exhibeant longiorem, ita tamen ut in nullo laedatur regula voluntariae paupertatis, **16** id est ne alia quidem nobis sint vestimenta ad procedendum praeparata et alia ad usum domesticum et rursum alia in aliud tempus vel in ‹die alia et in›[31] nocte alia, **17** sed oportet unum illud ipsum tale esse indumentum quo nobis sufficere possit ad omnia, ut et in die honestum videatur indumentum et in nocte expleat necessitatem. **18** Ex hoc enim fit, ut et habitus noster communis et similis atque unius formae sit omnium, et Christianum etiam visio ipsa designet; **19** ea enim quae uno prospectu ac proposito geruntur, similia immo eadem esse omnibus debent.

20 Utile autem est etiam ex ipsa proprietate vestis et habitus intellegi unumquemque et professionem eius agnosci in ea vita qua secundum deum vivit, **21** ut sciat sibi etiam actus consimiles esse debere, et ad eos qui nos vident secundum habitum nostrum aequales etiam in actibus apparere debemus. **22** Non enim similiter turpe est in quolibet alio si inhoneste quid agat, sicut in his qui vitam sobriam etiam ipso habitu profitentur. **23** Si enim quis videat de trivio aliquem hominem caedentem alium aut vapulantem publice vel turpiter proclamantem aut in tabernis aliisque locis vitam cum dedecore ducentem, **24** ne observabit quidem facile huiusmodi hominem vel notabit, sciens eum consequenter haec a reliquam vitam suam gerere. **25** Si vero eum qui religiosam vitam profitetur videat quis vel parum[32] aliquid contra quam condecet facere, observant omnes et increpant et ad religonis opprobrium ducunt. **26** Itaque velut paedagogus quis est infirmioribus habitus este religiosior, ut etiam invitos eos ab opere inhonesto indecentique custodiat.

---

[31] *In* ‹die alia et in› restored L² 76–77, with *in die alia* B, *in die* P, MZ, and J. A copyist obviously skipped from *in* to *in*: *alia in aliud tempus vel in nocte alia*, Zelz. following the other MSS that omit *in die*.

[32] *Parum* C, G, H, J, P, MT, Z Hol., confirmed L² 65 (cf. 115.1, where *parum* is used for ὀλίγον); *parvum* Zelz. following S, W.

13 However, since there is another purpose of clothing for us, that we are warmed and protected, it is evident that we must coordinate its use for both purposes: **14** so that nakedness may be seen to be covered and the force of the cold and all harm from the elements be kept at bay. **15** However, since in these matters some clothes are better and others less so, it follows that we should prefer whatever affords us the most comprehensive use, providing that the rule of voluntary poverty[63] is in no way hindered, **16** that is, we do not have one set of clothes prepared in which to go out, and another for use at home, or again different ones for different times, whether one for the day, and another for the night, **17** but we ought to have such a covering that can suffice us for all our purposes, that will appear decent in the daytime and fulfil our need at night. **18** Hence it is fitting that our habit is both common and that it be alike and of one form for all, and that even the very appearance should designate the Christian. **19** For those things that bear on the same purpose and goal should surely be alike or the same in all things.

20 It is also useful that an individual is understood from the proper character of his clothing and habit, and that his profession of life by which he lives according to God be recognized, **21** so that he knows that his deeds too ought to be consistent with himself and that we should appear to those who see us in our habit to correspond also in our deeds. **22** If someone behaves dishonourably, it is not equally disgraceful in anyone you meet and in one of those who profess the life of sobriety by their very habit. **23** If one were to see any fellow at the cross-roads giving or receiving blows in public, or bellowing obscenities, or conducting his life shamefully in taverns or other such places, **24** one would not readily pay attention to or note such a man, knowing that he is behaving in this way consistently with the rest of his life. **25** But if one sees him who has professed a life of piety do something small contrary to what is fitting, everyone pays attention and rebukes him and regards him as a reproach to religion. **26** Thus the more religious habit is like a kind of pedagogue for those who are weaker, in that it guards them from dishonourable and unbecoming deeds, even against their will.

---

[63] LR 22.2 980A: τὸν τῆς ἀκτημοσύνης . . . λόγον, the principle of voluntary poverty, "non-acquirement" or "dis-possession" proclaimed in Matt 19:16-30; Mark 10:23-31; Luke 18:18-30. QF: "the word of God which calls us to poverty."

27 Denique et apostolus *episcopum ordinatum esse* designat, quae res ad habitum magis revocatur, sed et de mulieribus dicit *in habitu ordinato* eas esse debere; **28** ordinatus autem habitus Christiani dicitur is qui secundum propositum ac professionem eius aptus intellegitur. **29** Sicut enim est proprium aliquid militi in habitu vestimenti et alius est habitus senatoris, ex quo praecipue intellegitur vel iste quod senator est vel ille quod miles est, **30** ita etiam Christianus habere aliquid proprium, etiam ex ordinatione indumenti ipsius debet.

31 Sed et de calciamentis eadem ratio observabitur, ut quod simplex est et paratius et aptum proposito et usibus sufficiens id assumatur.

32 Zonae quoque usum ostendunt necessarium esse etiam qui praecesserunt nos sancti, **33** nam *Iohannes zona pellicia* constringere *lumbos suos* dicitur et *Helias* antea, tamquam enim proprius quidam habitus ipsius designatur cum dicitur *Vir hirsutus et zonam pelliciam habens circa lumbos suos,* **34** sed et Petrus zona usus ostenditur, sicut ex verbis angeli quae ad eum dicta sunt recognoscimus: *Accingere,* inquit, *et calcia te caligas tuas.* **35** Sed et beatus Paulus zona usus ostenditur per Agabi prophetiam dicentis *Virum* enim *cuius est zona haec ita alligabunt in Hierusalem*; sed et Iob audit a domino *Accingere*[33] *sicut vir lumbos tuos.* **36** Virtutis namque cuiusdam et prompti ad opera animi signum videtur esse usus cinguli; sed et discipulis domini zonae usus fuisse videtur ex more, quibus prohibebatur *ne pecuniam* haberent *in zonis* suis.

37 Re vera enim necessarium videtur eum qui manuum opere uti in aliquo debet succinctum esse et in omnibus praeparatum ac sine ullo impedimento inveniri ad omne ministerium boni operis, **38** unde et cingulo indiget, ut vel colligata circa corpus sit tunica, ex qua et magis confoveri possit cum undique constrictus sit, vel non impediri ad omnem rem quam agere parat.

39 De numero autem indumentorum nihil possumus dicere, cum manifesta definitione perscriptum sit, in quo[34] dicit **40** *Qui habet duas tunicas det non habenti,* ex quo sine dubio plures habere illicitum ducitur. **41** Quibus ergo habere duas tunicas non licet, his quomodo aliquid de diversitate indumentorum praecipi potest?

---

[33] This middle voice imperative is attested in α (C before correction, JHS), confirmed L¹ 590—cf. 11.34, and it is closer to the Greek ζώσασθαι; the active imperative *accinge* (a conjecture betraying unawareness of the Greek accusative of respect) Zelz. following β.

[34] *Quo* most MSS, confirmed L¹ 589; *in qua* Zelz., following P, J after correction. Zelz. regards *quo* in all other MSS as an archetype mistake. According to Lundström this is a mistaken conjecture—*in quo* is correct, = *in eo quod . . . .*

27 Last, the Apostle indicates that the *bishop should be orderly* (1 Tim 3:2), which refers more to his outward habit, and of the women also he says that they should be *dressed in orderly habit* (1 Tim 2:9). **28** By a Christian's "orderly habit" is meant that which befits his purpose and profession. **29** For just as there is one habit of clothing proper to a soldier, while a senator's habit is of another kind, through which one understands in advance that this one is a senator and that one a soldier, **30** so a Christian too, ought to have something proper by way of the established form of his own clothing.

31 And concerning footwear the same principle shall be observed: whatever is simple, easily obtained, in keeping with our purpose and sufficient for our use, let this be taken up.

32 The saints also who have gone before us show the necessity of using a belt, **33** for *John* girded *his loins with a leather belt*, it is said (cf. Matt 3:4; Mark 1:6), as did *Elijah* before him, for indeed his proper habit was described when it says *he was a hairy man, having a leather belt around his loins* (2 Kgs 1:8). **34** Yes, and Peter is shown to have used a belt, as we know from the words of the angel who said to him: *Gird yourself*, it says, *and fasten your sandals* (Acts 12:8). **35** The blessed Paul is also shown to have used a belt through the prophecy of Agabus when he said: *The man whose belt this is, they shall likewise bind in Jerusalem* (Acts 21:11). Yes, and Job heard from the Lord: *gird your loins like a man* (Job 38:3; 49:2). **36** For the use of a belt appears to be the sign of a certain virtue and readiness for work. Yes, and the use of the belt appears to have been customary among the disciples of the Lord, since they were forbidden to keep *any money in their belts* (cf. Matt 10:9; Mark 6:8).

37 For indeed it appears necessary that one who is to make use of his hands for some work should be girded well, so that he is found in all ways prepared and without any impediment for the service *of every good work* (2 Tim 2:21). **38** Hence he needs a belt, so that his tunic may be gathered around his body, whereby he can be kept warmer since it is caught in all round him and he is unimpeded for any task he is ready to undertake.

39 Concerning the number of garments, however, we can say nothing, since it is written out in a manifest definition, in which it says, **40** *Whoever has two tunics, let him give to one who has none* (Luke 3:11; cf. Matt 10:10; Mark 6:9), whereby we surely infer that to possess several is forbidden. **41** To those therefore who are forbidden to possess *two tunics*, how can they be instructed concerning a variety of clothing?

Interrogatio XII
(Zelzer 58–60, QF 14, SR 1 [PG 31.1079–1082])

I: Si licet alicui ex proprio sensu dicere quod sibi videtur bonum absque testimoniis scripturarum?

R: 1 Domino nostro Iesu Christo dicente de spiritu sancto *Non enim loquetur a se sed quaecumque audierit haec loquetur,* de se ipso autem *Non potest filus a se facere quicquam,* **2** et iterum *Ego a me ipso non sum locutus, sed qui misit me pater ipse mihi dedit mandatum qui dicam et quid loquar, et scio quia mandatum eius vita aeterna est. Quae ergo loquor ego sicut dixit mihi pater ita loquor,* **3** quis potest in tantum temeritatis progredi, ut audeat a se quicquam vel loqui vel cogitare? **4** Immo vero sciendum est quia omnes duce itineris indigemus spiritu sancto, ut ipse nos in viam dirigat veritatis et in cogitatione et in verbis et in actibus. **5** Caecus est enim et in tenebris degit omnis qui est absque sole iustitiae, qui est dominus noster Iesus Christus cuius mandatis velut radiis quibusdam illu-minamur, **6** *Mandatum* enim, inquit, *domini lucidum illuminans oculos.*

7 Quia ergo in omnibus negotiis quae inter nos versantur vel verbis quaedam quidem per mandatum dei in divinis scripturis distinguuntur, quaedam vero reticentur, **8** de his quidem quae scripta sunt nulla prorsus licentia permittitur cuiquam vel admittere quod prohibitum est vel praeterire quod praeceptum est, **9** cum ipse dominus ita praeceperit dicens *Et custodi verbum hoc quod ego mando tibi hodie, non adicies ad illud neque auferes ab eo.* **10** Sed et *terribilis quaedam* est *exspectatio iudicii et ignis zelus qui consumpturus est adversarios* et eos qui aus sunt tale aliquid operari.

Question 12

Q: Is it permissible to anyone to say from his own sensibility[64] whatever seems to him to be good, without the testimonies of the Scriptures?

R: 1 Since our Lord Jesus Christ says of the Holy Spirit: *he shall not speak from himself, but whatever he shall hear, that he will speak* (John 16:13), and moreover says of himself: *the Son can do nothing of himself* (John 5:19), **2** and again, *I have not spoken from myself; rather, the Father who sent me has himself given me commandment what I should speak and what I should say and I know that in his commandment is eternal life. What therefore I speak, I speak as the Father has told me* (John 12:49), **3** who then can have gone so far in effrontery as to dare to speak or think anything from himself? **4** No, it needs to be understood that we all have need of the Holy Spirit as guide for the journey (cf. Ps 142:10), to *direct us into the way of truth* (John 16:13) in thought and in word and in deed. **5** For he is blind and dwells in darkness (cf. John 12:35; Luke 1:79), who is without *the Sun of Righteousness* (cf. Mal 4:2), that is our Lord Jesus Christ, by whose commandments we are illumined as with rays (cf. Ps 33:5)? **6** For the *commandment of the Lord,* it says, *is bright, illumining the eyes* (Ps 18:8).

7 Inasmuch as some of the practises or sayings in common use among us are specified by the commandment of God in the divine Scriptures, while others are passed over in silence, **8** when it concerns what is actually written down, no authority whatever is given to anyone to admit what is forbidden or to omit what is prescribed. **9** For the Lord himself declared, saying: *And you shall keep this word which I command you this day. Neither shall you add to it nor shall you subtract from it* (Deut 4:2). **10** Yes, and there is a *fearful prospect of judgment and a fury of fire which shall consume the adversaries* and those who dare to do any such thing (Heb 10:27).

---

[64] Thus Rufinus interprets "to allow himself" of the Greek (and Syriac) text. Cf. RBas 203.2. On Basil's commitment to Scripture see *Contra Eunomium* II.27; PG 29 663B; *Moralia* 26.1, 70.22.

11 De his vero quae scriptura reticuit, regulam nobis apostolus posuit evidentem dicens *Omnia licent sed non omnia expediunt, omnia licent sed non omni aedificant; nemo quod suum est quaerat sed quo alterius.* **12** Itaque omnimodo non quae nobis licita sunt sed quod aedificat proximos agere debemus, et non nobis placere sed proximis ad aedificationem; **13** scriptum est enim *Subiecti invicem in timore Christi,* sed et rursum dominus ait *Qui vult in vobis esse maior fiat omnium novissimus et omnium servus.* **14** Quod utique qui implere vult sine dubio proprias sibi amputat voluntates secundum imitationem ipsius domini dicentis **15** *Descendi de caelo non ut faciam voluntatem meam sed voluntatem eius qui me misit patris,* et iterum praecepit dominus **16** *Si quis te angariaverit mille passus, vade cum illo alia duo.*

Interrogatio XIII
(Zelzer 61–63, QF 15, SR 114 [PG 31.1159–1160])

I: Si oportet omnibus vel quibuscumque oboedire?

R: 1 Eorum quidem qui imperant differentia vel diversitas non debet impedire oboedientium proposito, quia neque Moyses intemperans exstitit socero suo Iothor, cum utilia moneret ac iusta.

11 Now concerning matters which the Scriptures pass over in silence, the Apostle has laid down a manifest rule for us: *All things may be permissible but not all things are expedient, all things may be permissible but not all things build up; let no one seek his own advantage, but rather that of another* (1 Cor 10:23). **12** Thus in every way we are to do not what is permitted us, but what builds up our neighbours, and to please not ourselves but our neighbours for their upbuilding, **13** for it is written: *subject yourselves to one another in reverence for Christ* (Eph 5:21), and again the Lord says: *Whoever wants to be greater among you, let him be the last and the servant of all* (cf. Matt 20:26; Mark 9:34; 10:43; Luke 22:26). **14** Whoever wishes to fulfil this assuredly cuts off his own will, in imitation of the Lord himself who says: **15** *I have come down from heaven not to do my own will, but the will of the Father who sent me* (John 6:38),[65] and again the Lord prescribes: **16** *If anyone shall compel you a thousand steps, go with him two thousand* (Matt 5:41).[66]

Question 13

Q: Do we owe obedience to everyone and anyone?

R: 1 A difference or diversity among those who give orders ought not hinder the obedience to what is proposed, since, for example, Moses did not refuse to hear his father-in-law Jethro, when he gave useful and just counsel (cf. Exod 18:19).

---

[65] Cf. RB 7.31-32.

[66] Like the RBas, QF 14.16, 13 place Matt 5:41 at the end of one question/answer, to which Eph 5:21 is added (placed earlier in the Latin). In the Greek, both these citations are transferred to the following question, SR 114.Q.

2 Commonitionum sane non parva est diversitas, aliae namque contrariae videntur esse mandatis dei, **3** aliae vero vel interrumpere mandatum vel contaminare illud videntur, aliae vero ad explendum id atque aedificandum veniunt. **4** Necessarium ergo est meminisse apostolici praecepti dicentis *prophetias nolite spernere, omnia probate, quod bonum est tenete, ab omni specie mala abstinete vos,* **5** et iterum *Cogitationes* purgantes vel *destruentes et omnem altitudinem extollentem se adversus scientiam dei et captivantes omnem intellectum ad oboediendum Christo.* **6** Si quid ergo est quod conveniat cum mandato et animae expediat et hoc nobis ab aliquo fuerit imperatum, **7** velut voluntatem dei prompte et libenter debemus accipere et explere quod dictum est, *obtemperantes invicem in caritate Christi.*

8 Si autem contrarium aliquid mandatis dei vel quod ea corrumpere videatur aut contaminare facere iubemur ab aliquo, tempus est nos dicere *Obtemperare oportet deo magis quam hominibus,* **9** et rursum meminisse domini dicentis *Alieni autem vocem non sequuntur, sed fugiunt ab eo quoniam nesciunt alienorum vocem.* **10** Sed et sancti apostolici memores esse debemus, qui ad nostram cautelam ausus est ne angelis quidem parcere dicens **11** *Etiamsi nos aut angelus de caelo evangelizaverit vobis praeterquam quod evangelizavimus vobis, anathema sit.* **12** Ex quo edocemur, ut etiamsi valde nobis carus sit aliquis, etiamsi magnificus habeatur et in admiratione sit positus, **13** qui prohibet nos facere quod a domino praeceptum est, vel rursum imperat fieri quod dominus fieri prohibuit, exsecrabilis debet esse qui eiusmodi est omnibus qui diligent dominum.

2 But certainly there is no small diversity in the things commanded, for some are seen to be contrary to the commandments of God, **3** others are seen to dissolve the commandment or adulterate it, while others help to fulfil and to build it up. **4** It is therefore necessary to remember the apostolic precept that says: *Do not despise prophesyings, but test all things, hold fast to the good, abstain from every semblance of evil* (1 Thess 5:20), **5** and again: Purging[67] or *demolishing arguments and every high thing exalted against the knowledge of the Lord, taking every thought captive for obedience to Christ* (2 Cor 10:4-5).[68] **6** So therefore, if what we have been ordered to do by someone accords with the commandment and is expedient for the soul, **7** then we ought to receive it promptly and willingly as the will of God, fulfilling what is written: *obeying one another in the love of Christ* (Eph 4:2 + 5:21).

8 But if we are ordered to do what is contrary to the commandments of God or what appears to dissolve or to adulterate it, it is time for us to say: *We ought to obey God rather than men* (Acts 5:29), **9** and to be mindful of the Lord who says: *They do not follow the voice of a stranger, but flee from him, because they do not recognize the voice of strangers* (John 10:5). **10** And we ought to be mindful of the Apostle, who, for our assurance, dared even not to spare the angels when he said: **11** *Even if we ourselves or an angel from heaven should proclaim a gospel to you other than the one we have already announced to you, let him be anathema* (Gal 1:18). **12** By which we are taught that even if someone is very dear to us, and even of exalted status and held up for admiration, **13** who hinders us from doing what the Lord has prescribed, or orders us to do what the Lord has forbidden to be done, such a one ought to be execrated by all who love the Lord.

---

[67] Rufinus duplicates the καθαιροῦντες, as if translating a very similarly spelt καθαροῦντες.

[68] This verse is used in *De Iudicio* PG 31 669A at an important juncture of Basil's argument that all disobedience is liable to judgment and that no sin may be regarded as small.

Interrogatio XIIII

(Zelzer 61–63, QF 16, SR 157 [PG 31.1185–1186])

I: Quali affectu debet quis servire deo, et iste ipse affectus quid est?

R: 1 Affectum bonum vel animum illum esse ego arbitror, cum deside-rium vehemens et inexplebile[35] atque immobile inest nobis placendi deo. **2** Impletur autem iste affectus per θεωρίαν vel scientiam per quam intueri et perspicere possumus magnificentiam gloriarum dei, et per cogitationes pias et puras et per memoriam eorum bonorum quae a deo nobis collata sunt; **3** ex quorum recordatione venit animae dilectio domini dei sui ut eum diligat *ex toto corde suo et ex tota anima sua et ex tota mente sua,* **4** se-cundum illum qui dicebat *Sicut cervus desiderat ad fontes aquarum, ita desiderat anima mea ad te deus.* **5** Cum hoc ergo tali affectu servire oportet domino adimplentes illud quod ab apostolo dictum est **6** *Quis nos sepa-rabit a caritate Christi? Tribulatio an angustia an persecutio an fames an nuditas an periculum an gladius?* et reliqua.

---

[35] *Inexplebile* Zelz., confirmed L² 37, SR 157 1185A: διάθεσιν ἀγαθὴν ἡγοῦμαι εἶναι ἐπιθυμίαν . . . σφοδρὰν καὶ ἀκόρεστον καὶ πεπηγυῖαν καὶ ἀμετάθετον. κατορθοῦται δὲ αὕτη ἐν θεωρίᾳ συνετῇ καὶ διηνεκεῖ τῆς μεγαλότητος τῶν δοξῶν τοῦ θεοῦ. The paradox that an insatiable (*inexplebile*) desire could be fulfilled (*impletur*) tripped up some copyists. As Lundström comments, it concerns disposition, the *desiderium* to please God as much as possible. There is no question here that the human being can attain what he or she wants. *Inexplicabile* C, LG, P; *inexplicabili* W.

Question 14

Q: In what disposition[69] ought one serve God and that disposition itself, what is it?

R: 1 I consider it a good disposition or mind when there is in us an eager, unquenchable, and unshakable desire to be pleasing to God. **2** Such a disposition is attained through θεωρίαν or the knowledge through which we are able to look towards and perceive the majesty of the glories of God, and by devout and pure thoughts and through remembrance[70] of the benefits that have been bestowed on us by God. **3** From the recollection of which there arises the soul's love for the Lord her God, so that she loves him with *all her heart and all her soul and all her mind* (cf. Mark 12:30), **4** like the one who said: *as the deer that yearns for fountains of water, so my soul yearns for you O God* (Ps 41:1). **5** Such is the disposition with which we must serve the Lord, fulfilling the saying of the Apostle: **6** *Who shall separate us from the love of Christ? Shall tribulation or anguish, or persecution, or hunger or nakedness or danger or the sword?* and the rest (Rom 8:35).

---

[69] SR 157 1185A: ποταπῇ διαθέσει, *diathesis* (= *affectus*) in its various forms derives from medical terminology. It is a key term in Basil's ascetic vocabulary, occurring some forty-two times in the RBas. See John Eudes Bamberger, "ΜΝΗΜΗ-ΔΙΑΘΕΣΙΣ The Psychic Dynamisms in the Ascetic Theology of Saint Basil," *Orientalia Christiana Periodica* 34 (1968): 233–51.

[70] SR 157 1185A λογισμοῖς τε εὐγνώμοσι καὶ ἀδιαλείπτῳ μνήμῃ. Bamberger also studies the function of memory in Basil's asceticism in the essay noted above.

Interrogatio XV
(Zelzer 64–65, QF 17, SR 98 [PG 31.1149–1152])

I: Quid sentire de se debet is qui praest in quibus praecipit vel imperat?

R: 1 Apud deum quidem *sicut minister Christi et dispensator mysteriorum dei* timens ne praeter voluntatem dei vel praeter quod in sanctis scripturis evidenter praecipitur vel dicat aliquid vel imperet **2** et inveniatur tamquam *falsus testis dei* aut sacrilegus vel introducens aliquid alienium a doctrina domini vel certe subrelinquens et praeteriens aliquid eorum quae deo placita sunt.

3 Ad fratres autem esse debet *tamquam si nutrix foveat parvulos suos;* paratus secundum voluntatem domini et secundum quod unicuique expedit communicare cum eis *non solum evangelium dei sed etiam animam suam,* **4** memor praecepti domini ac dei nostri dicentis *Mandatum novum do vobis ut diligitatis invicem sicut et ego dilexi vos.* **5** *Maiorem hac caritatem nemo habet quam ut ponat quis animam suam pro amicis suis.*

Question 15

Q: What mind in himself ought the one who presides[71] have towards those he commands or rules?

R: 1 Before God he should be *as a minister of Christ and steward of the mysteries of God* (1 Cor 4:1), fearing lest he say or prescribe anything apart from the will of God or apart from what is clearly[72] attested in the Scriptures, **2** and be found *bearing false witness to God* (1 Cor 15:15) or sacrilegious, whether by introducing anything foreign to the Lord's teaching, or indeed by allowing to pass or by overlooking anything that is pleasing to God.

3 Towards the brothers, however, he should be *as a nurse cherishing her children* (1 Thess 2:7), being prepared according to the will of the Lord and according to the better good of each, *to share with them not only the Gospel of God, but even his own life* (1 Thess 2:8), **4** mindful of the commandment of *our Lord and God* (John 20:28), who said: *A new commandment I give to you, that you love one another, even as I have loved you. Greater love has no man than this, that a man lay down his life for his friends* (John 15:12-13).

---

[71] Ὁ προεστὼς, RBas 15.Q: *qui praest*. This is the earliest occurrence of the singular term for the superior, and it notably appears in the *Small Asketikon*. The office receives here its scriptural characterization. Other occurences of the singular term in the *Small Asketikon* (excluding interpolations by Rufinus): RBas 44.Q, RBas 197.Q, and RBas 198.Q in feminine form, RBas 80.Q, RBas 96.1, RBas 106.Q. These cases show that such an office—or two, one male, one female—existed even at the earliest stage of the cenobitic community as envisaged by Basil. Plural terms sometimes denote a body of elders within the community, or a body of subordinate officials; see RBas 9.6, RBas 105.1 and note, RBas 36.3, RBas 69.6, RBas 81.1, RBas 94, RBas 176.1.

[72] 1149D: τι παρὰ τὸ θέλημα τοῦ Θεοῦ τὸ ἐν ταῖς Γραφαῖς ὁμολογούμενον. QF: "apart from the will that our Lord has revealed in the Holy Scriptures." Cf. RB 2.4: *abbas nihil extra praeceptum Domini quod sit debet aut docere aut constituere vel iubere*. Neither SR 98 nor QF has a parallel for *vel praeter quod*. Gribomont ("Commentaries," 249) recognizes the Greek text as the more authentic version and implies that Rufinus has inserted *vel praeter quod*, saying, "The translator Rufinus is no longer capable of understanding the unity of these ideas." Nonetheless, a *vel praeter quod* would be quite compatible with Basil's thinking at an early stage, in Letter 2: "A most important path to the discovery of duty is **also** the study (καὶ ἡ μελέτη) of the divinely-inspired Scriptures." (Def I, 14–15). Interestingly, this καὶ has dropped out of two manuscripts of Basil's letters. One may ask whether the "*vel*" functions as it does in many of Rufinus's "doublets," when it adduces a synonym, meaning "or alternatively" or "that is to say . . .," so that the sense of his translation is: ". . . anything apart from the will of God, that is to say: apart from what is clearly attested in the Scriptures."

Interrogatio XVI
(Zelzer 65–66, QF 18, SR 3 [PG 31.1083–1084])

I: Peccantem quodmodo corripiemus vel ebendabimus?

R: 1 Sicut praeceptum est a domino dicente *Si peccaverit in te frater tuus, vade et argue eum inter te et ipsum solum. Si audierit te, lucratus es fratrem tuum.* **2** *Si vero non te audierit, assume tecum alium unum vel duos, ut in ore duorum vel trium testium stet omne verbum.* **3** *Quodsi etiam ipsos non audierit, dic ecclesiae, si autem nec ecclesiam audierit, sit tibi sicut gentilis et publicanus,* si forte *increpatio haec quae fit a pluribus* eveniat ei in salutem; **4** et sicut dixit apostolus *Argue increpa consolare in omni patientia et doctrina,* **5** et rursum *Si quis non oboedit verbo nostro per epistolam, hunc notate, ut non commisceamini cum eo,* sine dubio ad mensam.

Question 16

Q: How shall we correct or amend the sinner?

R: 1 Just as we were enjoined by the Lord who said: *If your brother sins against you, go and confront him, between you and him alone. If he heeds you, you have gained your brother.* **2** *But if he does not heed you, take with you one or two others, for "in the mouth of two or three witnesses every word is established"* (Deut 19:15). **3** *But if he does not heed them, tell it to the church; if he does not heed even the church, then let him be to you as the pagan and the tax-collector* (Matt 18:15-17), if perhaps *this rebuke coming from the many may suffice* (2 Cor 2:6) for his salvation. **4** And, as the Apostle said: *confront, rebuke, appeal with all patience and teaching* (2 Tim 4:2) **5** and again, *If anyone does not obey our word through this letter, mark such a one and do not associate with him* (2 Thess 3:14), that is, doubtless, at table.[73]

---

[73] SR 3 1084B and QF 18.5 finish with the scriptural phrase: *that he may be ashamed* (ἵνα ἐντραπῇ). Curiously, Rufinus's gloss can be retranslated into Greek as ἵνα ἐν τραπέζῃ.

Interrogatio XVII
(Zelzer 66–67, QF 19, SR 4 [PG 31.1083–1086])

I: Si quis etiam in parvis delictis affligere voluerit fratres dicens quia Debetis paenitere per singula, ne forte et ipse immisericors videatur et dissolvere caritatem?

R: 1 Cum affirmaverit dominus quia *Iota unum vel apex unus non transiet a lege usquequo omnia finat*, et rursum definierit quoniam *De omni sermone otioso quemcumque locuti fuerint homines reddent pro eo rationem in die iudicii*, **2** nihil oportet contemni tamquam parvum, *qui enim spernit minima paulatim defluit*. **3** Sed et quomodo quis audebit dicere breve aut parvum delictum, cum apostolus dicat manifesteque definiat quia *per praevaricationem legis* deus exhonoratur? **4** Sed et *aculeus mortis peccatum* esse dicitur, et non dixit tale vel tale peccatum, sed omne peccatum. **5** Magis ergo immisericors est qui intermittit et neglegit quam ille qui arguit, sicut is qui in morsu serpentis permittit delitescere venenum quam ille qui educit et abstrahit. **6** Sed et caritatem destruit ille qui secundum quod scriptum est *parcens baculo odit filium suum, qui autem diligit diligenter corripit*.

Question 17

Q: If someone taxes the brothers even for small sins, saying "You should repent of each of them!" does not such a one appear to lack compassion and to dissolve love?[74]

R: 1 Since the Lord affirmed that *not one iota, not one little stroke shall pass from the Law till all is accomplished* (Matt 5:18) and again laid it down that *for every idle word that men utter, they shall render account for it on the day of judgment* (Matt 12:6), **2** nothing ought be despised as small,[75] *for he who spurns little things will fall little by little* (Sir 19:1; cf. Prov 13:13).[76] **3** How indeed shall anyone dare to say that a sin is slight or small when the Apostle has said and manifestly declared that *through your trangression of the law, you dishonour God* (Rom 2:23)? **4** And if it is said that *the sting of death is sin*, he did not say this sin or that, but every sin (1 Cor 15:56).[77] **5** So the one who does nothing and neglects it is far more wanting in compassion than one who rebukes, as is one who leaves the venom to fester in another bitten by a snake than one who draws it out and removes it. **6** Indeed, he dissolves love who, as it is written: *by sparing the rod, hates his son; but he who loves, chastises diligently* (Prov 13:24).

---

[74] On the dispositions necessary in administering correction see RBas 46.45 and RBas 78.

[75] Here in the *Small Asketikon* Basil teaches the so-called "equivalence of sins," or at any rate that no sin whatever may be regarded as "small" or treated lightly. See also RBas 12.8, and the discussion on the *De Iudicio* by W. K. L. Clarke in his *The Ascetic Works of Saint Basil* (London: SPCK, 1925), 15, 55–56, and by Paul J. Fedwick in "A Chronology of the Life and Works of Basil," in *Basil of Caesarea, Christian, Humanist, Ascetic* (Toronto: Pontifical Institute of Medieval Studies, 1981), 14 n. 81. In asserting that the doctrine of the equivalence of sins is not found in the *Small Asketikon* Fedwick appears not to have noticed the present text. Since he uses this assertion to argue for a late dating of the *De Iudicio*, that also must be considered questionable.

[76] Both the Greek and the Syriac cite Prov 13:13, which turns on the verb καταφρονῶ, just used by Basil. SR 4 1084C: *whoever despises a matter, will be slighted by it* (ὁ καταφρονῶν πράγματος καταφρονηθήσεται ὑπ᾽ αὐτοῦ). RBas 17.2, however, uses a passage from Sir 19:1, similar in meaning but different in vocabulary, which turns on the theme of "small": *qui enim spernit* (ὁ ἐξουθενῶν) *minima paulatim defluit* (κατὰ μικρὸν πεσεῖται)—he who spurns little things will fall little by little.

[77] SR 4 1084D: . . . this sin or that, but clearly, inasmuch as it is undefined, every sin. "But . . . every sin" is lacking in Voss. and Reg. prim. (*Ask* 3), which is curious, since part of it is here in the RBas. An early editor, Combefi, in choosing to omit the clause, censured it for Stoic severity. There is no doubt, however, that the thought is authentically Basilian.

Interrogatio XVIII
(Zelzer 67–68, QF 20, SR 5 [PG 31.1085–1086])

I: Quomodo quis debet paenitere in unoquoque delicto?

R: 1 Affectum illum in se recipiens quem gerebat ille qui dicit *Iniquitatem odio habui et abominatus sum,* sed et ea quae scripta sunt sexto psalmo atque in aliis quam plurimis, vel illa quae apostolus dixit ad eos qui *secundum deum contristati* sunt: **2** *Quantum operatum est,* inquit, *vobis, sollicitudinem; sed excusationem, sed indignationem, sed aemulationem, sed vindictam. In omnibus exhibuistis vos castos esse negotio.* **3** Sed et his ipsis in quibus deliquit agens multa contraria sicut et Zacchaeus fecit.

Interrogatio XVIIII
(Zelzer 68, QF 21, SR 287 [PG 31.1283–1284])

I: Qui sunt *fructus digni paenitentiae?*

R: 1 Opera quae contraria sunt peccato, isti sunt fructus iustitiae quos debet afferre ille qui vult secundum quod scriptum est *in omni opere bono fructifica*re.

Interrogatio XX
(Zelzer 68–69, QF 22, SR 6 [PG 31.1085–1086])

I: Qui se verbo dicit paenitere, peccatum autem suum non emendat, quid est?

R: 1 De isto scriptum est *Si te rogaverit inimicus tuus magna voce, non acquiescas ei: septem enim nequitiae sunt in anima eius,* **2** et alibi *Sicut canis revertens ad vomitum suum odibilis fit, ita homo qui per malitiam suam revertitur ad peccatum suum.*

Question 18

Q: How should one repent for each sin?

R: 1 By taking upon oneself the disposition which he showed who said: *Iniquity I hated and abhorred* (Ps 118:163) and also what is written in the sixth psalm (Ps 6) and in many other places, and what the Apostle said *to those who were grieving according to God:* **2** *What earnestness it worked in you, what giving account of yourselves, what indignation, what emulation, what putting of things right! In all ways you have shown yourselves pure in the affair* (2 Cor 7:11). **3** Yes, and by multiplying deeds contrary to those by which one has failed, as did Zaccheus (cf. Luke 19:8).

Question 19

Q: What are the *fruits worthy of repentance*? (Matt 3:8; Luke 3:8)

R: 1 These are works that are contrary to the sin, those fruits of righteousness which he ought to bring forth who wants, as it is written, *to bear fruit in every good work* (Col 1:10).

Question 20

Q: One who professes in word that he repents but does not amend his sin—what is he?

R: 1 Concerning such a one it is written: *If your enemy entreats you in a loud voice, do not be persuaded by him, for there are seven wickednesses in his soul* (Prov 26:25), **2** and elsewhere: *As odious as a dog returning to his vomit, so is a man who through his own malice returns to his sin* (Prov 26:11 LXX).

Interrogatio XXI
(Zelzer 69–70, QF 23, SR 288 [PG 31.1283–1286])

I: Qui vult confiteri peccata sua, si omnibus debet confiteri et quibuslibet aut certis quibusque?

R: 1 Clementia dei erga eos qui deliquerunt manifesta est secundum scriptum est quia *Non vult mortem peccatoris, sed ut revertatur et vivat.* **2** Quia ergo et conversionis modus aptus esse et convertentis se a peccato fructus dignus ostendi debet per paenitentiam secundum quod scriptum est *Facit fructus dignos paenitantiae,* **3** ne forte secundum comminationem illam eveniat his qui non paenitent quod scriptum est *Omnis arbor quae non facit fructum bonum, excidetur et in ignem mittetur,* **4** necessarium videtur his quibus *dispensa*tio *mysteriorum dei* commissa est confitenda esse peccata. **5** Sic enim et qui antiquitus paenitebant inveniuntur apud sanctos confessi esse peccata sua. **6** Scriptum est enim in evangelio quia Iohanni baptistae confitebantur peccata sua, et in actibus apostolorum apostolis a quibus et baptizabantur.

Interrogatio XXII
(Zelzer 70–72, QF 24, SR 289 [PG 31.1285–1286])

I: Qui paenituerunt pro aliquo peccato et rursum in hoc ipsum peccatum inciderunt quid faciant?

R: 1 Is qui semel deliquit et iterum in idem peccatum incurrit, indicare de se videtur hoc primum, quod ab illo priori peccato non fuerit expurgatus, ex quo velut a radice quadam pessima eadem quae antea pullularunt. **2** Sicut enim quis arboris ramos excidens si radicem relinquat, ubi radix fixa permanet virgulta denuo eiusdem seminis germinabit, ita etiam peccatum: **3** quoniam non omnes qui delinquunt ex ipsis peccatis initium sumunt, sed ex aliis interdum delicti occasio nascitur, **4** necessarium ergo ei est qui vult omnimodo purgare se a peccato, primas ipsas causas culpae succidere.

Question 21

Q: Ought one who wishes to confess his sins confess them to all and sundry, or only to certain ones?

R: 1 God's loving-kindness toward sinners is clear from what is written: *I do not desire the death of the sinner, but that he should be converted and live* (Ezek 33:11). **2** Since the manner of repentance should be appropriate and worthy fruit be shown by those turning from sin through their repentance, as it is written: *Bring forth fruits worthy of repentance* (Matt 3:8; Luke 3:8), **3** lest for those who do not repent it turns out according to that threat which is written: *every tree*, it says, *which does not bear fruit is cut down and cast into the fire* (Matt 3:10; 7:19; cf. Luke 3:9), **4** it seems[78] necessary that sins be confessed to those entrusted with *the stewardship of the Mysteries of God* (cf. 1 Cor 4:1). **5** For thus also those who repented of old are found to have confessed their sins before the saints. **6** For it is written in the gospel that they confessed their sins to John the Baptist (cf. Matt 3:6; Mark 1:5) and in the Acts of the Apostles, to the apostles, by whom they were also baptized (cf. Acts 2:37).

Question 22

Q: What shall they do who have repented of some sin but fall into the same sin again?

R: 1 He who has offended[79] once and incurs this same sin again is seen to indicate this about himself: first that he is not purified of what is prior to the sin, from which, as from a kind of noxious root there sprout the same ills as before. **2** It is as if someone cuts off the branches of a tree but leaves behind the root. As long as the root remains in the ground it will eventually generate shoots from the same stock. So also with sin: **3** since not all who commit an offence take their impulse from the sins themselves—rather the cause of the offence arises from yet other offences— **4** it is therefore necessary for him who wishes to purify himself wholly from sin to cut out from below the very first causes of defect.

---

[78] *Videtur*: there is no correlate of *videtur* in either the Greek or the Syriac; simply: "it is necessary. . . ."

[79] Both Greek and Syriac: *repented*.

5 Verbi gratia, si ex contentione vel ex invidia fuerit, non a se sumpsit exordium, sed radicem habet ex arrogantia et cupidate humanae gloriae venientem; **6** dum enim gloriam quaerit unusquisque ab hominibus, aut contentionibus studet aut recte agentibus invidet, huic scilicet per quem videtur ipse minus in laude vel in admiratione haberi.

7 Si quis ergo semel notatus fuerit invidiae vel contentionis vitio et rursum in hoc ipsum inciderit, **8** sciat se primam illam causam de qua superius diximus, ex qua invidia vel contentio nascitur, in interioribus medullis habere reconditam. **9** Oportet ergo eum et per contraria atque adversa curare, id est per humilitatis exercitium; exercitia vero humilitatis sunt, si se vilioribus officiis subdat et ministeriis indignioribus tradat. **10** Ita namque arrogantiae et humanae gloriae vitium curare poterit, ut in consuetudine humilitatis effectus ultra iam non incidat arrogantiae et vanae gloriae delictum.

11 Sed et in singulis huiuscemodi vitiis cura similis adhibebitur.

Interrogatio XXIII
(Zelzer 72, QF 25, SR 99 [PG 31.1151–1152])

I: Quali affectu vel quali sensu oportet increpare eum qui increpat?

R: 1 Ad deum quidem tali mente esse debet qualem indicat beatus David dicens *Vidi non servantes pactum et tabescebam, quia eloquia tua non custodierunt.* **2** Ad eos autem quos increpat hunc debet affectum servare quem pater et medicus erga aegrotantem filium servat, et tunc maxime, cum qualitas curae tristior videtur et gravior.

Interrogatio XXIIII
(Zelzer 73, QF 26, SR 158 [PG 31.1185–1186])

I: Quali affectu debet quis suscipere correptionem?

R: Sicut aeger filius patris aut medici de vita sua solliciti. Qui etiamsi asperum aliquid offerat vel amarum ad curandum filium, scit utique filius, quod nec pater in aliquo neglegere potest se salute filii nec medicus falli.

5 For example, if there has been something of *strife and envy* (cf. Rom 13:13, et al.), it does not take a beginning from itself, but has a root of arrogance and the love of human glory; **6** for he who seeks glory from men either harries with disputes or envies those who act uprightly, that is, with anyone through whom he appears to be held in less praise or admiration.

7 Therefore, if someone who has been censured once for the vice of envy or contention falls into the same again, **8** let him recognize that the primary cause of which we spoke above from which arises envy or contentiousness is the love of glory which he has lurking in his innermost marrow. **9** He therefore ought to be cured by the contrary and opposite, that is, by exercises of humility. Such exercises of humility are that he submit himself to menial tasks and give himself to lowly acts of service. **10** In this way the vice of arrogance and human glory shall be able to be cured, so that, once he is established in the disposition of humility, he will not fall again into the offence of arrogance and vainglory.

11 And let this manner of treatment be applied likewise to each of these vices.

Question 23

Q: With what kind of disposition or what sensibility should he who rebukes rebuke?

R: 1 Towards God he should be of such mind as was shown by blessed David when he said: *I saw that they were faithless and I fainted because they did not keep your words* (Ps 118:158). **2** Towards those whom he rebukes, he ought to adopt the disposition which a father and physician adopts towards his own ailing son, especially when the manner of the treatment appears more distressing and grievous.

Question 24

Q: In what kind of disposition should one accept correction?

R: 1 Just as the ailing son of one who is both his father and physician, who is solicitous for his life. Though he prescribes something sharp and bitter for the son's cure, the son nevertheless knows that the father cannot neglect anything to save his son, and as a physician cannot be deceived.

Interrogatio XXV
(Zelzer 73, QF 27, SR 159 [PG 31.1185–1186])

I: Qui tristatur adversus eum qui se increpat qualis est?

R: 1 Neque periculum peccati agnovit iste, et maxime ad deum, neque lucrum paentitentiae, nec credidit illi qui dixit quia *Qui diligit diligenter corripit.* **2** Sed et se ipsum alienum facit ab illa utilitate dicentis *Corripiet me iustus in misericordia et increpabit me,* **3** sed et laesionem ceterorum iste talis permanet inter fratres, resolvit enim et impedit animos eorum qui possunt proficere.

Interrogatio XXVI
(Zelzer 74, QF 28, SR 7 [PG 31.1085–1088])

I: Quale iudicium esse debet de his qui peccantes defendunt?

R: 1 Ut mihi videtur gravius ab illo quod dixit dominus quia *Expedit illi ut suspendatur mola asinaria ad collum eius et praecipitetur in mare quam ut scandalizet unum de minimis istis,* **2** non enim iam correptionem ad emendationem, sed defensionem ad confirmandum peccatum suum suscipit qui delinquit, sed at alios ad simile provocat malum, **3** ita ut conveniat ei qui peccantes defendit illud quod dictum est quia *Si non ostenderitis fructus dignos paenitentiae, excide*mini *et in ignem mitte*mini, **4** vel rursum quod a domino dictum est quia *Si oculus tuus dexter scandalizaverit te, eice eum et proice abs te,* **5** *expedit enim tibi ut pereat unum de membris tuis et non omne corpus tuum mittatur in gehennam.*

Interrogatio XXVII
(Zelzer 75, QF 30, SR 8 [PG 31.1087–1088])

I: Paenitentem ex corde quomodo oportet suscipi?

R: 1 Sicut dominus ostendit cum dicit quia *Convocavit amicos et vicinos dicens Congratulamini mihi quia inveni ovem meam quam perdideram.*

Question 25

Q: He who is resentful against the one who rebukes him, of what kind is he?

R: 1 He ackowledges neither the peril of sin—and above all towards God—nor the gain that comes from repentance, nor does he believe him who said: *Whoever loves, diligently chastises* (Prov 13:24). **2** And he has made himself a stranger to the benefit received by the one who said: *Let the righteous chastise me in mercy and reprove me* (Ps 140:5). **3** Indeed, such a one remains a source of harm to others among the brothers, for he undermines and hinders the souls of those capable of making progress.

Question 26

Q: What ought to be the judgment of those who justify sinners?[80]

R: 1 A heavier judgment, it seems to me, than that which the Lord said: *It would be better for him if a millstone were hung round his neck and he were cast into the sea than that he should scandalize one of these little ones* (Matt 18:9; Luke 17:2), **2** for the one who has offended no longer receives a rebuke leading to amendment but a justification leading to confirmation in his sin, and he provokes others to the same vice. **3** Hence there applies to him who defends sinners the saying: *if you do not* show forth *fruits worthy of repentance you shall be cut off and cast into the fire* (cf. Matt 3:8 + 3:10), **4** and again what was said by the Lord, *If your right eye scandalizes you, pluck it out and cast it from you,* **5** *for it is better for you that one of your limbs should perish, than that your whole body be cast into Gehenna* (Matt 5:29; cf. 18:9).

Question 27

Q: How ought we to receive back one who repents from the heart?

R: 1 As the Lord shows when he says: *he called his friends and neighbours together saying: Rejoice with me, for I have found my sheep which I had lost* (Luke 15:6).

---

[80] Cf. RB 69: That no one should presume to defend another in the monastery, "whence can spring the most serious incidence of scandals" (RB 69.3); see Gribomont, "Commentaries," 269.

Interrogatio XXVIII
(Zelzer 75, QF 29, SR 9 [PG 31.1087–1088])

I: Erga eum qui pro peccato non paenitet qualiter esse debemus?

R: 1 Sicut dominus praecepit dicens *Sit tibi sicut gentilis et publicanus*, et sicut apostolus docuit dicens *Subtrahite vos ab omni fratre inquiete ambulante et non secundum traditionem quam* tradidimus vobis.

Interrogatio XXVIIII
(Zelzer 76, QF 31, SR 85 [PG 31.1143–1144])

I: Si debet habere aliquid proprium qui inter fratres est?

R: 1 Hoc contrarium est illi testimonio quod in actibus apostolorum de illis qui credebant primitus scriptum est, **2** ibi enim ita dicit quia *Nemo quicquam ex bonis suis proprium dicebat esse, sed erant illis omnia communia.* **3** Si quis[36] ergo proprium sibi esse dicit aliquid, sine dubio alienum se facit ab electis dei et a caritate domini qui docuit verbo et opere complevit et qui *animam suam po*suit *pro amicis suis.* **4** Si ergo ipse *animam suam pro amicis* dedit, quomodo nos etiam ea quae extra animam sunt propria vindicamus?

Interrogatio XXX
(Zelzer 77, QF 32, SR 86 [PG 31.1143–1144])

I: Si quis dicat quia Neque accipio a fratribus neque do, sed contentus sum meis propriis, quid de hoc observare debemus?

R: 1 Si non acquiescit doctrinae domini dicentis *Diligite invicem sicut et ego dilexi vos,* acquiescat apostolo dicenti *Auferte malum ex vobis ipsis,* ne forte accidat ut *modicum fermentum totam massam corrumpat.*

---

[36] *Si quis* Zelz., most MSS, confirmed L² 24; *si qui* CEP, an archetype error.

Question 28

Q: How should we act toward one who is unrepentant for sin?

R: 1 As the Lord enjoined, saying: *let him be to you as the gentile and the tax-collector* (Matt 18:17), and as the Apostle taught, saying: *Withdraw yourselves from every brother who walks disorderly and not according to the tradition which* we delivered to you[81] (2 Thess 3:6).

Question 29

Q: Should someone who is among the brothers have anything of his own?

R: 1 This is contrary to the testimony written in the Acts of the Apostles concerning those who first believed, **2** for there it speaks thus: *Not one of them said that any of his possessions was his own, but all things were common to all* (Acts 4:32). **3** If someone therefore says that anything is his own, he without doubt makes himself a stranger to the elect of God[82] and from the love of the Lord who taught in word and completed it in deed and who *laid down his life for his friends* (cf. John 15:13). **4** Now if he himself gave *his life for his friends*, what claim have we on our possessions, which are, after all, external to our life?

Question 30

Q: If someone says, "I neither take anything from the brothers nor do I give, but am content with my own," what should we observe in his regard?[83]

R: 1 If he will not yield to that teaching of the Lord, who said *Love one another as I have loved you* (John 13:34), then let him yield to the Apostle, who said *Cast out the evil from among yourselves* (1 Cor 5:13), lest it happen that a *little leaven corrupts the whole lump* (1 Cor 5:6).

---

[81] SR 9 1088B: ἣν παρέλαβον παρ᾿ ἡμῶν *which they received from us.* "Two ancient books" have ἣν παρελάβετε *which you received* (Garnier, n. 69); QF 29.1: you have learnt. The second person plural of the two Greek MSS, RBas and QF might reflect a variant reading of the Greek NT originally used by Basil.

[82] SR 85 1144A: τῆς τοῦ Θεοῦ Ἐκκλησίας "to the church of God," confirmed in QF.

[83] This individualistic or "idiorrythmic" arrangement is so much at odds with Basil's teaching that perhaps the superior asking the question is dealing with a new-comer with wrong-headed ideas, or perhaps an aggregation of "sarabaites" or free-lancing ascetics is endeavouring to upgrade itself in accordance with Basil's teaching. Since this occurs in the *Small Asketikon*, the latter is preferable.

Interrogatio XXXI
(Zelzer 77–78, QF 33, SR 187 [PG 31.1207–1208])

I: Si debet quis a carnalibus propinquis accipere aliquid?

R: 1 Propinquos quidem reddere quae sua sunt his qui ad servitium dei accedunt necessarium est et nihil subtrahere, ut non crimen sacriliegii incurrant. **2** Verumtamen haec praerogari in conspectu eorum ad quos visa sunt pertinere, et illis ipsis occasionem praestat elationis ac superbiae et aliis fratribus eiusdem propositi pauperioribus tristitiam generat, **3** ita ut accidat illud in quo Corinthii increpabantur ab apostolo dicente quia *Confunditis non habentes.*

4 Et ideo his qui per loca singula ecclesiis praesunt, si sint fideles et prudentes dispensatores, ipsis offerri debent secundum imitationem eorum qui in actibus apostolorum id fecisse perscribuntur, **5** de quibus dicitur quia *Afferentes pretia* praediorum suorum *ponebant ante pedes apostolorum.*

6 Certe quoniam non est omnium huiuscemodi dispensationes explere fideliter, illis offerri convenit qui apud omnes in hoc officio probat habentur. **7** Verumtamen etiam de his probabit ille qui praeest, per quem debeant dispensari.

Interrogatio XXXII
(Zelzer 78–79, QF 34, SR 188 [PG 31.1207–1208])

I: Quomodo debemus videre eos qui nobis aliquando vel familiares vel consanguinei fuerunt et proximi?

R: 1 Sicut dominus ostendit tunc cum ei nuntiaverunt quia *Mater tua et fratres tui foris stant volentes te videre*, ad quos cum increpatione respondit dicens **2** *Quae est mater mea et quis sunt fratres mei? Qui enim fecerit voluntatem patris mei qui in caelis est, iste meus frater et soror et mater est.*

Question 31

Q: Should one accept anything from relatives in the flesh?

R: 1 It is necessary that relatives render to those coming to the Lord what is their due and subtract nothing, that they may not incur the judgment for sacrilege. **2** But to disburse these things before the eyes of those to whom they appeared to belong often becomes an occasion of inflation and pride for themselves and a cause of grief for the other brothers who came poor to the same way of life, **3** so that there happens what was indicted among the Corinthians by the Apostle where he says: *You put to shame those who have nothing* (1 Cor 11:22).

4 Therefore, if those who preside over the churches in each place[84] are faithful and prudent administrators, let it be brought to them **5** in imitation of those in the Acts of the Apostles who did this, of whom it is said that *bringing the proceeds of their estates they laid it at the feet of the apostles* (Acts 4:35).

6 But inasmuch as it is not everyone's duty to fulfil faithfully administrations of this kind, it is fitting that it be brought to those who have been approved in this office before all. **7** However, the one who presides, through whom all ought to be dispensed, shall exercise discretion even concerning these things.

Question 32

Q: How should we regard those who were once our companions and blood-relatives and neighbours?[85]

R: 1 Just as the Lord showed when they told him: *Your mother and brothers are standing outside wanting to see you* (Luke 8:20; Matt 12:47),[86] to whom he replied with a rebuke, saying: **2** *Who is my mother and who are my brothers? For anyone who does the will of my Father who is in heaven is my brother and sister and mother* (Matt 12:48, 50).

---

[84] SR 187 1208B uses the singular: ὁ τὴν φροντίδα τῶν κατὰ τόπον Ἐκκλησιῶν πεπιστευμένος: "the one entrusted with the responsibility of the churches in that place." Bishops appears to be meant. The reference disappears in the QF, which speaks of the responsibility for the church of the one dispensing his own goods.

[85] SR 188 1208C: τούς ποτε συνοίκους ἡμῶν, ἢ συγγενεῖς, ἐρχομένους πρὸς ἡμᾶς. The last phrase, "who come to us," is confirmed in QF: Did Rufinus misconstrue some form of the last phrase of the Greek as *"proximi"?* Garnier (PG 31.1208, n. 58) notes variants in the text at this point.

[86] For the same teaching and citation see *Morals* 22.2, where John 8:47; 15:14, and Rom 8:14 are also added.

Interrogatio XXXIII

(Zelzer 79, QF 35, SR 189 [PG 31.1209–1210])

I: Quodsi deprecantur nos volentes ut eamus cum ipsis ad domos eorum, si oportet eis acquiescere?

R: 1 Siquidem pro aedificatione fidei aliquis ire potest, si probaverit ille qui praeest, mittatur. **2** Si vero propter humanam aliquem gratiam, audiat dominum dicentem ad illum qui dixit ei, Magister, *permitte mihi primo* ire et *renuntiare his qui in domo sunt*, quia *Nemo mittens manum suam in aratrum et retro respiciens aptus est regno* caelorum. **3** Quodsi pro renuntiando hoc dictum est volenti ire ut renuntiaret, quid dicimus de ceteris?

Interrogatio XXXIIII

(Zelzer 80, QF 36, SR 21 [PG 31.1197–1198])

I: Unde vagatur mens nostra et cogitationes diversae ascendunt in corde, et quomodo hoc possumus emendare?

R: 1 Vagatur quidem mens interdum etiam otio, dum non occupatur in necessaria sollicitudine, sed in remissione posita et securitate non credit praesentem esse deum *scrutan*tem *corda et renes*. **2** Si enim hoc crederet, faciebat hoc quod superius dictum est, *Providebam dominum in conspectu meo semper, quia a dextris est mihi ne commovear*. **3** Qui enim haec agit vel horum similia, neque vacabit[37] umquam neque habebit otium vanis cogitationibus indulgere vel aliquid cogitare quod non ad aedificationem fidei pertineat et ad aliquam animae utilitatem exspectet. **4** Quanto magis nihil audebit, quod adversum sit deo et non ei placeat cogitare.

Interrogatio XXXV

(Zelzer 81, QF 37, SR 22 [PG 31.1097–1098])

I: Unde nocturnae phantasiae inhonestae et turpes accidunt nobis?

R: 1 Veniunt quidem haec maxime ex diurnis animae motibus et actibus indignis et incongruis. **2** Si enim vacet in iudiciis dei et expurgetur anima per meditationem legis divinae et studium verbi dei ibique indesinentem curam gerat semper requirens et scrutans quid sit quod placeat deo, talia habebit etiam somnia.

---

[37] *Vacabit* Zelz. most MSS, confirmed L² 30; *vagabit* (will wander) C (before correction), B (after correction); *vagabitur* (be led astray) C (after correction), J.

Question 33

Q: But what if they appeal to us, wanting us to come home with them? Should we yield to them?

A: 1 If it is possible for someone to go for the upbuilding of the faith, let him be sent, if the one who presides has approved. 2 But if it is merely for some human satisfaction, let him hear the Lord answer the one who asked him: *Master, first let me* go and *bid farewell to those at home: No one who puts his hand to the plough and looks back is fit for the kingdom of heaven* (Luke 9:61-62). 3 If this is the judgment concerning one who wanted to bid farewell once and for all, what have we to say in other cases?

Question 34

Q: Why does our mind wander and various reasonings arise in the heart, and how can we remedy this?

R: 1 The mind wanders during a time of idleness when it is not engaged in the care of necessities. Instead, finding itself at ease and without a care, it does not believe that God is present *who tries hearts and inmost parts* (Ps 7:9). 2 For if it believed this, it would be doing what was said above: *I kept the Lord always in view before me; since he is at my right hand, I shall not be shaken* (Ps 15:8). 3 Whoever does this and other sayings like it will never be unoccupied[87] and will never have the leisure to indulge in vain reasonings or to reason about anything that does not serve the upbuilding of faith and promise some benefit for the soul. 4 Much more so, he will never dare to think on what is forbidden or displeasing to God.

Question 35

Q: Why do the unseemly and shameful fantasies of the night come upon us?

R: 1 They come especially from the movements of the soul through the day and from unworthy and incongruous deeds. 2 But if the soul devotes itself to the judgments of God and is purified through meditation on the divine law and zeal for the word of God and exercises unceasing care, ever seeking and testing what may be pleasing to God, then it shall also have corresponding dreams.

---

[87] 1097B: τολμήσει, will dare; QF 36.3 ܢܡܪܚ dare.

Interrogatio XXXVI
(Zelzer 81–82, QF 38, SR 160 [PG 31.1187–1188])

I: Quali affectu debemus infirmis fratribus ministrare?

R: 1 Sicut ipsi domino offerentes obsequium qui dixit quia *Cum feceritis uni ex minimis istis fratribus meis, mihi fecistis.* **2** Expedit autem ad conservandum huiuscemodi affectum in obsequiis, ut et hi qui obsequia a nobis suscipiunt tales sint quibus merito deferri obsequium debeat. **3** Et ideo oportet eos qui praesunt curam gerere, uti ne hi quibus ministratur tales sint qui carni indulgeant et ventri, **4** set potius in amore dei et Christi Iesu probabiles inveniantur et per patientiam suam ac vitae meritum fratrum mereantur obsequia, **5** ut habeantur ad gloriam Christi et opprobrium diaboli, sicut et sanctus Iob.

Interrogatio XXXVII
(Zelzer 82, QF 39, SR 161 [PG 31.1187–1188])

I: Cum quali humilitate debet quis obsequium suscipere a fratribus?

R: 1 Sicut servus a domino et sicut ostendit Petrus apostolus cum ei dominus ministraret, in quo simul etiam periculum eorum qui nolunt recipere obsequia fratrum docemur.[38]

Interrogatio XXXVIII
(Zelzer 83, QF 40, SR 162 [PG 31.1187–1188])

I: Qualem debemus habere caritatem ad invicem?

R: 1 Qualem dominus ostendit et docuit dicens *Diligite invicem sicut et ego dilexi vos; maiorem hac caritatem nullus habet quam ut quis animam suam ponat pro amicis suis.* **2** Si autem et animam poni oportet, quanto magis in aliis votum et studium debet ostendi, **3** sine dubio non secundum humanas voluntates, sed secundum illum prospectum in quo est commune omnium propositum placendi deo.

---

[38] *Docemur* Zelz. following most α MSS, reflecting Gk: παιδευόμεθα, confirmed L²40; *docemur* omitted β.

Question 36

Q: In what disposition ought we to serve the sick brothers?

R: **1** As offering our service to the Lord himself who said: *When you did it to the least of these my brothers, you did it to me* (Matt 25:40). **2** Yet it helps us to preserve such a disposition in our ministry, if those who receive services from us are such to whom service is deservedly offered. **3** So those who preside ought to take care that they to whom service is done are not such as indulge the flesh and the stomach, **4** but instead are found proven in the love of God and Christ Jesus as those who through their own patience and the merit of their life deserve the services of their brothers, **5** whereby they are a boast for Christ and a reproach to the devil, as was holy Job.

Question 37

Q: With what humility ought one accept a service from the brothers?

R: **1** As a slave from his lord, and such as the apostle Peter showed when the Lord served him (cf. John 13:6-9), in which we also learn the danger of those who do not accept services from the brothers.

Question 38

Q: What kind of love ought we to have for one another?

R: **1** Such as the Lord showed and taught, when he said: *Love one another even as I have loved you; no-one has greater love than to lay down his life for his friends* (John 15:12-13). **2** For if it is necessary to lay down even one's life, then how much more ought we to show devotion and zeal in lesser matters, **3** not of course to accommodate human wishes, but to benefit each towards the goal proposed in common to all of being well pleasing to God.

Interrogatio XXXVIIII

(Zelzer 83–85, QF 41, SR 163 [PG 31.1187–1190])

I: Quomodo poterit quis implere caritatem circa proximam?

R: 1 Primo quidem metuens iudicium praevaricantis mandatum domini, quia ipse dixit *Qui non crediderit filio non habebit vitam, sed ira dei manet super eum,* **2** tum deinde velut cupiens ad aeternam vitam pervenire, quia *mandatum eius vita aeterna est.*

3 *Primum* autem *et magnum mandatum est: diliges dominum deum tuum ex toto corde tuo et ex tota mente tua et ex tota anima tua; secundum vero simile illi: Diliges proximum tuum sicut te ipsum.* **4** Etsi quis desiderat similis effici domino dicenti *Mandatum novum do vobis, ut diligatis invicem sicut* et *ego dilexi vos.*

5 Sed ex communi sensu sentire hoc possumus, quia si beneficium consequimur a fratre, in eo quod diligimus fratrem, debitores ei efficimur, ut eum merito diligamus, **6** quod etiam inter gentiles observari solet sicut et dominus in evangelio dicit *Si diligitis eos qui vos diligent quae vobis est gratia, quia et peccatores* et gentiles *diligentes se diligunt.*

7 Si autem in aliquo vel laedit nos vel adversatur quis, hunc[39] non solum propter mandatum, sed et propter hoc ipsum quia plus nobis praestat in quo laedit diligere debemus, **8** siquidem credimus domino dicenti *Beati estis cum exprobrabunt vos et persequentur et dicent omne malum adversum vos mentientes propter me:* **9** *Gaudete et exsultate, quoniam merces vestra multa est in caelis.*

---

[39] *Hunc* Zelz. most MSS, confirmed L¹ 589; *hoc* CS, an archetype error in α.

Question 39

Q: How shall one be able to fulfil *love for one's neighbour*? (cf. Matt 22:36)

R: 1 In the first place, by fearing the judgment against those who trespass the commandment of the Lord, for he himself said: *Whoever does not believe in the Son shall not have life, but the wrath of God shall stay over him* (John 3:36). **2** Second, by yearning to reach eternal life, for *his commandment is eternal life* (John 12:50).

3 Now *the first and the great commandment is: "You shall love the Lord your God with all your heart and with all your mind and with all your soul," and the second is like it: "You shall love your neighbour as your very self"* (Matt 22:36, 39). **4** Then if one desires to be made like the Lord who said: *A new commandment I give you, that you love one another, even as I have loved you* (John 13:34).

5 But we can appreciate this even from common sense, since if we have received a benefit from a brother for which we love the brother, we have become his debtors and love him deservedly. **6** This is customarily observed even among the Gentiles, as the Lord said in the gospel: *if you love those who love you, what credit is it to you, since even sinners* and pagans *love those who love them* (Luke 6:32; Matt 5:46-47).

7 If on the other hand a brother ill-treats us in some way or opposes us, then we ought to love him not only on account of the commandment, but on account of that something more which he offers us in the very fact that he harms us, **8**—that is, if we believe the Lord who said: *Blessed are you when they reproach you and persecute you and speak all manner of evil against you for my sake:* **9** *Rejoice and leap for joy, for great shall be your reward in heaven* (Matt 5:11-12).

Interrogatio XXXX

(Zelzer 85–86, QF 42, SR 23 [PG 31.1097–1100])

I: Usque ad quae *verb*a *otios*us sermo iudicatur?

R: **1** Generaliter omnis sermo qui non proficit ad aliquem gratiam fidei Christi otiosus est, et tantum est periculum huiuscemodi sermonis **2** ut, etiamsi bonum esse videatur quod dicitur et[40] ad aedificationem fidei non pertineat; **3** non in sermonis bonitate ille qui locutus est periculum effugit, sed in eo quod non proficit ad aedificationem sermo prolatus, contristat spiritum sanctum dei. **4** Hoc enim manifeste demonstrat apostolus dicens *Omnis sermo malus de ore vestro non procedat, sed si quis bonus ad aedificationem fidei, ut det gratiam audientibus,* **5** et super haec adiecit *Nolite contristare spiritum sanctum dei, in quo signati estis in die redemptionis;* quo utique gravius malum nullum esse poterit.

Interrogatio XXXXI

(Zelzer 86, QF 43, SR 24 [PG 31.1099–1100])

I: Quid est *maledicus* id est λοίδορος?

R: **1** Omnis sermo qui ob hoc profertur ut infamet aliquem vel male commendet maledicus est, etiamsi videatur non esse iniuriosus. **2** Et hoc manifestum est ex sententia evangelii, cum dicit de Iudaeis quia *Maledixerunt eum dicentes Tu sis discipulus illius.*

---

[40] *Et* S, C, B after correction, P, MTZ, confirmed L² 62–63, as reflecting the δὲ in the Greek, SR 23 1100A: καὶ τοσοῦτός ἐστι τοῦ τοιούτου ῥήματος ὁ κίνδυνος, ὅτι, κἂν ἀγαθὸν ᾖ τὸ λεγόμενον, μὴ πρὸς οἰκοδομὴν δὲ τῆς πίστεως οἰκονομῆται, which represents two concessive clauses followed by an apodosis: οὐκ ἐν τῇ ἀγαθότητι τοῦ ῥήματος ὁ λαλήσας ἔχει τὸ ἀκίνδυνον, ἀλλ' ἐν τῷ μὴ πρὸς οἰκοδομὴν οἰκονομῆσαι τό ῥηθὲν λυπεῖ τὸ Πνεῦμα τό ἅγιον τοῦ Θεοῦ; *et* here has the force of *et tamen; et* omitted by Zelz. following WLG.

Question 40

Q: For what *words* is speech judged *idle*? (cf. Matt 12:36)

R: 1 In general, any speech that does not lead to some grace of faith in Christ is *idle*. So great is the peril of such speech that **2** even though what is said may appear to be good, and yet fails to serve the upbuilding of faith, **3** the speaker shall not escape peril through the excellence of his speech—rather, because his conversation does not serve this upbuilding, he grieves the Holy Spirit of God. **4** The Apostle taught this clearly when he said: *Let no corrupt speech proceed from your mouth, but only what is good for the upbuilding of faith, that it might give grace to the hearers* (Eph 4:29), **5** and he then adds this: *Do not grieve the Holy Spirit of God in whom you were sealed unto the day of redemption* (Eph 4:30). And a greater evil than this there cannot be.

Question 41

Q: What is a *reviler*, that is λοίδορος? (cf. 1 Cor 5:11)

R: 1 Any speech uttered for the purpose of defaming or disparaging another, even if it does not seem to be insulting, is *reviling*. **2** And this is clear from that saying of the gospel where it says of the Jews that *They reviled him saying: You be his disciple!* (John 9:28).

Interrogatio XXXXII
(Zelzer 86–87, QF 44, SR 25 [PG 31.1099–1100])

I: Quid est *detractatio* vel derogatio?

R: 1 Duas opinor esse causas in quibus licet alicui dicere et retractare aliena mala. **2** Si quando consilium habere necesse est cum ceteris qui in hoc ipsum videntur assumi, quomodo corrigatur is qui peccavit vel male aliquid egit, **3** et rursum si quando necesse est praeveniri aliquem et commoneri, ne forte incurrat in consortium alicuius mali dum eum putat esse bonum, **4** quia apostolus dicit *Nolite commisceri cum huiusmodi*, et Salomon *Noli manere cum homine iracundo ne forte sumas laqueum animae tuae.* **5** Quod et ipsum apostolum fecisse invenimus per hoc quod scribit ad Timotheum dicens *Alexander aerarius multa mala mihi ostendit, quem tu quoque devita, valde enim resistit nostris sermonibus.*

6 Praeter huiusmodi autem necessitates quicumque dicit aliquid adversus alium ut vel deroget ei vel obtrectet, istud est detrahere, etiamsi vera videantur esse quae dicit.

Interrogatio XXXXIII
(Zelzer 88, QF –, SR 26 [PG 31.1101–1102])

I: *Qui detrahit de fratre* aut audit detrahentem et patitur, quid dignus est?

R: 1 Excommunicari. *Detrahentem* enim, inquit, *occulte adversus proximum suum hunc persequebar*, et alibi dictum est *Noli libenter* audire *detrah*entem, *ne* forte *eradiceris.*

Interrogatio XXXXIIII
(Zelzer 88, QF –, SR 27 [PG 31.1101–1102])

I: Quodsi de eo qui praeest detraxerit, quomodo eum observabimus?

R: 1 Et in hoc manifestum est iudicium iracundiae dei, quae facta est super Mariam cum detraxit de Moyse, et peccatum eius ne ipso quidem Moyse orante inultum deus esse permisit.

Question 42

Q: What is *detraction* or *slander*? (cf. Rom 1:30; 2 Cor 12:20; 1 Pet 2:1)

R: 1 I consider that there are two occasions when it is permissible to speak of or to discuss another's vices. **2** If it is necessary to take counsel with others who appear to be trustworthy in this matter, how one who has sinned or done something evil is to be corrected, **3** and again, when it is necessary to prevent someone or warn them, lest perhaps they fall into the company of someone wicked whom they think is good. **4** For the Apostle says: *Do not associate with such a one* (2 Thess 3:14), and Solomon: *Do not continue with a wrathful man lest one acquire a snare for one's soul* (Prov 22:24).[88] **5** And this is what the Apostle demonstrated clearly when he wrote to Timothy saying: *Alexander the coppersmith has done me much harm. . . . Be on your guard against him, for he fiercely opposed our words* (2 Tim 4:14).

6 But apart from necessary occasions of this kind, whoever says anything against another in order to slander or traduce him, that one is a detractor, even if what he says appears to be true.

Question 43

Q: What does he deserve *who slanders a brother* or listens to someone else slandering and tolerates it? (cf. Jas 4:11)

R: 1 To be excommunicated.[89] For *the one who slanders his neighbour in secret*, it says, *against him I took vengeance* (Ps 100:5) and elsewhere it is said: *Do not listen willingly to a slanderer, lest* perhaps *you are cut off* (Prov 20:13).

Question 44

Q: But what of someone who slanders him who presides? What shall be our approach towards him?

R: 1 The judgment against such is manifest in the wrath of God that came upon Miriam when she slandered Moses. God did not leave her sin unpunished, even though Moses himself entreated (cf. Num 12).

---

[88] SR 25 1100C: *do not associate with such a one lest you acquire some snare for your own soul*, largely confirmed in QF. Basil's amazing memory of Scripture appears to have conflated two distinct passages. Rufinus sorts them out and amplifies the second.

[89] SR 26 1101A: Both deserve separation (ἀφορισμοῦ). This is the penalty of a temporary exclusion *within* the community, not a definitive departure *from* the community. See RBas 76.

Interrogatio XXXXV
(Zelzer 89, QF 45, SR 28 [PG 31.1101–1102])

I: Si quis acerbiori sermone vel insolentiori voce respondeat et admonitus dicat quia nihil mali habeat in corde, si oportet ei credi?

R: 1 Non omnes passiones animae manifestae sunt omnibus, sed ne ipsis quidem qui patiuntur eas. **2** Sicut enim sapientioribus medicis signa quaedam dantur absconsa et occulta ex corporum motibus quae ipsos qui patiuntur effugiunt et latent, **3** ita etiam in anima sunt quaedam vitia etiamsi non sentit ille qui peccat, sed credere oportet domino dicenti quia *Malus homo*[41] *de malo thesauro* cordis sui *profert mala.*

4 Et ideo non potest fieri, ut malus de corde malo bonum proferat sermonem nec bonus de corde bono malum proferat verbum, sed interdum quidem potest esse mali cordis bonitas simulata, bonum autem cor malum non potest simulare. **5** Dicit enim apostolus quia *Providemus bona non solum coram deo set etiam coram hominibus.*

Interrogatio XXXXVI
(Zelzer 90, QF 47, SR 29 [PG 31.1101–1104])

I: Quomodo possit aliquis non irasci?

R: 1 Si deum omnia credat inspicere et dominum praesentem semper intueatur—quando quidem neque is qui iudici suo subiectus est, ausus est in oculis iudicis sui aliquid suae indignationis ostendere—**2** id est cum non ipse sibi alios putat esse subiectos sed se praeparat ad alterius oboedientiam, hoc est enim *omnes ducere superiores sibi.* **3** Si enim[42] ad suos usus vel ad suam utilitatem oboedire sibi quaerit eos qui oboediunt, scire debet quoniam sermo domini unumquemque docet aliis obsequi vel ministrare. **4** Quod etiamsi videat aliquem mandatum domini praeterire, non ira erga eum movetur, sed miseratione et compassione secundum eum qui dicit **5** *Quis infirmatur et ego non infirmor?*

---

[41] *Homo* B, H, WLG, MP Hol., confirmed L² 31; omitted Zelz. following SC, J, through misunderstanding it as a Vulgate normalization. But the Greek has ὁ πονηρὸς ἄνθρωπος.

[42] *Non* added in most manuscripts and in Hol. Zelzer considers that it may derive from a mistake in Rufinus's Greek original (εἰ μὴ γὰρ for εἰ μὲν γὰρ?), that is, that it is an archetype error, and includes it in square brackets.

Question 45

Q: If someone answers with an over-sharp speech and insolent voice, but when admonished says that in his heart he meant no harm, ought we believe him?

R: 1 Not all passions of the soul are evident to everyone, not even to those suffering them. **2** Just as from the motions of bodies there are certain obscure and hidden signs given to the more skilled physicians, which escape and elude the awareness of the sufferers, **3** so also in the soul are certain vices, even if the sinner is not aware of it, who ought instead to believe the Lord who says: *the evil man brings forth evil things from the evil store of his heart* (Matt 12:35; Luke 6:45)

4 And therefore it cannot be that someone wicked brings forth good speech from an evil heart, and that someone good also brings forth an evil word from a good heart,[90] for while indeed it is possible that goodness is simulated by a wicked heart, yet a good heart cannot simulate evil. **5** For the Apostle says: *we take forethought for what is good, not only before God, but also before men* (2 Cor 8:21; cf. Rom 12:17).

Question 46

Q: How can one avoid giving way to anger?

R: 1 If one believes that God watches over all things, and one looks always to the Lord who is present—for when indeed did anyone subject to judgment dare before the eyes of his judge to show any indignation?—**2** that is, if instead of thinking others to be subject to oneself, he prepares himself for obedience to others, this is to *consider* all *as better than oneself* (Phil 2:3).[91]

3 If he requires that those who obey, obey him for his own use and advantage, he must know that the word of the Lord teaches each of us to yield to and to serve others (cf. Matt 20:26-27; Mark 9:35; Luke 22:26-27). **4** Even if he sees someone transgressing a commandment of the Lord, let him not be moved by anger towards him, but by pity and compassion, according to him who said: **5** *Who is made weak and I am not made weak?* (2 Cor 11:29).

---

[90] Thus far, 45.4 appears to be Rufinus's own introduction to the antithesis that completes the verse. The antithesis alone appears in both the Greek and Syriac.

[91] On obedience not only to one's superiors but to one another in community, see RB 71.1, Cassian, *Institutes*, Book 4.30; 12.31, Augustine, *City of God*, 13.20.

Interrogatio XXXXVII
(Zelzer 91, QF 48, SR 191 [PG 31.1211–1212])

I: Quis est *mansuetus*?

R: 1 Qui non transfertur a iudiciis suis quibus statuit vel studet deo placere.

Interrogatio XXXXVIII
(Zelzer 91, QF 49, SR 126 [PG 31.1167–1168])

I: Quomodo quis non vincatur in voluptate ac libidine ciborum?

R: 1 Si statuat expetendum esse non id quod delectat sed id quod expedit et quod usui non voluptati sufficiat.

Interrogatio XXXXVIIII
(Zelzer 91–92, QF 50, SR 30 [PG 31.1103–1104])

I: Quodmodo excidimus vitium mali desiderii?

R: 1 Desiderio meliore, si magis ignimur et acccendimur ad amorem dei secundum illum qui dixit *Eloquium domini ignivit eum*, **2** et *Iudicia domini vera iustificata in semet ipsa, desiderabilia super aurum et lapidem pretiosum multum et dulciora super mel et favum.* **3** Semper enim desiderium meliorum, si in opere sit et in re et possideat totos animos nostros atque eorum quae desideramus ‹usu›[43] perfrui contendamus, contemnere nos facit et despicere inferiora, sicut docuerunt omnes sancti, **4** quanto magis ea quae mala sunt et turpia.

---

[43] Lundström elucidates the confusion of the Latin text here, L² 66–67. Zelz. brackets in cruces: †*si in opere . . . desideramus perfrui contendamus*†, and says that what Basil said can only be understood from the Greek. Lundström restores ‹*usu*› as the object of *perfrui*, which was omitted in the archetype by haplography after *desideramus*. However, in the phrase "*si in opere sit et in re et possideat*" one notices the multiplication of the letterings "*si*" and "*et*" in close sequence. It may be suspected that some form of dittography has occurred and that the original text may have stood: *si in opere et in re possideat totos animos nostros*: "if in deed and reality it possesses/governs our whole souls." This reading has the merit of steering closer to the Greek text, ἐν ἐξουσίᾳ καὶ δυνάμει ἔχουσα . . .

Question 47

Q: Who is *the meek*? (Matt 5:5)

R: 1 One who is not diverted from the decisions by which he is resolved and determined to please God.

Question 48

Q: How is one not to be conquered by the delight and pleasure of food?

R: 1 If one makes it a rule to seek not what pleases, but rather what is helpful and what is sufficient for use and not for delight.

Question 49

Q: How shall we cut out the passion of base desire?

R: 1 By a better desire—if we are more on fire and ablaze for the love of God as was he who said: *The word of the Lord has set him on fire* (Ps 104:19 LXX), **2** and: *the judgments of the Lord are all of them true, more desirable than gold and very precious stone, yes, sweeter beyond honey and honeycomb* (Ps 18:9-10). **3** For always the desire of better things, if it is in deed and in reality and possesses our whole souls, and we strive to enjoy the benefit of those things we desire, causes us to despise and spurn the lesser, as all the saints have taught, **4** and how much more things that are vicious and shameful.

Interrogatio L
(Zelzer 92, QF 51, SR 192 [PG 31.1211–1212])

I: Quae est *tristitia secundum deum* et quae secundum *saecu*lum?

R: 1 *Secundum deum* est *tristitia* cum pro mandati neglegentia vel prae-varicatione tristamur secundum quod scriptum est *Tristitia tenuit me pro peccatoribus derelinquentibus legem tuam,* **2** *saeculi autem tristitia* est cum aliquid de rebus humanis vel quae ad saeculum pertinent contristamur.

Interrogatio LI
(Zelzer 93, QF 52, SR 193 [PG 31.1211–1212])

I: Quod est in domino gaudium vel quid facientes gaudere debemus?

R: 1 Si qua secundum mandatum domini gerimus vel in gloriam dei agimus, hoc est in domino gaudium, vel cum pro nomine domini aliquid patimur et gaudemus vel aliis recte agentibus congratulamur.

Interrogatio LII
(Zelzer 93, QF 53, SR 194 [PG 31.1211–1212])

I: Quomodo *luge*re debemus ut beatitudinem consequi mereamur?

R: 1 Cum illa interrogatione in qua exposuimus quae est *secundum deum tristitia,* etiam ista interrogatio continetur, **2** id est si pro peccatis lugemus vel si eos deflemus qui *per praevaricationem legis deum non honor*ant, vel propter eos qui periclitantur in peccato, **3** quia *anima quae peccaverit ipsa morietur,* secundum illum qui dixit *Et lugeam multos ex his qui ante peccaverunt.*

Interrogatio LIII
(Zelzer 94, QF 54, SR 31 [PG 31.1103–1104])

I: Si ex toto *ride*re non licet?

R: 1 Cum dominus eos *qui nunc ride*nt condemnet manifestum est quia numquam tempus est risus fideli animae, **2** et maxime cum tam plurimi sint qui *per praevaricationem legis deum non honor*ent et in peccatis suis moriantur, pro quibus utique tristari indesinenter convenit et lugere.

Question 50

Q: What is *grief according to God* and grief according to *the world*? (cf. 2 Cor 7:10)

R: 1 *Grief according to God* is when we grieve over the neglect or transgression of the commandment of God, as it is written: *Grief has seized me because of sinners who forsake your law* (Ps 118:53), **2** but it is *grief according to the world* when we are grieved over some aspect of human affairs or of those things which pertain to the world.

Question 51

Q: What is *joy in the Lord* (cf. Phil 3:1, 4:4), and what ought we to find joy in doing?

R: 1 When we act according to the commandment of the Lord, or do anything for the glory of God, this is *joy in the Lord*, or when we suffer in some way for the name of the Lord, or share in the joy of others who act uprightly.

Question 52

Q: How should we *mourn* that we may be worthy to attain blessedness? (Matt 5:4)

R: 1 This question is also covered by the question in which we explained *grief according to God* (cf. 2 Cor 7:10), **2** that is, if we mourn over sins either because we weep over those who *through their transgression of the law dishonour God* (Rom 2:23), or because of those who are in peril through sin, **3** for *the soul that sins, itself shall die* (Ezek 18:4, 20) according to him who said: *that I may mourn over many who have sinned till now* (2 Cor 12:21).

Question 53

Q: Is *laughter* altogether disallowed? (cf. Luke 6:25)

R: 1 Since the Lord condemns those *who laugh now* (Luke 6:25), it is clear that for the faithful soul there is never a time for laughter, **2** especially since there are so many who *through their transgression of the law dishonour God* (cf. Rom 2:23) and are *dying in their sins* (cf. John 8:24), over whom it is fitting to sorrow and to groan unceasingly.

Interrogatio LIIII
(Zelzer 94, QF 55, SR 88 [PG 31.1143–1144])

I: Quae est *sollicitudo saecul*aris?

R: **1** Omnis sollicitudo animi etiamsi nihil habere videatur illicitum, tamen si non at religionem pertineat et ad virtutem saecularis est.

Interrogatio LV
(Zelzer 95, QF 56, SR 32 [PG 31.1103–1104])

I: Unde nobis accidit importune dormitare, et quomodo possumus hoc abicere?

R: **1** Evenit quidem dormitare importune tunc cum languidior est anima erga memoriam dei et cum iudiciorum eius eam incessit oblivio. **2** Abicere autem id possumus, cum dignum de deo assumpserimus cogitationem et ad voluntates eius extendimus desideria nostra secundum illum qui dixit **3** *Si dedero somnum oculis meis et palpebris meis dormitationem, usquequo inveniam locum domino, tabernaculum deo Iacob.*

Interrogatio LVI
(Zelzer 95–96, QF 57, SR 195 [PG 31.1211–1212])

I: Quomodo quis ad *gloriam dei facit omnia*?

R: **1** Cum omnia propter deum vel ex mandato dei facimus et in nullo sectamur hominum laudes et in omnibus meminimus domini dicentis **2** *Luceat lux vestra coram hominibus, ut videant bona opera vestra et glorificent patrem vestrum qui in caelis est.*

Interrogatio LVII
(Zelzer 96, QF 58, SR 196 [PG 31.1211–1214])

I: Quodmodo *manducat* quis et *bibit in gloriam dei*?

R: **1** Si in memoria semper habeat eum a quo pascitur deum, et si non solum anima verum etiam corpore per singula contestetur se et gratias agere et non securum manducare, **2** sed quasi operarium dei ab ipso refici, ob hoc quod ad laborem vel expletionem sufficiat mandatorum.

Question 54

Q: What is a care *of this life*? (cf. Matt 13:22)

R: 1 Every *care* of the mind, even though it seems to involve nothing forbidden, if it does not lead to piety and to virtue, is *of this life*.

Question 55

Q: Why does untimely sleep come upon us and how can we thrust it off?

R: 1 Untimely sleep comes about when the soul slackens in the remembrance of God and when forgetfulness of his judgments overcomes it. **2** We can thrust it off when we resume thoughts that are worthy of God and *stretch out our* desires towards the will of God as did the one who said: **3** *I shall give no sleep to my eyes, or slumber to my eyelids, till I find a place for the Lord, a tabernacle for the God of Jacob* (Ps 131:4-5).

Question 56

Q: How does one *do all for the glory of God*? (1 Cor 10:31)

R: 1 When we do everything for God's sake, that is, according to the commandment of God, and in no way seek the praises of human beings and are mindful in all things of the Lord who said: **2** *Let your light so shine before men that they may see your good works and glorify your Father who is in heaven* (Matt 5:16).

Question 57

Q: How does one *eat and drink . . . to the glory of God*? (1 Cor 10:31)

R: 1 By always keeping in mind God who feeds us, and by bearing witness in every aspect, not only in soul but also in body, that he gives thanks and does not eat carelessly, **2** but rather as God's worker who is being refreshed by him,[92] for which reason let there be sufficient for labour and the fulfilment of the commandments.

---

[92] SR 196 1214A: ἐργάτης θεοῦ, QF: ꙍ. The theme of God's worker appears three times in the RBas: here and in 95.2 and 173.2.

Interrogatio LVIII
(Zelzer 96–97, QF 59, SR 197 [PG 31.1213–1214])

I: Quomodo facit *dextera* quod non cognoscat *sinistra*?

R: 1 Cum intenta mente et fixo desiderio placendi deo agimus opera dei et omni sollicitudine constringimur ne decidamus a via recta et ab opere legitimo, **2** tunc nullius prorsus extrinsecus neque membri nostri alicuius recepimus cogitationem nisi dei solius et eius operis quod explemus, **3** tamquam si artifex faciens vas indesinenter et eius meminit qui opus iniunxit et vas quod versat in manibus si recte et fabre veniat intuetur.

Interrogatio LVIIII
(Zelzer 97–98, QF 60, SR 33 [PG 31.1103–1106])

I: Quomodo apparebit is qui *hominibus* vult *placere*?

R: 1 Cum praesentibus quidem his qui laudare possunt agit aliquid operis boni, nullo autem tali praesente vel etiam his qui vituperare possunt adstantibus segnis est et pigrior in opere. **2** Si enim domino placere vellet, semper utique et in omni loco idem esset atque eadem gereret adimplens illud quod scriptum est **3** *Per arma iustitiae a dextris et sinistris, per gloriam et ignobilitatem, per infamiam et bonam famam, ut seductores et veraces.*

Interrogatio LX
(Zelzer 98, QF 61, SR 34 [PG 31.1105–1106])

I: Quomodo quis effugiat vitium *hominibus placen*di vel captandi laudem ab hominibus?

R: 1 Si certus sit de praesentia dei et fixam habeat sollicitudinem deo placendi et multo desiderio teneatur earum beatitudinum quae a domino repromissae sunt. **2** Non enim oportet sub praesentia domini placere conservis ad iniuriam domini et sui perniciem, non domino sed conservorum nutibus intuens.

Question 58

Q: How does *the right hand* act so that *the left hand does not know?* (cf. Matt 6:3)

R: 1 When, with mind intent and a desire fixed on pleasing God, we do the works of God and strive with all care lest we fall from the right path or from a lawful task, **2** then we take no thought for anything external or for any other limb, but only for God and for his work which we are to fulfil. **3** just as a craftworker who is fashioning a vessel keeps constantly in mind the task he has been enjoined to do and looks carefully to the vessel he is turning in his hands, that it may come out true and well-made.

Question 59

Q: How shall one who wants *to court human favour* be manifest?[93] (Gal 1:10)

R: 1 He is one who does some good work when those who can offer him praise are present, but when no-one like that is present and especially when there are those at hand able to censure him, he is tardy and sluggish in his tasks. **2** For if he wanted to please the Lord he would always and everywhere be and do the same, fulfilling what is written: **3** *With the armour of righteousness on the right hand and on the left, whether in glory or dishonour, in bad report or good, taken as deceivers though we are truthful* (2 Cor 6:7-8).

Question 60

Q: How does one escape the vice of *courting human favour* (Gal 1:10), or of seeking praise from human beings?

R: 1 If one is certain of the presence of God and maintains an undistracted solicitude (cf. 1 Cor 7:35) for pleasing God and is possessed by a great desire for the blessedness promised by the Lord. **2** For no-one in the presence of his master ought to be pleasing a fellow-servant, to the insult of his master and his own condemnation by not looking to his Master, but to the nods of fellow-servants.

---

[93] SR 33 1104C: πῶς ἐλέγχεται ὁ ἀνθρωπάρεσκος, "How is the *courter of human favour* (or 'men-pleaser') exposed?"

Interrogatio LXI

(Zelzer 98–99, QF 62, SR 35 [PG 31.1105–1106])

I: Quomodo intellegitur *superbus* vel quomodo curatur?

R: 1 Intellegitur quidem ex eo, quod semper ea quae eminentiora sunt quaerit, curatur autem si credat sententiae eius qui dixit *Superbis deus resistit.* **2** Illud sane sciendum est, quod quomodo quis timeat damnationem superbiae impossibile est curare hoc vitium, nisi abstrahat se et secedat ab omnibus occasionibus elationis, **3** sicut impossibile est exstingui linguam[44] alicuius vel gentis loquelam vel artificium aliquod, nisi quis omni genere se penitus abstrahat, **4** non solum ab agendo vel loquendo vel movendo,[45] sed etiam ab audiendo eos qui loquuntur vel videndo eos qui agunt id quod oblivisci cupit. **5** Et hoc observandum est de omnibus vitiis.

Interrogatio LXII

(Zelzer 99–100, QF 63, SR 198 [PG 31.1213–1214])

I: Quid est *humilitas* et quomodo eam implere possumus?

R: 1 *Humilitas* quidem est haec, ut omnes homines aestimemus *superiores* nobis secundum definitionem apostoli; **2** implere autem id possumus si memores fuerimus domini dicentis *Discite a me quia mansuetus sum et humilis corde,* quod in multis saepe et ostendit et docuit, et credere ei debemus promittenti quia *Qui se humiliaverit exaltabitur;* **3** deinde ut indesinenter et absque ulla cessatione in omnibus actibus et in omni negotio humiliores ceteris inveniri studeamus et in hoc exercitium nostrum ponamus. **4** Vix enim sic poterimus a nobis pristinae arrogantiae abolere memoriam et affectum humilitatis assumere, sicut etiam in artificiis fieri solet. **5** Idemque modus erit etiam in ceteris virtutibus obtinendis quae ex mandato domini nostri Iesu Christi veniunt.

---

[44] *Linguam,* restored L² 79–80 with BCHMZ; *linguae* Zelz. following most MSS; an archetype error, rightly corrected by some MSS. Rufinus rendered διάλεκτος by means of a doublet, *lingua* and *loquela.*

[45] *Vel movendo* Zelz. following most MSS, QF 62.4; *illo modo* restored L² 29, 79, who considered it an archetype error; omitted CP.

Question 61

Q: How is the *proud* recognized and how is he cured? (cf. Ps 88:11; Luke 1:51; Rom 1:30; 1 Tim 6:4; 2 Tim 3:2, et al.)

R: 1 He is recognized by this: that he constantly seeks things of greater prominence. He is cured when he believes the judgment of him who said: *God resists the proud* (Jas 4:6; 1 Pet 5:5). **2** Yet it should be understood that however much one might fear the judgment for pride, this vice cannot be cured unless one withdraws and cuts oneself off from every occasion of inflation. **3** Likewise, it is impossible to unlearn a language of any kind or a local dialect or whatever craft unless one withdraws oneself utterly from everything to do with it, **4** not only from doing and speaking or stirring oneself, but even from hearing those who speak or from seeing them practise what one wishes to forget. **5** And this needs to be observed with regard to all the vices.

Question 62

Q: What is *humility* and how shall we fulfil it? (cf. Phil 2:3)

R: 1 Humility is this: that we *consider* all human beings *better than* us according to the Apostle's definition (cf. Phil 2:3). **2** Now we can accomplish it if we are mindful of the Lord who said: *Learn from me for I am meek and humble in heart* (Matt 11:29), which he often showed and taught in many ways; and we ought to believe him who has promised: *Whoever humbles himself shall be exalted* (Matt 23:12; Luke 14:11). **3** Second, we should strive unremittingly and unceasingly in all our deeds and affairs to be found humbler than others, and by working hard at this practice. **4** For thus we shall be able with difficulty to remove from ourselves the memory of our primal arrogance and to attain the condition of humility, as also usually happens with crafts. **5** The same method applies to accomplishing all the other virtues which come from the commandment of our Lord Jesus Christ.

Interrogatio LXIII

(Zelzer 100–1, QF 64, SR 36 [PG 31.1105–1106])

I: Si oportet honorem quaerere?

R: 1 *Redd*ere quidem *cui honorem honorem* edocti sumus, requirere autem honorem prohibiti domino dicente **2** *Quomodo potestis credere gloriam* quaerentes *ab invicem, et gloriam quae est ab uno deo non quaeritis?* **3** Itaque requirere ab hominibus gloriam vel honorem indicium est infidelitatis et alienos nos esse a pietate dei, maxime cum et[46] apostolus dicat *Si adhuc hominibus placerem Christi servus non essem.* **4** Si ergo hi qui oblatam sibi ab hominibus gloriam suscipiunt ita condemnantur, qui ne oblatam quidem sibi requirunt, quali iudicio digni sunt?

Interrogatio LXIIII

(Zelzer 101, QF 65, SR 115 [PG 31.1161–1162])

I: Quomodo invicem oboedire debemus?

R: 1 Sicut servi dominis,[47] secundum quod praecepit dominus quia *Qui vult in vobis esse magnus fiat omnium novissimus et omnium servus.* **2** Quibus addidit ut magis nos inclinet ad humilitatem, *Sicut filius hominis non venit ministrari sed ministrare,* sed et illud quod ab apostolo dictum est, *Per caritatem spiritus servite invicem.*

Interrogatio LXV

(Zelzer 102, QF 66, SR 116 [PG 31.1161–1162])

I: Usque ad quem modum oboedire oportet eum qui placendi deo implere regulam cupit?

R: 1 Apostolus ostendit proponens nobis oboedientiam domini qui *factus* est, inquit, *obediens usque ad mortem, mortem autem crucis,* et praedixit *Hoc sentite in vobis, quod et in Christo Iesu.*

---

[46] *Et* BMST Hol., confirmed L² 29, 41; omitted Zelz. with C, γ, HJ.

[47] *Dominis* Zelz. following CP, WL, confirmed L² 25, 63; *domini* ("of the Lord") BGHJMSTZ, an archetype error.

Question 63

Q: Is it right to seek honour? (cf. Rom 2:7)

R: 1 Though we are taught to *give honour to whom honour is due* (Rom 13:7), we are forbidden to seek honour, since the Lord says: **2** *How can you believe, you who seek glory from one another, while the glory which is from the only God you do not seek?* (John 5:44) **3** Therefore to seek glory and honour from human beings is a mark of infidelity and an estrangement from piety towards God, especially when the Apostle too says: *If I were still courting human favour, I would not be a servant of Christ* (Gal 1:10). **4** If those who accept the glory offered them by human beings are so condemned, what judgment do they deserve who seek a glory not even offered them?

Question 64

Q: How ought we to obey *one another*?[94] (cf. Eph 5:21; Phil 2:3; 1 Pet 5:5)

R: 1 As servants do their masters, just as the Lord prescribed: *Whoever wants to be great among you, let him be the last of all and the servant of all* (Mark 9:34; 10:43-44). **2** So as to further persuade us to humility he added to this: *Just as the Son of Man came not to be served, but to serve* (Matt 20:28; cf. Mark 10:45), and there is that saying of the Apostle: *serve one another through the love of the Spirit* (Gal 5:13).

Question 65

Q: What ought to be the measure of obedience of one who desires to fulfil the rule of being well pleasing to God?

R: 1 The Apostle shows when he sets before us the obedience of the Lord, *who was made obedient* he says, *unto death, even death on a cross* (Phil 2:8), and he prefaced it with: *have this mind in you which was also in Christ Jesus* (Phil 2:5).

---

[94] For the same theme and vocabulary of mutual obedience, cf. RB 71 title and RB.1: *ut oboedientes sibi sint invice*; cf. de Vogüé, "Twenty-five Years," 412.

Interrogatio LXVI

(Zelzer 102–3, QF 67, SR 37 [PG 31.1107–1108])

I: Qui piger est erga mandatum quomodo potest industrius et vigilans effici?

R: 1 Si certus sit praesentiam domini dei ubique esse et omnia intueri, et comminationem illam quae adversum pigrum prolata est ante oculos habeat et spem multae retributionis dei **2** qui repromisit per Paulum apostolum dicens quia *Unusquisque propriam mercedem accipiet secundum suum laborem,* **3** et si qua similia in scripturis sanctis inveniuntur, quae de labore patientiae et operum sollicitudine ad dei gloriam referuntur.

Interrogatio LXVII

(Zelzer 103, QF 68, SR 117 [PG 31.1161–1162])

I: Si quis[48] non contentus cotidie sibi aliquid iniungi de his quae pro mandato dei incidunt, sed artificium vult discere, quali vitio aegrotat aut si oportet ei acquiescere?

R: 1 Iste talis et praesumptor est et sibi placens et infidelis, qui non timuit sententiam domini dicentis *Estote parati, quia qua hora non putatis filius hominis veniet.* **2** Si enim cotidie exspectat quis dominum, sollicitus est et trepidus quomodo praesentem diem non transeat otiosus et nihil amplius quaerit. **3** Si autem imperatur ei artificium discere, oboedientiae suae habeat lucrum et in hoc placeat deo, et non in eo quod sibi placet assumat iudicium.

---

[48] *Si quis* Zelz. following most MSS, confirmed L² 24; *si qui* C, an archetype error.

Question 66

Q: How can someone who is indolent towards the commandment recover his zeal and vigilance?

R: **1** If he is resolved that the presence of the Lord God is everywhere and watches over all things, and keeps before his eyes[95] the warning which is put before the indolent and the hope of a great recompense from God, **2** who through the apostle Paul promises, saying that *each shall receive his own reward according to his own labour* (1 Cor 3:8). **3** And other like passages are found in the Holy Scriptures that concern the labour of patience and zeal in works to the glory of God.

Question 67

Q: If someone is discontented with the tasks he is charged to do daily, which accord with the commandment of God, but wants instead to learn a craft, with what kind of vice is he ailing and ought he be tolerated?

R: **1** Such a one is presumptuous and a self-pleaser and wanting in faith, who does not fear that judgment of the Lord who says: *Be prepared, for the Son of Man is coming at an hour you do not expect* (Luke 12:40). **2** For if someone is expecting the Lord daily he is careful and anxious that the present day does not pass by idle and he busies himself with nothing else. **3** But if he has been ordered to learn a craft, let him hold fast the profit of obedience and in this please God and not incur judgment for pleasing himself.[96]

---

[95] Cf. RB 19.1, *Ubique credimus divinam esse praesentiam, et* oculos Domini in omni loco speculari bonos et malos (Prov 15:3).

[96] SR 117 1161B: ἐν τῇ ὑποκοῇ ἐχέτω τὸ κέρδος τῆς πρὸς Θεὸν εὐαρεστήσεως καὶ μὴ ἐν τῇ ἐπερθέσει τὸ κρῖμα, "let him by his obedience cleave to the profit of being well-pleasing to God and not incur the judgment for delay." Rufinus rearranges the argument somewhat and at the end gives an alternative object of "judgment." This Rufinian paraphrase of Basil appears to be the source of the Benedictine "boon of obedience" (RB 71:1) *Oboedientiae bonum . . . exhibendum est.*

Interrogatio LXVIII

(Zelzer 104, QF 69, SR 118 [PG 31.1161–1162])

I: Si quis industrius sit et promptus ad implenda mandata, agat autem non quod ei[49] iniungitur sed quod ipse vult, quam mercedem habet?

R: 1 Merces eius illa ipsa est quod sibi placet. Cum autem apostolus dicat *Unusquisque vestrum proximo suo placeat in bono ad aedificationem*, **2** et ut amplius inclinaret et constringeret audientes addidit et dicit quia et ipse *Christus non sibi placuit*, scire debet unusquisque periculum suum esse in eo quod vult sibi placere, simul enim et inoboediens invenitur.

Interrogatio LXVIIII

(Zelzer 104–5, QF 70, SR 119 [PG 31.1161–1164])

I: Si licet alicui excusare opus quod ei iniungitur et aliud quaerere?

R: 1 Cum definitum sit mensuram *oboedien*tiae *usque ad mortem* esse, qui devitat[50] hoc quod ei iniungitur et aliud quaerit primo omnium inoboedientiae reus est et manifeste ostenditur quia nondum *neg*avit *semet ipsum*.

2 Deinde multorum malorum causa efficitur tam sibi quam etiam ceteris, quia aditum contradictionis pluribus aperit et se ipsum ad contradicendum insuescit, **3** et cum non possint singuli discernere quod melius est et eligere, potest fieri, si talis sit licentia, ut aliquis quod deterius est eligat.

4 Tum deinde etiam suspicionem dabit fratribus, quod passione aliqua vel ad opus illud quod eligit adstringatur vel certe erga eos cum quibus id necesse est operari.

5 Itaque omnimodo non oboedire multorum malorum causa est et radix, **6** si autem ratio est aliqua, qua sibi recte excusare videatur opus illud quod exscusat, exponat hanc ipsam huic qui praeest et relinquat eius iudicio, ut ipse probet si excusatione dignum est quod allegat.

---

[49] *Ei* SCP, confirmed L² 24; omitted by Zelz. following most other MSS.

[50] *Qui devitat* Zelz. following BCGHJLMWZ, confirmed L¹ 589; *quid debet ad* CS, an archetype error; *qui vitat* P.

Question 68

Q: What if someone is diligent and prompt in fulfilling the commandments, but does what he wants rather than what is enjoined on him, what is his reward?

R: 1 His reward is the same as for self-pleasing. Since the Apostle says *Let each one please his neighbour for his benefit, to his upbuilding* (Rom 15:2), **2** and that he might the more persuade and constrain his hearers adds that even *Christ did not please himself* (Rom 15:3), each ought to recognize his danger in this wanting to please himself, for it reveals at the same time that he is disobedient.

Question 69

Q: Is it permissible for anyone to excuse himself from the work he is charged to do and to seek something else?

R: 1 Since it is defined that the measure of obedience is *even unto death* (Phil 2:8), anyone who avoids what he is charged to do and seeks something else is first of all guilty of disobedience and manifestly shows that he has not yet *denied himself* (Matt 16:24; Mark 8:34; Luke 9:23).

2 Second, he becomes the cause of many more ills both for himself and for others. For he opens the door of contradiction to the many and accustoms himself to contradicting, **3** and since not everyone is able to discern what is better and to choose it, it can happen that with such licence someone chooses what is worse.

4 Third, he fosters a suspicion among the brothers that he is motivated by some passion, either for the work he chooses or even in regard to those with whom he must work.

5 And so, not to obey is in every way the cause and root of many evils. **6** But if there is some reason whereby it seems to him he might rightly excuse himself from that task which he is excusing himself, let him put it before the one who presides and leave it to his judgment so that he may examine whether the plea he submits has merit.

Interrogatio LXX
(Zelzer 106, QF 71, SR 38 [PG 31.1107–1108])

I: Si iniunctum fuerit aliquid fratri et contradixerit, *postea autem* sua sponte *abierit,* quid est?

R: 1 In eo quidem quod contradixit quasi non obtemperans iudicandus est et velut ceteros ad simile concitans malum, **2** in quo sciat se illi sententiae obnoxium quae dicit[51] *Contradictiones suscitat omnis malus, dominus autem angelum immisericordem immittit ei.* **3** Cum autem certus sit quia non homini obtemperat sed domino, dicenti quia *Qui audit vos me audit et qui spernit vos me spernit,* **4** si compunctus est recordatione mandati prius satisfaciat et ita si permittitur impleat quod iniunctum est.

Interrogatio LXXI
(Zelzer 107, QF 72, SR 39 [PG 31.1107–1108])

I: Si autem oboediens quis murmuret?

R: 1 Apostolo dicente *Omnia facite sine murmurationibus et haesitationibus* alienus sit a fratrum unitate qui murmurat et opus eius abiciatur. **2** Manifestus est enim iste qui talis est quia infidelitate aegrotat et certam futurae spei fiduciam non gerit.

Interrogatio LXXII
(Zelzer 107–8, QF 73, SR 40 [PG 31.1107–1110])

I: Si frater fratrem contristaverit quomodo debet emendare?

R: 1 Siquidem contristaverit sicut apostolus dixit *Contristati enim esti ut in nullo detrimentum pateremini ex nobis,* non ille qui contristavit emendare debet sed ille qui contristatus est, et indicia eius tristitiae quae secundum deum est debet ostendere.

---

[51] *Dicit* Zelz. following C, E, P, WLG, J, confirmed L^2 41; *dixit* (influenced by *contradixit*) BHMSTZ Hol.

Question 70

Q: If a brother was commanded something and refused, but *afterwards* of his own accord *goes off*, what is he? (cf. Matt 21:28-29)

R: 1 By his refusal he ought to be judged as a contradictor and an inciter of others to the same kind of evils. **2** Let him know therefore that he is subject to this judgment which says: *A contradictor stirs up every evil, but the Lord sends upon him an angel of unmercy* (Prov 17:11). **3** But when he is resolved to obey not man[97] but the Lord who says: *whoever listens to you listens to me and whoever rejects you rejects me* (Luke 10:16), **4** if he is pierced by remembrance of the commandment, let him first apologize and then, if he is permitted, fulfil what was commanded.

Question 71

Q: What of someone obeying who murmurs?

R: 1 Since the Apostle says: *Do all things without murmurings or hesitations* (Phil 2:14), a murmurer is estranged from the unity of the brothers and his work is rejected. **2** For such a one is manifestly sick with want of faith and does not have the sure confidence of hope for the future.

Question 72

Q: If a brother grieves a brother, how ought he to be corrected?

R: 1 If he grieved him according to the saying of the Apostle: *But you were grieved so that you suffered no loss from us* (2 Cor 7:9), then it is not the one who caused the grief who needs correction, but the one aggrieved who ought to show the signs of that *grief* which is *according to God* (cf. 2 Cor 7:10).

---

[97] SR 38 1108B ἀνθρώπῳ, De Vogüé ("Twenty-five Years," 446) asks: "Who is 'the man' whom the brother has refused to obey? This short text does not say, but the reader of the *Little Asketikon* who has just read Question 69, irresistibly thinks of the 'superior' of whom Rufinus was speaking." But strictly, the Greek does not speak of "*the* man," or even of "*a* man," but simply ἀνθρώπῳ without article, i.e., a generically *human* reference whether one or several superiors are envisaged, the contrast being between obedience considered merely as a human matter or in a divine perspective. This may be more exactly conveyed using the standard English inclusive meaning of "man" without article, as here.

2 Si vero indifferenter contristavit, id est non secundum deum, memor sit is qui contristavit apostoli dicentis **3** *Si autem propter escam frater tuus constristatur iam non secundum caritatem ambulas.* **4** Et cum cognoverit tale delictum esse suum, impleat illud quod a domino dictum est **5** *Si offeres donum tuum ad altare et recordatus fueris ibi quia frater tuus habet aliquid adversum te, relinque ibi donum tuum ante altare et vade prius reconciliari fratri tuo et tunc veniens offeres donum tuum.*

Interrogatio LXXIII
(Zelzer 108, QF 74, SR 41 [PG 31.1109–1110])

I: Quodsi non acquiescit ut satisfaciat?

R: 1 Implere debemus in eo illud quod a domino dictum est de eo qui peccavit et non egit paenitentiam, cum dixit *Si autem et ecclesiam non audierit sit tibi sicut gentilis et publicanus.*

Interrogatio LXXIIII
(Zelzer 109, QF 75, SR 42 [PG 31.1109–1110])

I: Quodsi satisfaciente eo qui contristavit noluerit reconciliari is qui contristatus est?

R: 1 Manifesta est et de hoc domini sententia quae refertur in illa parabola de servo qui rogatus a conservo suo noluit patienter agere, *Et videntes,*[52] inquit, *conservi renuntiaverunt domino suo.* **2** *Iratus autem dominus* revocavit omnem gratiam quam concesserat debiti et *tradidit eum tortoribus usquequo redderet omne debitum.*

Interrogatio LXXV
(Zelzer 109–10, QF 76, SR 43 [PG 31.1109–1110])

I: Quomodo debet quis habere eum qui ad orationem suscitat fratres?

R: 1 Si quis cognoscit damnum quod de somno patitur, cum neque sui ipsius sensum habet, et intellegit quantum sit lucrum vigiliarum et praecipue cum vigilatur ad glorificandum deum in orationibus, **2** ita debet habere eum qui ad hoc se invitat et suscitat dormientem tamquam eum per quem divina lucra et caelestia dona consequatur, **3** sive is ad orationem sive ad aliud quodcumque mandatum dei invitat et provocat.

---

[52] *Videntes* W and δ, restored according to the Vulgate, confirmed L² 78 as in keeping with ἰδόντες; *audientes* Zelz. following C, S, P, LG, J, an archetype error.

2 But if he caused grief over an indifferent matter, that is, not *according to God*, then let him who caused the grief be mindful of the Apostle who said: **3** *If your brother is grieved on account of food, you are no longer walking according to love* (Rom 14:15). **4** And when he has acknowledged that such a sin is his, let him fulfil what was said by the Lord: **5** *If you are offering your gift at the altar and there you remember that your brother has something against you, leave your gift there before the altar and go, be reconciled with your brother first, and then come and offer your gift* (Matt 5:23-24).

Question 73

Q: What if he cannot bring himself to apologize?

R: 1 In his case we ought to fulfil what was said by the Lord concerning the sinner who does not repent when he said: *But if he will not listen to the church, let him be to you as the pagan and the tax-collector* (Matt 18:17).

Question 74

Q: What if the one who caused the grief apologizes, but the one grieved does not wish to be reconciled?

R: 1 The judgment of the Lord in such a case is clear which is told in the parable of the servant who, besought by a fellow-servant, would not show patience: *And seeing this*, it says, *his fellow servants told their master* (Matt 18:31). **2** *At this the Master was wrathful* and revoked the favour he had bestowed on the debtor *and handed him over to the torturers till he should repay all the debt* (Matt 18:34).

Question 75

Q: How should someone regard him who wakens the brothers for prayer?

R: 1 If he realizes the loss suffered from sleep, when he has no awareness of himself, and if he understands how great is the profit of vigils and especially when vigil is kept to glorify God in the prayers, **2** he ought to regard him who invites him to this and awakens the sleeper as one through whom divine benefits and heavenly gifts are obtained, **3** whether he invites and summons to prayer or to any other of God's commandments.

Interrogatio LXXVI

(Zelzer 110, QF 77, SR 44 [PG 31.1109–1112])

I: Quodsi contristatur ille qui excitatur aut etiam si irascitur, quid dignus est?

R: 1 Interim excommunicari et non manducare, si forte compunctus agnoscat quantis et qualibus bonis semet ipsum insipienter defraudet, et ita conversus recipiat gratiam eius qui dixit *Memor fui dei et laetatus sum.*

2 Quodsi permanserit in stultitia non intellegens gratiam abscidatur tamquam putrefactum membrum a corpore, **3** scriptum est enim quia *Expedit ut pereat unum membrorum tuorum et non omne corpus tuum mittatur in Gehennam.*

Interrogatio LXXVII

(Zelzer 111–12, QF 78, SR 164 [PG 31.1189–1192])

I: Qui est *Nolite iudicare ut non iudicemini, nolite condemnare ut non condemnemini?*

R: 1 Cum dominus aliquando dicat *Nolite iudicare ut non iudicemini,* aliquando vero *Iustum iudicium iudicate,* non utique omni modo iudicandi prohibet facultatem, **2** sed differentiam iudicii nosse nos docet[53] ut sciamus in quibus oporteat[54] iudicare et in quibus non.

3 De hoc autem manifeste nobis apostolus tradidit dicens de his causis quae in uniuscuiusque arbitrio esse debent, *Tu autem qua re iudicas fratrem tuum?* et iterum *Non ergo invicem iudicemus.*

---

[53] *Docet* Zelz. most MSS, confirmed L² 37; *docet et* by diplography CS, LW, P.
[54] *Oporteat* Zelz. and most MSS, confirmed L² 37; *oportet* C, P, WLG.

Question 76

Q: If someone is annoyed or even irate when awoken from sleep, what does he deserve?

R: 1 To be excommunicated[98] and to be without food for a time, that he might perhaps experience compunction and come to realize how great and many are the benefits of which he has stupidly defrauded himself, and, thus converted, regain the grace he had who said: *I remembered my God and was glad* (Ps 76:4 LXX).

2 But if he continues in his stupidity not understanding the grace, let him be cut off[99] as a rotten limb from the body, **3** for it is written: *It is better that one of your members perish, than that your whole body be cast into Gehenna* (Matt 5:29).

Question 77

Q: What is: *Do not judge that you may not be judged, do not condemn that you may not be condemned?* (Luke 6:37)

R: 1 Since in one place the Lord says: *Do not judge that you may not be judged* (Luke 6:37), while in another: *Judge with just judgment* (John 7:24), he does not altogether forbid the faculty of judging, **2** but teaches us to recognize that there are different kinds of judging, that we might know in what cases we ought to judge and in what cases not.

3 On this matter the Apostle has clearly handed down to us, speaking of those cases which ought to lie at the discretion of each: *But you, why do you judge your brother?* and again: *therefore let us not judge one another* (Rom 14:10, 13).

---

[98] SR 44 1109D ἀφορισμοῦ: of being separated. This does not mean "excommunication" in the sense of put out of the community, but temporary exclusion from common exercises. Cf. RB 25, where those at serious fault are suspended from meals, prayers, and speech with the brothers.

[99] SR 44 1112A ἀποκοπτέσθω, i.e., excommunication absolute. On the use of "amputation" as a last resort, cf. also RB 28:6, *tunc iam utatur abbas ferro abscisionis*; cf. Gribomont, "Commentaries," 260.

4 In his vero actibus quae deo non placent notat eos qui non iudicant, et ipse suam sententiam prodit per haec quae dicit **5** *Ego quidem* sicut *absens corpore, praesens autem spiritu iam iudicavi tamquam praesens eum qui haec ita operatus est in nomine domini nostri Iesu Christi,* **6** *congregatis vobis et meo spiritu cum virtute domini nostri Iesus Christi tradere huiusmodi hominem satanae in interitum carnis ut spiritus salvus fiat in die domini nostri Iesus Christi.*

7 Si quid itaque in nostra est potestate vel arbitrio positum et incertum est, non oportet de his iudicare fratrem secundum hoc quod apostolus dicit tamquam de his quae ignorantur **8** *Itaque nolite ante tempus quid iudicare usquequo veniat dominus qui illuminabit occulta tenebrarum et manifestabit consilia cordium.*

9 Dei autem iudicia vindicare omnimodis necessarium est, ne forte et nos simili ira dei absorbeamur si quiescimus erga peccantes et silemus, **10** nisi forte quis eadem faciens fiduciam non habeat arguendi neque auctoritatem iudicandi fratrem domino dicente **11** *Eice primum trabem de oculo tuo et tunc videbis eicere festucam de oculo fratris tui.*

Interrogatio LXXVIII
(Zelzer 112–13, QF 79, SR 165 [PG 31.1191–1192])

I: Quomodo intelleget quis si zelo dei movetur adversus peccantem fratrem aut propria iracundia?

R: 1 Si ad omne peccatum fratris patitur illud quod scriptum est *Consumpsit me zelus tuus,*[55] *quoniam obliti sunt verborum tuorum inimici mei.* **2** Manifestus est enim et in hoc dei zelus; verumtamen etiam in his oportet prudenter omnia dispensari. **3** Si ergo hunc affectum etiam antea non habuit in anima sua, motus suos sciat magis ex passione quam ex deo descendere et in nullo posse se officium pietatis implere.

---

[55] *Zelus tuus* ("your zeal") CJPS; *zelus domus tuae* ("zeal for your house") BGHLM-TWZ Hol.; SR 15 1192A: ὁ ζῆλός σου ("your zeal"); QF ܚܣܡܐ "zeal/jealousy."

4 But concerning those actions which are not pleasing to God, he censures those who do not judge and himself gives his own judgment in these words: **5** *I myself, even if absent in body, am present in spirit and as if present have already in the name of our Lord Jesus Christ judged him who has perpetrated such a deed.* **6** *When you have come together and my spirit is with you, with the power of Our Lord Jesus Christ you are to hand over such a man to Satan for the destruction of the flesh, in order that his spirit might be saved in the day of our Lord Jesus Christ* (1 Cor 5:3-5).

7 Thus, if a matter lies within our power or discretion and is uncertain, we ought not to judge our brother, according to this saying of the Apostle concerning matters of which we are ignorant: **8** *Therefore, do not judge anything before the right time, until the Lord comes, who will surely illumine the things hidden in darkness and will manifest the deliberations of hearts* (1 Cor 4:5).

9 But it is in every way necessary to vindicate the judgments of God, lest perhaps we also are overtaken by a like wrath from God, if we have kept quiet toward sinners and remained silent—**10** except that someone doing the same thing has neither warrant to reprove nor authority to judge a brother, since the Lord says: **11** *Cast the beam from your own eye first; then you shall see clearly to cast the speck from your brother's eye* (Matt 7:5).

Question 78

Q: How shall one know whether one is moved by a zeal for God against a brother who sins, or by one's own anger?

R: **1** If towards any sin of a brother one experiences what is written: *Your zeal has consumed me, because my foes have forgotten your words* (Ps 118:139; cf. 68:10), **2** for in this case it is clearly a zeal for God. Nevertheless, even in these cases one still needs to dispense all things prudently. **3** But if he did not already have such a disposition in the soul, then let him know that his motives derive more from passion than from God, and they cannot in any way fulfil the service of piety.

Interrogatio LXXVIIII
(Zelzer 113–14, QF 80, SR 127 [PG 31.1167–1168])

I: Dicunt quidam quia Impossibile est non irasci hominem.

R: Sane possibile[56] est militi in conspectu sui regis[57] irasci, sed ne sic quidem habebit rationem hoc quod dicitur. **2** Humanus enim vultus—eiusdem[58] formae hominis ad hominem propter unitatem naturae—ubi cum sola dignitatis sit eminentia tamen prohibet passionem,[59] **3** quanto magis deus quem certi sumus etiam cordi nostro praesentem esse et omnes motus nostros inspicere. **4** Cuius manifestum est quanta sit eminentia etiam hoc ipso quod *scruta*tur *corda et renes* et videt motus animae.

Interrogatio LXXX
(Zelzer 114–15, QF 81, SR 120 [PG 31.1163–1164])

I: Si oportet ire quocumque non commonito eo qui praeest?

R: **1** Cum dominus dicat *Non* enim *veni ut a me faciam quicquam, sed* ille *me misit*, quanto magis unusquisque nostrum sibi permittere nihil debet. **2** Qui enim sua auctoritate aliquid agit, manifestissime superbiae morbo tenetur et subiectus est illi sentientiae quae dicit *Quod in hominibus superbum est abominatio est in conspectu domini.* **3** Sed et in omnibus sua sponte vel auctoritate aliquid agere culpabile est.

Interrogatio LXXXI
(Zelzer 115, QF 82, SR 96 [PG 31.1149–1150])

I: Si omne volenti litteras discere vel lectioni vacare indulgendum est?

R: **1** Apostolo dicente *Uti non quae vultis faciatis* in omni negotio sua voluntate permittere unumquemque agere perniciosum est, sed oportet illud suscipere quod ab his qui praesunt iniungitur, **2** etiamsi contra voluntatem sit eius cui iniungitur, secundum domini exemplum dicentis *Pater non mea voluntas sed tua fiat.*

---

[56] *Sane possibile* restored L[1] 589, L[2] 68. According to Lundström *ne* is too well indicated to be ignored—it is in CSP, an archetype error. He explains that in the MSS the response would have begun *"epsc sane," "epsc"* meaning *episcopus*, i.e., Basil, and that *"sa-"* dropped out through haplography. Zelz. reasonably conjectures *"Si possibile,"* following the Greek εἰ δύνατον ἐστι'.

[57] *Sui regis* SJ, P, HMT, confirmed L[2] 39; *regis sui* Zelz. following C, WLG, B.

[58] *Eiusdem* Zelz. most MSS, confirmed L[2] 28; *et eiusdem* SC, P, J, an archetype error.

[59] Zelz. places v. 2 in cruces as corrupt. Lundström, however, elucidates its sense, L[2] 70; his punctuation has been adopted here.

Question 79

Q: Some say it is impossible for a human being to avoid anger.

R: 1 Although it is possible for a soldier to become angry in the presence of his king, yet even so, this assertion shall have no reasonable foundation. **2** For if the sight of a man—of the same human form with another human being through unity of nature—forbids passion merely through the preeminence of his rank, **3** how much more so with God, whom we are assured is present even to our heart and gazes on all our motives. **4** How great is his preeminence is shown in this fact, that he is *the searcher of hearts and inward parts* and sees the movements of the soul (Ps 7:9; cf. Jer 11:20; 17:10; 20:12, Acts 2:23).

Question 80

Q: Ought one go anywhere without a mention from the one who presides?

R: 1 Since the Lord says: *I have not come that I might do anything of myself, but it was he who sent me* (John 7:28), how much less ought each of us to give himself permission! **2** For whoever does anything by his own authority is manifestly gripped by the disease of pride, and liable to that judgment which says: *That which is exalted among human beings is an abomination in the sight of God* (Luke 16:15). **3** So then, to do anything at all of one's own accord or authority is blameworthy.

Question 81

Q: Should everyone who wishes to learn letters or to devote himself to reading be permitted?

R: 1 Since the Apostle says *That you may not do the things you wish* (Gal 5:17), it is harmful in any matter to permit anyone a private choice according to his own will. Instead, he should undertake all that is enjoined by those who preside,[100] **2** even if it is contrary to the will of him who receives the order, in accordance with the example of the Lord who says: *Father, not my will but yours be done* (Luke 22:42).

---

[100] SR 82 1149A ὑπὸ τῶν προεστώτων.

Interrogatio LXXXII
(Zelzer 116–17, QF 83, SR 121 [PG 31.1163–1166])

I: Si licet unicuique vitare opus quo gravius videtur?

R: 1 Qui fideliter et pure deum diligit et certus est de retributione domini, **2** nec sufficere sibi putat ea quae iniunguntur sed semper augmenta operis quaerit et maiora quam iniunguntur desiderat et exoptat, etiamsi supra vires videatur esse quod facit, **3** nec aliquando securus est tamquam opere expleto sed e contrario sollicitus est et anxius tamquam qui[60] nihil dignum praeceptis evangelicis egerit, **4** memor illius dominici sermonis dicentis *Cum autem feceritis omnia quaecumque praecepi vobis, tunc dicetis Servi inutiles sumus, quod debuimus facere fecimus.*

5 Sed et imitabitur apostolum, cui cum *mundus* esset *crucifixus et* ipse *mundo*, non erubescit dicere quia **6** *Ego me ipsum nondum aestimo apprehendisse, unum autem, ea quidem quae retro sunt obliviscens ad ea autem quae inante sunt me extendens, secundum propositum sequor ad palmam supernae vocationis dei in Christo Iesu.* **7** Et qui cum haberet potestatem ut *evangelium annuntians de evangelio vivere*t, *Magis in labore et fatigatione*, inquit, *nocte et die operans* vixi, **8** *non quia non haberemus potestatem, sed ut nos formam daremus vobis ut imitaremini nos.*

9 Quae cum ita sunt, quis ita vel stultus est vel infidelis ut putet se maioribus quam debet oneribus praegravari, cum hoc quod mensura poscit nondum possit implere?

Interrogatio LXXXIII
(Zelzer 117–18, QF 84, SR 199 [PG 31.1213–1216])

I: Quomodo quis promptus fiat etiam ad pericula propter mandata domini?

R: 1 Primo quidem ut consideret quia et ipse dominus *oboediv*it[61] patri pro nobis *usque ad mortem*, et certus sit quia *Mandata* domini *vita aeterna est* sicut scriptum est. **2** Tum deinde etiam ut credat domino dicenti quia *Quicumque voluerit animam suam salvam facere perdet eam, qui autem perdiderit animam suam propter me et propter evangelium salvam faciet eam.*

---

[60] *Qui*, the majority text, confirmed L² 10–11 as being closer to the Greek: οὐκ ἀμεριμνεῖ ὡς πληρώσας τὸ μέτρον· ἀγωνιᾷ δὲ ἀεὶ ὡς ἀπολιμπανόμενος τοῦ πρὸς ἀξίαν; *si* Zelz. following CS, an achetype error in α.

[61] *Oboedivit* B after correction, C after correction, HJ after correction, LG, MP after correction, TZ Hol., confirmed L² 64–65; *oboedit* W; *oboediit* Zelz. following S.

Question 82

Q: Is it permissible for anyone to avoid a work that seems to be heavier?

R: 1 One who loves God faithfully and purely and is assured of recompense from the Lord **2** is not content to think of the tasks enjoined, but is always seeking an increase of the work and desiring and reaching for something greater than what is enjoined. Even though he seems to be working beyond his strength, **3** he is never free of care as if he had fulfilled his task, but on the contrary is careful and anxious as one who has performed nothing worthy of the Gospel precepts, **4** mindful of that utterance of the Lord which says: *When you shall have done all that I have commanded you, then say "We are unprofitable servants, we have only done what it was our duty to do"* (Luke 17:10).

5 Yes and he will imitate the Apostle to whom *the world* had been *crucified and* himself *to the world* (cf. Gal 6:14), and is not ashamed to say **6** *I do not consider myself to have taken possession yet. There is but one thing: forgetting what lies behind and straining forward to what lies ahead, I press on towards the goal, to the prize of the upward call of God in Christ Jesus* (Phil 3:13-14). **7** This is he who, though he had the right *as a preacher of the Gospel, to live from the Gospel* (cf. 1 Cor 9:14), said: I have lived *in* greater *toil and fatigue, working night and day,* **8** *not as though I did not have the right, but that we might give you a pattern so that you might imitate us* (2 Thess 3:8-9).

9 Since that is how things are, who then is so stupid and wanting in faith as to think that he is weighed down with burdens too heavy or toilsome when this man begs for a measure he is not yet able to fulfil?

Question 83

Q: How may one be ready even *for dangers on account of* the commandments *of the Lord*? (Acts 15:26; 2 Cor 11:26)

R: 1 In the first place when one considers that the Lord himself *obeyed* the Father *even unto death* (Phil 2:8) and one is assured that the *commandment* of the Lord *is eternal life* as it is written (John 12:50); **2** then also when he believes the Lord who said: *Whoever wants to save his life, shall lose it, whoever loses his life for my sake and the sake of the Gospel, shall save it* (Mark 8:35; cf. Luke 9:24).

Interrogatio LXXXIIII
(Zelzer 118–19, QF 85, SR 166 [PG 31.1191–1192])

I: Cum quali affectu oboedire oportet ei qui nos ad opus mandati cohortatur?

R: 1 Eo affectu quo esuriens parvulus nutrici obtemperat ad ubera invitanti, vel quo affectu omnis homo suscipit ab aliquo ea quae ad vitam pertinent, **2** immo et si quid amplius, pro eo quod multo est pretiosior futura vita quam praesens, sicut et dominus dixit *Quia mandata mea vita aeterna est.* **3** Sicut ergo praesens vita constat in cibo panis, ita aeterna vita constat in opere mandati, sicut et ipse dominus iterum dicit **4** *Meus cibus est ut faciam voluntatem eius qui me misit, patris.*

Interrogatio LXXXV
(Zelzer 119, QF 86, SR 167 [PG 31.1191–1192])

I: Quali animo debet esse quis pro hoc ipso quod dignus habitus est in opere dei inveniri?

R: 1 Eo quo erat ille qui dicebat *Quis ego sum, domine, aut quae est domus patris mei, quoniam dilexisti me?* explens per singula id quod scriptum est **2** *Gratias agentes deo patri qui idoneos nos fecit in partem sortis sanctorum in lumine, qui et liberavit nos de potestate tenebrarum et transtulit in regnum filii caritatis suae.*

Question 84

Q: With what disposition ought we to obey him who urges us to the work of the commandment?

R: 1 With the same disposition with which a hungry little child obeys the nurse who invites it to her breasts, or with the same disposition with which any human being accepts from anyone the things necessary for life. **2** And indeed, even more so, inasmuch as the future life is more precious than the present life, just as the Lord said: my *commandment is eternal life* (John 12:50). **3** Accordingly, as this present life is secured in the eating of food, so eternal life is secured in the doing of the commandment, just as the Lord himself again says: **4** *My food is to do the will of the Father who sent me* (John 4:34).

Question 85

Q: In what mind ought he to be who is found worthy of abiding in the work of God?[101]

R: 1 As was he who said: *What am I, Lord, and what is my* father's *house that you have loved me?* (2 Sam 7:18), fulfilling each part of what is written: **2** *Giving thanks to the Father who has made us fit us to partake in the inheritance of the saints in light; who has freed us from the power of darkness and transferred us to the kingdom of the Son whom he loves* (Col 1:12).

---

[101] SR 167 1192C: ἐν τῷ ἔργῳ τοῦ Θεοῦ, QF: of being found among God's workers. "Basil's answer does not reveal the exact sense in which *opus* is used; probably it means the entire monastic life including the Divine Office" (Clarke [1925], 290 n. 6). The topic is continued in RBas 86.Q immediately following, where it is clear that Basil's "work of God" refers to the entire project of piety, the purposeful way of life in the Christian ascetic community, not too unlike the *conversatio morum* of RB 58.17. In RB 67.2, 3 the term *Opus Dei* is used for the choral prayer of the church.

Interrogatio LXXXVI

(Zelzer 119–20, QF 87, SR 200 [PG 31.1215–1216])

I: Quomodo debent hi qui praecesserunt in labore operis dei instruere vel instituere eos qui nuper accedunt?

R: 1 Si quidem corpore adhuc vegeti sunt, per hoc quod impigre ad cuncta humilitatis officia semet ipsos paratos exhibent aedificant eos et formam eis utilem ad omnem profectum praestant. **2** Si vero infirmiores sunt corpore, per hoc quod ostendunt eis se in omnibus vel actibus vel motibus vel etiam ipso vultu dei semper habere et cogitare praesentiam, **3** sed et in his quae ab apostolo enumerata sunt specialibus caritatis affectibus quibus ait **4** *Caritas patiens est, benigna est, non zelatur, non peperam agit, non inflatur, non dehonestatur, non quaerit quae sua sunt, non irritatur, non cogitat malum,* **5** *non gaudet iniquitati, congaudet autem veritati, omnia sustinet, omnia sperat, omnia patitur, caritas numquam cadit.* **6** Haec enim omnia etiam in infirmo corpore impleri possible est.

Interrogatio LXXXVII

(Zelzer 121–22, QF 88, SR 97 [PG 31.1149–1150])

I: Si dicat quis Volo apud vos parum[62] aliquid temporis facere ut proficiam ex vobis, si oportet eum suscipi?

R: 1 Domino pronuntiante quia *Venientem ad me non eicio foras,* **2** et apostolo nihilominus dicente *Propter subintroductos autem falsos fratres qui subintroierunt explorare libertatem nostram quam habemus in Christo Iesu, quibus nec ad horam cessimus subiectioni, ut veritas evangelii permaneat apud vos,* **3** concedi quidem ei convenit ingressum propter incertos exitus rerum. **4** Interdum enim potest fieri ut per tempus proficiat et delectetur sanctitate vitae et permaneat ‹in›[63] coeptis, sicut et frequenter factum scimus, sed et manifesta fiet veritas institutionum nostrarum de quibus fortassis homines aliter opinantur.

5 Oportet tamen circa eum cautius agi et diligentius, ut sive in *verita*te *permanet* proficiat, sive institutionum nostrarum *liberta*s *explora*tur[64] probabilis inveniatur et pura. **6** Ita namque et nos deo placebimus et ille aut proficiet si verax est aut si simulator est erubescet.

---

[62] *Parum* C, W after correction LG, P, MT, Z Hol., confirmed L² 65, *parum aliquid temporis* translates ὀλίγον χρόνον (compare 115.1, where *parum* is used for ὀλίγον); *parvum* Zelz. following S, W before correction, J.

[63] ‹*In*› *coeptis* restored L² 65–66, following *inceptis* in CL after correction (for in *c[o] eptis,* but contracted through lack of space), and *in coeptis,* Holste's correct conjecture; *coeptis* Zelz. with most MSS, an archetype error.

[64] *Explora*tur Zelz. most MSS, confirmed L¹ 589; *exprobatur* CS, an archetypal error.

Question 86

Q: How ought those who have long been labouring in the work of God instruct and train those who have lately come?

R: 1 If they are still vigorous in body, they edify them and present a good example of every virtue by showing themselves energetic and prepared for all the services of humility, **2** but if they are weaker in body,[102] by showing them in all their actions and movements and even in their very face that they always possess and ponder the presence of God. **3** and also by all the characteristic dispositions of love enumerated by the Apostle where he says: **4** *Love is patient, is kindly, is not envious, does not vaunt itself, is not inflated, is not unseemly, does not seek its own, is not provoked, does not contrive evil,* **5** *finds no joy in wickedness, but rejoices rather in the truth, sustains all things, hopes all things, suffers all things. Love never fails* (1 Cor 13:4-8). **6** For all these can be fulfilled even in a weak body.

Question 87

Q: If someone says "I wish to spend only a short time with you, that I may profit from you," ought he be welcomed?

R: 1 The Lord declared that *Whoever comes to me I do not cast out* (John 6:37), **2** and the Apostle nevertheless says: *Moreover on account of false brothers brought in surreptitiously who slipped in to spy out the freedom which we have in Christ Jesus—to them we did not yield submission, even for an hour, that the truth of the gospel might continue with you* (Gal 2:4-5). **3** It is therefore suitable to allow him entry because it is uncertain what the end of it will be. **4** Meanwhile it can come about that with time he finds profit and delight in the holiness of the life and so continues in what he began, as has happened frequently we know, and the truth of our observances will be manifest concerning which men have perhaps thought otherwise.

5 Around such a one, however, we must conduct ourselves cautiously and carefully so that if he *continues in the truth* he may profit, or if he is *spying out the liberty* (Gal 2:4) of our observances, we shall be found equal to the test and blameless. **6** Thus shall we please God and such a one will either be benefited if he is genuine, or discomfited if he is a dissembler.

---

[102] Basil himself suffered much from bodily infirmity; see especially the report in his letters to Eusebius of Samosata, e.g., 136, 138, 141.

Interrogatio LXXXVIII
(Zelzer 122–23, QF 89, SR 128 [PG 31.1167–1168])

I: Si quis[65] supra vires vult abstinere ita ut etiam in opere mandatorum impediatur per nimietatem abstinentiae, si oportet ei concedi?

R: 1 Interrogatio vestra non mihi videtur competenter adhibita. **2** Non enim continentiam in cibis solum esse diximus, nam haec ab apostolo etiam culpari invenitur si non cum fide et ratione fiat, cum dixit *Abstinentes se a cibis quos deus creavit*, **3** sed illam diximus esse perfectam continentiam, qua se quis a propriis suis voluntatibus continet. **4** Quantum autem habeat periculi qui voluntatem propriam facere vult et non domini, certum est ex his quae apostolus dicit, *Facientes voluntates carnis et cogitationum eramus natura filli irae sicut et ceteri.*

Interrogatio LXXXVIIII
(Zelzer 123, QF 90, SR 129 [PG 31.1169–1170])

I: Qui satis ieiunat et in refectione non potest communem cibum cum omnibus sumere, quid magis eligere debet: ieiunare cum fratribus et cum ipsis reficere aut propter maiora ieiunia alios cibos requirere?

R: Ieiunii mensura non debet ex uniuscuiusque voluntate pendere, sed ex usu et institutione eorum qui communiter deo serviunt, **2** sicut et illorum in omnibus unanimitas et consonantia refertur qui in actibus apostolorum *cor et anima*m *una*m habuisse signantur. **3** Si quis ergo rationabiliter et fideliter ieiunat, etiam virtutem ut sustinere possit a domino consequitur, *fidelis enim est qui repromisit.*

Interrogatio LXXXX
(Zelzer 124, QF 91, SR 130 [PG 31.1169–1170])

I: Quomodo oportet ieiunare cum necessarium ieiunium iniungitur, si quando aliquid quod religio deposcit explendum est, tamquam ex necessitate an voluntarie?

R: 1 Domino dicente *Beati qui esurient et sitiunt iustitiam* omne quod ad religionem pertinet nisi ex proposito et devotione fiat periculum generat; debet ergo ieiunio sociari devotio.

---

[65] *Si quis* Zelz. most MSS, confirmed L² 24; *si qui* C, an archetype error.

Question 88

Q: If someone wants to practise self-control beyond his strength, so that through excessive abstinence he is hindered even in the work of the commandments, ought this be allowed him?

R: 1 Your question does not appear to me to be well put. **2** For we did not say that self-control consists solely in abstinence from foods, for this is even found blameworthy by the Apostle, if it is done without faith and reason, when he says: *Those who abstain from foods which God has created* (1 Tim 4:3). **3** But what we did say is that that self-control is perfect in which someone restrains himself from his own will. **4** But how great is the peril of one who wishes to do his own will and not the Lord's, is affirmed in the words of the Apostle: *Fulfilling the desires of the flesh and of our thoughts, we were as much children of wrath as were all the rest* (Eph 2:3).

Question 89

Q: One who fasts much but at a meal is unable to take the common food with all the others, what should he rather choose: to fast with the brothers and to eat with them, or, because of his excessive fasting to seek other foods?

R: 1 The measure of fasting must not depend on the will of each, but serve the use and order of those who serve God in common, **2** in the same way that unanimity and concord in all things is reported of those who in the Acts of the Apostles are described as having *one heart and soul* (Acts 4:32). **3** If anyone, therefore, fasts reasonably[103] and faithfully, he can obtain from the Lord the very strength to be able to sustain it, for *He who promised is faithful* (Heb 10:23).

Question 90

Q: When a necessary fast is enjoined, if on occasion some piety requires that it be fulfilled, how must we fast, with constraint or willingly?

R: 1 Since the Lord says: *Blessed are those who hunger and thirst after righteousness* (Matt 5:6), anything done for piety begets danger unless it is done with resolve and with zeal; fasting therefore should be joined with zeal.

---

[103] Perhaps *"rationabiliter"* might be translated in the context as "according to this principle" (of community concord, just argued).

2 Quia autem necessarium sit ieiunium in talibus quibusque causis, et maxime cum desideramus aliquid impetrare de domino, etiam sanctus apostolus docet **3** qui inter ceteras suas virtutes addidit etiam hoc dicens quia *In ieiuniis frequenter*.

Interrogatio LXXXXI
(Zelzer 124–25, QF 92, SR 131 [PG 31.1169–1170])

I: Qui non vult uti ipsis cibis ex quibus fratres reficiunt sed alios requirit, si recte facit?

R: 1 Specialiter hoc ipsum requirere cibum contra mandatum est domini dicentis *Nolite quaerere quid manducetis vel quid bibatis*. **2** Et ut magis nos attentos faceret ad ea quae dicebat addidit *Haec enim omnia gentes requirunt*. **3** Sane debet sollicitudo esse eius qui praeest, ut impleat illud quod scriptum est *Dividebatur autem uniquique secundum id quod opus erat*.

Interrogatio LXXXXII
(Zelzer 125–26, QF 93.1-4, SR 132 [PG 31.1169–1170])

I: Qui dicit quia Laedit me hoc, et contristatur si ei alius cibus non fuerit datus?

R: 1 Apparet quia hic non est fixus in spe illa quam *Lazarus* habuit, nec de caritate eius qui praeest et sollicitudinem tam sui quam omnium gerit certus est. **2** Verumtamen absolute neque de his quae laedunt[66] neque de his quae prosunt permittitur unicuique suo iudicio vel voluntate aliquid agere, **3** sed eius qui praeest iudicio committendum est ut unicuique prout res vel necessitas expetit consulat, **4** primo omnium in his quae animae prosunt, tum deinde secundo loco etiam ut in corporalibus usibus secundum dei voluntatem moderetur.

---

[66] *Neque . . . laedunt* Zelz. most MSS, confirmed L² 10; omitted through haplography from *neque* to *neque* CPS, an archetype error in α.

2 But that fasting is necessary on such occasions especially when we desire to implore something from the Lord, the Apostle also teaches **3** who among his other virtues tells of this one too saying: *In fasts often* (2 Cor 11:27).

Question 91

Q: Does he do well who does not want to use the same foods from which the brothers refresh themselves, but seeks something else?

R: 1 To be seeking foods is especially contrary to the commandment of the Lord who said: *Do not seek what you are to eat or what you are to drink* (Luke 12:29; cf. Matt 6:31). **2** And to impress this on us all the more, he added: *For the nations seek all these things* (Matt 6:32). **3** Still, the one who presides[104] must take care to fulfil what is written: *It was distributed to each according to his need* (Acts 4:35).[105]

Question 92

Q: But what if someone says "This does me harm!" and is upset if another food is not given him?

R: 1 Clearly he is not established in that hope which *Lazarus*[106] had (cf. Luke 16:20-21) and is uncertain that the one who presides loves him and fulfils this responsibility both for him and for all. **2** Nonetheless, in no way is it permitted anyone to do anything by his own judgment or will, neither concerning what is harmful nor what is beneficial, **3** but it is entrusted to the judgment of the one who presides who is to consult for each as circumstance or necessity demand, **4** making arrangements first of all in respect of what benefits the soul and then secondly also for bodily needs according to the will of God.

---

[104] SR 131 1169C: the one assigned/appointed (τοῦ δὲ ἐπιτεταγμένου). The Greek appears to be referring to a subordinate official, i.e., the one entrusted with the task of distributing food. The same shift between the Greek and Latin terms appears in RBas 94.

[105] The same text is quoted at RBas 94.3 and at RB 34.1 and 55.20.

[106] *Lazarus* in Garnier's Greek text, in QF, and in Zelzer; *Eleazar* in HMTZ Hol. and, strangely, in Clarke's translation. The reference is to the beggar who welcomed whatever scraps were given him, rather than the martyr who indeed had a sure hope (2 Macc 6) but whose virtue was tested precisely in observing distinctions between foods.

Interrogatio LXXXXIII
(Zelzer 126, QF 93.5-6, SR 133 [PG 31.1171–1172])

I: Si vero etiam quis murmuret propter escam, quae erga eum sententia servabitur?

R: 1 Ea quae circa illos qui murmuraverunt in deserto; dicit enim apostolus *Neque murmuraveritis sicut quidam eorum murmuraverunt et perierunt ab exterminatore.*

Interrogatio LXXXXIIII
(Zelzer 126–27, QF 94, SR 135 [PG 31.1171–1172])

I: Si oportet eum qui plus laborat requirere plus aliquid a consuetudine?

R: 1 Si propter retributionem dei laborem suscipit, non hic requirere debet laboris sui mercedem vel requiem, sed pro his ad promissa domini festinare, **2** sciens quia sicut pro laboribus mercedes paravit dominus, ita etiam pro angustiis consolationes. **3** Verumtamen hi qui praesunt observabunt regulam illam quae dicit *Dividebatur autem unicuique prout opus erat*; debet enim unumquemque praevenire ut secundum laborem etiam solacia refectionis inveniat.

Interrogatio LXXXXV
(Zelzer 127–28, QF 95, SR 168 [PG 31.1193–1194])

I: Quali affectu oportet accipere vel vestimentum vel calciamentum qualecumque fuerit?

R: 1 Si quidem breve aut grande est ad mensuram staturae suae hoc indicare debet, sed cum omni verecundia et mansuetudine. **2** Si vero pro abiectiori vel viliori moveatur aut quia non est novum, meminerit mandati domini dicentis quia *Dignus est* non quicumque, sed *operarius mercede sua.* **3** Discutiat se ipsum si digne operatus est opera dei et adimplevit omnia quaecumque praecepta sunt et tunc non aliud requiret, sed de eo ipso quod ei datur adhuc erit sollicitus quia supra meritum suum accepit. **4** Hoc enim quod de esca dictum est etiam de omni re quae ad usus corporis pertinet eadem forma observari potest.

Question 93

Q: But what if someone murmurs about food, what judgment shall be observed towards him?

R: 1 The judgment concerning those who *murmured* in the desert (cf. Num 11:1); for the Apostle says: *And do not murmur, as some of them murmured and perished by the destroyer* (1 Cor 10:10).

Question 94

Q: Should one who labours more seek something more than the usual?

R: 1 If he undertook the labour in view of the reward from God, such a one ought not to seek compensation or respite for his toil, but hasten for these things to the promises of the Lord, **2** knowing that as the Lord has prepared a reward for his labours, he has also prepared consolations for his distresses. **3** Nevertheless, those who preside shall[107] observe that rule which says: *It was distributed to each according to his need* (Acts 4:35); for they must anticipate each individual, so that he finds the solace of refreshment appropriate to the labour.

Question 95

Q: In what disposition ought one to receive clothing or footwear, whatever it may be?

R: 1 If it is too short or too long for the measure of his size he must make this known, yet with all modesty and gentleness. **2** But if he is upset because it is of a poorer or cheaper quality, or because it is not new, let him be mindful of that commandment of the Lord, who says: *Worthy is, not anyone at all, but the labourer of his hire* (Luke 10:7; cf. Matt 10:10). **3** Let him examine himself, whether he has accomplished the works of God worthily and fulfilled all precepts whatever they may be, and then he will not seek anything else, but rather be anxious about the very thing even now given to him, whether he has received more than he deserves. **4** For what was said about food can be observed as a rule for every other matter concerning the needs of the body.

---

[107] 1172C ὁ ἐπιτεταγμένος: "the one appointed," i.e., the one entrusted with the distribution of food. On the question of one or several superiors in the community see RBas 15.Q and note.

Interrogatio LXXXXVI
(Zelzer 128, QF 96, SR 134 [PG 31.1171–1172])

I: Si quis iratus nolit suscipere aliquid eorum quae ad usus praebentur?

R: 1 Iste talis dignus est ut etiam si quaerat[67] non accipiat usquequo probet is qui praeest, et cum viderit vitium animi curatum tunc etiam corporis usibus quod necessarium fuerit praebebit.

Interrogatio LXXXXVII
(Zelzer 128–29, QF 97, SR 136 [PG 31.1171–1172])

I: Si necesse est omnes convenire ad horam prandii, eum qui remanet et post prandium venit quomodo transimus?

R: 1 Si quidem necessitate vel loci vel operis remansit a communi ordine, qui praeest probabit et ignoscet. **2** Si vero cum posset non satis egit occurrere, fateatur culpam neglegentiae suae et maneat sine cibo usque ad horam illam qua convenitur ad cibum in posterum diem.

Interrogatio LXXXXVIII
(Zelzer 129–30, QF 98, SR 100 [PG 31.1151–1152])

I: Pauperes venientes ad ostium et petentes quomodo dimittemus, et si debet unusquisque porrigere panem vel quodcumque aliud, aut oportet hoc ad eum qui praeest pertinere?

R: 1 Cum dominus dixerit *Non est bonum tollere panem filiorum et mittere canibus,* sed et canes manducare *de micis quae cadunt de mensa puerorum* libenter acceperit, is cui dispensatio iniuncta est cum consideratione debet hoc facere. **2** Si quis autem praeter illius voluntatem facere hoc praesumit, tamquam inquietus et indisciplinatus confundatur usquequo discat loci sui ordinem custodire **3** secundum quod apostolus dixit *Unusquisque in quo vocatus est in eo permaneat.*

---

[67] *Quaerat* Zelz. following WLG, MZ, and Hol., confirmed L² 40, 47; *qu(a)erit* (the subjunctive, cf. κἂν ζητῷ), all other MSS.

Question 96

Q: What of someone who angrily refuses something that is given for his needs?

R: 1 Such a one deserves to receive nothing at all even if he asks, until the one who presides assesses, and when he sees that the vice of his soul is cured then he shall also provide for the needs of the body.

Question 97

Q: If it is necessary that all gather at the hour of the meal, how are we to deal with one who stays behind and arrives after the meal?

R: 1 If it was due to some necessity of place or of work that he stayed back from the common order, he who presides will assess and acknowledge. **2** If however he was able, but did not sufficiently bestir himself, let him acknowledge the charge of his negligence and remain without food till the prescribed hour of the meal the next day.

Question 98

Q: How are we to send on their way the poor who come to the door begging? Must each provide them with bread or whatever else, or should this be the task of the one to whom the one presiding has assigned it?

R: 1 Since the Lord said: *It is not good to take the children's bread and give it to the dogs*, yet willingly accepted that *dogs too eat the scraps that fall from the children's table* (Matt 15:26-27), it is for the one charged with the distribution to perform this task prudently. **2** But if anyone else presumes to do so without his approval, let him be rebuked as restless and undisciplined, until he learns to keep to the order of his place, **3** as the Apostle said: *Let each remain in that wherein he was called* (1 Cor 7:20).

Interrogatio LXXXXVIIII

(Zelzer 130, QF 99, SR 87 [PG 31.1143–1144])

I: Si licet unicuique veterem *tunicam* suam aut calciamentum dare cui voluerit misericordiae causa propter mandatum?

R: 1 Dare aliquid mandati gratia pro misericordia non est omnium sed eorum quibus istud officium creditum est. **2** Is ergo ad quem pertinet dispensatio, sive novum sive vetus vestimentum ipse da‹bi›t cui dare debet et ipse suscipiet a quo suscipi debet.

Interrogatio C

(Zelzer 131, QF 100, SR 169 [PG 31.1193–1194])

I: Si frater iunior iussus fuerit docere aliquem seniorem secundum aetatem, quomodo debet agere cum eo?

R: 1 Tamquam ministerium exhibens ad implendum praeceptum domini cum omni reverentia, timens illam sententiam quae dicit **2** *Maledictus qui facit opera domini neglegenter,* observet autem *ne elatus in iudicium incidat diaboli.*

Interrogatio CI

(Zelzer 131–32, QF 101, SR 141 [PG 31.1177–1178])

I: Si debent peregrini intrare usque ad illa loca ubi fratres operantur, vel etiam si alii de eodem monasterio debent relictis suis locis intrare ad alios?

R: 1 Praeter illum cui creditum est requirere operantes, id est ad quem opus pertinet dispensationis, si quis alius inventus fuerit hoc faciens **2** tamquam interturbans disciplinam et ordinem fratrum a communi conventu excludatur et omnino etiam a licitis progressibus inhibeatur,[68] **3** et sedens in uno loco in quo iudicaverit is qui praest apto ad correptionem et vindictam nusquam prorsus permittatur abscedere, **4** sed urgeatur in opus multo plus quam consuetudo est et cotidie exigatur, usquequo discat implere hoc quod apostolus dixit *Unusquisque in quo vocatus est in eo permaneat.*

---

[68] *A licitis progressibus inhibeatur* all β MSS, confirmed L¹ 590 and L² 9; *a licitis ingressibus prohibeatur* (be forbidden permissible entries) Zelz. With α (CS). According to Lundström β preserves the original reading, reflecting the Greek προόδου. *Ingressibus* is a mistaken reading of προσόδου. The issue is not entry into others' places but departure from one's own assigned place.

Question 99

Q: Is anyone allowed to give away his old *tunic* or footwear wherever he wishes as an alms on account of the commandment (cf. Matt 10:10; Mark 6:9)?

R: 1 To give or receive anything as an alms according to the command-ment is not for everyone, but for those to whom this office is entrusted.[108] **2** Therefore the one who has the responsibility for distribution shall give the clothing, whether new or old, to whom he ought to give it, and himself shall receive it from whom he ought to receive it.

Question 100

Q: If a younger brother has been ordered to teach something to another senior in years, how should he behave toward him?

R: 1 As performing a service in fulfilment of the Lord's precept with all reverence, fearing that judgment which says: **2** *Cursed is anyone who does the works of the Lord negligently* (Jer 48:10), and taking care *lest, being inflated, he falls into the condemnation of the devil* (1 Tim 3:6).

Question 101

Q: Ought visitors enter as far as the places where the brothers work, or even some from the same monastery leave their own places to enter the places of others?[109]

R: 1 Except for the one entrusted with overseeing the workers, that is, to whom belongs the task of distribution, let anyone else found doing this **2** be excluded from the common gathering and wholly checked even from permitted exits, as one who upsets the discipline and order of the brothers, **3** and sitting in one place, which the one who presides has judged suitable for correction and chastisement, let him not be permitted to go anywhere at large, **4** but be urged to apply himself to his work far more than was his custom and to exercise himself in it daily, until he learns to fulfil what the Apostle said: *Let each remain in that wherein he was called* (1 Cor 7:20).

---

[108] The reference is to one or more in the community charged with distribution of the community's goods, the οἰκονόμος, the *cellarius* of RB 31. Medieval monasteries developed the office of almoner for dispensing help outside the community. In SR 91 Basil restates the point made here even more strongly. Cf. RB 33.2.

[109] See Letter 22, Def I, 136–37: "He should not be found going from one workshop to another."

Interrogatio CII
(Zelzer 132, QF 102, SR 142 [PG 31.1177–1178])

I: Si oportet eos qui noverunt artificia suscipere ab aliquo opus absque conscientiae vel iussione eius qui praeest et operum sollicitudinem gerit?

R: 1 Furti res erit eiusmodi vel similis his qui furibus concurrunt.

Interrogatio CIII
(Zelzer 132–33, QF –, SR 143 [PG 31.1177–1178])

I: Quomodo debent hi qui operantur curam gerere ferramentorum vel utensilium eorum de quibus operantur?

R: 1 Primo quidem sicut vasis dei vel his quae deo consecrata sunt uti debent, deinde tamquam qui non possint sine ipsis devotionis et studii sui emolumenta consequi.

Interrogatio CIIII
(Zelzer 133, QF 103, SR 144 [PG 31.1177–1178])

I: Quodsi per neglegantiam pereat aliquid ex his aut per contemptum dissipetur?

R: 1 Is quidem qui contemnit velut sacrilegus iudicandus est et qui perdidit per neglegentiam, et ipse simile crimen incurrit pro eo quod omni ad usus servorum dei deputata deo sine dubio consecrata sunt.

Interrogatio CV
(Zelzer 133, QF 104, SR 145 [PG 31.1177–1178])

I: Quodsi a se ipso commodare voluerit alicui aut accipere ab alio?

R: 1 Tamquam insolens et temerarius habendus est; haec enim eorum qui praesunt et curam dispensationis gerunt officia propria sunt.

Question 102

Q: Should those who know crafts accept a task from anyone without the recognition or order of him who presides and bears the responsibility for these matters?[110]

R: 1 Someone like this will be guilty of theft, and likewise those who collude with his thefts.[111]

Question 103

Q: How must workers care for the tools or utensils they use for work?

R: 1 First they must use them as God's instruments, that is, as consecrated to God. Second, as being unable without them to obtain the benefits of their own devotion and zeal.[112]

Question 104

Q: What if one of them is lost through neglect, or damaged through contempt?

R: 1 One who treats it with contempt should be judged sacrilegious and one who loses it through neglect also incurs a like judgment, since everything that is assigned to the use of the servants of God is without doubt consecrated to God.

Question 105

Q: What if someone chooses of himself to lend to another or to receive from another?

R: 1 He ought to be regarded as presumptuous and rash; for these things are the proper concern of those who preside and have the care of stewardship.[113]

---

[110] Gribomont points to RBas 102 as the background of RB 57: "Concerning the Craftsmen of the Monastery"—"Commentaries," 258 #12.

[111] SR 142 1177B: Let either of them, the giver and the receiver, be subject to the judgment of the thief or of the thief's accomplice.

[112] SR 143 1177B ὡς (σκευῶν) Θεῷ ἐπονομασθέντων καὶ ἀνατεθέντων, "as vessels dedicated and consecrated to God." There is little doubt that RB 31.10 has borrowed this phrasing: "*Omnia vasa monasterii cunctamque substantiam ac si altaris vasa sacrata conspiciat*"; see Gribomont, "Commentaries," 259 #16: "*De Ferramentis vel Rebus Monasterii.*"

[113] 1177D τοῦ ἐπιτεταγμένου τὴν φροντίδα, καὶ οἰκονομοῦντος: "of the one entrusted with the responsibility and of the one who exercises stewardship." For ambiguities

Interrogatio CVI
(Zelzer 134, QF –, SR 146 [PG 31.1177–1180])

I: Quodsi necessitas poscat et is qui praeest requirat ab aliquo eorum vas vel ferramentum, et contradixerit?

R: 1 Qui se ipsum et membra sua tradiderit in alterius potestatem propter mandatum domini, quomodo licebit de utensilibus contradicere, huic praecipue cui cura commissa est?

Interrogatio CVII
(Zelzer 134–35, QF –, SR 147 [PG 31.1179–1180])

I: Si is qui circa cellarium vel coquinam vel alia huiuscemodi opera occupatus est non occurrat adesse in ordine psallentium vel ad orationem, nihil damni patitur in anima?

R: 1 Unusquisque in opere suo observare debet propriam regulam sicut membrum in corpore, et damnum habebit si neglexerit in eo quod iniunctum est ei, sed et communem fratrum utilitatem neglegens amplius pereclitabitur. **2** Et ideo mente et devotione complere debet id quod scriptum est *Cantantes et psallentes in cordibus vestris domino.* **3** Si enim corporaliter non occurrit adesse cum ceteris ad orationis locum, in quocumque loco inventus fuerit quod devotionis est expleat. **4** Oportet tamen observare ne forte quis possit complere in tempore suo quod complendum est et occurrere, sed dum loqui vult occasiones nectit tamquam in ministerii opere occupatus. **5** Quod qui facit et offendiculum ceteris praestat et ipse neglegentis crimen incurrit.

Question 106

Q: What if necessity requires and the one who presides asks someone for a vessel or a tool, and he objects?

R: 1 How can one who has handed over himself and his members into the power of another for the sake of the Lord's commandment be at liberty to dispute about tools, especially with one to whom the responsibility is entrusted?

Question 107

Q: If someone engaged in work in the store-room or the kitchen or a similar task[114] does not hasten to be present at the order of psalmody and of prayer, does his soul suffer no loss?

R: 1 Each in his own work must keep to his proper rule as a member of the body, and will suffer loss if he neglects what he is enjoined to do, and indeed be in greater peril if he neglects the common purpose of the brothers. **2** So then, he must fulfil with mind and devotion what is written: *chanting and singing psalms in your hearts to the Lord* (Eph 5:19). **3** For if he does not hasten to be bodily present with the others at the place of prayer, let him fulfil what pertains to piety in whatever place he finds himself. **4** Care however ought to be observed lest someone perhaps is able to complete in time what needs to be completed and to hasten, but wants to allege excuses as if he had been detained in a work of service. **5** Anyone who does this answers for a stumbling-block for the others and incurs the penalty of the negligent.

---

over singular or plural and over "entrusted" or "appointed" with regard to superiors or subofficers, see LR 43, SR 132 (RBas 92), 135 (RBas 94) and note, 142 (RBas 102), 146 (RBas 106), 235, 252 (RBas 173), Letter 22, Def I, 131–33, Letter 199, Def III, 104, *Virgins of God*, 70 n. 37, and Philip Rousseau, *Basil of Caesarea* (Berkeley: University of California Press, 1994), 212–13.

[114] SR 147 1180A τοῦ κελλαρίου, ἢ τοῦ μαγειρείου, ἢ περί τι ἄλλο τοιοῦτον ἀσχολούμενος. On the kitchen see RBas 131.Q.

Interrogatio CVIII
(Zelzer 135–36, QF –, SR 201 [PG 31.1215–1216])

I: Quomodo obtinebit quis ut in oratione sensus eius non vagetur?

R: 1 Si certus sit assistere se ante oculos dei; si enim quis iudicem suum videns vel principem et loquens cum eo non sibi credit licitum esse vagari oculo[69] et aliorsum aspicere[70] dum ipse loquitur, **2** quanto magis qui accedit ad deum nusquam debet movere oculum cordis, sed intentus esse in eum qui *scruta*tur *renes et corda*, **3** ut impleat illud quod scriptum est *Levantes sanctas manus sine ira et disceptatione.*

Interrogatio CVIIII
(Zelzer 136, QF –, SR 202 [PG 31.1215–1216])

I: Si possibile est obtinere hominem ut in omni tempore et loco non vagetur mens sua, vel quomodo id fieri potest?

R: 1 Quia possibile est ostendit ille qui dixit *Oculi mei semper ad dominum,* et iterum, *Providebam dominum in conspectu meo semper, quia a dextris est mihi ut non commovear.* **2** Quomodo autem possibile sit praediximus, id est si non demus animae otium, sed in omni tempore de deo et de operibus ac beneficiis eius et donis cogitemus **3** et haec cum confessione et gratiarum actione semper volvamus in mente sicut scriptum est.

Interrogatio CX
(Zelzer 137, QF –, SR 279 [PG 31.1279–1280])

I: Quid est *Psalliter sapienter*?

R: 1 Quod est in omnibus cibis gustus quo unumquodque dinoscitur cuius saporis sit, hoc est et in verbis sanctae scripturae prudentiae et[71] sensus; **2** *fauces* enim, inquit, *escas gustabunt, sensus autem verba discernit.* **3** Si quis ergo ita animam suam intendat in singula verba psalmorum sicut gustus intentus est ad discretionem saporis ciborum, iste est qui complet hoc quod dicitur *Psallite sapienter.*

---

[69] *Oculo* restored L[1] 589, L[2] 15-16 with S and the Greek τὸ ὄμμα; *oculis* Zelz. following L, P, TMZJ.

[70] *Aspicere* most MSS, confirmed L[2] 16; *respicere* Zelz., following CJB.

[71] *Prudentiae et sensus* CPJ, confirmed L[2] 25; *et* omitted Zelz. following S.

Question 108

Q: How can one ensure that in prayer his senses do not wander?

R: 1 If he is resolved that he stands before the eyes of God, for if someone who sees his judge or ruler[115] and converses with him does not allow his eye the liberty to roam about or look away elsewhere while he is engaged in speaking, **2** how much more ought someone who approaches God never divert the eyes of his heart but remain intent on him who *searches hearts and inward parts* (Ps 7:9), **3** so that he fulfils what is written: *Lifting up holy hands without anger and argument* (1 Tim 2:8).

Question 109

Q: Is it possible for a human being to ensure that always and everywhere his mind does not wander, and how can this be done?

R: 1 That it is possible he shows us who said: *My eyes are always on the Lord* (Ps 24:15) and again: *I kept the Lord always in view before me; since he is at my right hand I shall not be shaken* (Ps 15:8). **2** How it may be possible we have already said: that is, if we allow no idleness to the soul, but at all times think on God and his works and benefits and gifts **3** and ponder these things in our mind with *confession* and *thanksgiving* as it is written (cf. Ps 33:1; 1 Tim 2:1).

Question 110

Q: What is it to *sing psalms wisely*?[116] (Ps 46:7 LXX)

R: 1 Just as with all foods, the flavour of each is discerned through taste, so also are prudence and discernment with the words of Holy Scripture. **2** *For the throat*, it says, *tastes foods, but the sense*[117] *discerns words* (cf. Job 12:11; 34:3 LXX). **3** Therefore if one's soul is intent on each word of the psalms, as taste is intent on distinguishing the flavour of foods, such a one fulfils that which is said: *sing psalms wisely* (Ps 46:7).

---

[115] SR 201 1216B ἄρχοντά τις ἢ προεστῶτα: "ruler or one who presides." See RBas 46.1. RB 20.1-2 also uses the approach to eminent or important persons as an analogy for the proper disposition of prayer.

[116] *Psallite sapienter* is also the reading of the Latin Vulgate. SR 279 1280A: ψάλατε συνετῶς, "sing psalms wisely," Garnier: *intelligenter*.

[117] SR 279 1280A νοῦς: the mind / thought. The Septuagint, following the Hebrew, has οὖς . . . ῥήματα διακρίνει. A very minor change from οὖς (ear) to νοῦς (mind) occurs in some Septuagint manuscripts, and this is the version used by Basil.

Interrogatio CXI

(Zelzer 137–38, QF –, SR 148 [PG 31.1179–1180])

I: Qua mensura temperare debet potestatem dispensationis suae is cui cellarii cura commissa est?

R: 1 Erga eum quidem qui ei credidit huiuscemodi dispensationem meminisse debet domini dicentis *Non possum ego a me ipso facere quicquam.* **2** Ad ceteros vero sollicite scire debet quid unusquisque opus habeat, ut compleat illud quod scriptum est *Dividebatur autem unicuique prout opus erat.* **3** Eadem autem ratio observari debet ab omnibus quibuscumque aliqua ministerii vel dispensationis sollicitudo commissa est.

Interrogatio CXII

(Zelzer 138–39, QF –, SR 149 [PG 31.1179–1182])

I: Quae sententia observabitur erga dispensantem si aliquid secundum *personae acceptio*nem vel per *contentio*nem faciat?

R: 1 Apostolo praecipiente aliquando quidem *Ne quid facias* secundum favorem vel *in alteram partem declinando,* **2** aliquando autem dicente quia *si quis videtur contentiosus esse nos talem consuetudinem non habemus neque ecclesia dei,* si quis hoc facit notetur usquequo corrigatur.

3 Verumtamen oportet cum summa diligentia et probatione discutere et considerare ad quam partem unusquisque aptus sit vel opportunus, et ita ei iniungi quodcumque illud est operis vel officii, **4** ut neque illi qui iniungunt ex hoc ipso condemnentur quod non aptum alicui officium iniunxerint, et inveniantur mali esse dispensatores sive animarum sive mandatorum domini, **5** neque illi ipsi quibus iniungitur occasionem peccati ex hoc habere videantur.

Question 111

Q: With what measure ought he who is entrusted with the care of the store-room administer the authority of his stewardship?[118]

R: 1 Towards the one who entrusted him with this stewardship, he must be mindful of the Lord who said: *I can do nothing of myself* (John 5:30). **2** Towards the others let him be attentively aware of the need of each so that he fulfils what is written: *it was distributed to each according to his need* (Acts 4:35). **3** The same principle must also to be observed by all who are entrusted with the responsibility of any service or stewardship.

Question 112

Q: What judgment shall be observed concerning a steward who does anything with *respect of persons* (cf. Deut 10:17; Matt 22:16; Rom 2:11; Eph 6:9), or from *contentiousness*? (cf. 2 Cor 12:20; Gal 5:20)

R: 1 Since the Apostle at one time commands: *Do nothing* from *favoritism* or from *partiality* (1 Tim 5:21), **2** and at another time says: *If anyone appears to be contentious, we have no such custom, and neither does the church of God* (1 Cor 11:16), if someone does this let him be reprimanded until he emends.

3 All the same, he ought to weigh and to consider with all diligence and testing what part each is suited or fitted to, and thus to each is entrusted whatever the task or office may be, **4** lest those who assign the work are themselves condemned thereby, because they have assigned to someone an unsuitable office and are found to be bad stewards, whether of souls or of the commandments of the Lord, **5** and lest those who are assigned the task appear to have in this a pretext for sin.[119]

---

[118] τὴν φροντίδα τοῦ κελλαρίου. Cf. RB 30.3-5 for the same teaching concerning the "cellarer," or supervisor of material distribution in the monastery.

[119] Following this verse is a passage in GLMWZ Hol. which largely duplicates RBas 92.3-4 with minor variations of wording: ". . . or do something by their own will; but let the judgment of the one who presides be entrusted to each individual as principle or necessity requires. Let him consult first of all for those things in which souls benefit, then in the second place let him also accommodate bodily needs according to the will of God."

Interrogatio CXIII

(Zelzer 139, QF –, SR 150 [PG 31.1181–1182])

I: Si autem neglexerit dare fratri quod opus est?

R: 1 Manifesta est de hoc sententia ex ipsis domini verbis dicentis *Discedite a me maledicti in ignem aeternum quod praeparatum*[72] *est diabolo et angelis eius. Esurivi enim et non dedistis mihi manducare, sitivi et non dedistis mihi bibere* et ea quae sequuntur, **2** et quia *Maledictus* est omnis *qui facit opera domini neglegenter.*

Interrogatio CXIIII

(Zelzer 140, QF –, SR 203 [PG 31.1217–1218])

I: In profectibus mandatorum dei una mensura est omnium an alius amplius, alius minus habet[73] aliquid?

R: 1 Quia non est una mensura in omnibus sed quia alii plus creditur et alii minus, manifestum est ex ipsis domini verbis nunc quidem dicentis **2** *Aliud semen cecidit super terram bonam* et *hic est qui audit verba* mea *et intellegit et fructum affert, aliud centesimum, aliud sexagesimum, aliud tricesimum.* **3** Hoc idem autem etiam in his qui *mnas*[74] susceperunt invenitur, cum dicitur alii quidem datas esse *quinque* mnas, *alii du*as, *alii un*am.

Interrogatio CXV

(Zelzer 140–41, QF –, SR 170 [PG 31.1193–1194])

I: Si oportet aequaliter haberi eos qui plus proficiunt et eos qui minus?

R: 1 Illud observandum est in hoc quod et de remissione peccatorum dominus statuit dicens *Remissa sunt ei peccata sua multa quoniam dilexit multum, cui autem parum remittitur parum diligit,* **2** et iterum quod de presbyteris apostolus statuit dicens *Qui bene praesunt presbyteri duplici* honore *honorentur, maxime qui laborant in verbo et doctrina.* **3** Hoc in omnibus huiuscemodi causis observari consequens puto.

---

[72] *Quod praeparatum* S, B after correction, J, confirmed L¹ 590, L² 52, cf. the Greek: εἰς τὸ πῦρ τὸ αἰώνιον τὸ ἡτοιμασμένον τῷ διαβόλῳ . . .; *qui praeparatus* Zelz. with C and most β MSS.

[73] *Habet* Zelz. following CP, with Gk. ἔχει; confirmed L² 25, 61; *habeat* S, an archetype error.

[74] SR 203 1217A τὰς μνᾶς. Zelzer follows P (after correction), which transliterates the Greek. The forms of the word in the Latin are almost as various as the number of the codices: J has *talenta* for the first *mnas*; GLMW Hol. use *talenta* in place of the second *mnas*.

Question 113

Q: But what if he neglected to give a brother what he needs?

R: 1 His judgment is clear from the very words of the Lord who says: *Depart from me you accursed into the eternal fire, that which is prepared for the devil and his angels. For I was hungry and you did not give me to eat, I was thirsty and you did not give me to drink*—and the rest (Matt 25:42), **2** and also: *cursed* is anyone *who does the works of the Lord negligently* (Jer 48:10).

Question 114

Q: In regard to progress made in the commandments of God, is there a single measure among them all or does one have more and another less?

R: 1 That there is not one measure among all, but that one is credited with more and another with less, is clear from the very words of the Lord who in one place says: **2** *Some seed fell upon good earth,* and *this is he who hears my words and understands and brings forth fruit, one a hundredfold, another sixtyfold, another thirtyfold* (Matt 13:23; Luke 8:8). **3** This same thing is found also with those who received the *minas* (cf. Luke 19:13), where it is said that *five minas* were given to one, *to another two, to another one* (Matt 25:15).

Question 115

Q: Should those making greater progress and those making less be regarded equally?

R: 1 That should be observed what the Lord laid down concerning the forgiveness of sins when he said: *her sins, though many, are forgiven her, this is why she has loved much; who has been forgiven little, loves little* (Luke 7:47), **2** and again what the Apostle laid down concerning elders, saying: *Let elders who preside well be honoured with double honours and especially those who labour in the word and in teaching* (1 Tim 5:47)—**3** this, I consider, is suitably observed in all such cases.

Interrogatio CXVI
(Zelzer 141–42, QF –, SR 171 [PG 31.1193–1196])

I: Quodsi contristetur is qui minus honoratur, cum praeferri sibi viderit eum qui in timore domini praecedit, quomodo eum habebimus?

R: 1 Is qui talis est certum est quia malignitatis vitio non caret secundum evangelii parabolam **2** in qua dicit dominus ad eos qui contristati sunt quia aequaliter cum ipsis honorati sunt alii, *Aut,* inquit, *oculus tuus malus est quia ego bonus sum?* **3** Et manifesta est de his talibus dei sententia quae dicit per prophetam *Ad nihilum deductus est in conspectu eius malignus, timentes autem dominum magnificat.*

Interrogatio CXVII
(Zelzer 142–43, QF –, SR 10 [PG 31.1087–1090])

I: Anima post multa peccata et post multas vitae miserias cum quali timore et qualibus lacrimis debet recedere a peccatis et cum quali spe et affectu accedere ad dominum?

R: 1 Primo quidem odisse debet illam suam priorem notabilem vitam et ipsam memoriam eius perhorrescere atque exsecrari; **2** scriptum est enim *Iniquitatem odio habui et abominatus sum, legem autem tuam dilexi.*

3 Deinde ut maiorem timorem habeat magistro utatur ignis aeterni metu et poenae perpetuae, sed et lacrimarum tempus agnoscat per paenitentiam. **4** sicut David docuit in sexto psalmo purgationem peccatorum fieri posse ubertate lacrimarum in sanguine Christi per potentiam misericordiae eius et multitudinem miserationum dei, **5** qui dixit quia *Si fuerint peccata vestra sicut phoenicium, ut nivem dealbabo, si autem fuerint sicut coccum, ut lanam candidam efficiam.*

6 Et post hoc recepta virtute et facultate placendi deo dicit *Convertisti planctum meum in gaudium mihi, disrupisti saccum meum et praecinxisti me laetitia ut psallam tibi gloria mea.* **7** Et ita accedens ad dominum psallit et dicit *Exaltabo te domine, quoniam suscepisti me et non laetificasti inimicos meos super me.*

Question 116

Q: What if someone who is less honoured is sullen at seeing another who surpasses him in the fear of the Lord preferred to himself? How should we regard him?

R: 1 Such a one is certainly not without the vice of ill-will,[120] according to the parable of the gospel **2** in which the Lord says to those who are grieved that others have received equal honour with themselves: *Is it, he asks, that your eye is evil because I am generous?* (Matt 20:15) **3** Moreover, the judgment of God concerning such as these is clear when it says through the prophet: *the wicked is brought to nothing before him, but he honours those who fear the Lord* (Ps 14:4).

Question 117

Q: With what fear and in what tears ought a soul after many sins and many miseries of life withdraw from its sins and with what hope and disposition draw near to the Lord?

R: 1 In the first place, it ought to hate its former reprehensible life, and shudder and be repelled at the very memory of it; **2** for it is written: *Iniquity I hated and abhorred, but your law I have loved* (Ps 118:163).

3 Second, let it use the dread of eternal judgment and of everlasting punishment as a teacher, that it may gain a livelier fear, and let it acknowledge a season of tears through repentance, **4** just as David taught in the sixth psalm (Ps 6:6-8), that the purification of its sins can be achieved through an abundance of tears in the blood of Christ by the power of his mercy and the multitude of God's compassions, **5** who said: *Although your sins be as crimson, I will make them white as snow; although they be as scarlet, I will make them white as wool* (Isa 1:18).

6 After it has received the power and the capacity to please God, it says: *You have changed my lamentation into joy for me, you have torn away my sackcloth and girded me with gladness, that I may sing psalms to you in my glory*[121] (Ps 29:11-12). **7** And so it draws near to the Lord singing psalms and saying: *I will extol you, Lord, since you have upheld me and have not let my enemies rejoice over me* (Ps 29:2).

---

[120] SR 171 1193D: is clearly condemned for wickedness (ἐπὶ πονηρίᾳ κατεγνωσμένος), i.e., bitterness, spite, malignity, malice, envy.

[121] SR 10 1088C uses the verb in the third person: that my glory may sing psalms to you (ψάλῃ σοι ἡ δόξα μου).

204 The Rule of St Basil in Latin

Interrogatio CXVIII

(Zelzer 144, QF –, SR 89 [PG 31.1143–1146])

I: Quoniam scriptum est *Redemptio animae viri divitiae eius*, nobis quibus non accidit dispergere pro animae redemptione divitias quid faciemus?

R: 1 Si quidem voluimus et non potuimus memores simus responsionis domini ad Petrum, **2** cum de hac re sollicitus esset et diceret *Ecce nos dimisimus omnia et secuti sumus te, quid ergo erit nobis?* respondit ei dicens **3** *Omnis qui reliquerit domum aut fratres aut sorores aut patrem aut matrem aut uxorem aut filios aut agros propter me* et propter evangelium *centuplum accipiet et vitam aeternam consequetur.*

4 Quodsi per neglegentiam accidit cuiquam omisisse divitias vel nunc adhibeat propensius studium ut ex opere manuum largiens neglectum resarciat censum. **5** Quodsi ne nunc quidem vel tempus nobis superest vel virtus ad huiuscemodi ministerium, consoletur nos apostolus dicens *Non quaero quae vestra sunt sed vos.*

Interrogatio CXVIIII

(Zelzer 145–46, QF 105, SR 45 [PG 31.1111–1112])

I: Si quis audiens sermonem domini dicentis quia *Servus qui cognovit voluntatem domini sui et non fecit secundum voluntatem eius vapulabit multum, qui vero non cognovit et fecit digna plagis vapulabit paucis,* neglegat et dissimulet scire voluntatem domini, si habet aliquid excusationis?

R: 1 Manifestus est qui huiusmodi est quia simulat ignorantiam nec ullo genere effugiet peccati sententiam: **2** *Si* enim *non venissem,* inquit dominus, *et locutus eis fuissem, peccatum non haberent; nunc vero excusationem non habent pro peccato suo.* **3** Si ergo sancta scriptura omnibus et ubique voluntatem dei denuntiat, non inter eos qui ignorant iste talis iudicatur, **4** sed cum illis magis de quibus scriptum est quia *Sicut aspides surdae et obturantes aures suas ne exaudiant vocem incantantium* et curentur *medicamento quod componitur a sapiente.*

Question 118

Q: Since it is written *The ransom of a man's soul is his riches* (Prov 13:8), what shall we do if it happens that we have not distributed wealth for the soul's ransom?

R: 1 If we really wanted to but were unable, let us remember the Lord's answer to Peter, **2** who, being troubled about this matter, said: *Behold, we have given up all things and followed you, what therefore shall there be for us?* (Matt 19:27) He answered him: **3** *Everyone who has left house or brothers or sisters or father or mother or wife or children or lands on my account and that of the gospel shall receive a hundredfold and obtain eternal life* (Matt 19:29; cf. Luke 18:29).

4 But if it happened through carelessness that someone neglected his wealth, then let him now display a greater zeal in order that, through bestowing freely from the work of his hands, he may restore the neglected estate. **5** But if we now no longer have left the time or strength for such service, the Apostle consoles us saying, *I seek not what is yours but you* (2 Cor 12:14).

Question 119

Q: If someone who hears that saying of the Lord: *The servant who knew the will of his master but did not do* according to his will *shall be beaten with many blows; but he who did not know it and did things worthy of blows shall be beaten with fewer* (Luke 12:47-48), neglects and pretends not to know the will of the Lord—does he have any excuse?

R: 1 Manifestly, such a one is feigning ignorance and shall not in any way escape the judgment of his sin. **2** For *If I had not come,* says the Lord, *and spoken to them, they would not be in sin; but now they have no excuse for their sin* (John 15:22). **3** If therefore Holy Scripture everywhere announces the will of God to all, such a one is not judged among those who are ignorant, **4** but rather with those of whom it is written: *as deaf adders that stop up their ears lest they hear the voice of the charmers and are cured with a medicine compounded by the wise*[122] (Ps 57:4-5 LXX).

---

[122] SR 45 1112B: φαρμακοῦ τε φαρμακευομένη παρὰ σοφοῦ. The word φαρμακον and its field comprehend both curative drugs and medical treatment, poisons and sorcery. The nuance has often to be decoded from the context. Here, clearly, Basil and Rufinus both understand it in a medical sense. RBas casts the passage in the plural. Cf. RBas 135.1.

5 Verum is qui praeest et verbi dei ministerium exhibet, si neglexerit annuntiare unicuique et intimare de singulis velut homicida iudicabitur animarum secundum scripturas.

Interrogatio CXX
(Zelzer 146, QF 106, SR 283 [PG 31.1281–1282])

I: Si is qui facit voluntatem alicuius, particeps eius est vel socius eius cuius fecerit voluntatem?

R: 1 Si credimus domino dicenti quia *Qui facit peccatum servus est peccati,* et iterum *Vos ex patre diabolo estis et desideria patris vestri facere vultis,* **2** scimus quia non solum socium et participem, sed et dominum sibi ac patrem adscribit eum cuius opus facit. **3** Testatur autem et de his apostolus dicens *Aut nescitis quia cui exhibetis vos servos ad oboediendum servi estis eius cui oboeditis, sive peccati in mortem sive oboedientiae ad iustitiam?*

Interrogatio CXXI
(Zelzer 147–48, QF 107, SR 46 [PG 31.1111–1114])

I: Si is qui consentit alterius peccato si etiam ipse peccati reus est?

R: 1 Haec sententia manifesta est ex verbis domini quibus ait ad Pilatum dicens *Qui tradidit me tibi maius peccatum habet.* **2** Manifestum namque est ex hoc et Pilatus acquiescens his qui tradiderunt[75] dominum peccatum habebat, licet minus quam illi. **3** Ostenditur autem hoc etiam in eo, quod Adam acquiescit vel consentit Evae, quae acquieverat serpenti. **4** Nullus enim ex ipsis ut innocens iudicatus est aut impunitus abscessit, sed et ipsa dei indignatio quae adversum eos habita est hoc ipsum indicat. **5** Cum enim Adam pro excusatione sua obiecisset quia *Mulier quam dedisti mihi ipsa mihi dedit et manducavi,* **6** *Quia audisti,* inquit Deus, *vocem mulieris tuae et manducasti de ligno de quo praeceperam tibi ne de solo ipso[76] manducares, maledicta terra in operibus tuis.*

---

[75] *Acquiescens his qui tradiderunt* (perfect), translating . . . ἀνεχόμενος (variant reading: ἀνασχόμενος) τῶν παραδεδωκότων, BHMPSTZ Hol., confirmed as both archetype and Rufinus's text, L² 36; *tradiderant* (pluperfect) Zelz. following C, WLG.

[76] *De solo ipso* Zelz. following SP, and also B, J, T, in which some form of *solo* appears. But the case is complicated, says Lundström, L² 54, and for once he is noncommittal. If the reading is genuine, it is Rufinus's gloss, as it does not appear in the Greek.

5 But if he who presides and exercises the ministry of the word of God neglects to declare it to each and make it known in detail,[123] he shall be adjudged a murderer of souls according to the Scriptures (cf. Ezek 33:8).

Question 120

Q: Is he who does another's will an accomplice and associate of him whose will he does?

R: 1 If we believe the Lord who says: *anyone who commits sin is the slave of sin* (John 8:34) and again: *you are from your father, the devil, and it is the desires of your father you wish to accomplish* (John 8:44), **2** we know that one like this is not only an accomplice and associate but claims as his lord and father him whose work he does. **3** The Apostle also bears witness to this when he says: *Do you not know that if you yield yourselves to anyone as slaves for obedience, you are slaves of the one whom you obey, either of sin that leads to death, or of obedience that leads to righteousness?* (Rom 6:16).

Question 121

Q: If someone consents to another's sin, is he himself guilty of that sin?

R: 1 The condemnation for this is clear in the words which the Lord spoke to Pilate, saying: *The one who handed me over to you has the greater sin* (John 19:11). **2** From this it is clear that Pilate, in yielding to those who handed over the Lord, did sin, although less than they did. **3** This is also shown clearly from the fact that Adam yielded and consented to Eve, just as Eve had yielded to the serpent (cf. Gen 3:6), **4** for not one of them was judged innocent or escaped with impunity. Indeed, the very ire of God displayed against them, when carefully considered, shows this. **5** For when Adam objected as an excuse: *It was the woman you gave me. She gave it to me and so I ate* (Gen 3:12), God said: **6** *Because you heeded the voice of your wife and ate from the tree from which alone I forbade you to eat . . . cursed be the earth in all your works* (Gen 3:17).

---

[123] It seems *"de singulis"* refers to particular "offences" or "sins" as in Ezekiel, and Clarke even inserts it in a gloss, but it is not actually expressed in either the Greek or the Latin.

Interrogatio CXXII

(Zelzer 148–51, QF 108, SR 47 [PG 31.1113–1116])

I: Si oportet peccantibus fratribus silere et quiescere?

R: 1 Quia non oportet manifestum est ex ipsis domini praeceptis, quibus in vetere quidem testamento dicit *Argues proximum tuum et non assumes ex eo peccatum.* **2** In evangelio autem dicit *Si peccaverit in te frater tuus, vade et argue eum inter te et ipsum solum.* **3** *Si audierit te, lucratus es fratrem tuum, si vero non audierit te, assumes adhuc tecum alium unum aut duos ut in ore duorum vel trium testium stet omne verbum.* **4** *Si autem et ipsos non audierit, dic ecclesiae; si vero nec ecclesiam audierit, sit tibi sicut gentilis et publicanus.*

5 Quantum autem sit crimen huius peccati dinoscitur primo quidem ex sententia domini qua dicit *Qui incredulus fuerit filio non habebit vitam* aeternam sed *ira dei manet super eum,* **6** tum deinde ex historiis quae vel in veteri vel in novo testamento referuntur. **7** Nam Achar ille cum furatus est[77] linguam[78] auream, super omnem populum facta est ira domini, et quidem[79] populo peccatum quod commiserat ignorante usquequo manifestatus est, et pertulit cum omni domo sua horrendum illum ac famosissimum interitum.

8 Sed et Heli sacerdos, et quidem[80] cum non siluisset peccantibus filiis qui errant filii pestilentiae, immo et frequenter commonens et castigans et dicens **9** *Nolite filii, non bona audio ego de vobis* et cetera, quae vel peccatum arguerent vel de dei iudicio commonerent, **10** tamen quoniam non vindicavit neque digno zelo dei adversum eos motus est, in tantum dei iracundiam provocavit, **11** ut etiam universus populus pariter cum filiis suis exstingueretur et arca testamenti ab alienigenis raperetur, et ipse insuper omnibus subversi miseranda morte corrueret.

---

[77] *Furatus est* Zelz. following ESJ; *furatus esset* (normal syntax of a *cum* clause) in all other MSS. Lundström, L^2 51, is uncertain of the preferable reading, though he points out that *cum furatus est* is an exact translation of of ἡνίκα ἔκλεψε.

[78] *Linguam* Zelz. following EJS and Greek γλῶσσαν μίαν χρυσῖν, confirmed L^2 50; *regulam* (Vulgate normalization) C, P, G, THMZ; other variants.

[79] *Et quidem* most MSS, Hol., confirmed L^2 61; *e[t]quidem* (= *equidem*) conj. Zelz. following the Greek καίτοιγε.

[80] *Et quidem* most MSS, Hol., confirmed L^2 61; *equidem* conjectured by Zelz. following ES (καίπερ).

Question 122

Q: Should we keep silent and be quiet towards brothers who sin?

R: 1 That we should not is clear from the very precepts of the Lord, first in the Old Testament where he says: *Indeed you shall reprove your neighbour and in this way not contract sin on his account* (Lev 19:17). **2** Further, in the gospel he says: *If your brother sins against you, go and confront him, between you and him alone.* **3** *If he listens to you, you have gained your brother; if he does not listen, then take with you one or two others, since "in the mouth of two or three witnesses every word is established"* (Deut 19:15). **4** *But if he refuses to listen to these, tell it to the church; if however he refuses to listen even to the church, let him be to you as the Gentile and the tax-collector* (Matt 18:15-17).

5 But how great is the condemnation of this sin can be learned first of all from that pronouncement of the Lord where he says: *Whoever disobeys the Son shall not have eternal life, but the wrath of God stays over him* (John 3:36), **6** and second, from stories related in both the Old and New Testaments. **7** For when that Achan (cf. Josh 7:20-26) stole the wedge of gold, the wrath of God came down on the whole people as well—even though the people were ignorant of the sin committed till it was brought to light—and he with all his house suffered that fearful and most famous destruction.

8 Yes and there is Eli the priest too (cf. 1 Sam 2:22–4:18).[124] Although he did not pass over in silence the sins of his own sons—who were baleful sons indeed—but warned them frequently and chastised them saying: **9** *No, my sons, the things I hear about you are not good* (1 Sam 2:24) and so on, and pointed out the sin and warned of the judgment of God, **10** yet because he neither put things right nor was moved by a fitting zeal for God against them, he provoked such a wrath from God **11** that the whole people itself, together with his sons, were destroyed and the Ark of the Covenant was snatched by alien hands, while he himself, overwhelmed by all these disasters, fell backwards in a miserable death.

---

[124] For Basil, Eli's failure to *effectively* correct his sons was a great cautionary tale, teaching the responsibility of superiors to confront sins and ensure that they are remedied. See the extended treatment in *De Iudicio* 5–6 (PG 31 664D–665B, Clarke, 83), where Basil combats the idea that there are "small" sins that can be treated lightly and is vitally concerned to inculcate the practice of evangelical correction.

12 Quodsi vel in populum ignorantem de unius peccato vel in patrem qui commonuerat et corripuerat filios pro peccato tanta dei iracundia accensa est, **13** quid sperandum est de his qui cognoscunt aliorum delicta et reticent nec qualemcumque adhibent correptionem? **14** Quos utique conveniret observare illud quod apostolus ad Corinthios dicit, *Qua re non potius luctum habuistis ut tolleretur e medio vestrum qui hoc opus fecit?* et aliqua, **15** vel illud, *Ecce enim hoc ipsum, secundum deum contristari, quantum operatum est vobis, sollicitudinem; sed excusationem, se indignationem, sed timorem, sed desiderium, sed aemulationem, sed vindictam.*

16 Unde et metuere debent ne forte etiam nunc similem veteribus interitum sumant hi qui similiter neglegunt, immo et gravius quanto spernere legem Christi perniciosius est quam legem Moysi. **17** Et his competit illud aptari quod dixit *Septies vindicatum est de Cain, de Lamech vero septuagies septies.*

Interrogatio CXXIII
(Zelzer 151–53, QF 109, SR 16 [PG 31.1091–1094])

I: Cur aliquotiens animae etiamsi non satis agat sponte tamen quodam genere incidit ei[81] dolor quidam cordis et compunctio timoris dei, aliquotiens autem tanta securitas et neglegentia animum tenet, ut etiamsi cogat se homo non possit dolorem aliquem vel compunctionem cordis assumere?

R: **1** Huiuscemodi quidem compunctio ex dei dono venit ad provocandum desiderium, ut degustans anima dulcedinem huiuscemodi compunctionis vel doloris provocetur et invitetur a imitandam similem gratiam. **2** Ostenditur enim quia si datur etiam non satis agentibus, quanto magis dabitur et his qui desiderant et laborant semper esse in compunctione timoris dei, **3** et ut sint inexcusabiles qui per neglegentiam istam gratiam perdunt.

---

[81] *Ei* B, J, WLG, MT, H, Hol., confirmed L² 28; omitted by Zelz. following SCP.

12 Now if so great a wrath from God blazed out against the people ignorant of one sin, and against a father who warned and corrected his sons for their sin, **13** what hope do they have who know of the sins of others and remain silent and apply no correction whatever? **14** It assuredly behooves them to observe what the Apostle said to the Corinthians: *Why did you not mourn instead, so that the one who did this deed might be removed from your midst?* (1 Cor 5:2) and so on, **15** and also: *Behold, through this very thing which caused grief according to God, what great things it accomplished in you! What anxiety, what clearing of yourselves, what indignation, what fear, what longing, what emulation, what putting of things right!* (2 Cor 7:11).

16 Hence they too must fear lest even now they incur a similar destruction as they did of old who were negligent in like fashion, or rather incur something even graver, inasmuch as to spurn the Law of Christ is more calamitous than to spurn the Law of Moses (cf. Heb 10:28-29). **17** And on this it is fitting to apply what was said: *Cain was avenged sevenfold, but Lamech seventy-sevenfold* (Gen 4:24).

Question 123

Q: Why is it that sometimes upon the soul, without much effort, spontaneously as it were, a kind of sorrowing of heart falls upon it, and a compunction from the fear of God, while at other times so great a listlessness or negligence holds down the soul that even though a man forces himself, he cannot assume any sorrow or compunction of heart?

R: 1 Such a compunction comes from the gift of God to stir up desire, that the soul, having tasted the sweetness of such compunction or sorrow, might be stirred and drawn to imitate such a grace. **2** For it is shown that if it is given even to those who have not much stirred themselves, how much more shall it be given to those who desire and labour always to be in the compunction of the fear of God, **3** and that those who lose this grace through indolence are without excuse.

4 Quod vero aliquotiens compellimus nosmet ipsos et non possumus obtinere indicatur ex hoc quod in alio tempore multum neglegimus. **5** Non enim possible est ut is qui neque meditationibus neque institutionibus divinis se ipsum iugiter exercuit subito veniat ad orationem et continuo obtineat quod requirit, **6** sed et ostenditur per hoc huiuscemodi animam aliis vitiis vel passionibus praegravari, quorum dominatione ad ea quae vult habere non permittitur libertatem **7** secundum illud quod apostolus tractat dicens quoniam *Ego carnalis sum venundatus sub peccato; non enim quod volo hoc ago sed quod odio hoc facio*, **8** et rursum *Nunc autem non ego operor illud sed quod habitat in me peccatum.*

9 Quod et ipsum permittit nobis deus pro nostra utilitate provenire, ut per haec ipsa quae contra voluntatem anima patitur corrigatur aliquando et convertatur ad eum qui relevet eam ab oneribus suis **10** et cognoscat tandem semet ipsam ac resipiscat et intellegat quod in *laqueis diaboli* capta detinetur, **11** in quos[82] sua quidem sponte incidit, sed iam quasi captiva non quod vult agit, sed quod odit illud facit. **12** Sed si se convertat[83] ad dominum qui liberet eam de corpore mortis huius statim inveniet misercordiam, si integre et corde paeniteat.

Interrogatio CXXIIII
(Zelzer 154, QF 111, SR 204 [PG 31.1217–1218])

I: Quomodo quis dignus efficitur *particeps* fieri *spiritus sancti*?

R: 1 Dominus noster Iesus Christus docuit dicens *Si diligitis me mandata mea servate et ego rogabo patrem, et alium paraclitum dabit vobis, spiritum veritatis quem hic mundus non potest accipere*. **2** Donec ergo non servamus omnia mandata domini nec sumus tales, ut ipse de nobis testimonium ferat dicens *Quia* vos *non estis de* hoc *mundo*, spiritus sancti participium habere non possumus.

---

[82] *Quos* (i.e., *laqueos*) Zelz. following SJ, G Hol., confirmed L² 49; a great variety in other MSS, beginning with *quo*, an archetype error, in C.

[83] *Se convertat* Zelz. following SJ, B after correction, confirmed L² 52–53; *se* omitted in all other MSS "In β, *se* surely dropped out through haplography," Lundström.

4 But the fact that sometimes we force ourselves and yet are unable to obtain it is proof thereby that we are negligent at other times—**5** for it is impossible that one who has not continually exercised himself either in meditations or in the divine ordinances should suddenly turn to prayer and immediately obtain what he seeks. **6** Yes, and it shows thereby that a soul of this kind is oppressed by other vices and passions, the ascendancy of which does not allow it the freedom for those things it wishes to possess, **7** according to what the Apostle dealt with, saying: *I am carnal, sold under sin; for what I want, this I do not perform, but what I hate, this is what I do* (Rom 7:14-15) **8** and again: *But now it is no longer I who am doing this, but rather sin that dwells in me* (Rom 7:17).

9 God has permitted this very thing to befall us for a good purpose, so that through the very things that the soul suffers against its will, it may in time be corrected and converted to him who will allieviate it of its burdens (cf. Ezek 18:23; 33:11) **10** and at length come to know itself and recover its senses and understand that it has been seized and held down in *the snares of the devil* (cf. 1 Tim 3:7; 6:9; 2 Tim 2:26), **11** into which it has fallen of its own accord, so that as a captive *what it does not want it performs and what it hates it does* (cf. Rom 7:15). **12** But if it turns to the Lord so that he may *liberate* it *from the body of this death* (Rom 7:24), immediately it shall discover mercy, provided it repents wholly and from the heart.

Question 124

Q: How is someone made worthy of becoming a *partaker of the Holy Spirit?* [125] (Heb 6:4)

R: 1 Our Lord Jesus Christ taught us when he said: *If you love me, keep my commandments and I myself will ask the Father and he will give you another Paraclete, the Spirit of truth, whom the world cannot receive* (John 14:15-17). **2** Therefore, insofar as we do not keep all the commandments of the Lord and are not such of whom he bears testimony, saying: *you are not of this world* (John 15:19), we cannot have participation in the Holy Spirit.

---

[125] Here Basil brings the "mystical" pretentions of Eustathian and pre-Messalian enthusiasts back to base with the Johannine call of concrete obedience to the commandments. See also RBas 2.2 and note and RBas 168.

Interrogatio CXXV

(Zelzer 154–55, QF 112, SR 205 [PG 31.1217–1218])

I: Qui sunt *pauperes spiritu*?

R: 1 Domino dicente aliquando quidem quia *Verba quae ego locutus sum vobis spiritus et vita est,* **2** aliquando autem quia *Spiritus sanctus ipse vos docebit omnia et commonebit vos quae dixi vobis, non enim loquitur a se, sed omnia quae audiet haec loquitur,* **3** isti sunt *pauperes spiritu* qui non alia aliqua causa pauperes sunt nisi doctrinam domini dicentis *Vade et vende* omnia *quae habes et da pauperibus.*

4 Si autem quis etiam quacumque ex causa impositam sibi paupertatem secundum voluntatem domini dispenset et ferat sicut ille *Lazarus,* etiam iste a beatitudine non erit alienus **5** domino praecipiente *Nolite solliciti esse quid manduce*tis *vel biba*tis *vel quid indua*mini.

Interrogatio CXXVI

(Zelzer 155–56, QF 113, SR 206 [PG 31.1219–1220])

I: Usque ad quem modum est observatio mandati vel quomodo adimpleri potest?

R: 1 Mandati quidem observatio est usque ad mortem, quia et dominus *oboediens factus est usque ad mortem;* adimpleri autem potest per hoc quod habet unusquisque desiderium et amorem dei. **2** Dominus enim cum exclusisset *sollicitud*inem *saecul*i coniungi statim promissionis spem dicens *Scit enim pater vester quibus opus habetis antequam vos petatis.*

3 Sed et apostolus dicit quia *Ipsi in nobis ipsis responsum mortis habuimus ut non simus fidentes in nobis sed in deo qui suscitat mortuos.* **4** Secundum propositum ergo nostrum et animae praeparationem *cotidie mori*mur, voluntate autem dei reservamur. **5** Propter quod et apostolus cum omni fiducia dicebat *Ut morientes et ecce vivimus.*

Question 125

Q: Who are the *poor in spirit*? (Matt 5:3)

R: 1 Since the Lord at one time says: *The words which I have spoken to you are spirit and life* (John 6:63), **2** and at another time: *The Holy Spirit will teach you all things and bring to your remembrance all that I have said to you . . . for he shall not speak as from himself, but all the things that he shall hear, these he will speak* (John 14:26; 16:13), **3** the *poor in spirit* are those who are poor for no other cause but for that teaching of the Lord who said: *Go and sell all that you have and give to the poor* (Matt 19:21).[126]

4 But even if someone governs the poverty imposed on him from whatever cause and and bears it like Lazarus (cf. Luke 16:19-25), such a one will not be a stranger to blessedness either, **5** since the Lord commanded: *Do not be anxious about what you shall eat or what you shall drink or what you shall put on* (Matt 6:31).[127]

Question 126

Q: Up to what measure is the observance of the commandment, and how can it be fulfilled?

R: 1 The keeping of a commandment is *even to death*, for the Lord himself *became obedient even to death* (Phil 2:8). It can be fulfilled by means of the desire and love that each has for God. **2** For when the Lord had excluded *the anxiety of the world* (cf. Matt 6:31), he immediately added the hope of a promise, saying: *For your Father knows what you need before you ask him* (Matt 6:8 + 6:32).

3 The Apostle also says: *We received the sentence of death, in order that we might trust not in ourselves, but in God who raises the dead* (2 Cor 1:9). **4** Hence, in accordance with our resolve and preparedness of soul *we die daily* (cf. 1 Cor 15:31), but we are kept safe in the will of God. **5** This is why the Apostle could say with all confidence: *as dying and behold, we live!* (2 Cor 6:9).

---

[126] Basil seems to mean here that only *intentional* poverty for the Lord merits the title of poverty of spirit. Yet, as he shortly points out, even economic poverty, "worldly" poverty so to speak, can be turned to poverty of spirit through the dispositions in which it is lived.

[127] This scriptural passage forms the introduction to the next question in both the Greek and Syriac text. RBas has mistakenly appended it to RBas 125.

6 Iuvat autem huiuscemodi propositum etiam circa mandata dei ardentior animus et desiderium insatiabile, quo qui constringitur non habebit otiosum ad haec[84] tempus occupari erga corporales usus vel actus.

Interrogatio CXXVII
(Zelzer 156–58, QF 114, SR 207 [PG 31.1219–1222])

I: Si ergo neque sollicitudinem habere oportet de necessariis usibus ad vitam, et aliud praeceptum est domini dicentis *Operamini cibum qui non perit*, superfluum est manibus operari?

R: 1 Ipse dominus in alio loco praeceptum suum explanavit, nam ibi quidem dixit non oportere quaeri aliquid ad vitam cum dicit **2** *Nolite quaerere quid manducetis aut quid bibatis, haec enim omnia gentes* huius *mundi requirunt*, et addidit *Quaerite autem regnum dei et iustitiam eius.*

3 Et quomodo oporteat quaeri indicavit; cum enim dixisset *Nolite operari cibum qui perit*, addidit *Sed eum qui permanet in vitam aeternam.* **4** Et quid hoc esset ipse in alio loco ostendit dicens *Meus cibus est ut faciam voluntatem eius qui me misit, patris*; voluntas autem patris est *esuri*entibus cibum dare, *siti*entibus potum, *nudos operi*re et ceterea huiusmodi. **5** Tum deinde necessarium est et apostolum imitari dicentem *Omnia ostendi vobis quia ita oportet* nos *laborantes suscipere infirmos*, **6** et cum iterum docet *Magis autem laboret* unusquisque *manibus suis operans quod bonum est, ut possit impertire necessitatem patienti.*

7 Cum ergo haec ita nobis vel dominus in evangelio vel apostolus tradat, manifestum est quia pro nobis ipsis quidem solliciti esse non debemus neque laborare, **8** propter mandatum autem domini et propter necessitates proximorum solliciti esse debemus et operari attentius **9** et[85] maxime quod dominus in se ipsum recipit ea quae in servos eius fecerimus et regnum caelorum pro huiusmodi promittit obsequiis.

---

[84] *Otiosum ad haec* restored L[2] 67–68, following *otiosum* in C before correction, S, and the omission of *nec* in S; *otium nec* Zelz. following *otium* C after correction, and *ocia* P.

[85] *Et* Zelz. most MSS, confirmed L[2] 29, 62; *eo* CPJ.

6 Aiding such a resolve is a burning zeal and an insatiable desire for the commandments of God, so that anyone constrained in this way will have no leisure time left over from this to be taken up with the needs and activities of the body.

Question 127

Q: Well then, if we ought *not to be anxious* about the necessities of life (Matt 6:31) and there is the other precept of the Lord that says: *Do not labour for the food that perishes* (John 6:27), is it superfluous to work with our hands?[128]

R: 1 The Lord himself explained his own precept in another place. For there he said that we must not seek anything for this life when he says: **2** *Do not seek what you shall eat or what you shall drink, for these things all the nations of* this *world seek,* and added: *Seek rather the kingdom of God and his justice* (Luke 12:29-30 + Matt 6:31-33).

3 He also indicated how we ought to seek, for in the same place, having said: *Do not labour for the food which perishes,* he added: *but for that which endures to eternal life* (John 6:27). **4** And what this might be he showed in another place, saying: *My food is to do the will of the Father who sent me* (John 4:34; cf. 6:38-39). Now the Father's will is that we give food to *the hungry* and drink to *the thirsty, clothe the naked* and the rest like this (cf. Matt 25:35-36). **5** Then it is necessary that we also imitate the Apostle who says: *I have given you example in all things that by so labouring you ought to support the weak* (Acts 20:35), **6** and again when he teaches: *Let each do honourable work with his own hands that he may have something to give to one who is suffering necessity* (Eph 4:28).

7 When therefore the Lord in the gospel or the Apostle delivers these things to us, it is clear that we ought not be anxious or labour for ourselves, **8** but we ought to be anxious and to work diligently on account of the Lord's commandment and on account of our neighbours' necessities, **9** and that above all because the things that we do for his servants the Lord receives to himself and promises in return for these services the kingdom of heaven (cf. Matt 25:40).

---

[128] The questioner voices the thinking of some hyperascetics that "higher" spirituality emancipates from the necessity of mundane work. This was an identifying trait of the Messalians at century's end. Basil typically cures the error by a summons to the Gospel realism of service to the poor.

Interrogatio CXXVIII
(Zelzer 158–59, QF 115, SR 17 [PG 31.1093–1094])

I: Si quis in corde suo cogitet de cibis, tum deinde notet se ipsum et arguat, si et hic quasi cogitans de talibus iudicandus sit?

R: 1 Si quidem non id temporis est quo naturaliter requirere cibos famis necessitate commonemur, manifestum est id esse vagae mentis indicium et animae erga praesentia affectum gerentis, et erga voluntatem dei desidis et remissae, **2** proximam tamen habet dei misericordiam, et pro hoc ipso quod se ipsum arguit et notavit nota criminis exuitur, si tamen servet de cetero cogitationum lapsus **3** memor dominici sermonis quo ait *Ecce sanus factus es, iam noli peccare, ne quid tibi deterius fiat*. **4** Si autem id temporis sit quo naturaliter de cibis appetendis commonemur, mens autem in melioribus occupata inferiora spernit et despicit, non recordatio ciborum notabilis, sed contemptus laudabilis invenitur.

Interrogatio CXXVIIII
(Zelzer 159, QF 116, SR 90 [PG 31.1145–1146])

I: Si licet nocturnam tunicam habere alteram vel cilicium vel aliam quamlibet?

R: 1 Cilicii quidem usus habet propriam tempus, non enim propter usum corporis, sed propter afflictionem eius inventum est huiuscemodi indumentum et pro humilitate animae. **2** Cum autem *duas tunicas* habere prohibeat sermo divinus, quomodo potest hoc suscipi nisi ad eos usus de quibus supra diximus?

Question 128

Q: If someone thinks in his heart about *eating*, then condemns and reproves himself, is he to be judged for thinking about such things (cf. Matt 6:25)?

R: 1 If the thought arose before the due time when we are naturally urged by the necessity of hunger to seek food, it is manifestly an indication of a wandering mind and of a soul attached to present things and listless and indolent towards the will of God. **2** Even so, he has God's mercy at hand. For inasmuch as he has condemned and reproved himself for this, the sting of the offence is drawn—if he only keeps himself from another lapse of his thoughts, **3** mindful of the Lord who said: *Behold you are made whole; do not sin again, lest something worse befall you* (John 5:14). **4** But if it occured at the proper time in which we are urged naturally by the appetite for food, but the mind, in its devotion to better things spurns and disdains the lesser then it is not the thought of eating that deserves blame, but its disregard that deserves praise.

Question 129

Q: Is it permissible to have a separate night tunic, whether of hair-cloth or anything else?

R: 1 The use of hair-cloth has its proper time;[129] for such a garment is not used for bodily need, but for the affliction and humbling of the soul. **2** But since the divine word forbids having *two tunics* (Matt 10:10; cf. Mark 6:9), how can this be adopted apart from those uses of which we spoke above?

---

[129] See Cassian, *Institutes* 1.2 (NPNF, ser. 2, vol. 11, 202): "(The fathers) utterly disapproved of a robe of sackcloth being visible to all and conspicuous, which from this very fact will not only confer no benefit on the soul but rather minister to vanity and pride and be inconvenient and unsuitable for the performance of necessary work."

Interrogatio CXXX
(Zelzer 160, QF 117, SR 151 [PG 31.1181–1182])

I: Si licet ei qui ministrat maiore voce id est cum *clamor*e loqui?

R: 1 Vocis mensuram definit audiendi modus; si ergo brevior fuerit et pressior vox quam res poscit, prope est ut murmur potius vel susurratio videatur quam sermo. **2** Si vero maior sit quam res requirit, cum possit audire ille cui loquimur etiamsi levius loquamur, hoc iam non erit vox sed *clamor*, **3** quod est notabile nisi si[86] forte gravior sit auditus eius cui loquimur et necessitas nos cogat ad clamandum. **4** Propterea enim et de domino scriptum est quia *Et*[87] *Iesus*, inquit, *clamabat dicens Si quis credit in me non credit in me sed in eum qui me misit.* **5** Clamare enim dicitur pro his quorum interior auditus surdus et obturatus erat.

Interrogatio CXXXI
(Zelzer 161, QF 118, SR 152 [PG 31.1181–1182])

I: Si quis die suo quo ministrat in coquina laboraverit supra vires ita ut impediatur et non possit etiam reliquis diebus exercere opus suum, si oportet imperare ei huiuscemodi officium?

R: 1 Iam supra diximus quia is cui iniuncta est operum cura et qui praeest consideratius observare debet uniuscuiusque vel vires vel possibilitatem **2** et prout quis aptus est ita etiam opus iniungere, ne audiat et ipse quod scriptum est *Qui fingit laborem in praecepto.* **3** Ille tamen cui iniungitur contradicere non debet, quia *oboedien*tia *usque ad mortem* servari definita est.

Interrogatio CXXXII
(Zelzer 161–62, QF 159, SR 153 [PG 31.1181–1184])

I: Et illa cui lana credita est, quomodo debet habere hanc curam et quomodo observare eas quae operantur?

R: 1 Lanam quidem tamquam opus dei sibi commissum, sorores autem ut absque ulla *contentio*ne vel *personarum acceptio*ne unicuique sorori opus apte et competenter iniungat.

---

[86] *Si* S, confirmed L² 54; cf. 137.4; *si* omitted Zelz. following C and most MSS.

[87] *Et* SC (after correction), P, J (after correction), confirmed L² 24; omitted by Zelz. following most other MSS.

Question 130

Q: Is it permissible for anyone ministering to speak with a loud voice, that is, with *crying out*? (Eph 4:31)

R: 1 The mode of hearing defines the measure of the voice. So if the voice is lower or more subdued than occasion requires, it would seem to be nearer to murmuring or whispering rather than speech. **2** But if it is louder than the occasion requires, such that the one to whom we speak could hear if we spoke in a softer voice, this will not be a "voice," but that *crying out* (Eph 4:31) **3** which is blameworthy, unless the hearing of him to whom we speak is harder, and necessity constrains us to *cry out*. **4** For as far as that goes, it is even written of the Lord: *And Jesus*, it says, *cried out saying "If anyone believes in me, he believes not in me, but in the one who sent me"* (John 12:44). **5** For it was spoken with a *crying out* because of those whose inner hearing was dull and obdurate (cf. Ps 94:8).

Question 131

Q: When someone serves in the kitchen on his own day, but works beyond his strength, so that he is hindered and unable to perform his own work for days afterward, should we assign him such an office?

R: 1 We already said above that the one entrusted with the arrangement of tasks and the one who presides ought to note carefully the strength and capacity of each, **2** and, as each is suited, so also assign the task, lest he should hear what is written: *those who frame toil by decree* (Ps 93:20). **3** The one obeying, however, must not contradict, for the limit of *obedience* to be observed is *unto death* (cf. Phil 2:8).

Question 132

Q: And she to whom the wool is entrusted, how ought she approach this responsibility and how keep watch over the workers?

R: 1 The wool, on the one hand, as the work of God entrusted to her, and her sisters, on the other, such that without any *contentiousness* (cf. 2 Cor 12:20; Gal 5:20) or *respect of persons* (cf. Deut 10:17; Matt 22:16; Rom 2:11; Eph 6:9) she appropriately and fittingly assigns to each sister her task.

Interrogatio CXXXIII
(Zelzer 162, QF 119, SR 122 [PG 31.1165–1166])

I: Si quis condematus est ut eulogiam non accipiat et dicit quia Si non accepero eulogiam non manduco, si debemus audire eum?

R: 1 Si quidem tantimodi est culpa pro qua condemnatus est ut dignum sit etiam a cibo eum vetari probet ille qui praeest. **2** Si autem a sola benedictione aliquis abstentus est et indulgetur ei cibus, condemnatus autem et inoboediens est, etiam in hoc *contentio*si notam suscipere debet et cognoscere quia per hoc non curat culpam sed multiplicat delictum.

Interrogatio CXXXIIII
(Zelzer 162–64, QF 120, SR 172 [PG 31.1195–1196])

I: Quali timore vel fide vel affectu percipere debemus corporis et sanguinis Christi gratiam?

R: 1 Timorem quidem docet nos apostolus dicens *Qui manducat et bibit indigne iudicium sibi manducat et bibit.*

2 Fidem vero docet nos sermo domini dicens *Hoc est corpus meum quod pro* multis *datur, hoc facite in mei commemorationem,* **3** et sermo Iohannis dicens quia *Verbum caro factum est et habitavit in nobis et vidimus gloriam eius, gloriam sicut unigeniti a patre pleni gratiae et veritatis,* **4** sed et apostolus scribens quia *Cum in forma dei esset non rapinam arbitratus est esse se aequalem deo, sed semet ipsum exinanivit formam servi accipiens,* **5** *in similitudine hominum factus et habitu repertus ut homo humiliavit se ipsum, factus oboediens usque a mortem, mortem autem crucis.*

Question 133

Q: If someone is punished by not receiving a blessing and says: "If I am not to receive a blessing, I will not eat," must we listen to him?

R: 1 Whether the fault for which he is punished is such as to merit his exclusion from meals is entirely for the one who presides to decide. **2** But if someone is kept only from the blessing, while food is allowed him, yet though already censured, disobeys as well, then he ought to receive blame also for *contentiousness* (cf. 1 Cor 11:16) and realize that by this means he is not curing his fault but multiplying his offence.

Question 134

Q: With what fear or faith[130] or disposition should we partake of the gift of the Body and Blood of Christ?[131]

R: 1 The fear, at any rate, the Apostle teaches when he says: *Whoever eats and drinks unworthily, eats and drinks judgment upon himself* (1 Cor 11:29).

2 As to the faith, the word of the Lord teaches which says: *This is my body which is given for many, do this as a commemoration of me* (Luke 22:19; 1 Cor 11:24), **3** and the discourse of John which says: *the Word became flesh and dwelt among us and we saw his glory, the glory as of the only-begotten of the Father, full of grace and truth* (John 1:14), **4** and further, the Apostle writes: *though he was in the form of God, he did not deem equality with God as something to be grasped, but emptied himself, accepting the form of a slave,* **5** *being made in the likeness of human beings; and being found in human form, he humbled himself and became obedient unto death, even death on a cross* (Phil 2:6-8).

---

[130] SR 172 1196A ἢ ποίᾳ πληροφορίᾳ. Rufinus frequently translates πληροφορίαν, "conviction," with *fides*, a reasonable approximation. Yet Basil, when revising the Greek text that lay behind RBas 134.2, used the actual Greek word for faith, πίστις.

[131] Cf. the liturgical echoes of RBas 2.44-50 and notes. For similar teaching on the manner of approaching the Eucharist, using the same texts, see *Morals* 21.2, 3.

6 Cum ergo anima fidem habet his dictis et considerat magnificentiam gloriae ipsius et admiratur nimietatem humilitatis, quomodo tantus et talis *oboediens* fuit patri *usque a mortem* pro nostra vita, **7** puto quia possit provocari ad affectum et dilectionem et ipsius dei et patris qui unico *filio non perpercit, sed pro nobis omnibus tradidit eum*; **8** et ad amorem unigeniti eius eo amplius provacabitur, cum videat *mortem turpissimum* pro nostra redemptione tolerasse. **9** Sicut et apostolus de eo dicebat quia *Caritas Christi constringit nos iudicantes hoc, quod si unus pro omnibus mortuus est, ergo omnes mortui sunt, et pro omnibus mortuus est, ut qui vivunt iam non sibi vivant, sed ei qui pro ipsis mortuus est et resurrexit.*

10 Talem ergo affectum vel fidem praeparare debet in animo suo is qui panem et calicem percipit.

Interrogatio CXXXV
(Zelzer 164–65, QF 121, SR 239 [PG 31.1241–1242])

I: Quid est *bonus thesaurus* et quis *malus*?

R: 1 Prudentia quidem et sensus qui in Christo est, et virtus animi quae ad dei gloriam pertinet, *thesaurus* est *bonus*; prudentia autem et sensus malitiae, et in his sapere quae deus fieri non vult, *thesaurus* est *malus*. **2** Ex quibus proferuntur secundum domini vocem suo quoque tempore utrique fructus vel boni vel mali in operibus et verbis.

6 When the soul therefore has faith in these sayings and considers the majesty of his glory and wonders at the excess of his humility, that one so great and of such a nature was obedient to the Father *even unto death, that we might live,* **7** I think the soul might well be stirred to affection and love for that same God and Father *who did not spare his only son, but delivered him up for us all* (Rom 8:32), **8** and to love for his Only-begotten to which it will be stirred even more when it sees how he bore *a most shameful death for our redemption* (cf. Wis 2:20). **9** Just so the Apostle spoke of this: *the love of Christ constrains us when we consider this, that if one man died for all, therefore all have died. And he died for all so that those who live might live no longer for themselves but for him who died for them and rose again* (2 Cor 5:14-15).

10 Such then is the disposition and the faith he must prepare in his own mind who partakes of the Bread and the Cup.

Question 135

Q: What is the *good treasure* and what the *evil*? (cf. Matt 12:35; Luke 6:45)

R: 1 The *good treasure* is the prudence and sensibility in Christ and the virtue of the mind which leads to the glory of God; whereas the *evil treasure* is the shrewdness and sensibility of malice with which to discern all that God wills should not be done. **2** From these are brought forth, according to Lord's utterance, each in its own kind, either good or evil in deeds and in words (cf. Luke 6:45; Matt 7:17-20; 12:33-35).

Interrogatio CXXXVI
(Zelzer 165–66, QF 122, SR 208 [PG 31.1221–1222])

I: Si bonus est penitus tacere?

R: 1 Silentium et taciturnitas tunc bonum est cum vel ad personas vel ad tempus aptatur sicut a sancta scriptura edocemur, quae dicit aliquando quidem quia *Qui intellegit in illo tempore tacebit, quia tempus malum est,* **2** aliquando autem *Posui ori meo custodiam, dum consistit peccator adversum me, obmutui et humiliatus sum et silui a bonis,* **3** et alibi *Quodsi alii sedenti revelatum fuerit prior taceat,* et iterum, *Mulieres vestrae in ecclesiis taceant.* **4** Sed et alio tempore his qui incontinentem habent linguam dicitur *Omnis sermo malus de ore vestro non procedat, sed si quis bonus ad aedificationem fidei.* **5** Necessaria vero est taciturnitas usquequo vitia si qua illa sunt linguae vel sermonum temeritas resecetur, et discat opportune et in tempore et utiliter loqui **6** ut sicut scriptum est *Sermo eorum sale conditus sit, ut det gratiam audientibus.*

Interrogatio CXXXVII
(Zelzer 166–67, QF 123, SR 173 [PG 31.1197–1198])

I: Si oportet tempore orationum vel psalmorum loqui aliquem in domo?

R: 1 Praeter eos qui ministerii sollicitudinem generunt vel eos quibus disciplinae cura permissa est vel dispensationis operum, qui et ipsi tamen consideratius agere debent **2**—ut quantum necessitas exigit hoc solum loquantur, et hoc ipsum cum quiete et honestate ne interturbent aut offendiculum faciant ceteris—cunctos reliquos silentium habere convenit.

3 si enim prophetis in ecclesia docentibus apostolus dicit quia *Si sedenti revelatum fuerit prior taceat,* quanto magis in tempore psalmorum vel orationum tacere et silentium agere cunctis convenit **4** nisi si[88] quem forte ut superius diximus communis providentiae causa aliquid proloqui cogit.

---

[88] *Nisi si* CS, B, confirmed L¹ 389, L² 54 as Rufinus's text; *si* omitted by Zelz. with β.

Question 136

Q: Is it good to practise complete silence?

R: 1 Silence and taciturnity are good when they befit the time and the person, as we are taught by the holy Scripture, which says on one occasion: *He who understands will keep silent at that time, for it is an evil time* (Amos 5:13), **2** and again on another occasion: *I set a guard over my mouth, when the sinner rose up against me; I was dumb and humbled myself and kept silent even from good things* (Ps 38:1-2), **3** and elsewhere: *If a revelation is made to one seated, let the one who was speaking first keep silent* (1 Cor 14:30) and again: *let the women among you keep silent in the churches* (1 Cor 14:34). **4** And there is also another occasion when it says to those who have an incontinent tongue: *Let no evil speech proceed from your mouth, but only what is good for the upbuilding of the faith* (Eph 4:29). **5** Now taciturnity is necessary at all times until the vices of the tongue and rashness of speech are pruned and one learns to speak appropriately and at the right time and beneficially, **6** as it is written: *Let their speech be seasoned with salt . . . that it may impart grace to the hearers* (Col 4:6; Eph 4:29).

Question 137

Q: Should anyone be speaking in the house during the hour of prayers or psalmody?[132]

R: 1 Except for those who have the responsibility of service, or those whom the care of discipline or the arrangement of tasks permits, and they too ought to take great care **2** that they speak only as necessity requires and do so quietly and respectfully, refraining from making any disturbance or even a small annoyance for the others. It is fitting that all the rest maintain silence.

3 For if the Apostle says even to prophets who are teaching in the church: *If there is a revelation to one seated, let the one who was speaking first fall silent* (1 Cor 14:30), then how much more at the time of psalmody or prayers is it fitting that all refrain from speech and observe silence, **4** unless perhaps as we said above, because of the common supervision there is need of speech.

---

[132] SR 173 1197A: Should there be any speech at the hour of psalmody in the house (ἐν τῇ ὥρᾳ τῆς κατ᾽ οἶκον ψαλμῳδίας). QF 123.Q: Should anyone be speaking during the hour of psalmody? The *"vel"* in *orationum vel psalmorum* suggests a Rufinian hendiadys, in which the psalms themselves are considered *"orationes."* Cf. RBas 107. On this point see the section "Psalms and Silent *Oratio*" in Gribomont, "Commentaries," 253 n. 60. Clarke, 293, offers this translation of the Greek: "at the hour of the

Interrogatio CXXXVIII

(Zelzer 167, QF 124, SR 209 [PG 31.1221–1222])

I: Quomodo possumus timere iudicia dei?

R: 1 Naturaliter exspectatio omni mali timorem incutit; ita namque etiam bestias timemus et principes, scientes imminere ex his aliquid quod ad vitae exitum pertinet. **2** Si ergo credamus quia verae sunt comminationes futuri iudicii dei et recordemur terribile illud futuri examinis tribunal, timebimus iudicia dei.

Question 138

Q: In what way are we to fear the judgments of God? (cf. Heb 10:27)[133]

R: 1 The expectation of anything evil naturally strikes fear. Thus, we fear both wild beasts and rulers, knowing that what comes from them is something that threatens the end of life. **2** If therefore we believe that the warnings of God's future judgment are true, and keep in mind the terrible tribunal of our future examination, we shall fear the judgments of God!

Office in the several houses" (κατ᾽ οἶκον) and then goes on to query whether there were individual "houses" within the community, such that the Office was prayed separately in each of them. He points to examples from *Lausiac History* 7.2, 5, "where the Nitrian monks are said to live either alone or in groups and 'the strains of psalmody arise from each habitation' and Jerome's version of Pachomius's rules, where the *praepositi domorum* are the superiors of the various houses within the big monastery (Ladeuze, *Cénobitisme pakhomien*, p. 293)." However, the known character of Macrina's community and Basil's high cenobitic doctrine do not support the idea of separate liturgies in separate houses. In the *Great Asketikon* LR 3 and 7 and LR 15.1 we read of the constituent "houses" forming a single *adelphotes* praying in the one "house of prayer" (ἐπὶ τὸν οἶκον τῆς προσευχῆς). See also Letter 207 (Def III, 186–87), which surely reflects arrangements at Annisa. Consequently, τῆς κατ᾽ οἶκον ψαλμῳδίας refers either to "house" as a figure for the entire community, or more probably to the "house of prayer" itself and whether there may be extraneous speech there during the actual hour of psalmody. The mention shortly of "the place" (τοῦ τε τόπου) and the ease with which those at psalmody might be disturbed also suggests proximity in a single locale, the "house of prayer" itself. An instance might occur when others who are legitimately absent (see RBas 107) find it necessary to come in with an urgent message for the superior or other officials. Cf. RB 42.10-11 on speech during the night silence: *excepto si necessitas hospitum supervenerit, aut forte abbas alicui aliquid iusserit, quod tamen et ipsum cum summa gravitate et moderatione honestissima fiat.*

[133] This response illustrates Basil's pragmatic view of emperors and the imperial system. Like Athanasius, Basil was no subscriber to the Eusebian / Constantinian ideology of a merging of church and empire. This is unsurprising since most of his adult years were spent under the Arian emperors of the East, Constantius and Valens; the latter in particular was emperor all through his years as bishop. Basil in many ways harked back to an ante-Nicene, early Christian view of church/state relations.

Interrogatio CXXXVIIII
(Zelzer 167–68, QF 125, SR 240 [PG 31.1243–1244])

I: Quomodo *lata est porta et spatiosa via quae ducit ad* mortem?

R: 1 Dominus pro multa clementia sua et nominibus et verbis his utitur quibus possit nobis in notitiam adducere dogmata veritatis. **2** Sicut ergo hi qui ambulant in via, si a recto itinere declinent quod certis lineis et manifesto[89] calle concluditur, spatia multa et vaga incident,[90] **3** ita ergo, ait, et is qui excesserit viam[91] quae ducit ad regnum caelorum multam latitudinem erroris incurrit per quam ad perditionem pervenitur.

Interrogatio CXXXX
(Zelzer 168–69, QF 126, SR 241 [PG 31.1243–1244])

I: Quomodo *angusta porta et arta via est quae ducit ad vitam*?

R: 1 Et hic similiter angustum et artum hoc indicat quia via haec id est vita nostra angustatur et coartatur in tribulationibus, **2** constringimur enim ex utraque parte nos qui iter agimus ne prorsus in aliud aliquid declinemus. **3** Periculum enim est in utramlibet[92] partem declinare, sicut in exigui pontis transitu ubi ex utraque parte eum qui forte declinaverit conciti fluminis unda rapiat et auferat. **4** Propterea ergo scriptum est *Ne declinaveris in dexteram neque in sinistram*, et David ait *Iuxta semitam scandalum posuerunt mihi*.

---

[89] *Manifesto* Zelz. most MSS, confirmed L² 39; *manifesta* C after correction, W.

[90] *Incident* (future of *incido*: fall into, be caught up in, meet with) B before correction, G, confirmed L² 46-47; *incidunt* (present tense) B after correction, HJPST; *incedunt* (*incedo*: tread upon) Zelz. following C, WL, M.

[91] *Viam* Zelz. following S, P, J, confirmed L² 56; *de via* (*-am* W) β; *a via* C.

[92] *Utramlibet* restored L¹ 389, L² 80, B after correction also has it by correct conjecture; *utramquamlibet* Zelz. following C after correction, an archetype error; a great variation in the other MSS. Lundström explains the process by which this latter impossible reading was generated.

Question 139
(Zelzer 167–68, QF 125, SR 240 [PG 31.1243–1244])

Q: How is it that *the gate is wide and the way is broad that leads to* death? (Matt 7:13)

R: 1 The Lord in his manifold loving kindness uses terms and vocabulary with which he is able to bring to our awareness the dogmas of the truth.[134] **2** Just as those walking along the road who stray from the direct route which continues within definite boundaries and a clear passageway will fall into vast and wandering spaces, **3** so too, he says, one who leaves the way which leads to the kingdom of heaven runs into a great breadth of error through which he arrives at perdition.

Question 140

Q: In what way *is the gate narrow and the way straitened that leads to life?*[135] (Matt 7:14)

R: 1 And here likewise, "narrow" and "straitened" indicate that this way which is our life, is narrowed and straightened by tribulations, **2** for we who make the journey are constrained on both sides, lest we in any way deviate to this side or that. **3** For it is perilous to deviate to either side, as on the narrow passage of a bridge, where if perhaps someone does deviate, the swift current of the river on either side snatches and bears him away. **4** For this reason it is written: *Do not stray to the right hand or to the left* (Deut 17:11), and David says: *They have laid stumbling blocks for me in my path* (Ps 139:5).

---

[134] SR 240 1244A: "uses the vocabulary of recognizable realities (ῥήμασι τῶν γινωσκομένων πραγμάτων), to present the dogmas of truth (πρὸς παράστασιν τῆς ἀληθείας δογμάτων).

[135] Eight or nine kilometers from Annisa, a Roman bridge, built in the time of Pompey, crossed over the river Iris, just downstream from its confluence with the river Lycus, before it enters the gorge country. The bridge is still there today, having remained in continuous use until the early twentieth century. When the river is in full spate the current becomes very turbulent. Basil's brother Naucratius died in those swirling waters only a couple of kilometers downstream—though not from falling off a bridge. Cf. Letter 365, Def IV, 346–51 to Emperor Theodosius, petitioning for the construction of a bridge. It describes the unpredictable Cappadocian climate and the "violent character" of the river Halys in the vicinity of Caesarea. Cf. also Gregory of Nyssa's *Life of Gregory the Wonderworker* (GNO X.I, 32), where he describes from familiar experience the havoc wrought on the surrounding countryside by the "wild, savage river Lykos" (= "wolf") in Pontos.

Interrogatio CXXXXI

(Zelzer 169–70, QF 127, SR 48 [PG 31.1115–1116])

I: *Avaritia* usque ad quem modum definitur?

R: 1 Cum transgressus quis fuerit modum legis statutum, quod designatur secundum vetus quidem testamentum in eo, si plus se diligat, quis vel plus in pecunia vel in necessariis de se sit sollicitus quam de proximo, **2** scriptum est enim *Diliges proximum tuum sicut te ipsum.*

3 Secundum evangelium vero si quis plus sollicitus sit quam de praesenti die, sui videlicet causa vel corporis, iste sine dubio audiet **4** *Stulte, hac nocte repetent abs te animam tuam, et quae praeparasti cuius erunt?* quibus addit dominus dicens *Ita* erit et is *qui sibi thesaurizat et non est in deo dives.*

Interrogatio CXXXXII

(Zelzer 170, QF –, SR 49 [PG 31.1115–1116])

I: Quid est *perperam agere*?

R: 1 Quicquid non propter usus necessarios sed vel ornatus causa vel decoris alicuius fit, hoc est *perperam agere.*

Interrogatio CXXXXIII

(Zelzer 170–71, QF 128, SR 210 [PG 31.1221–1224])

I: Quis est qui ab apostolo dicitur *habitus ordinatus*?

R: 1 Is qui secundum propositum uniuscuiusque honestus est usus vel secundum locum vel secundum tempus vel secundum personam. **2** Non enim idem usus homini esse potest in tempore hiemis et in tempore aestatis, neque idem habitus operantis et quiescentis nec militis idem est et privati neque viri idem qui mulieris.

Question 141

Q: As far as what measure is *avarice* judged? (cf. Luke 12:15)

R: 1 When someone has exceeded the limits laid down by the law, which according to the Old Testament is indicated in this: if he loves himself more, whether he is more solicitous for himself than his neighbour in the matter of money or in necessities, **2** for it is written: *love your neighbour as yourself* (Lev 19:18; Matt 22:39).

3 But according to the Gospel, if one is solicitous for more than the present day (cf. Matt 6:34), that is, on account of oneself or the body, such a one shall doubtless hear: **4** *Fool! This very night they shall require your soul and these things you have prepared, whose shall they be?* To this the Lord adds, saying: *So shall he be who lays up treasure for himself and is not rich before God* (Luke 12:20-21).

Question 142

Q: What is it to *vaunt oneself*?[136] (cf. 1 Cor 13:4)

R: 1 Anything done not on account of practical necessity, but for show or any kind of display, this is to *vaunt oneself.*

Question 143

Q: What is the *orderly dress* handed down by the Apostle? (1 Tim 2:9)

R: 1 It is that use which respects each one's purpose, according to place or time or person. **2** For the same use is not possible to a human being in winter time and in summer time, nor is the dress of a worker and of one at rest the same, nor of a soldier and a civilian, nor of a man and a woman.

---

[136] SR 49 1116C: περπερεύεσθαι, a NT hapax. Clarke, 248, compares Clement of Alexandria, *Paedagogue* III.1, and says that Basil's answer here is quoted in canon 16 of the Second Council of Nicaea.

Interrogatio CXXXXIIII

(Zelzer 171, QF 129, SR 50 [PG 31.1115–1118])

I: Si quis pretiosas vestes abiciat, ipsa autem indumenta viliora quibus utitur vel calciamenta ita composite utatur ut studeat decorem inde aliquem capere, si peccat aut vitio aliquo id facere putandus est?

R: 1 Qui vult per decorem habitus *place*re *hominibus,* manifestum est eum huius ipsius vitii aegritudine laborare, id est *hominibus place*ndi, et certum est mentem eius a deo longius evagari, **2** sed et hoc ipsum est vitium *perperam agere,* cum indumentis vel calciamentis non usus causa sed decoris.

Interrogatio CXXXXV

(Zelzer 171–72, QF 130, SR 51 [PG 31.1117–1118])

I: Quid est *racha*?

R: 1 Provincialis id est gentis[93] illius sermo est velut lenioris convicii, qui domesticis et his quorum fiduciam quis gerit dici solet.

Interrogatio CXXXXVI

(Zelzer 172, QF 131, SR 52 [PG 31.1117–1118])

I: Quod dicit apostolus *non efficiamur inanis gloriae cupidi,* et iterum *Non ad oculum servientes quasi hominibus placentes,* quis est *inanis gloriae cupidus* et quis *hominibus placens*?

R: 1 Puto quod *inanis gloriae cupidus* est qui propter solam gloriam saeculi, id est qui propter eos qui vident et audiunt de se aliquid quod vel laudare possint vel admirari, facit aliquid vel dicit. **2** *Hominibus* autem *placens* ille est qui ad voluntatem alicuius hominis ut placeat ei facit aliquid vel dicit, etiamsi indignum sit et iniuriosum hoc ipsum quod facit.

---

[93] *Gentis* Zelz. following SJ, G, HT, confirmed L² 38; *gentilis* (influence of *provincialis*) C, P, WL, BM Hol.

Question 144

Q: If someone rejects the more expensive clothing, yet even with the cheaper sort, whether tunic or footwear, wants what he thinks suits himself to attract the attention of others, does he sin or is he to be reckoned as acting with some other vice?[137]

R: 1 Whoever wishes through the outward form of his clothing to *court human favour*, manifestly labours under the malady of this very passion, that is, of *courting human favour* (cf. Gal 1:10; Eph 6:6). His mind has certainly wandered far from God **2** since he uses clothing and footwear not by reason of use but for outward adornment and this very thing is the vice of *vaunting oneself* (1 Cor 13:4).

Question 145

Q: What is *raca*? (Matt 5:22)

R: 1 It is a vernacular word of that nation, of lighter reproach, which is commonly spoken among familiars, or those with whom one has some understanding.

Question 146

Q: Since the Apostle says in one place: *Let us not be vainglorious* (Gal 5:26) and in another: *Not in eye-service as courters of human favour* (Eph 6:6), who is *vainglorious* and who a *courter of human favour*?

R: 1 I consider that he is *vainglorious* who does or says anything merely for worldly glory, that is, before those who see or hear something from him that they can applaud or marvel at. **2** But he is a *courter of human favour* (Eph 6:6; Gal 1:10) who does or says anything according to the wish of another in order to please him, even if what he does is dishonourable and harmful.

---

[137] Here Basil corrects the hyper-ascetics' penchant for ostentatiously shabby clothing, censured by the Council of Gangra, Preamble 4, Canons 12 and 13. See also RBas 155.

Interrogatio CXXXXVII
(Zelzer 173–74, QF 132, SR 53 [PG 31.1117–1118])

I: Quid est *inquinamentum carnis et* inquinamentum *spiritus* et quomodo ab his emundari possumus, et quae est *sanctificatio* et quomodo eam possumus obtinere?

R: 1 *Inquinamentum carnis* est commisceri his qui illicita et nefanda committunt, *spiritus* autem inquinamentum est, cum indifferenter habemus commisceri eis qui de fide impie sentiunt.

2 Emundamur autem ab his cum implemus illud quod apostolus dicit, *Cum eiusmodi nec cibum sumere*, et quaecumque his similia statuit, **3** vel certe cum illud patimur in corde nostro quod ait David, *Tristitia tenuit me a peccatoribus derelinquentibus legem tuam*, **4** vel cum ostenderimus talem nostram tristitiam qualem Corinthii ostenderunt cum obiurgati sunt a Paulo, cur erga eum qui peccaverat indiscrete egerint, cum dicit *In omnibus exhibuisitis vos castos esse negotio.*

5 *Sanctificatio* autem est adhaerere deo ex integro et sine aliqua intermissione in omni tempore sollicitum esse et studium gerere placendi ei, **6** quoniam quidem neque pollutum aliquid in donis dei offerri potest vel sanctificari **7** neque rursum quod semel oblatum est deo et sanctificatum est ad communem humani ministerii usum adduci potest; alioquin et sacrilegum erit et impium.

Interrogatio CXXXXVIII
(Zelzer 174, QF 133, SR 280 [PG 31.1279–1280])

I: Quis est *mundus corde*?

R: 1 Qui se ipsum non reprehendit, quia vel praevaricatus sit mandatum dei vel contempserit vel neglexerit.

Interrogatio CXXXXVIIII
(Zelzer 174–75, QF 134, SR 11 [PG 31.1089–1090])

I: Quomodo potest aliquis odium habere adversus peccatum?

R: 1 Semper ex his quae tristem et infaustum finem habent odium nascitur hominibus adversum eos qui causa sibi huiuscemodi negotii exstiterint. **2** Si quis ergo certus sit quantorum et qualium malorum causa nobis fiunt peccata, sponte et sine ulla commonitione ex intimo affectu odium ei adversum ea nascitur, **3** sicut ostendit ille qui dicebat *Iniquitatem odio habui.*

Question 147

Q: What is *pollution of the flesh* and pollution *of the spirit* and how shall we be cleansed from them, and what is *sanctification* and how do we obtain it? (cf. 2 Cor 7:1)

R: 1 *Pollution of the flesh* is to mingle with those who practise forbidden and unspeakable things, whereas pollution *of the spirit* is when we associate indifferently with those of impious sentiments concerning the faith.

2 We are cleansed from these things when we fulfil what the Apostle says: *With such a one do not even eat* (1 Cor 5:11) and other such precepts, **3** or when we experience in our heart what David says: *Grief has seized me because of sinners who forsake your law* (Ps 118:53), **4** or when we manifest such a sorrow as the Corinthians manifested when they were accused by Paul of behaving indifferently towards one who had sinned, when, he says: they had *in all ways shown* them*selves pure in this matter* (2 Cor 7:11).

5 *Sanctification* is to cleave to God entirely, and to be unceasingly anxious and zealous to please him at all times, **6** since indeed nothing polluted can be among the gifts dedicated and sanctified to God **7** and again, nothing which has been once offered and sanctified to God can be assigned to the common use of human service; otherwise it would be sacrilegious and impious (cf. Lev 27:28).

Question 148

Q: Who is *pure of heart*? (Matt 5:8; Pss 23:4; 50:10)

R: 1 One who does not have to reprimand himself for transgressing the commandment of God, or overlooking it, or being negligent about it.

Question 149

Q: How can one gain a *hatred for sins*? (cf. Ps 118:163)

R: 1 Hatred always arises in human beings from grievous and unfortunate events, against those who are the causes of such trouble. **2** If therefore one is assured how many and how great are the evils of which sins are the cause, then spontaneously and without any encouragement, and from inner disposition a hatred arises in him against them, **3** as he showed who said: *Iniquity I hated* (Ps 118:163).

Interrogatio CL
(Zelzer 175–76, QF 135, SR 174 [PG 31.1197–1198])

I: Quomodo potest aliquis ex animo et ex affectu facere mandata domini?

R: 1 Naturaliter delectamur his quae bona sunt et prosunt. **2** Si ergo credimus de his quae promissa sunt, ex eo ipso quod speramus inseritur animae nostrae affectus et desiderium ad explenda ea quibus id consequi possumus quod desideramus. **3** Si quis ergo *odium habu*erit et exsecratus fuerit *iniquitatem* et emundaverit se ab omni peccato, ex quo sicut corpus a languore delectationem non habet cibi, ita et anima a peccati morbo non habet desiderium erga mandata dei, **4** si recordetur quia *mandatum dei vita aeterna est* et omnibus qui custodiunt illud permanet adimpletio promissorum, **5** potest per haec nasci animae affectus ille de quo dixit *Iudicia dei vera, iustificata in semet ipsa, desiderabilia super aurum et lapidem pretiosum nimi et dulciora super mel et favum,* **6** *nam et servus tuus custodit ea, in custodiendo illa retributio multa.*

Interrogatio CLI
(Zelzer 176, QF 136, SR 211 [PG 31.1223–1224])

I: Quae est mensura in caritate dei?

R: 1 Ut super vires quis semper *extendat* animam suam ad voluntatem dei prospiciens et desiderans ea quae ad gloriam dei pertinent.

Question 150

Q: How can one fulfil the commandments of the Lord with inward disposition and with eagerness?

R: 1 We naturally delight in those things which are good and beneficial. **2** If therefore we believe in the things that have been promised, then from the very thing that we hope for there is implanted in our soul the disposition and desire to fulfil everything by which we can attain that which we desire. **3** Therefore if anyone *hates and detests iniquity* (Ps 118:163) and purifies himself from all sin—for just as through infirmity the body loses delight in food, so through the disease of sin the soul loses desire for the commandments of God—**4** and if one recalls that *the commandment of God is eternal life* (John 12:50) and that for all who keep it there will be a fulfilment of the promises, **5** then by such means that disposition of soul can arise of which it says: *The judgments of the Lord are true and all of them just, they are more desirable than gold and very precious stone, and sweeter than honey and the honeycomb,* **6** *for indeed your servant keeps them and in keeping them there is great reward* (Ps 18:9-11).

Question 151

Q: What is the measure of love for God?

R: 1 That one ever stretches[138] one's soul (cf. Phil 3:13) beyond its strength towards the will of God, looking towards and desiring whatever leads to the glory of God.

---

[138] SR 211 1224A: τὴν ψυχὴν ἐπεκτείνεσθαι. The importance of *epektasis* (stretching or reaching beyond) in the spiritual life will be much developed by Gregory of Nyssa.

Interrogatio CLII
(Zelzer 176–77, QF 137, SR 212 [PG 31.1223–1224])

I: Quomodo quis obtineat ut possit habere in se caritatem dei?

R: 1 Si grati et fideles exsistamus erga beneficia eius, quod etiam in mutis animalibus fieri videmus; nam et canes interdum diligunt eos qui sibi cibum praebent. **2** Sed et Esaias propheta hoc docet cum arguit ingratam gentem et dicit ex persona domini **3** *Filios genui et exaltavi, ipsi autem me spreverunt. Agnovit bos possessorem suum et asinus praesepe domini sui, Israel vero me non cognovit et populus meus me non intellexit.* **4** Sicut enim bovi et asino pro eo beneficio quod pascitur dilectio spontanea nascitur erga pastorem, ita etiam nos, si grate et fideliter beneficia dei suscipiamus, sine dubio diligimus beneficiorum praebitorem deum **5** et absque ulla doctrina naturali quodam instinctu in eius concitamur affectum, si tamen sanitas sua animae praesto sit.

Interrogatio CLIII
(Zelzer 177, QF 138, SR 213 [PG 31.1223–1224])

I: Quae sunt indicia esse in nobis caritatem dei?

R: 1 Quae dominus docuit dicens *Si diligitis me, mandata mea servate.*

Interrogatio CLIIII
(Zelzer 178, QF 139, SR 54 [PG 31.1119–1120])

I: Quid est se ipsum diligere vel quomodo vitium suum cognoscit qui se ipsum diligit?

R: 1 Multa abusive dicuntur sicut et illud, *Qui amat animam suam perdet eam, et qui odit animam suam in hoc mundo in vitam aeternam servabit eam.* **2** Philautus ergo graece dicitur qui se ipsum diligit; intellegi autem potest is qui talis est hoc modo, si ea quae facit pro semet ipso facit, etiamsi videantur secundum mandatum dei esse quae facit.

Question 152

Q: How may one obtain within oneself the ability to love God?

R: 1 If we show ourselves grateful and faithful for his benefits, which we see happens even with dumb animals; for dogs for the most part love those who provide them with food. **2** Indeed, the prophet Isaiah teaches this when he takes to task an ungrateful people and says in the person of the Lord: **3** *I begot children and I brought them up, but they have spurned me. The ox knows its owner and the ass its master's crib, but Israel has not known me and my people has not understood* (Isa 1:2-3). **4** For just as love is born spontaneously in the ox and the ass toward their shepherd for the benefit of their pasturage, so also with us. If we receive the benefits of God gratefully and faithfully, we shall without doubt love God the provider of the benefits, **5** and without being taught, by a certain natural instinct, such a disposition is awakened towards him—if one's soul is in a sound condition.

Question 153

Q: What are the signs within us of love for God?

R: 1 What the Lord taught us, saying: *If you love me, keep my commandments* (John 14:15).

Question 154

Q: What is self-love and how does *the lover of self* (cf. 2 Tim 3:2) recognize his vice?

R: 1 Many things are said in a misapplied way,[139] such as: *Whoever loves his life shall lose it, and whoever hates his life in this world will keep it unto life eternal* (John 12:25). **2** *Philautus* therefore, in the Greek, expresses one who loves himself. Someone like this can be recognized if whenever he does something, he does it for himself, even though what is done appears to be according to the commandment of God.

---

[139] 1120A Πολλὰ καταχρυστικῶς λέγεται: "Many things are said in a fuller sense." For the interpretation of the Greek adverb here, see G. W. H. Lampe, *A Patristic Greek Lexicon* (Oxford: Clarendon Press, 1961), καταχράομαι, 1. And καταχρῆσις 1. Both Garnier and Rufinus interpret it in the sense of "misuse," which in the context does not make much sense. QF 139.1: "Many things are said in an assumed/applied sense (ܪܠܪ ܪܐ ܪܐܐܐ)."

3 Qui enim pro sua requie patitur aliquid deesse necessitati vel usibus fratris sive eorum quae ad animam necessaria sunt sive ad corpus, 4 manifeste philautus id est se ipsum diligens deprehenditur, cuius vitii finis interitus est.

Interrogatio CLV
(Zelzer 178–79, QF 140, SR 175 [PG 31.1197–1200])

I: Quomodo apparet qui diligit fratrem secundum mandatum domini, et quomodo arguitur qui non diligit?

R: 1 Caritatis duo ista praecipua sunt, cum contristamur et graviter ferimus in his in quibus laeditur ille quem diligimus, **2** et cum vel satis agimus ut fiant vel gaudemus si provenerint aliqua in quibus utilitas vel profectus est eius qui diligitur. **3** Beatus ergo est qui luget super eum qui delinquit, cuius videt vitae imminere periculum, et gaudet pro eo qui proficit et suum lucrum deputat profectum proximi sui. **4** Contestatur autem hoc ipsum et apostolus Paulus dicens *Si patitur unum membrum compatiuntur omnia membra*, quod utique secundum rationem caritatis Christi dicebat, *et si glorificatur unum membrum congaudent omnia membra*. **5** Qui autem talem non habet affectum erga fratrem, certum est quod non secundum caritatem diligit proximum suum.

Interrogatio CLVI
(Zelzer 180–81, QF 141, SR 176 [PG 31.1199–1200])

I: Qui sunt inimici quos diligere iubemur, et quomodo *diligi*mus *inimicos* no*stros*: praestantes eis beneficia tantummodo aut etiam affectum eis exhibentes, et si hoc possibile est fieri?

R: 1 Inimici proprium est laedere et insidiari et ideo omnis qui quo modo laedit aliquem inimicus dicitur, maxime autem hi qui peccant. **2** Isti enim, quod in se est, laedunt diversis modis, et insidiantur vel his qui se vident vel his qui simul vivunt. **3** Et quoniam ex corpore et anima constat homo, secundum animam quidem diligamus eos arguentes et commonentes et omni modo ad conversionem eos provocantes, **4** secundum corpus vero praestemus eis beneficia et misericordiam si indigent victum, quoniam nemo dubitat quod caritas in affectu sita sit.

3 For if, for the sake of his own ease, he leaves undone anything needed for the service of a brother whether in soul or in body, **4** manifestly he is caught out as a *philautos*, that is, one who loves himself, the end of which vice is destruction.

Question 155

Q: How is he manifest who loves his brother according to the commandment of the Lord, and how is he to be reproved who does not so love?

R: 1 These are the two criteria of love: that we are grieved and saddened over the things by which the one whom we love is harmed, **2** and that we strive that it should be well and rejoice at those things which turn out to the benefit or advancement of the one who is loved. **3** *Blessed*, then, is anyone *who mourns* over a sinner (cf. Matt 5:4), who sees the danger that threatens his life, and rejoices over one who is making progress and considers his neighbour's gain as his own. **4** The apostle Paul also bears witness to this very thing, saying: *If one member suffers, all the members suffer with it*—which he was certainly teaching according to the principle of the love of Christ—*and if one member is glorified, all the members share the joy* (1 Cor 12:26). **5** He who does not have such a disposition towards a brother certainly does not love his neighbour according to charity.[140]

Question 156

Q: Who are the *enemies* we are ordered to love, and how do we *love* our *enemies* (cf. Matt 5:44)—simply by providing them with benefits, or also displaying to them some disposition, and whether it is possible to do this?

R: 1 The character of an enemy is to do harm and to lie in wait, and so anyone who in any way harms another is called an enemy, but especially those who sin. **2** For these, as far as they can, do harm in various ways and lie in wait against those they see or those who live with them. **3** Now since man consists of both body and soul, in regard to the soul, let us love such as these by reproving them and warning them and stirring them in every way to conversion, **4** and in regard to the body, let us provide them with benefits and alms if they are in need of sustenance, since no-one doubts that charity is in the disposition.

---

[140] So Rufinus "unpacks" the original μὴ ἀγαπῶν τὸν ἀδελφόν (PG 31.1200A).

5 Quod autem possibile sit docuit dominus per caritatem dei patris et per suam *oboedien*tiam *usque ad mortem,* quia[94] utique pro inimicis adhuc et impiis nobis sustinuit, **6** sicut et apostolus testatur dicens *Commendat autem suam caritatem deus in nobis, quia cum adhuc peccatores essemus Christus pro nobis mortuus est.*

7 Sed et nos a hoc ipsum cohortatur dicens *Estote ergo imitatores dei sicut filii carissimi et ambulate in caritate sicut et Christus dilexit nos et semet ipsum tradidit pro nobis oblationem et hostiam deo.* **8** Numquam autem praeciperet hoc iustus et clemens deus nisi utique etiam possibilitatem nobis donasset. **9** Inesse enim hoc naturae nostrae ostenditur, cum etiam bestiis vel animalibus erga eos qui beneficii aliquid praestiterint inest naturalis affectus.

10 Quis autem tantum beneficii amicus praestat quantum inimicus, cum nobis causa beatitudinis efficitur illius quam dicit dominus **11** *Beati estis cum persequentur vos et exprobrabunt et dicent omne malum adversum vos mentientes propter me, gaudete et exsultate, quia merces vestra multa est in caelis.*

Interrogatio CLVII
(Zelzer 182, QF 142, SR 243 [PG 31.1245–1246])

I: Quid est quod dicit apostolus *Irascimini et nolite peccare et sol non occidat super iracundiam vestram,* cum in aliis dixerit *Omnis amaritudo vel ira vel indignatio auferatur a vobis?*

R: 1 Arbitror in hoc loco apostolum secundum imitationem domini haec locutum. **2** Sicut enim in evangelio dominus dicebat *Audistis quia dictum est antiquis* illud vel illud et ipse addebat dicens *Ego autem dico vobis* hoc vel hoc, **3** ita etiam hic apostolus cum prius meminisset antiquitatis per hoc quod dicitur *Irascimini et nolite peccare,* paulo post addidit quod ex se erat et quod nobis conveniret dicens *Omnis amaritudo et ira et indignatio et clamor auferatur a vobis.*

---

[94] *Quia* CS, confirmed L² 17–18; *quam* Zelz. Following β.

5 That it is possible, the Lord has taught us through God the Father's love and through his own *obedience unto death* (Phil 2:8), since he assuredly suffered for us while we were still enemies and impious, **6** as the Apostle testifies when he says: *But God proves his love for us in that Christ died for us while we were still sinners* (Rom 5:8).

7 And he exhorts us to do the same when he says: *Therefore be imitators of God as his very dear children and walk in love even as Christ loved us and delivered himself for us as a sacrifice and an offering to God* (Eph 5:1-2). **8** For he who is just and merciful would never have commanded this, unless he also granted to us the capacity to do so. **9** This is shown to be implanted in us of our very nature since even beasts and animals have in them a natural affection toward those who provide them with some benefit.

10 Moreover, what benefit does a friend bestow as great as that of an enemy who provides us with an occasion for that blessedness of which the Lord speaks: **11** *Blessed are you when they persecute you and revile you and speak every kind of evil word against you, falsely, on my account; rejoice and leap for joy, for great is your reward in heaven!* (Matt 5:11-12)

Question 157

Q: What does the Apostle mean when he says: *Be angry but do not sin;* and: *do not let the sun go down on your anger* (Eph 4:26), whereas elsewhere he says: *Let all bitterness and wrath and indignation be put away from you?* (Eph 4:31)

R: **1** I consider that here the Apostle has spoken in imitation of the Lord. **2** For just as in the gospel the Lord would say first: *You have heard that it was said of old,* and then would add: *But I say to you* this and this (Matt 5:21, 27, 33, et al.), **3** so also here the Apostle first brings to mind what was once said of old: *Be angry but do not sin* (Ps 4:5) and shortly adds something from himself that applies to us, saying: *Let all bitterness and wrath and indignation and shouting out be put away from you* (Eph 4:31).

Interrogatio CLVIII
(Zelzer 182–83, QF 143, SR 244 [PG 31.1245–1246])

I: Quid est *Date locum irae?*

R: 1 *Non resistere malo* secundum quod scriptum est *Sed et ei qui percusserit te in dexteram maxillam praebe et alteram,* **2** et implere ea omnia quae sequuntur vel illud *Cum persecuti vos fuerint in una civitate fugite in alteram.*

Interrogatio CLVIIII
(Zelzer 183–84, QF 144, SR 55 [PG 31.1119–1120])

I: Quae est diferentia *amaritud*inis et *furor*is et *irae* et *clamor*is et irritationis?

R: 1 Furoris quidem et irae differentiam puto in animo constare et motu, quia qui irascitur intra animos suos adhuc vitium volvit, sicut ex hoc ipso indicatur quod dicit *Irascimini et nolite peccare.* **2** Qui vero furit iam plus aliquid per motum gerit; *furore nim,* inquit, *eis secundum similitudinem serpentis.* **3** Vehementius vero furorem concitare irritatio nominatur, *amaritudo* autem illa est *cum malitia* in corde etiam arte quadam componitur et armatur.

Interrogatio CLX
(Zelzer 184, QF 145, SR 215 [PG 31.1225–1226])

I: Quis est qui a domino beatificatur *pacificus?*

R: 1 Qui Christi adiutor est secundum quod dicit apostolus *Pro Christo legatione fungimur tamquam deo exhortante per nos; obsecramus pro Christo, reconciliamini deo,* et iterum, *Iustificati ergo ex fide pacem habeamus ad deum.* **2** Illa enim alia pax repudiata est a Christo dicente *Pacem meam do vobis, non sicut hic mundus dat* etiam *ego do vobis.*

Question 158

Q: What does *Give place to wrath* mean? (Rom 12:19)

R: 1 *Not to resist one who is evil*, as it is written, *but instead, to him who strikes you on the right cheek, offer the other too* (Matt 5:39), **2** and to fulfil all that follows, such as that saying: *when they persecute you in one city, flee to another* (Matt 10:23).

Question 159

Q: What is the difference between *bitterness* and *wrath* and *anger* and *shouting out* and paroxysm?[141] (Eph 4:31; Ps 57:5)

R: 1 The difference between wrath and anger lies I think in the disposition and the motive, since the vice of one who is stirred to anger extends only to the disposition, as he makes clear who says: *Be stirred to anger, but do not sin* (Eph 4:31; Ps 4:5). **2** But one who is wrathful has already gone further in motive; *their wrath*, it says, *is like a serpent* (Ps 57:4). **3** But to stir up a still more vehement wrath is called paroxysm, whereas bitterness is with *malice* in the heart, even compounded and armed with a certain deliberation.[142]

Question 160

Q: Who is the *peacemaker* called *blessed* by the Lord? (cf. Matt 5:9)

R: 1 One who is Christ's assistant, as the Apostle says: *We act as ambassador for Christ, as though God were appealing through us; we beseech you on behalf of Christ: be reconciled to God* (2 Cor 5:20), and again: *having been justified by faith, we have peace with God* (Rom 5:1). **2** Yet there is another kind of peace disowned by Christ where he says: *My peace I give to you, but not as the world gives do I give to you* (John 14:27)

---

[141] The Greek and the Syriac name four qualities, the Latin five. The Greek and the Latin appear to line up as follows: bitterness/πικρίας/*amaritud*inis; rage/θυμοῦ/*furor*is; anger/ὀργῆς/*irae*; shouting out (*nil* in Greek, otherwise κραυγὴ as in Eph 4:31)/*clamor*is; paroxysm/παροξυσμοῦ/*irritation*is; "et irritationis" omitted in GLW.

[142] SR 55 1120B: "[bitterness] expresses a more terrifying (δεινότεραν) premeditated *malice*." Hol. (no codex is recorded as its source) adds: "and shouting out is when one is moved by anger and rage to indignant cries, or to blasphemy or is carried away into cursing."

Interrogatio CLXI
(Zelzer 184–85, QF 146, SR 216 [PG 31.1225–1226])

I: Quomodo *converti* quis potest *et fieri sicut infans*?

R: 1 Ipsa lectio evangelii docet nos omnem causam in qua hoc ostenditur, uti ne arrogantiam requiramus vel elationem, sed aequitatem naturae cognoscamus et exaequemus nos eis qui videntur inferiores. **2** Hoc enim est proprie infantum aequales esse his quibus non nobilitate sed aetate iungunter, donec processu temporis et monitorum nequitia elationis inficiantur venenis.

Interrogatio CLXII
(Zelzer 185–86, QF 148, SR 245 [PG 31.1245–1246])

I: Quid est *prudentem esse sicut serpentem et simplicem sicut columbam*?

R: 1 *Prudens* quidem *ut serpens* est qui circumspecte et considerate quae sint possibilia et quae honesta vel utilia pervidens doctrinam suam dispensat et aptat ea arte qua suaderi auditores ad audentiam possint. **2** *Simplex* autem *ut columba* est qui nec in cor prorsus recipit cogitationem ulciscendi in eos qui laedunt, sed permanet in benefaciendo secundum quod apostolus dicit *Vos autem nolite deficere benefacientes.*

3 Dominus ergo ad praedicationem mittens discipulos haec eis praecipiebat, **4** ubi sine dubio opus erat sapientia ad suadendum eos qui docebantur et patientia adversum eos qui insidiabantur, **5** ut sicut ibi serpens per prudentiam intellexit, quam personam ad persuadendum aggredi deberet—**6** eam scilicet quae fragilior videbatur ad persuadendum, quo eam a deo abstractam peccato sociaret—**7** ita et nos personam et mores et tempus considerare et deligere debemus et omnimodo ita ordinare *sermones* nostros *in iudicio*, ut possimus abstrahere homines a peccato et sociare deo.

Question 161

Q: How can one be *converted and become as little children*? (cf. Matt 18:3)

R: 1 This very reading of the gospel teaches us the whole reason why this was revealed, that we are not to seek arrogance or haughtiness, but recognize our equality of nature and put ourselves on an equal basis with those who seem to be our inferiors. **2** For it is characteristic of little children to be equal with those associated with them not by rank but by age, until, with the passage of time and the baseness of their guardians, they are infected with the poison of haughtiness.[143]

Question 162

Q: What is it *to be wise as a serpent and simple as a dove*? (cf. Matt 10:16)

R: 1 He is w*ise as a serpent* who in dispensing his teaching discerns circumspectly and thoughtfully what may be possible and what honourable or useful, adapting it with that skill which can persuade his hearers to listen. **2** He on the other hand is *simple as a dove* who never admits into his heart a thought of vengeance against those who harm him, but perseveres in doing good, as the Apostle says: *But as for you, do not weary of doing good* (2 Thess 3:13).

3 For the Lord gave these instructions when he sent out his disciples to preach, **4** in which no doubt there was need of wisdom to persuade those who were being taught and of patience with those who would lay snares against them. **5** Accordingly, just as the serpent through his wisdom knew which person he ought to approach to persuade—**6** her at any rate who seemed more susceptible to persuasion—whereby once she was drawn away from God, he might join her to sin (Gen 3:1-6), **7** so we also ought to consider and choose the person and the manner and the occasion and in every way so *dispense* our *words with judgment* (Ps 111:5) that we withdraw human beings from sin and join them to God.

---

[143] See also *Morals* 45.1: *That it is impossible for them to be deemed worthy of the Kingdom of heaven who in their dealings with one another do not imitate the equality observed by little children among themselves.*

Interrogatio CLXIII
(Zelzer 186–87, QF 147, SR 217 [PG 31.1225–1226])

I: Quomodo debemus suscipere *regnum* dei sicut infans?

R: 1 Si tales fuerimus ad doctrinam domini qualis est infans in discendo, **2** qui neque contradicit doctoribus neque rationes et verba componit adversum eos resistens, sed fideliter suscipit quod docetur et cum metu obtemperat et acquiescit.

Interrogatio CLXIIII
(Zelzer 187–88, QF 149, SR 56 [PG 31.1119–1122])

I: Domino dicente quia *Qui se exultat humiliabitur,* et apostolo praecipiente *Noli superbum*[95] *sapere,* et alibi *arrogantes superbi inflati,* et iterum *Caritas non inflatur,* quis est elatus et quis est iactans vel arrogans, quis vero superbus et quis inflatus vel tumens?

R: 1 Elatus est qui se ipsum effert pro his quae forte ei recte vel prospere gesta sunt, et pro hoc magnus sibi videtur et elatus secundum illum pharisaeum qui et ipse inflatus dici potest; **2** sicut et Corinthios arguit quibus dicit *Et vos inflati estis.*

3 Iactans autem vel arrogans est ille qui non acquiescit his quae a patribus statuta sunt pro utilitate communi, **4** nec acquiescit verbis apostoli dicentis *Ut eadem sentiatis et unum sapiatis,* sed propriam quandam viam iustitiae ac sanctitatis inquirit.

5 Superbus vero est qui etiam nihil in se virtutis aut rectorum gestorum habens elatus est et erectus et videri vult plus esse quam est. **6** Similis autem esse hic potest etiam is qui inflatus dicitur vel tumens secundum hoc quod apostolus dicit *Sed inflatus est nihil sciens.*

---

[95] *Superbum* C, P, W, M, confirmed L² 26; *superbe* Zelz. with other MSS: "*superbe* has surely been picked up through assimilation to a manuscript with the Vulgate," Lundström.

Question 163

Q: How must we receive *the kingdom* of God *as a little child*? (cf. Matt 18:3)

R: 1 If towards the teaching of the Lord we become as a little child at his lessons, **2** who neither contradicts his teachers nor puts arguments and words together to oppose them, but faithfully accepts what he is taught and respectfully obeys and complies.

Question 164

Q: Since the Lord says: *Whoever exalts himself shall be humbled* (Luke 14:11; 18:14) and the Apostle charges: *Do not be haughty-minded* (Rom 11:20), and elsewhere: *Arrogant, proud, inflated* (2 Tim 3:2), and again: *Love is not puffed up* (1 Cor 13:4), who is haughty, and who boastful or arrogant, while who proud and who inflated or puffed up?[144]

R: 1 The haughty-minded is one who puts himself forward for things which have perhaps been done rightly and successfully by him, and who thereby seems to himself to be great and lofty, like that Pharisee who can well be called inflated, **2** just as he rebuked the Corinthians to whom he said: *You yourselves are inflated* (1 Cor 5:2).

3 The boastful or arrogant, however, is one who does not observe the things laid down by the Fathers for the common good, **4** or obey the words of the Apostle who says: *That you may be of the same mind and of one accord* (Phil 2:2), but seeks after his own way of righteousness and holiness.

5 The proud is one who, though he has nothing of virtue or of upright deeds in himself, is haughty-minded and lofty and wants to appear to be more than he is. **6** Like him can be one who is called inflated or puffed up, according to this saying of the Apostle: *he is inflated, yet he knows nothing* (cf. 1 Tim 6:4).

---

[144] There are six adjectives in the RBas, five in the Greek, four in the Syriac. The Greek seems to have expanded one as a hendiadys, and Rufinus yet another.

Interrogatio CLXV
(Zelzer 188–89, QF –, SR 246 [PG 31.1247–1248])

I: Quid est *Caritas non dehonestatur*?

R: 1 Sicut si quis dicat De statu honestatis suae non deducitur; est enim propria quaedam honestas caritatis et habitus eius atque ornatus, **2** ille sine dubio, quem per singulas caritatis virtutes enumeravit apostolus, quae singulae honestas quaedam eius sunt et ornatus.

Interrogatio CLXVI
(Zelzer 189–90, QF 150, SR 247 [PG 31.1247–1248])

I: Scriptura dicente *Nolite gloriari neque loqui alta,* et apostolo confitente quia *Quae loquor non secundum dominum loquor sed sicut in insipientia in hac substantia gloriandi,* et rursum *Factus sum insipiens gloriando,* et iterum ipso dicente quia *Qui gloriatur in domino glorietur,* quae est gloriatio in domino et quae est culpabilis gloriatio?

R: 1 Apostoli quidem manifestum est propositum quod adversum vitia loquebatur; **2** non enim ut se ipsum commendaret haec dicebat, sed ut quorundam insolentiam arrogantiamque retunderet. **3** Gloriatio ergo in domino est cum quis ea quae recte gerit non sibi sed domino adscribit dicens *Omnia possum* sed *in eo qui me confortat Christo.*

4 Culpabilis autem gloriatio duplici ratione dinoscitur, vel secundum hoc quod dicit *Quia laudatur peccator in desideriis animae suae,* et *Quid gloriatur in malitia qui potens est in iniquitate?* **5** vel secundum illud, cum *faciunt* aliquid boni operis *ut videantur ab hominibus* et per hoc ipsum quod volunt laudari, gloriantur in his quae fecerunt. **6** Sed huiusmodi homines etiam sacrilegi designantur, cum gratiam quae a deo data est propriam faciunt et gloriam quae deo debetur in semet ipsos convertere conantur.

Question 165

Q: What is: *Love is not dishonourable?* (1 Cor 13:5)

R: 1 It is as if someone should say "it is not drawn aside from its state of integrity," for there is a certain honourable character and manner and form proper to love, **2** that which doubtless the Apostle enumerated in each of the virtues of love, which are as it were its specific honourable character and form.

Question 166

Q: Since Scripture says: *Do not boast or speak high-sounding words* (cf. 1 Sam 2:3) and the Apostle confesses: *What I speak, I do not speak from the Lord, but as if in folly, in this confidence of boasting* (2 Cor 11:17), and again: *I have become a fool* in my boasting (2 Cor 12:11) and again he says: *Whoever boasts, let him boast in the Lord* (1 Cor 1:31; 2 Cor 10:17), what is *boasting in the Lord* and what is culpable boasting?

R: 1 It is clear that the Apostle's purpose was to speak against the vices. **2** For he did not say these things in order to commend himself, but to curb the insolence and arrogance of some. **3** Therefore *boasting in the Lord* is when one ascribes what one does rightly not to oneself but to the Lord, saying: *I can do all things*—only *in Christ who strengthens me* (Phil 4:3).

4 Culpable boasting is recognized in a twofold form, either according to this saying: *The sinner boasts of his soul's desires* (Ps 9:24) and: *Why do you boast in your malice, you who are mighty in iniquity?* (Ps 51:1) **5** or according to this: *since they do* any good work *in order to be seen by men* (Matt 6:5) and through this very fact that they wish to be praised, they boast in what they do. **6** Moreover, men such as these may also be called sacrilegious, since they appropriate as their own the grace given by God, and strive to turn to themselves the glory that is due to God.

Interrogatio CLXVII
(Zelzer 190–91, QF 151, SR 218 [PG 31.1225–1228])

I: Qualem intellectum vel prudentiam a deo petere debemus vel quomodo eam possumus promereri?

R: 1 Intellectus quidem quid sit ab ipso deo per prophetam discimus dicente *Non glorietur sapiens in sapientia sua nec glorietur fortis in fortitudine sua nec glorietur dives in divitiis suis, sed in hoc glorietur qui gloriatur in intellegendo at cognoscendo dominum,* **2** et iterum per apostolum sic dicit *Sed intellegentes quae sit voluntas domini.*

3 Possumus autem hoc modo promereri si faciamus illud quod scriptum est *Vacate et cognoscite quoniam ego sum dominus* **4** et si credamus omne verbum dei verum esse, *Si enim,* inquit, *non credideritis neque intellegetis.*

Interrogatio CLXVIII
(Zelzer 191–92, QF 152, SR 248 [PG 31.1247–1250])

I: Si *dominus dat sapientiam et a facie eius scientia et intellectus* est, et si *alii quidem per spiritum datur sermo sapientiae, alii sermo scientiae,* quomodo increpat dominus discipulos suos dicens quia *Et vos adhuc insensati estis et non intellegitis,* et apostolus culpat *Galat*as *insensat*os?

R: 1 Si quis scit bonitatem dei volentis *omnes homines salvos fieri et ad agnitionem veritatis venire* et studium spiritus sancti didicit, quo unicuique dividit gratiam dei, **2** iste cognoscit tarditatem intellectus non ex culpa eius descendere qui dona distribuit, sed ex eorum qui desidia et infidelitate sua id suscipere non merentur. **3** Et ideo recte culpatur insipiens vel insensatus qui velut sole orto claudit oculos suos ne videat sed in tenebris ambulat.

Question 167

Q: What is the understanding or wisdom we ought to ask of God (cf. Jas 1:5), and how can we become worthy of it?

R: 1 The understanding which is from God himself we learn through the prophet who says: *Let not the wise glory in his wisdom, nor the strong glory in his strength, nor the rich glory in his riches, but let him who glories glory in this, that he understands and knows the Lord* (Jer 9:23-24), **2** and again through the Apostle who speaks thus: *but understanding what is the will of the Lord* (Eph 5:17).

3 Now in this way we can be made worthy of it, if we do what is written: *Desist and know that I am the Lord* (Ps 45:10) **4** and if we believe that every word of God is true, for *if you will not believe*, it says, *neither shall you understand* (Isa 7:9 LXX).

Question 168

Q: If *the Lord gives wisdom and from his face are knowledge and understanding* (Prov 2:6), and if *to one is given through the Spirit the word of wisdom, to another the word of knowledge* (1 Cor 12:8), how is it that the Lord rebukes his own disciples, saying: *Are you still senseless and do you not understand?* (Matt 15:16-17) and the Apostle reproaches the *Galatians* as *senseless* (cf. Gal 3:1)?

R: 1 If one knows the goodness of God who *wills that all men be saved and come to a knowledge of the truth* (1 Tim 2:4) and has learned the solicitude of the Holy Spirit by which he distributes the grace of God to each, **2** then one comes to know that slowness of the understanding does not derive from the fault of him who distributes the gifts, but from the fault of those who through their own indolence and want of faith do not deserve to receive it. **3** Therefore he is rightly reproached as foolish and senseless who, as it were, shuts his eyes at sun-rise lest he see, and walks in the darkness instead (cf. Ps 33:5).

Interrogatio CLXVIIII
(Zelzer 192, QF 153, SR 219 [PG 31.1227–1228])

I: Si ab aliquo quid beneficii consequamur, quomodo poterimus et domino digne et integre gratias agere et ei qui beneficium praestitit, quali mensura uti debemus in utroque?

R: 1 Si deum auctorem et consummatorem omnium bonorum esse credamus, eum vero per quem boni aliquid consecuti sumus ut ministrum dei gratiae et muneris agnoscamus.

Interrogatio CLXX
(Zelzer 193, QF 154, SR 249 [PG 31.1249–1250])

I: Quid est dignum vel sanctum quod Graeci ὅσιον dicunt, et quid est iustum?

R: 1 Ὅσιον quidem id est sanctum vel dignum esse arbitror hoc quod decet et debetur ab inferioribus deferri superioribus secundum hanc ipsam rationem qua eminentiores videntur, **2** iustum autem hoc quod pro operis merito unicuique retribuitur. **3** Et in illo quidem alio optimorum quorumque indicatur obsequium, in hoc vero tam boni quam mali retributio designatur.

Interrogatio CLXXI
(Zelzer 193–94, QF 155, SR 250 [PG 31.1249–1250])

I: Quomodo dat quis *sanctum canibus* et mittit *margaritas ante porcos,* aut quomodo accidit illud quod additur, *ne forte conculcent eas pedibus suis et conversi disrumpant vos*?

R: 1 Manifeste nobis tradit[96] apostolus ex his quae adversum Iudaeos dicit quia *Qui in lege gloriaris per praevaricationem legis deum inhonoras.* **2** Iniuriam ergo hanc quam *per praevaricationem* verbo dei inferre dicuntur hi de quibus sermo est, prohibet hic et abdicat dominus. **3** Ex qua evenit ut etiam infideles et non credentes cum vident nos praevaricari mandata, contemptum habeant religionis et doctrinae domini, **4** et ex his ipsis arguant nos quae scripta sunt in lege nostra, et velut rumpant nos et afficiant exprobrantes et confutantes tamquam legis propriae transgressores.

---

[96] *Tradit* Zelz., following CPJ, confirmed L² 25; *tradidit* most other MSS.

Question 169

Q: If we receive a benefit from someone, how shall we be able to thank worthily and wholeheartedly both the Lord and the one who bestowed the benefit, with the measure we owe to each?

R: 1 If we are fully persuaded that God is *the author and finisher* of every good (cf. Heb 12:2), then we will acknowledge him through whom we received something good as the minister of God's grace and bounty.

Question 170

Q: What is "worthy or holy," what the Greeks call ὅσιον, and what is just? (cf. Titus 1:8)[145]

R: 1 Ὅσιον, that is, holy and worthy, is, I consider, whatever is fitting and due that is offered by subjects to their betters, according to the very principle by which they appear to be pre-eminent. **2** "Just," however, is the recompense made to each for the merit of his work. **3** With the former only the tribute of the best is meant, but with the latter, the recompense of both good and evil is denoted.

Question 171

Q: How does one *give to dogs what is holy* and *cast pearls before swine*, or how does it happen what is added: *lest perhaps they trample them underfoot and turn and rend you*? (Matt 7:6)

R: 1 The Apostle manifestly delivers this to us in what he says against the Jews, namely: *you who boast of the law dishonour God through your transgression of the law* (Rom 2:23). **2** The Lord therefore forbids and refuses that harm which they whom this saying concerns are said to bring against the word of God *through their transgression*. **3** Hence it happens that even those outside the faith and non-believers, when they see that we transgress the commandments, hold the piety and teachings of the Lord in contempt, **4** and they reprimand us with the very things which are written in our law, and as it were they *rend* and harry us, reproving and confounding us as transgressors of our own law.

---

[145] SR 249 1249A τί ἐστι τὸ ὅσιον καὶ τὶ ἐστι τὸ δίκαιον. Garnier translates τὸ ὅσιον as *honestum*, which seems more in keeping with the sense used in the response. Evidently the terms here discussed acquired their nuances from some unrecorded context concerning relations of subjects and superiors.

Interrogatio CLXXII

(Zelzer 194–95, QF 156, SR 251 [PG 31.1249–1252])

I: Quomodo aliquando quidem dominus prohibet portari *sacculum* vel *peram* in via, aliquando autem dicit *Sed nunc qui habet sacculum tollat similiter et peram et qui non habet* gladium *vendat vestimentum suum et emat* gladium?

R: 1 Hoc explanat ipse dominus dicens quia *Oportet adhuc et hoc compleri in me quod dictum est quia cum iniquis deputatus est.* **2** Denique posteaquam completa est prophetia de gladio ait ad Petrum *Converte gladium in locum suum; omnes enim qui accipiunt gladium in gladio peribunt,* **3** ita ut non videatur praeceptum esse quod dicitur *Nunc qui habet sacculum tollat,* sed prophetia praedicentis domini quia futurum erat ut apostoli obliti gratiae domini et legis eius assumerent gladium.

4 Quod autem videtur quasi imperativo modo dici ‹pro› propositivo,[97] haec verbi figura in scripturis propheticis satis frequenter invenitur, **5** sicut est illud *Fiant filii eius orphani* et *Diabolus stet a dextris eius* et multa alia similia.

Interrogatio CLXXIII

(Zelzer 196, QF 157, SR 252 [PG 31.1251–1252])

I: Quid est *Panem substantivem da nobis hodie,* quod in oratione dicere iubemur?

R: 1 Cum operantes manibus memores sumus domini dicentis *Nolite solliciti esse animae vestrae quid manducetis aut quid bibatis,* et apostoli prae-cipientis *Operamini ut habeatis unde praestare necessitatem patienti,* **2** id est cum non ad proprios usus, sed pro mandato domini operamur quoniam *dignus est operarius mercede sua,* **3** tunc *substantivum panem,* id est qui vitam cotidianum substantiae nostrae confert, a deo poscimus, et non nobis ipsis praesumimus, **4** sed ‹a deo petimus›[98] ut necessitati in quantum sufficit satisfiat et agnoscamus eum qui sufficientiam praestat.

---

[97] ‹*Pro*› *propositivo.* The ‹*pro*› restored by Zelzer, confirmed L² 61, 64; "*pro*" is om-mitted by haplography in CGJLPSW; *propositio* MT Hol., *non prepositivo* H.

[98] *Et non nobis . . . petimus›,* the whole passage restored L² 29, 72. The Greek SR 252 1252B: τότε τὸν ἐπιούσιον ἄρτον, τουτέστι τὸν πρὸς τὴν ἐφήμερον ζωὴν τῇ οὐσίᾳ ἡμῶν χρησιμεύοντα, οὐχ ἑαυτῷ ἐπιτρέπει, ἀλλὰ τῷ θεῷ ἐντυγχάνει περὶ τούτου (but turns to God with a request for it), καὶ τὴν ἀνάγκην τῆς ἐνδείας ἐπιδείξας (that is, in praying

Question 172

Q: How is it that in one place the Lord forbids us to *carry a purse or wallet for the way* (Luke 10:4), while in another place he says: *But now, whoever has a purse, let him take it and likewise a wallet and whoever does not have a sword, let him sell his cloak and buy a sword?* (Luke 22:36)

R: 1 The Lord himself explains this where he says: *For there must even now be fulfilled in me what is written: "he was reckoned among the wicked"* (cf. Luke 22:37; Isa 53:12). **2** For as soon as the prophecy of the sword is fulfilled, he says to Peter (cf. John 18:10): *Put your sword back in its place; for all who take up the sword shall perish by the sword* (Matt 26:51-52). **3** This was so that the saying: *now, whoever has a purse let him take it* (Luke 22:36) might not appear to be a precept, but a prophecy of the Lord foretelling what was going to happen, that the apostles, forgetting the grace of the Lord and his law, would take up the sword.

4 Besides, it seems as if the imperative mood used for the future tense is found quite often in the Scriptures as a figure for the prophetic,[146] **5** as in that saying: *Let his children become orphans* (Ps 108:9) and *Let an accuser stand at his right hand* (Ps 108:6), and many other like passages.

Question 173

Q: What is the *Give us this day our daily bread* which we are taught to say in prayer? (Matt 6:11; Luke 11:3)

R: 1 If, while we are working with our hands we are mindful of the Lord who said: *Do not be anxious about your life, what you shall eat and what you shall drink* (Matt 6:25), and of the Apostle who charges: *work that you may have something to give to those in need* (Eph 4:28), **2** that is, when we do not work for our own needs, but for the sake of the Lord's commandment— since *the worker is worthy of his hire* (Luke 10:7; cf. Matt 10:10), **3** then *the daily bread*, that which bestows daily life on our substance, we ask from God and do not arrogate for ourselves. **4** Instead we seek from God that he might satisfy us with sufficient for our need, and so acknowledge him who provides us with a sufficiency.

---

[146] SR 251 1252A τῷ προστακτικῷ εἴδει τοῦ λόγου ἀντὶ προφητικοῦ πολλάκις κέχρηται, "Scripture often uses the imperative mood of speech for the prophetic."

Interrogatio CLXXIIII

(Zelzer 196–98, QF 158, SR 220 [PG 31.1227–1228])

I: Si omni volenti accedere ad sorores oportet indulgere an certis quibusque et personis et temporibus, vel quomodo videndae sunt sorores?

R: 1 De his superius iam sufficientur diximus quia nec vir ad virum
accedere utcumque et sine causa ex arbitrio suo vel potestate debet, sed
cum omni observatione probante eo qui praeest, **2** id est ut vel prosit
quis ei quem videt vel proficiat ex eo: quanto magis erga mulieres id
observare convenit maiore cautela.

3 Si quis ergo meminit domini dicentis quia *De omni sermone otioso red-
de*tis *rationem in die iudicii,* timebit in omni negotio hanc sententiam.
4 Acquiescendum est enim et sancto apostolo dicenti *Sive manducatis sive
bibitis sive aliud quid facitis omnia in gloriam dei facite,* et iterum *Omnia ad
aedificationem fiant.* **5** Nihil ergo vel otiose vel inutiliter agendum est, sed
certus quis et certo tempore et certo in loco et certis personis vel apparere
vel loqui debet, **6** ut excludatur omnis nefanda suspicio et servemus sine
offensione esse apud omnes et ad aedificationem fidei uniquique
apparere.

7 Certe solum ad solam accedere nulla religionis ratio permittit, *melius
enim duo quam unus,* simul enim et fidelius et tutius res geritur; **8** *vae enim
uni quia si ceciderit non est qui erigat eum.*

---

the word "give us today our daily bread") οὕτως ἐσθίει τὸ διδόμνον παρὰ τοῦ . . .
ἐπιτεταγμμένου ποιεῖν . . . ; omitted Zelz. following CS; *et non nobis ipsis praesumimus
sed* GHLMW Hol. with slight variants, confirmed by Lundström as Rufinus's Latin
text, in which he recast the response in first person plural after the Our Father, as
corresponding with the Greek οὐχ ἑαυτῷ ἐπιτρέπει, ἀλλά, . . . ; omitted in α (CS), P,
J, T. ‹*A deo petimus*› is supplied by Lundström, which he says had already dropped
out in the archetype, creating a syntactical confusion leading to ad hoc deletions in
α. It corresponds to καὶ τὴν ἀνάγκην τῆς ἐνδείας ἐπιδείξας.

Question 174

Q: Should anyone who wishes to be allowed to meet the sisters, or only certain persons and times? And how ought the sisters to be seen?

R: 1 We have already spoken sufficiently about this above,[147] that one man ought not approach another man whenever and without cause, by his own decision or authority, but only after much testing with the approval of the one who presides, **2** that is, in order to benefit the other whom he sees or be helped by him. Then how much more fitting it is to observe a greater caution towards women!

3 But if one is mindful of the Lord who said: *For every idle word you shall render account in the day of judgment* (Matt 12:36), he will fear this sentence at every encounter. **4** For the holy Apostle must be obeyed who says: *whether you eat or drink or whatever you do, do all for the glory of God* (1 Cor 10:31); and again: *Let all be done so as to edify* (1 Cor 14:26). **5** Nothing therefore is to be done idly and aimlessly—instead, a definite person must appear and speak at a definite time, in a definite place with definite persons, **6** so that every base suspicion is excluded and we preserve ourselves blameless before all and appear to each for the upbuilding of the faith.

7 Surely no principle of piety permits a man alone to meet a woman alone,[148] *for two*, it says, *are better than one* (Eccl 4:9), and at the same time the meeting is conducted with greater credibility and assurance, **8** for *woe to one alone; if he falls there is no one to raise him up* (Eccl 4:10).

---

[147] SR 220 1228B: ἐν τοῖς κατὰ πλάτος, "in the extended sections," QF 158.1: "We have spoken plainly about this once before." This later insertion in the Greek shows that at some stage after the *Small Asketikon* was finished Basil himself edited or authorized the division of the *Asketikon* into Longer and Shorter Responses. See also SR 74 and 103. But what does the "*superius*" of the Latin here refer to? The topic is touched on in the *Small Asketikon*—not, however, "above," but rather "below" at RBas 198. Perhaps qualifying for "above" may be RBas 136 on the topic of silence.

[148] SR 220 1228C: Ἀλλ᾽ οὔτε ἓν πρόσωπον ἑνὶ συντυγχάνειν ἐπιτρέπει ὁ λόγος. In Greek, "one person" is neuter gender, whereas the Latin adjectival pronouns are rendered in masculine and feminine genders respectively. Second, ὁ λόγος might be translated as "reason" or "principle," as Rufinus seems to have understood it and then added "*religionis*," but in relation to what follows it may be better understood as the scriptural word.

Interrogatio CLXXV
(Zelzer 198–99, QF –, SR 57 [PG 31.1221–1222])

I: Si quis habeat aliquod vitium quod corrigere non potest et frequenter notatus in peius proficiat,[99] si expedit illum intermitti?

R: 1 Et de hoc alibi iam diximus quia oportet peccantes corripere patienter secundum eum quem supra ostendimus modum a domino positum. **2** Quodsi non *sufficit ei* ad emendationem sicut illi Corinthio *obiurgatio haec quae fit a pluribus, sicut gentilis* de reliquo *et publicanus* haberi debet qui eiusmodi est, **3** quia ei parcere quem dominus condemnavit nulli tutum est, maxime cum dominus dicat quia **4** *Expedit* unicuique *ut unum* oculum aut unam manum vel unum pedem *perd*at et ita intret in regnum, *quam* dum parcit uni ex his membris *totum corpus mittatur in gehennam* ignis, ubi est *fletus et strido dentium*. **5** Sed et apostolus de his ipsis testatur dicens[100] quia *Modicum fermentem totam massam corrumpit*.

Interrogatio CLXXVI
(Zelzer 199, QF 164, SR 123 [PG 31.1165–1166])

I: Si quis contristetur quod ei non permittitur facere illud quod non potest apte et recte facere, si debemus ei permittere?

R: 1 Et de his iam dictum est in multis quia propria voluntate nulli quicquam facere permittendum est, sed iudicio et probatione vel multorum vel eorum qui praesunt. **2** Qui autem non obtemperat his sententiam praesumptoris et contradicentis excipiat.

Interrogatio CLXXVII
(Zelzer 200, QF 165, SR 177 [PG 31.1199–1202])

I: Quomodo debent *fortiores infirmitates infirmorum portare*?

R: 1 Portare est tollere et curare secundum quod scriptum est *Ipse infirmitates nostras tulit et aegritudines nostras portavit*, **2** non quod in semet ipsum susceperit infirmitates, sed quia abstulit eas ab his in quibus erant et curavit eos. **3** Ita ergo et hic paenitentia interveniente curabuntur infirmiores ex constantia et integritate fortiorum qui dicuntur portare, id est exportare et auferre, infirmitates eorum qui invalidi sunt.

---

[99] *Proficiat* J, confirmed L² 64; *proficit* Zelz. with most MSS, an archetype error through assimilation to the following *expedit*.

[100] *Dicens* Zelz. following C, WLG, M, J, confirmed L² 40–41; omitted HPST.

Question 175

Q: If someone has a vice which he is unable to correct, and, although he is constantly reproved, he becomes worse, is it better to leave him alone?

R: 1 We have already spoken of this elsewhere, that we ought to correct sinners patiently in the manner which we showed above was set out by the Lord. **2** But if *the rebuke coming from the many is* not *enough for his amendment*, as it was for the Corinthian (2 Cor 2:6), then someone like this must be regarded henceforth *as the Gentile and the tax-collector* (Matt 18:17). **3** For to spare him whom the Lord has condemned is no way a safe course for anyone, especially since the Lord says: **4** *it is better* that someone *lose an eye or a hand or a foot and so enter into* the kingdom, *than that* he spare one of his members and *his whole body be cast into the Gehenna of fire*, where there is *weeping and grinding of teeth* (cf. Matt 5:29-30 + 13:42 + 18:8-9). **5** And the Apostle, too, bears witness concerning this when he says that *a little leaven corrupts the whole lump* (Gal 5:9).

Question 176

Q: If someone is saddened because he is not permitted to do what he cannot do fittingly and correctly, should we allow him?

R: 1 Concerning this it has already been said on many occasions that it ought not be permitted anyone to do anything according to his own will, but according to the judgment and approval of the many or of those who preside.[149] **2** Let anyone who does not obey them, incur the judgment of presumption and contradiction.

Question 177

Q: How ought *the strong bear the infirmities of the weak*? (Rom 15:1)

R: 1 To bear is to carry away and to cure according to what is written: *he took our infirmities and carried our diseases* (Isa 53:4; Matt 8:17), **2** not that he contracted the infirmities in himself, but that he took them away from those who were in such case and cured them. **3** So then in this case too, once repentance has entered in, the weak are cured by the steadfastness and integrity of the stronger who are said to *bear*, that is, to carry and take away, *the infirmities* of those who are frail.

---

[149] "Or of those who preside" is not found in the Greek or Syriac. It seems to be a gloss by Rufinus explaining who "the many" are. In LR 45, Basil himself warns against "democracy."

Interrogatio CLXXVIII
(Zelzer 200–1, QF 166, SR 178 [PG 31.1201–1202])

I: Quid est *Invicem onera vestra portate,* et *quam legem Christi adimplebi*mus hoc facientes?

R: 1 Idem est quod in superioribus explanavimus: gravia enim sunt peccata quae trahunt animam in profundum inferni, quae a nobis invicem auferimus et portamus, id est exportamus, ad conversionem provocantes eos qui peccant. **2** Portare autem pro auferre et exportare consuetudo est etiam ritu provincialium dici, sicut et ego saepe audisse me memini. **3** Legem autem Christi replebimus qui dixit *Non veni vocare iustos sed peccatores in paenitentiam.*

Interrogatio CLXXVIIII
(Zelzer 201–2, QF 167, SR 221[PG 31.1229–1230])

I: Domino dicente nos *ora*ndum esse uti *ne intre*mus *in temptationem,* si oportet orare nos ne accidant nobis dolores corporales, vel si inciderimus in eos quomodo oportet ferre?

R: 1 Non discrevit temptationum qualitatem, sed generaliter praecepit *ora*ndum esse *ne intre*mus *in temptationem.* **2** Si vero inciderimus ut det nobis exitum evadendi et *ut sustinere possi*mus a domino posci oportet, ut possimus implere quod dictum est quia *Qui permanserit usque in finem hic salvus erit.*

Interrogatio CLXXX
(Zelzer 202, QF 168, SR 222 [PG 31.1229–1230])

I: Quis est *adversarius* noster et quomodo ei *consenti*re debemus *in via?*

R: 1 Hic specialiter dominus eum qui auferre quid a nobis conatur adversarium nominavit. **2** Consentimus autem ei si servemus praeceptum domini dicentis *Si quis autem voluerit tecum iudicio contendere et auferre tunicam tuam dimitte ei et pallium;* quod et in omnibus similiter observari oportet.

Question 178

Q: What is *bear one another's burdens*, and in so doing, what is *the law of Christ* that we *shall fulfil*? (Gal 6:2)

R: 1 The same as was explained above, for sins are deadweights that drag the soul down to the abyss of Hell, which we take away and bear, that is, carry away from each other, when we rouse those who sin to conversion. **2** Moreover, in the vernacular use,[150] "to bear" is said for "to take away" and "to carry away," as I myself remember having heard often. **3** Now *the law of Christ* that we *shall fulfil* (Gal 6:2) is as he said: *I came not to call the just, but sinners to repentance* (Luke 5:32).

Question 179

Q: The Lord teaches us that we ought to *pray lest we enter into temptation.* Ought we then to pray that bodily distresses do not happen to us, or if we do fall into them, how ought we to bear them? (Matt 6:13; 26:41; Luke 11:4; 22:40)

R: 1 He made no distinction as to kinds of temptation, but commanded in general terms that we ought to *pray lest we enter into temptation.* **2** But if we have succumbed to it, we should ask from the Lord that he give us *a way out, so that* we may *be able to bear it* (cf. 1 Cor 10:13), and so be able to fulfil what was said: *he who endures to the end shall be saved* (Matt 10:22; 24:13).

Question 180

Q: Who is our *adversary* and how must we *agree with him on the way*? (cf. Matt 5:25)

R: 1 Here the Lord especially names as *adversary* one who tries to take away what is ours. **2** And we *agree with him* if we keep that precept of the Lord who said: *If anyone would contend with you at law and take away your tunic, let him have your cloak as well* (Matt 5:40) and it ought to be likewise observed in all matters.

---

[150] "Milligan–Moulton s.v. βαστάζω quote papyri instances showing that the meaning 'carry' developed into 'carry off,' 'take away.' Basil says this sense was well established in Cappadocia. Did Paul in Gal. 6.2 use a well-known local phrase in the sense 'take away'?" Clarke (1925), 296 n. 1.

Interrogatio CLXXXI
(Zelzer 202–3, QF 169, SR 137 [PG 31.1173–1174])

I: Si bonum est statuere ad certum tempus verbi causa abstinere se a tali vel tali cibo sive potu?

R: 1 Domino dicente *Non ut faciam voluntatem meam sed voluntatem eius qui misit me* omnis huiuscemodi definitio incongrua est. **2** Quod sciens David dicebat *Iuravi et statui custodire iudicia iustitiae tuae* non meae voluntatis.

Interrogatio CLXXXII
(Zelzer 203, QF 170, SR 58 [PG 31.1121–1122])

I: Si quis voluntate peccaverit condemnatur, an etiam ille qui per ignorantiam aliquid extra veritatem fuerit locutus?

R: 1 Iudicium dei etiam in his qui per ignorantiam peccant manifestum est cum dicit quia *Qui nescit et fecerit digna plagis vapulabit paucis.* **2** Ubique tamen digne gesta paenitentia veniae spem praesumit.

Interrogatio CLXXXIII
(Zelzer 204, QF 171, SR 59 [PG 31.1121–1122])

I: Si quis cogitaverit tantum facere aliquid et non fecerit, si et ipse mendax iudicandus est?

R: 1 Si secundum mandatum est quod cogitavit facere non solum ut mendax sed ut contemptor a domino condemnatur.

Question 181

Q: Is it good to resolve for a certain time to abstain, for example, from such and such a food or drink?[151]

R: 1 Since the Lord says: *I came not to do my own will, but the will of him who sent me* (John 6:38) any determination of this kind is out of place. **2** David knew this when he said: *I have sworn and resolved to keep the judgments of your justice* (Ps 118:106)—not of my own will.

Question 182

Q: Is it one who sins deliberately that is condemned, or also one who said something contrary to the truth, but in ignorance?

R: 1 That the judgment of God is also against those who sin in ignorance is clear since he says: *Whoever did not know, yet did things worthy of blows, shall be beaten with fewer* (Luke 12:48).[152] **2** But, as always, repentance worthily carried out presupposes the hope of forgiveness.

Question 183

Q: If someone only thought to do something, but did not do it, is he also to be judged a *liar*? (cf. 1 Tim 1:10)

R: 1 If what he thought to do was according to the commandment, he is condemned by the Lord not only as a liar but as a scorner.

---

[151] See Letter 99.28 to Amphilochius (Def III, 118–19): "One thing, however, seems to me ridiculous, that anyone should vow to abstain from swine's flesh. So do teach them to refrain from ignorant vows and promises, I beg you." See also Palladius, *Lausiac History*, Prologue 9.

[152] *Morals* 9.5 uses the same text to teach the same thing.

Interrogatio CLXXXIIII

(Zelzer 204–5, QF 172, SR 60 [PG 31.1121–1124])

I: Si quis praeventus fuerit ut definiat agere aliquid eorum quae non placent deo, quid oportet magis: in irritum devocare[101] quod male fuerat definitum an timore eo ne mendax sit implere peccatum?

R: 1 Cum dicit apostolus *Non quod ex nobis ipsis idonei sumus cogitare aliquid quasi ex nobis,* et dominus nihilo minus quia *Non possum ego a me ipso facere quicquam,* **2** et rursum *Verba quae ego loquor vobis a me ipso non loquor,* et in alio quoque loco *Descendi de caelo non ut faciam voluntatem meam sed voluntatem eius qui misit me patris,* **3** paenitentiam debet agere primum qui ita aliquid temere definit,[102] quodcumque illud fuerit quod definitum est, **4** quia ne ipsa quidem bona propria auctoritate et definitione facere oportet, multo autem magis ea quae non placent deo statuere non licet.

5 Quia autem oportet in irritum revocari quaecumque ex praesumptione contra mandatum domini statuuntur, manifeste ostenditur in apostolo Petro **6** qui temere quidem statuerat et dixerat *Non lavabis pedes meos in aeternum,* **7** audit‹a› autem a domino definita sententia quia *Si non te lavero non habebis partem mecum,* statim mutavit definitionem suam et ait *Domine, non tantum pedes, sed et manus et caput.*

---

[101] *Devocare* most MSS. confirmed L² 34; *revocare* Zelz. following C, WLG.

[102] *Definit* S, P, WLG, confirmed L² 64, as echoing the present tense in the Gk: τολμᾷ . . . ὁρίζειν ("dares to decide": the verbal senses are inverted in the Latin); *definiit* Zelz., a defective perfect, following C, HJM.

Question 184

Q: If someone is prevented from doing something he had determined to do of things that are displeasing to God, which is preferable: that he call off as invalid what was wickedly determined, or that for fear of being a liar he complete the sin?

R: 1 Since the Apostle says: *Not that we are sufficient of ourselves to think anything as from ourselves* (2 Cor 3:5) and the Lord no less: *I can do nothing from myself* (John 5:30), **2** and again: *The words I speak to you I do not speak as from myself* (John 14:10), and also in another place: *I have come down from heaven not to do my own will, but the will of the Father who sent me* (John 6:38), **3** he must do penance, because he determined so rashly to do something, whatever it may have been that he determined, **4** for he ought not even to perform good deeds by his own authority and determination, and then, much more so, it is not permitted to decide upon deeds displeasing to God.

5 But that he ought to revoke whatever he presumptuously decided contrary to the commandment of the Lord is clearly shown in the case of the Apostle Peter **6** who, having rashly decided and declared that: *You shall never wash my feet!* (John 13:8) **7** yet when he heard the sentence assigned by the Lord: *If I do not wash you, you shall have no part in me*, he immediately changed his own determination and said: *Lord, not only my feet, but my hands and head too!* (John 13:9).

Interrogatio CLXXXV

(Zelzer 207–8, QF 173, SR 101 [PG 31.1151–1154])

I: Si is cui commisa est dispensatio eorum quae domino offeruntur necessitatem habet implere mandatum illud quod dicitur *Omni petenti te da et eum qui vult abs te mutuum sumere non avertas*?

R: 1 Hoc quod dictum est *Omni petenti te da et volentem mutuari abs te non avertas*, quasi temptationis habet locum sicut ex consequentibus demonstratur; **2** propter malos enim praeceptum est non principaliter sed quasi quod in necessitate fieri debeat. **3** Principale enim praeceptum domini est *Vende omnia bona tua et da pauperibus*, et rursum *Vendite bona vestra et date misericordiam*. **4** Quod ergo aliis delegatum est vel deputatum, in alios transferre non est absque discrimine, domino dicente quia *Non sum missus nisi ad oves perditas domus Israel*, **5** et quia *Non est bonum tollere panem filiorum et mittere canibus*, sed et *abs te ipso debes iudicare quod iustum est*.

Interrogatio CLXXXVI

(Zelzer 206–7, QF 174, SR 91 [PG 31.1145–1146])

I: Quodsi frater nihil habens proprium petatur ab aliquo hoc ipsum quod vestitus est, quid debet facere, maxime si nudus sit ille qui petit?

R: 1 Sive nudus sive malus, id est sive vere necessitatem patiatur sive fallat,[103] vel si quid aliud est, semel dictum est quia dare vel accipere non est omnium sed illius solius cui commissum est istud officium. **2** Qui utique cum omni providentia et cautela huiuscemodi dispensationem debet implere, ut possit *unusquisque in* eo *quo vocatus est perman*ere.

---

[103] *Patiatur sive fallat* Zelz. following SP, confirmed L² 36; *patitur sive fallit* WLG, HJ; many other sub-variants.

Question 185

Q: Is it necessary that the one entrusted with the dispensing of the goods dedicated to the Lord fulfil that commandment which says: *Give to everyone who asks and from him who would borrow from you, do not turn away?* (Matt 5:42; Luke 6:30)

R: 1 This saying: *Give to everyone who asks and from him who would borrow from you, do not turn away* (Matt 5:42; Luke 6:30) has the function of a kind of trial, as is shown by what follows. **2** For it is not principally commanded for the sake of the wicked, but as something that should be done in necessity. **3** For the Lord's principal command is: *Sell your possessions and give to the poor* (Matt 19:21), and again: *Sell your possessions and give alms* (Luke 12:33). **4** Therefore what is set apart and assigned for some may not be transferred to others without peril,[153] for the Lord says: *I was sent only to the lost sheep of the house of Israel* (Matt 15:24), **5** and: *It is not right to take the children's bread and give it to the dogs* (Matt 15:26), yes and: *you must judge for yourself what is just* (cf. Luke 12:57).

Question 186

Q: What of a brother who, not having anything of his own, is asked by another for the very thing he is wearing? What is he to do, especially if the petitioner is naked?

R: 1 Whether naked or wicked, that is, whether he truly suffers necessity or deceives or whatever else, it has been said once that to give or to receive is not for everyone but only for the one to whom that office is entrusted. **2** He at any rate ought to fulfil this kind of stewardship with all forethought and caution, so that *each* can *abide in that wherein he was called* (1 Cor 7:20, 24).

---

[153] In Letter 150 (Def III, 368–69), Heracleidas reports of Basil: "He said that experience was needed in order to distinguish between one who is genuinely needy and one begging from avarice. For he who gives to the afflicted gives to the Lord, and from the Lord shall receive his reward. On the other hand, he who gives to every vagabond casts to a dog, which is troublesome indeed from his shamelessness, but deserving no pity on the ground of need." The translator of the Syriac adds a new passage in which he takes a cue from Matt 5:45 to say that despite legitimate cause for discernment, alms should be dispensed to all the needy regardless.

Interrogatio CLXXXVII
(Zelzer 205–6, QF –, SR 179 [PG 31.1201–1204])

I: Quomodo potest quis sine caritate tantam *fidem* habere *ut montes transfer*at aut substantiam suam pauperibus dividat, et *corpus* suum *trade*re *ut arde*at?

R: 1 Si memores sumus domini dicentis *Faciunt enim omnia ut videantur ab hominibus,* **2** sed et illud quod respondit illis dicentibus *Domine, nonne in tuo nomine daemonia eiecimus et in tuo nomine virtutes multas fecimus?* cum ait ad eos *Nescio vos unde estis*—**3** non quia mentiti sunt, sed quia dei gratia abusi sunt ad proprias voluntates, quod utique alienum est a caritate dei,—**4** si ergo horum meminimus facile quae dicta sunt advertimus.

5 Quia autem gratiam dei vel donum accipiant etiam indigni non est novum aut mirum, deus enim in tempore hoc *benignitatis et patientiae* suae etiam *solem suum oriri iubet super bonos et malos;* **6** interdum autem etiam ad profectum eorum qui adhuc infideles sunt, ut gloria eius multiplicetur, secundum quod apostolus dicit quia *Quidam per invidiam et contentionem, quidam autem et propter bonam voluntatem Christum annuntiant,* **7** et addidit his dicens Verumtamen *omni modo sive occasione sive veritatem Christus annuntietur et in hoc ego gaudeo.*

Interrogatio CLXXXVIII
(Zelzer 208–9, QF –, SR 62 [PG 31.1123–1124])

I: Quis est qui *abscond*ere dicitur *talentum* et propterea condemnatur?

R: 1 Qui quamcumque gratiam dei detinet et assumit in suis usibus et non ad aliorum utilitatem, iste tamquam occultati talenti crimine condemnatur.

Interrogatio CLXXXVIIII
(Zelzer 209, QF –, SR 67 [PG 31.1129–1130])

I: Quid est *immunditia* et quid est *impudicitia*?

R: 1 *Immunditia*m quidem lex ostendit; hoc enim nomine usa est super his qui inviti per naturalem necessitatem patiebantur ea quae homines pati consueverunt.

2 *Impudicitia* vere mihi videtur esse cum quis naturalem libidinis motum impudentius et inverecundius concitat et irritat.

Question 187

Q: How can anyone, without love, acquire *so great a faith as to move mountains*, or *give away* his *possessions* to the poor or *hand over* his *body to be burnt*? (cf. 1 Cor 13:2-3)

R: 1 If we remember the Lord who said: *They do all these things that they may be seen by human beings* (Matt 23:5; cf. 6:5), **2** and his answer to those who said: *Lord, Lord, did we not cast out demons in your name and do many mighty works in your name?* when he said to them: *I do not know you, or where you come from* (Matt 7:22-23)—**3** not because they had lied, but because they had misused the grace of God for their own will, which assuredly is alien to love for God—**4** if therefore we remember these things, we easily discern what was said.

5 Besides, there is nothing strange or surprising that some receive the grace or the gift of God unworthily, for God, in this season of *forbearance* and *patience* (cf. Rom 2:4) *orders his sun to rise upon the good and the bad alike* (Matt 5:45). **6** At the same time this also happens for the progress of those who do not as yet believe, that his glory might be multiplied, according to the Apostle who says: *Some proclaim Christ through envy and contention, while others from good will* (Phil 1:15), **7** and to this he adds shortly: *Only, in every way, whether in pretext or in truth, Christ is proclaimed and in this I rejoice* (Phil 1:18).

Question 188

Q: Who is the one said to *hide his talent* and on that account is condemned? (cf. Matt 18:25)

R: 1 Whoever holds back any grace from God and arrogates it for his own purposes and not for the benefit of others, such a one is condemned for the offence of *hiding his talent*.

Question 189

Q: What is *uncleanness* and what is *lewdness*? (2 Cor 12:21)

R: 1 The law has shown what *uncleanness* is, for it used this term for what happens without our unwilling it through the necessity of nature, when human beings undergo what they normally undergo.

2 But it seems to me that *lewdness* is when one wantonly and shamelessly provokes and stirs up a natural impulse of pleasure.

Interrogatio CLXXXX

(Zelzer 209–10, QF 175, SR 68 [PG 31.1129–1132])

I: Quid est proprium furoris et quid est proprium indignationis iustae, et quomodo aliquotiens quasi[104] ab indignatione incipientes invenimur decidere in furorem?

R: 1 Furoris quidem proprium est concitatio animae mala meditantis adversum eum qui se concitat et irritat. **2** Indignationis vero iustae proprium est peccantem corripere eo affectu vel proposito, quo avertimur a peccatis et quo displicet nobis quod non recte gestum est.

3 Quod autem interdum a bono incipiens anima decidit in malum nihil mirum est, multa etenim invenies huiusmodi propter quod meminisse oportet sanctae scripturae dicentis **4** *Iuxta semitam scandalum posuerunt mihi*, et iterum *Nisi* enim quis *legitime certaverit non coronatur.* **5** Et ideo in omnibus observanda est rerum mensura et tempus et ordo, quia ex aliqua horum causa accidit ut quod videtur bonum id inveniatur malum.

Interrogatio CLXXXXI

(Zelzer 208–9, QF 163, SR 182 [PG 31.1203–1204])

I: Ex quibus fructibus probari debet is qui ex affectu arguit fratrem peccantem?

R: 1 Primo omnium ex eo quod praecipuum est, si cum misericordia rem gerit et est in eo illud quod dicit apostolus quia *Si patitur unum membrum compatiuntur omnia membra*, vel illud *Quis scandalizatur et ego non uror?* **2** Tum deinde si in omni peccato similiter affligitur et contristatur et erga omnes qui peccant, vel si in se delinquat aliquis vel in alium, similiter contristatur et luget. **3** Et si *arguens* observat illam regulam quam dominus posuit, id est ut vel *inter se et ipsum solum* vel alio uno aut duobus adhibitis. **4** Super omnia autem si observat quod dixit apostolus *Cum omni patientia.*

---

[104] *Quasi* most MSS, confirmed L² 27: *quasi* conveys the δῆθεν ("naturally," "of course" or "understandably") of three MSS of the *Great Asketikon*. It is somewhat supported by QF 175.Q, which uses the adverb ܪܕܘܠܩ ("suitably," "fittingly"). See PG 31.1130 n.18; omitted Zelz. following SCP.

Question 190

Q: What is proper to wrath[154] and what is proper to just indignation[155] and how is it at times that we begin, as it were, with indignation, but find ourselves succumbing to wrath?

R: 1 Wrath is properly a provocation of the soul which meditates ill against one who has provoked and irritated it. **2** On the other hand, what is proper to just indignation is to correct the sinner in that disposition or purpose whereby we are repelled by sins and what has not been done uprightly displeases us.

3 But there is nothing to marvel at that a soul beginning with good succumbs to evil, for you might find many such instances. That is why we ought to be mindful of the holy Scripture which says: **4** *They have placed a stumbling block on my path* (Ps 139:6) and again, *no-one is crowned unless he contends lawfully* (2 Tim 2:5). **5** And so in all things moderation in affairs and timeliness and order needs to be maintained, lest it happen that from some such cause what seems to be good is discovered to be evil.

Question 191

Q: By what fruits must it be shown that one has rebuked a sinning brother with sympathy?[156]

R: 1 First of all by that which is the chief criterion, if he conducts himself with mercy and has in him what the Apostle says: *If one member suffers, all the members suffer with it* (1 Cor 12:26), or this: *Who is made to stumble and I do not burn?* (2 Cor 11:29) **2** Second, if he is afflicted and saddened in the same way towards every sin, and, whether someone offends against himself or another, he is saddened and mourns in the same way. **3** Third, if, when he rebukes someone, he observes that rule which the Lord laid down, that it is to be *between himself and the other alone*, or, *having brought along one or two others* (Matt 18:15-16; cf. Deut 19:1). **4** But above all, if he observes what the Apostle says: *With all patience* (2 Tim 4:2).

---

[154] SR 68 1129C: θυμοῦ.
[155] SR 68 1129C: ἀγανακτήσεως εὐλόγου.
[156] SR 182 1204C: ὁ συμπάθῶς ἐλέγχων.

Interrogatio CLXXXXII
(Zelzer 211, QF –, SR 105 [PG 31.1155–1156])

I: Si oportet qui ingrediunter ad fratres statim artificia discere?

R: 1 Qui praesunt probent.[105]

Interrogatio CLXXXXIII
(Zelzer 212, QF 176, SR 73 [PG 31.1155–1156])

I: Si quis non desiderio corrigenda fratres arguat eum qui delinquit sed sui vitii explendi gratia, quomodo hunc corrigi si post multam commonitionem in eidem permaneat?

R: 1 Iste velut suis commodis prospiciens et primatus desiderans notetur et emendationis ei modus ex institutionum disciplinis intimetur. **2** Quodsi permanserit in obstinatione manifesta est sententia eorum qui non paenitent pro delicto.

---

[105] *Add*: ut quem sociari voluerint corpori congregationis, artibus erudiant diversis, secundum modum et qualitatem propriae aetatis et conditionis: Ut verbi gratia: si ad meditanda vel agenda spiritualia minus inveniatur idoneus, alterius negotii solicitetur occupationibus, ne torpentem otio atque vacantem satanas, expositum quodammodo suis telis occupet. Dicit enim Apostolus: *Qui non laborat, non manducet*. Et Salomon: Otiositas inimica est animae. Hol.

Question 192

Q: Should those entering the brothers[157] begin to learn crafts immediately?

R: 1 Let those who preside decide.[158]

Question 193

Q: If someone reprimands an offender not from a desire to correct the brothers but for the sake of venting his own vice, how ought such a one be corrected if, despite many warnings, he persists in the same ways?

R: 1 Let such be censured as one looking to suit himself and desiring to dominate. Let him be shown the way to amend himself through the practices of the disciplined life. **2** If he persists in this obstinacy, it is clear his judgment is with those who do not repent for their offence.

---

[157] SR 105 1156A: εἰς ἀδελφοτήτα. One of several instances where the Latin text seems to be translating the Greek *adelphotes* "brotherhood/fraternity" by using "brothers."

[158] SR 1156A: οἱ προεστῶτες δοκιμάσουσιν. That is the sum of the response, both in the Latin and the Greek. Zelzer supplies in a note the continuance of the text in Holste's edition, without adducing M (a chief source of Hol.) or any other codex in support: ". . . [assess] whether they are to educate in various crafts one whom they want to associate with the body of the community, to the measure and in the kind suitable for their age and condition—for example: if he is found less fitted for the spiritual things that must be meditated and carried out, let him be accommodated with occupations of another sort, lest, grown sluggish with idleness and unoccupied, he may be exposed in a way to Satan's darts, who may then take up residence. For the Apostle says: *Whoever does not work, let him not eat* (2 Thess 3:10). And Solomon: *Idleness is the enemy of the soul.*" Grib 106 briefly notes the use of the singular *qui praeest* in printed editions (Bivar and Venise), following W and a short addition in L. He concludes: "En revanche, Holste ajoute neuf lignes, qui cherchent d'ailleurs à imiter la manière de Basile."

Curiously, there appear to be two verbal parallels in the RB to the Holste text, "*sociari voluerint corpori congregationis,*" namely, RB 61.7, "*sociari corpori monasterii*" and RB 61.8, "*suscipiatur congregationis sociandus.*" The concluding citation as if from Solomon does not appear in Scripture. Yet the same aphorism begins RB 48.1. Timothy Fry, ed., *RB 1980: The Rule of St. Benedict in Latin and English with Notes* (Collegeville, MN: Liturgical Press, 1980) indicates in the apparatus on p. 248 that RB is borrowing from RBas 192—evidently relying on Holste's edition. At the same place in the RB are several cross-references to Cyprian, who certainly was a source for the RB: *To Quirinus* (Testimoniorum 3, 1.3) *On the Lord's Prayer* 7, *To Fortunatus,* par. 1, *On Zeal and Envy* 16, *Letter* 38.2. Cf. Lienhard, "St. Basil's 'Asceticon Parvum' and the *Regula Benedicti,*" 236, and de Vogüé, "Twenty-five Years," 413 n. 37.

Interrogatio CLXXXXIIII
(Zelzer 212, QF 177, SR 106 [PG 31.1155–1156])

I: Qualibus correptionibus uti oportet inter fratres ad emendationem eorum qui delinquunt?

R: 1 Hoc sit in iudicio positum eorum qui praesunt vel quanto tempore vel quali modo corripi debeant, quia et aetas et eruditio multam habere facit differentiam poenae.

Interrogatio CLXXXXV
(Zelzer 213–14, QF 178, SR 75 [PG 31.1133–1136])

I: Si in omni peccato sive secundum cogitationem sive secundum verbum sive secundum actum satanan in causa esse convenit dici?

R: 1 Generaliter arbitror quod satanas ipse per se ipsum causa peccati exsistere nulli potest, sed motibus animae nostrae sive naturalibus sive etiam ex vitio conceptis abutitur ad voluntatem malitiae suae **2** et de nostris nos si forte non vigilemus trahit in hoc quod ipsi gratum est, id est in peccatum.

3 Naturalibus ergo motibus nostris abutitur sicut illud quod in domino facere conatus est, cum eum sensisset esurire, et ait ad eum *Si Filius dei es, dic ut lapides isti panes fiant.* **4** Motibus autem ex vitio conquisitis abutitur sicut fecit in Iuda, quem quoniam cupidum vidit et avaritiae morbo aegrotantem, abusus hoc vitio eius usque ad proditionis eum ob triginta argenteorum lucrum pertraxit ruinam.

Question 194

Q: What penalties ought to be used among the brothers[159] for the amendment of those who sin?

R: 1 Let this be left to the judgment of those who preside, both as to the time and the type of penalty that are due, since both age and understanding make a great difference as to punishment.

Question 195

Q: Is it fitting to say that Satan is the cause of every sin, whether of thought or word or deed?

R: 1 On the whole, I consider that Satan himself, on his own account, cannot be the cause of any sin, but that he abuses the motions of our soul, whether natural or from vice, into doing the will of his malice, **2** and from what is our own he tries to drag us, if perhaps we are not vigilant, into what pleases him, that is, into sin.

3 He abuses the natural motions just as he attempted to do with the Lord, when he perceived that he was hungry and said to him: *If you are the Son of God, tell these* stones *to become loaves* (Matt 4:3), **4** and he abuses the motions acquired through vice, just as he did with Judas. Once he saw his covetousness and his sickness with the disease of avarice, he abused this vice of his and dragged him down even to the ruin[160] of betrayal for a profit of thirty pieces of silver (cf. Matt 26:15).

---

[159] 1156A: ἐν ἀδελφότητι, QF 177.Q: ⲣⲇ̇ⲁⲩⲣ̇ ⲇ̇ⲁⲗ "toward the brotherhood." This is another instance where the Latin translates *adelphotes* with a form of "brothers."

[160] *Pertraxit ruinam*; a Vergilian echo (*Aeneid* II. 465-66)? The image is that of dragging him with the "hook" of the proffered money.

5 Quia autem mala ex nobis ipsis oriantur manifeste dominus ostendit dicens quia *De corde procedunt cogitationes malae* et reliqua. **6** Hoc autem accidit his qui per neglegentiam inculta et squalentia naturalium in se bonorum semina derelinquunt **7** sicut ait Salomon quia *Sicut agricultura* ita *vir insipiens et sicut vinea* ita *homo cui deest prudentia, si relinquas eam fiet deserta et ascendent in eam spinae et erit derelicta.* **8** Huic ergo animae quae ex huiusmodi neglegentia squaluerit et in desertum venerit consequens est suscipere illam sententiam quae dicit *Spinae et tribuli orientur in te,* **9** et pati illud quod scriptum est *Exspectavi ut faceret uvam,*[106] *fecit autem spinas,* de qua dixerat *Plantavi vineam Sorech.* **10** Et tunc merito dicitur ad eam illud quod per Ieremiam praedictum est a deo dicente **11** *Ego plantavi te vineam fructiferam totam veracem, quomodo conversa es in amaritudinem, vinea aliena?*

Interrogatio CLXXXXVI
(Zelzer 214–15, QF 179, SR 94 [PG 31.1147–1148])

I: Si quis relinquens fiscalia debita intret ad fratres, et parentes eius pro ipso exigantur et tribulentur: si non affert hoc culpam aliquem vel his qui eum susceperunt vel illi ipsi[107] qui ita egerit?

---

[106] *Uvam* CPJ, confirmed L² 26, in keeping with the Greek singular σταφυλήν; *uvas* Zelz. following most MSS; QF 178.9 also uses the plural ܥܢܒ̈ܐ, appearing in the oldest MSS. But the word is almost notorious in all three languages for connoting both a singular and a collective sense.

[107] *Illi ipsi* restored by Zelz. confirmed L² 11; *ipse ille* S; *ille ipse* corr. to *illi ipsi* C; *illi ipse* corr. to *ille ipse* P; *ipse* was an archetype error in α, L¹ 589.

5 Moreover the Lord shows clearly that evils spring from ourselves, for *from the heart*, he says, *proceed evil thoughts* and so on (Matt 15:19). **6** This is what happens to those who through negligence let the seeds of natural good lie uncultivated within them and going to waste, **7** just as Solomon says: *Like a field is a foolish man and like a vineyard the man lacking prudence; if you let it be, it will become a desert and thorns shall spring up in it and it shall become derelict* (Prov 24:30-31 LXX). **8** For it follows that a soul which through such negligence becomes derelict and a desert incurs that judgment which says: *Thorns and thistles shall spring up in you* (Gen 3:18) **9** and it experiences what is written: *I expected it to yield grapes, but it yielded thorns* (Isa 5:2 LXX), concerning which he had said: *I planted it a sorech vine* (Isa 5:4). **10** And then it deserves to hear said to it by God what was foretold through Jeremiah: *I planted you a fruitful vine, all true. How then are you changed into bitterness, an alien vine?* (Jer 2:21)

Question 196

Q: If someone enters the brothers[161] leaving behind tax debts, and his parents[162] are subject to demands and hard pressed because of him, does this not bring some blame either upon those who received him, or upon the one who so acted?[163]

---

[161] SR 94 1148B: ἀδελφότητι, QF 179.Q ܐܚܘܬܐ ("to the brotherhood"). Rufinus is clearly translating "brotherhood" with a form of "brothers."

[162] SR 94 1148B: οἰκεῖοι, family or relatives, likewise in QF.

[163] Clarke, 265 n. 5: "One of the motives for renouncing the world in the fourth century was the intolerable pressure of taxes. A landed proprietor who sold his land and retired to a monastery, either distributing the proceeds to the poor himself or inviting the superior to do so for him, would cause serious loss to the Exchequer. This question and answer suggest that there was a good deal of friction, which Basil as bishop tried to prevent." Except that Basil was not bishop at the time of this response, since the text is found in the *Small Asketikon*. On monks and taxation see also Letters 284 (Def IV, 172–75) and 285 (Def IV, 174–75). Deferrari observes (IV, 173 n. 1): "at this period the burdensome tax system inaugurated by Diocletian is still operative throughout the Roman Empire and . . . monks, unlike the clergy proper are laymen and are not therefore eligible to the immunities granted the clergy." In Letter 285 it is clear that the practice of handing over property to the church to administer, as Macrina did, was becoming a burden to Basil as bishop: "such is the property of the poor [Deferrari translates 'monks'] that we are always seeking someone to take it over, for the church spends more on it than any profit it gains from these possessions." In Letter 285 he seems to plead for a Christian property-owner who had been relieving Basil of some of this administrative burden.

R: 1 Dominus noster Iesus Christus his qui interrogaverunt se si *Licet dare censum Caesari aut non*, ait *Ostendite mihi denarium, cuius habet imaginem et superscriptionem?* **2** Cum autem dixissent quia *Caesaris*, respondit dicens *Reddite ergo quae Caesaris sunt Caesari et quae dei sunt deo.* **3** Ex hoc ergo manifeste docemur quia hi obnoxii sunt tributis Caesarum apud quos invenitur Caesaris census et imago. **4** Si quid ergo tale etiam iste veniens ad fratres secum detulit obnoxius est ad exsolvendum debitum, si vero omnibus derelictis in manibus propinquorum abscessit nullus vel ipsi[108] vel fratribus scrupulus debet exsistere.

Interrogatio CLXXXXVII
(Zelzer 215–17, QF 160, SR 108 [PG 31.1155–1156])

I: Si oportet eum qui praeest extra eam quae sororibus praeest loqui aliquid quod ad aedificationem fidei pertineat virginibus?

R: 1 Et quomodo servabitur praeceptum illud apostoli dicentis *Omnia vestra honeste et secundum ordinem fiant?*

---

[108] *Ipsi* most MSS, confirmed L² 11; *illi ipsi* Zelz. synthesized from *illi*, S and *illis*, C + *ipsi* of β, an archetype error in α.

R: 1 To those who asked him whether *it was permissible to pay tribute to Caesar or not*, our Lord Jesus Christ said: *"Show me a denarius; whose image and inscription does it have?"* **2** And when they had said: *"Caesar's,"* he replied: *"Render therefore to Caesar the things that are Caesar's and to God the things that are God's"* (Matt 22:17, 19-21; Luke 20:22-25). **3** From this we learn clearly that they are liable for the tribute to Caesar with whom Caesar's census mark and image are found. **4** If then the one coming to the brothers[164] brought such with him, then he is liable for the payment of the debts, but if when he departed he left all things in the hands of his relatives, then neither himself nor the brothers ought have any scruple about it.

Question 197

Q: Ought he who presides say anything for the upbuilding of the faith among the virgins,[165] apart from her who presides[166] over the sisters?[167]

R: 1 In that case, how is that precept of the Apostle to be observed which says: *Let all you do be done honorably and in order*? (1 Cor 14:40)

---

[164] SR 94 1148C: If he brought with him into the brotherhood (εἰς τὴν ἀδελφότητα) any of the things that are Caesar's. QF 179.4 also uses ܐܚܘܬܐ, "brotherhood."

[165] ἀδελφῇ τινι, "to a sister."

[166] SR 108 1156C: ἐκτὸς τῆς προεστώσης "apart from her who presides." Colb. (Ask 6) adds the phrase ἀδελφαῖς, The Syriac tends to confirm the phrase. QF 160.Q: ܐܚܘܬܐ ܕܐܚܬܐ ܕܩܝܡܐ ܐܝܕܐ ܡܢ ܠܒܪ, "apart from her who is head of the sisters."

[167] In the early days a female *proestosa* might sometimes have presided over the whole *adelphotes*, both men and women. In the 370s Macrina presided at Annisa, with a deaconess, Lampadium, in charge of the women, while Peter, her little brother and protégé, was in charge of the men and served the whole *adelphotes* as priest, a rare situation not easily replicated. The Theodora whom Basil addresses in Letter 173 (Def II, 448–53) belonged to a community of both men and women and may well have been their overall superior; Egeria's friend, the deaconess Marthana, governed a community of both men and women at St. Thecla's, in Seleucia of Isauria; see *Egeria: Diary of a Pilgrimage,* ed. George E. Gingras, ACW 38 (New York: Newman Press, 1970), chap. 22. Of course, devout aristocratic widows presided over their own households, including both men and women, e.g., Magna of Ancyra (Palladius, *Lausiac History,* 67), and this is how Annisa began, with the widow Emmelia as the mistress of the estate.

Interrogatio CLXXXXVIII
(Zelzer 216, QF 161, SR 109 [PG 31.1155–1156])

I: Si convenit eum qui praeest cum ea quae sororibus praeest frequenter loqui, et maxime si aliqui de fratribus pro hoc laeduntur?

R: 1 Apostolo dicente *Ut quid enim libertas mea iudicatur ab alia conscientia?* bonum est imitari eum dicentem quia *Non sum usus potestate mea uti ne offendiculum aliquod darem evangelio Christi.* **2** Et quantum fieri potest et rarius videndae sunt et brevius est sermocinatio finienda.[109]

Interrogatio CLXXXXVIIII
(Zelzer 216–17, QF 162, SR 110 [PG 31.1157–1158])

I: Si oportet cum soror aliqua confitetur quodcumque delictum suum presbytero etiam matrem monasterii adesse?

R: 1 Honestius mihi videtur esse et religiosius ut per seniorem matrem presbyter si quid illud sibi videtur statuat et modum vel typum[110] paenitentiae imponat ad emendationem eius quae corrigi desiderat a peccato.

---

[109] *Finienda* Zelz. With α and most β MSS, confirmed L² 58; *facienda* WLG, J.
[110] *Typum* Zelz. Following α and J, confirmed L² 32; *typus* β MSS.

Question 198

Q: Is it suitable for him who presides to converse frequently with her who presides over the sisters[168] and particularly if some of the brothers take offence at this?[169]

R: 1 Although the Apostle says: *why should my liberty be judged by another's conscience?* (1 Cor 10:29) it is well to imitate him who says: *I did not use this right, that I might not provide the least hindrance to the gospel of Christ* (1 Cor 9:12), **2** and, as far as possible, such meetings ought to be rare and their consultations be quickly brought to an end.

Question 199

Q: When a sister confesses some fault of hers to the presbyter, ought the mother of the monastery be present too?[170]

R: 1 It seems to me to be more honourable and more pious that through the senior mother the *presbyter* prescribes as it appears to him, the measure and kind of penance for the amendment of her who desires to be corrected from sin.[171]

---

[168] SR 109 1156C: τῆς προεστώσης. Again the Syriac tends to confirm the additional phrase. QF 160.Q: ܪܕܐܘܪܟܐ ܪܟܐ ܚܘܕܘܟܐ ܪܒܪܟ ܒܐ, "with her who is head of the sisters."

[169] While Basil has nothing *in principle* against frequent consultation between the two superiors in the one *adelphotes*, he advises prudent restraint for the sake of others' more vulnerable sensitivities. Clarke's "Yes, since the apostle said . . ." (p. 270) remarkably overinterprets a genitive absolute, on which it was unwise for Elm to rely (*Virgins of God*, 75). Rufinus had the advantage of conveying the Greek genitive absolute as a Latin ablative absolute, concessional in sense.

[170] SR 110 1157A Εἰ χρή, ἐξομολογουμένης ἀδελφῆς τῷ πρεσβυτέρῳ, καὶ τὴν πρεσβυτέραν παρεῖναι: "When a sister confesses to the *presbyter* should the *presbytera* be present too?" Rufinus paraphrases *presbytera* as *matrem monasterii*. Why would a sister be confessing to a *presbyter* and not a *presbytera*? Though it is difficult to recover the background with assurance, the solution may be that the sisters' confession to a male *presbyter* is a private "medicinal" confession before one who can be and increasingly *is* also a priest; but it is not the much later sacramental "confession of devotion." But there are several hints that Basil may have had a significant role in the development of private sacramental confession, long before the "Irish monks." See also SR 288 and SR 229.

[171] Rufinus's text is quite differently arranged to the Greek. SR 110 1157A: Confession to the *presbyter*, who is able to prescribe with knowledge the manner of repentance and amendment, shall take place with more seemliness and piety if the *presbytera* is present.

Interrogatio CC
(Zelzer 217–18, QF 180, SR 229 [PG 31.1235–1236])

I: Si oportet gesta turpia vel obscaena confitentem inverecundius enuntiare omnibus aut certis quibusque vel quibus illis?

R: 1 Confessio peccatorum hanc habet rationem quam habet vulnus aliquod corporis vel passio quae medico demonstranda est. **2** Sicut ergo non omnibus quis vitia vel vulnera corporis sui revelat nec quibuslibet, sed his tantummodo qui summae peritiae testimonium habent et curae ac medelae disciplinam, **3** ita et confessio peccatorum fieri debet apud eos tantummodo qui curare haec praevalent et emendare secundum quod scriptum est **4** Vos qui *fortiores* estis *infirmitates infirmorum* portate, hoc est auferte et exportate per curationem.

Interrogatio CCI
(Zelzer 218, QF –, SR 111 [PG 31.1157–1158])

I: Si ignoranter matre seniore presbyter aliquid fieri praecipiat sororibus recte videtur indignari senior mater?

R: 1 Et valde.

Question 200

Q: Ought one to confess shameful or unchaste deeds before all shamelessly, or only before some and who are they?[172]

R: 1 The confession of sins has the same principle as displaying a wound or condition of the body to a physician. **2** Just as one does not disclose the diseases or wounds of the body to anyone, but to those only who give evidence of thorough expertise and of training in cure and remedy, **3** so also confession of sins ought to be made only before those capable of treating and remedying them in accordance with what is written: **4** You *who are stronger, carry the weaknesses of the weak*, that is, bear away and carry them off through treatment (Rom 15:1).

Question 201

Q: If the presbyter has ordered something to be done among the sisters without the knowledge of the senior mother, does it seem right that the senior mother is indignant?

R: 1 Most certainly!

---

[172] Basil will not have "shameful" sins confessed in the assembly, but privately before those accredited in the community as "soul doctors." The principle of private confession which Basil teaches here in the domain of community life he carries through even in the church's system of canonical penance, for he indicates that there are occasions when private confession before the bishop is appropriate, e.g., canon 34, Letter 199 (Def III, 124–25). For whether priests as such are involved in the practice of confession in community, see the discussion in RBas 21 and 199.

Interrogatio CCII

(Zelzer 219–20, QF 182, SR 275 [PG 31.1273–1274])

I: Si potest impedire propositum sancti hominis satanas, quia scriptum est *Ego quidem Paulus et semel et bis, et impedivit nos satanas?*

R: 1 Eorum quae in domino geruntur quaedam[111] quidem solo proposito et iudicio animae efficiuntur, quaedam etiam per corpus adimplentur, id est vel labore vel patientia corporis. **2** Quaecumque ergo in animae proposito consistunt, haec impedire nullo modo potest satanas, **3** ea vero quae etiam ministerio corporis adimplentur frequenter permissu quidem[112] dei impedire possunt ad probationem eius qui impeditur, **4** ut appareat si a bono proposito nequaquam per huiuscemodi impedimenta mutatur, sicut hi qui *supra petram* seminati dicuntur, **5** *qui ad praesens quidem audientes verbum cum gaudio susceperunt, facta autem tribulatione vel persecutione continuo recesserunt,* **6** vel certe si permanserint in bonis, maioribus praemiis digni sunt quasi qui in certamine vicerint. **7** Sicut et ipse apostolus cum frequenter *proposui*sset Romam proficisci et *prohibitu*m se esse‹t, ut ipse› fatetur,[113] tamen non cessavit a proposito usquequo quod proposuerat expleret, sed per patientiam—**8** sicut sanctus Iob, qui tanta a diabolo passus est cogente se loqui aliquid impium adversus deum, et in nullo penitus ne in sermone quidem regulam pietatis excessit quominus ea sentiret de deo quae par erat, **9** sicut scriptum est de eo quia *In his omnibus nihil peccavit Iob labiis suis in conspectu domini nec dedit insipientiam deo.*

Interrogatio CCIII

(Zelzer 220–21, QF 183, SR 274 [PG 31.1271–1274])

I: Quomodo fit aliquis *in* praesenti *saeculo stultus?*

R: 1 Si timeat sententiam dei dicentis *Vae qui prudentes sunt apud semet ipsos et in conspectu suo sapientes,* et imitetur eum qui dixit *Sicut iumentum factus sum apud te.* **2** Et omnem arrogantiam prudentiae abiciens non prius credat sensibus suis inesse aliquid boni quam mandato domini illuminetur, **3** ut intellegat quid est quod placeat deo sive in opere sive in verbo sive in cogitatione, secundum quod et apostolus dixit **4** *Confidentiam autem talem habemus in Christo ad deum, non quia a nobis ipsis idonei sumus cogitare aliquid quasi ex nobis, se sufficientia nostra ex deo est.*

---

[111] *Et quaedam* CSP, an archetype error, L² 28; omitted Zelz. and most MSS.

[112] *Quidem* Zelz. Following α, confirmed L² 14; *tamen* β.

[113] *Se esse‹t, ut ipse› fatetur* restored L² 72, with Gk: καὶ κωλυθεὶς, ὡς αὐτος ὡμολόγησεν; *se esse fatetur* appears in CHJPS Hol.; *se esse fateretur* Zelz. following most β MSS. As Lundström explains, the archetype error here was *et prohibetus esse fatetur* through skipping from (*es)se(t)* to (*ip)se.*

Question 202

Q: Can Satan hinder the purpose of the holy man, since it is written, *I, Paul tried to come a first and a second time, but Satan hindered us?* (1 Thess 2:18)

R: 1 Of the deeds accomplished in the Lord some are effected solely through the purpose and judgment of the soul, while some are also fulfilled in the body, whether by zeal or patience. **2** What therefore resides in the purpose of the soul, Satan can in no way hinder. **3** Deeds however which are also accomplished through the ministry of the body, can indeed by God's permission often be hindered, for the testing of the one who is hindered, **4** that it may appear whether he changes from his good purpose through hindrances of this kind as they did who are said to have received the seed *upon rock,* **5** *who indeed as soon as they hear the word receive it with joy, but when tribulation or persecution comes, they immediately fall away* (cf. Matt 13:20-21; Luke 8:6, 13), **6** whereas surely if they had persevered in good works they would have been deemed worthy of the great rewards of those who conquer in battle. **7** Just so, the Apostle who, though he had often *proposed* to set out for Rome and been *prevented* as he tells (cf. Rom 1:13), did not, however, desist from his purpose until he fulfilled what he had proposed to do, but through patience, **8** like holy Job, who though he suffered so much from the devil who was urging him to utter some blasphemy against God, yet in absolutely nothing, not even in speech, did he depart from the rule of piety to think thoughts unworthy of God, **9** as it was written of him: *in all these things Job neither sinned with his lips before the Lord, nor gave folly to God* (Job 1:22; 2:10).

Question 203

Q: How does one *become a fool in this* present *world?* (1 Cor 3:18)

R: 1 If he fears that judgment of God who says: *woe to you who are wise in your own estimation and knowledgeable in your own eyes!* (Isa 5:21), and imitates him who said: *I have become as a beast of burden before you* (Ps 72:22). **2** And casting away all arrogance of understanding, he does not credit any good to his own sensibilities until he is illumined by the commandment of God **3** so that he understands what pleases God, whether in work or word or thought, as the Apostle said: *Such confidence, however, we have in Christ toward God, not that we are adequate of ourselves to think anything as coming from ourselves—rather, our sufficiency is from God* (2 Cor 3:4-5).

Appendix 1

Comparative Table of Recensions[1]

The following table[2] is aligned on the first column: the Latin *Regula Basilii*.

A1r RBas[3]	A1s QF	A2 Basiliad	A3 Caesarean/ Studite	A4 Pontic/ Vulgate
1	1	1	no number	LR 1
2:1-57	2:1-57	2	1	LR 2
2:58–69	2:58–69	3	2	LR 3
2:70–73	2:70–73	4	3	LR 4
2:74–93	2:74–93	5	4	LR 5
2:94–112	2:94–112	5 cont.	5	LR 6
3	3	6	6	LR 7
4	4	7	7	LR 8
5	5	8	8	LR 9
6	6	9	9	LR 10
7:14–15	7	9 cont.	11 cont.	LR 15
7:1–10	7 cont.	10	12	LR 14
8:1–25	8	11	13	LR 16
8:26–37	8 cont.	11 cont.	13 cont.	LR 17
9	9	11 cont.	14	LR 19
10	10	13	16	LR 21

11:1–31	11	14	17	LR 22
11:32–41	–	14 cont.	17 cont.	LR 23
	12			LR 23a
	13			LR 23b
12	14	45	42	SR 1
13	15	46	43	SR 114
14	16	47	44	SR 157
15	17	48	45	SR 98
16	18	49	46	SR 3
17	19	50	47	SR 4
18	20	51	48	SR 5
19	21	52	49	SR 287
20	22	53	50	SR 6
21	23	54	51	SR 288
22	24	55	52	SR 289
23	25	56	53	SR 99
24	26	57	54	SR 158
25	27	58	55	SR 159
26	28	59	56	SR 7
27	30	60	57	SR 8
28	29	61	58	SR 9
29	31	62	59	SR 85
30	32	63	60	SR 86
31	33	64	61	SR 187
32	34	65	62	SR 188
33	35	66	63	SR 189
34	36	67	64	SR 21
35	37	68	65	SR 22
36	38	69	66	SR 160
37	39	70	67	SR 161
38	40	71	68	SR 162
39	41	72	69	SR 163

40	42	73	70	SR 23
41	43	74	71	SR 24
42	44	75	72	SR 25
43	–	76	73	SR 26
44	–	77	74	SR 27
45	45	78	75	SR 28
–	46[4]	–	–	–
46	47	79	76	SR 29
47	48	80	77	SR 191
48	49	81	78	SR 126
49	50	82	79	SR 30
50	51	83	80	SR 192
51	52	84	81	SR 193
52	53	85	–	SR 194
53	54	86	142	SR 31
54	55	87	82	SR 88
55	56	88	83	SR 32
56	57	89	143	SR 195
57	58	90	144	SR 196
58	59	91	145	SR 197
59	60	92	84	SR 33
60	61	93	146	SR 34
61	62	94	85	SR 35
62	63	95	86	SR 198
63	64	96	87	SR 36
64	65	97	88	SR 115
65	66	98	89	SR 116
66	67	99	90	SR 37
67	68	100	91	SR 117
68	69	101	92	SR 118
69	70	102	93	SR 119
70	71	103	94	SR 38

71	72	104	95	SR 39
72	73	105	96	SR 40
73	74	106	97	SR 41
74	75	107	98	SR 42
75	76	108	99	SR 43
76	77	109	100	SR 44
77	78	110	147	SR 164
78	79	111	148	SR 165
79	80	112	149	SR 127
80	81	113	101	SR 120
81	82	114	102	SR 96
82	83	115	103	SR 121
83	84	116	150	SR 199
84	85	117	104	SR 166
85	86	118	105	SR 167
86	87	119	106	SR 200
87	88	120	151	SR 97
88	89	121	107	SR 128
89	90	122	108	SR 129
90	91	123	–	SR 130
91	92	124	109	SR 131
92	93	125	110	SR 132
93	93 cont.	126	111	SR 133
94	94	127	112	SR 135
95	95	128	113	SR 168
96	96	129	114	SR 134
97	97	130	115	SR 136
98	98	131	116	SR 100
99	99	132	117	SR 87
100	100	133	118	SR 169
101	101	134	119	SR 141
102	102	135	120	SR 142

103	–	136	121	SR 143
104	103	137	122	SR 144
105	104	138	123	SR 145
106	–	139	124	SR 146
107	–	140	125	SR 147
108	–	141	126	SR 201
109	–	142	153	SR 202
110	–	143	154	SR 279
111	–	144	127	SR 148
112	–	145	128	SR 149
113	–	146	129	SR 150
114	–	147	–	SR 203
115	–	148	130	SR 170
116	–	149	131	SR 171
117	–	150	132	SR 10
118	–	151	133	SR 89
119	105	152	134	SR 45
120	106	153	155	SR 283
121	107	154	135	SR 46
122	108	155	136	SR 47
123	109	156	137	SR 16
–	110[5]	–	–	–
124	111	157	138	SR 204
125	112	158	156	SR 205
126	113	159	157	SR 206
127	114	160	158	SR 207
128	115	161	159	SR 17
129	116	162	160	SR 90
130	117	163	139	SR 151
131	118	164	161	SR 152
132	159	–	311	SR 153
133	119	165	140	SR 122

134	120	166	162	SR 172
135	121	167	163	SR 239
136	122	168	164	SR 208
137	123	169	141	SR 173
138	124	170	165	SR 209
139	125	171	166	SR 240
140	126	172	167	SR 241
141	127	173	168	SR 48
142	–	174	169	SR 49
143	128	175	170	SR 210
144	129	176	171	SR 50
145	130	177	172	SR 51
146	131	178	173	SR 52
147	132	179	174	SR 53
148	133	182	175	SR 280
149	134	180	176	SR 11
150	135	181	177	SR 174
151	136	183	178	SR 211
152	137	184	179	SR 212
153	138	185	180	SR 213
154	139	186	181	SR 54
155	140	187	182	SR 175
156	141	188	183	SR 176
157	142	191	186	SR 243
158	143	192	187	SR 244
159	144	193	188	SR 55
160	145	194	189	SR 215
161	146	195	190	SR 216
162	148	196	191	SR 245
163	147	197	192	SR 217
164	149	198	193	SR 56
165	–	199	194	SR 246

166	150	200	195	SR 247
167	151	201	196	SR 218
168	152	202	197	SR 248
169	153	203	198	SR 219
170	154	204	199	SR 249
171	155	205	200	SR 250
172	156	206	201	SR 251
173	157	207	202	SR 252
174	158	208	203	SR 220
175	–	209	204	SR 57
176	164	210	205	SR 123
177	165	211	206	SR 177
178	166	212	207	SR 178
179	167	213	208	SR 221
180	168	214	209	SR 222
181	169	215	210	SR 137
182	170	216	211	SR 58
183	171	217	212	SR 59
184	172	218	213	SR 60
185	173	219	214	SR 101
186	174	220	215	SR 91
187	–	221	216	SR 179
188	–	227	222	SR 62
189	–	262	255	SR 67
190	175	263	256	SR 68
191	163	277	265	SR 182
192	–	281	302	SR 105
193	176	282	269	SR 73
194	177	283	270	SR 106
195	178	286	272	SR 75
196	179	288	292	SR 94
197	160	332	306	SR 108

198	161	233	307	SR 109
199	162	327	308	SR 110
200	180	289	293	SR 229
201	–	328	309	SR 111
–	181[6]			–
202	182	299	279	SR 275
203	183	295	275	SR 274

Footnotes to Appendix 1

[1] The table is selected and rearranged from BBV III, esp. 9–15.

[2] Cf. Gribomont's three hypothetical orders of question-answers: "X" (Gribomont 165–70) approximating to the *Small Asketikon* and A2; "Y" (Gribomont 171–79) approximating to A3; "V" approximating to A4, the Vulgate of the printed editions.

[3] On the several enumerations and arrangements of the RBas itself, see BBV 5–9. The sequence entered here is that of Holste's edition of 1661 and Zelzer's edition of 1986, which is also the most common in the manuscripts and hence may be considered the *ordo vulgatus*.

[4] One of three question-answers found only in the Syriac. The others are *Ask* 1s 110 and 181.

[5] One of three question-answers found only in the Syriac; the others are *Ask* 1s 46 and 181. *Ask* 1s 110 is edited in Gribomont, 139–41, with French translation.

[6] One of three question-answers found only in the Syriac. The others are *Ask* 1s 46 and 110.

Appendix 2

Three Extra Pieces from the
Questions of the Brothers

The following three *question-answers* do not appear in the RBas or the Greek text of the Great Asketikon. They survive only in the Syriac *Questions of the Brothers* as QF 46, 110, and 181. The Syriac text and translation presented here are drawn without critical apparatus from the author's own critical edition of the QF (with English translation), forthcoming from Brill in the Texts and Studies in Eastern Christianity series.

It may also be mentioned that there are another three extra pieces that appear in just one manuscript of the QF, the thirteenth-century Vat. sir. 126. Two of them concern the conduct of brothers who have been ordained priests, and the other the practice of individual dispossession in community. The third in particular gives a very good imitation of Basil. It seems, however, that these are late specimens of pseudepigraphy. They will be found in an appendix to my critical edition of the QF.

QF 46

Q: ܐܝܟ ܐܡܪܝܢ. ܐܚܐ ܐܢ ܓܝܪ ܠܐ ܡܦܢܐ ܫܠܡܐ ܠܐܚܘܗܝ، ܒܪ ܓܒܗ ܕܐܝܩܪܐ. ܐܝܟܢܐ ܢܣܝܡܝܘܗܝ.٭

R: ܦܘܢܝܐ ܐܡܪܝܢ. 1 ܐܝܢ ܕܡܝܐ ܗܘ ܐܝܟ ܗܘ ܓܘܢ ܟܐܢ ܡܢ ܦܘܩܕܢܐ ܟܠܗ ܡܠܐ ܗܘܐ. ܚܠܦܝܢ ܗܟܘܬ.

Q: The brothers say: If someone does not return the peace to his brother in his rank of honour, how are we to regard him?

299

R: Basil says: **1** One such as this is bereft of serenity and empty of all love. For among all the deeds of love, there is none more modest than the peace of the word. **2** Now if a blessing is given to *peace-makers* (cf. Matt 5:9), of necessity it is also upon those who return it, whereas the opposite of blessing, woe, is upon those who abstain from deeds of blessing, and their life constantly realizes the woe.

3 For David joins peace and righteousness in a single love so that they kiss (cf. Ps 84.10). **4** Hence one who holds aloof from the peace is also a stranger to righteousness, and with a haughtiness that is defiled before God he conducts his life in this world, **5** and is not very far from the punishment of one *whose heart is haughty, and whose spirit was hardened to act loftily*, as it is written (Dan 5:20; Ps 130:1).

QF 110

ܐܠܬ̈ܐ ܐܘܪ ܐܘܪ̈ܐ ܐܡܪ ܐ ܐܚܪ̈ܐ ܐܡܪ ܐܘܪ ܐ ܢ ܐܡܬܐ ܐ ܘ ܟ ܐܘܪ ܐܚܪ̈ܝ ܐ ܐ ܘ ܟ ܢ ܢ ܐܠܬ ܐܠܬ.
ܐܢ ܐܚܪ̈ܐ ܡ ܐܣܘܒܝܐ ܐܡ ܐ ܐ.

ܟܠܡܐ ܐܡܪ 1. ܐܡܪ ܐ ܣ ܐܣܘܝܬܐ ܐܠ ܐ ܡ ܐ ܐ ܐ.

(Syriac text — QF 110)

Q: The brothers say: when a sign of the impurity of the body appears in us during dreams, we want to learn whether this appearance is a sign of culpability?

R: Basil says: **1** In the teaching of Christ we do not have baptisms of purifications for these mishaps. But after that absolving immersion, we do have true compunction of soul which we use for all faults, **2** for it cleanses the uncleanness of a moment when it was not a willing passion, and the evening washes it away and there is no more groaning. **3** This was not a sin that is from the conscience. For the things that are appointed to nature, in which the will is not associated, Scripture does not condemn the effects of their movements as sins. **4** Hence all those things come during dreams, and the sign of the mind's deliberation in its wakefulness does not sully them. One in whom there is no witness of this is a stranger even to the shadow of sin.

5 But let us fear lest sin should overtake us in the wakefulness of our will, and that the form of our anxiety, arising from the vision of the night, should reveal to us the face of sin's wakefulness within us. **6** But if the testimony of good thoughts is in our movements, and it is the body draining away the impurity in its nature, and the flames do not press upon it from passions hissing within it, this mishap is not one of culpability.

7 Nevertheless, let us not pass over even this without a qualm, because it may be a testimony to us from the one who sees all, that not even with what happens to us by chance are we to be at ease, for if we were unable to annul this impulse, and it was stamped with the sign of sins, we possess a commandment concerning it from the teaching of our Lord. **8** Wherefore, let us seek to be delivered from sins that are consigned after the will, the doers of which are condemned by Scripture in the intention that runs with the deed.

QF 181

❖.ܪܟܣܐ ܪܟܘ̱ ܐ ܐܩ ܪܟܣܘ .ܪܟܠܝ ܐܩ ܪܟܣܐ ..ܝܗܣܐܪܟ ܪܟܘܐܪ :Q

ܗܝ ܪܟܠܝܝ 2 .ܪܟܠܐܝ ,ܡܐܘܪܟܣܣ ܪܟܡܝܟܠܐܝܐ ܪܟܐܗܪܟܣ ܗ݂ܗ݂ܝܐܪ ܪܟܘ̱ܐ ܐܗܟܣܝ 1 .ܝܗ݂ܝܐܪ ܥܠܝܣܣ :R
Q: The brothers say: What is *guile* and what is a *wicked mind*? (cf. Rom 1:28-29; Mark 7:21-22)

R: Basil says: **1** Wickedness of mind is a hatred concealed in the secret places of the heart, **2** whereas guile is wickedness veiled under a show of the good, which inflicts pain by a device that is undetected. And just as a trap has on it a sign of food in a device of death, so guile wears an outward face of friendship, so to accomplish its will by a wickedness concealed in common courtesy.

3 For those whose malice is plain, the many are on their guard against meeting them. 4 But that a man should speak with a double heart, and *speak peace with his neighbour, while he devises evil in his heart* (Ps 27:3), this is a great impiety learned from the craft of the Evil One, so that its remission is difficult, perhaps even with penitence.

Appendix 3

Index of Scriptural Citations and Allusions in the *Regula Basilii*

Scriptural references are made according to their appearance in the text of the *Regula Basilii*. Books of Scripture are listed in the order of the Septuagint and Vulgate. The psalms are listed according to their Septuagint and Vulgate numeration and their Septuagint versification (which largely corresponds with the Hebrew). "LXX" identifies a reading peculiar to the Septuagint. Where there are multiple references to a single passage, the earliest only is listed. So for example with the Synoptic Gospels, when some distinctive wording does not identify which gospel, Matthew is used as the default reference.

Genesis						
3:1-6	162.5-6					
3:6	8.10, 121.3					
3:12	121.5					
3:17	121.6					
3:18	195.8					
3:21	11.12					
4:24	122.17					
21:6	8.33					
25:33	8.10					

Numbers	
11:1	93.1
12	44.1
19:18	141.2

Deuteronomy	
4:2	12.9
10:17	112.Q, 132.1
17:11	140.4
25:33	8.12
32:7	Prol.2

2:24	122.9
2:25	7.15

2 Samuel	
7:18	85.1

1 Kings	
19:8	8.13

2 Kings	
1:8	11.33

Exodus	
18:19	13.Q

Joshua	
7:20-26	122.7

Job	
1:22	202.9
8:21	8.33
12:11	110.1
38:3; 49:2	11.35

Leviticus	
19:17	122.1
19:18	141.2
27:28	147.7

1 Samuel	
2:3	166.Q
2:22–4.18	122.8-11

Psalms

1:2	Prol.11
4:4	157.3, 159.1
6	18.1
6:6-8	117.4
7:9	34.1, 79.4,
	108.2
9:23	166.4
15:8	34.2, 109.1
18:8	12.6
18:10	2.111
18:9-10	49.2
18:9-11	150.5
26:4	2.24
29:2	117.7
29:11-12	117.6
33:1	109.3
33:5	12.5, 168.3
38:1-2	136.2
41:1	2.22,23, 14.3
45:10	167.3
46:7	110.Q,3
49:21	Prol.18
51:1	166.4
57:1-2	119.4
57:4	159.2
72:22	203.1
76:4	76.1
93:20	131.2
94:10	Prol.1
100:5	43.1
104:19	49.1
108:6	172.5
108:9	172.5
111:5	162.7
115:12	2.55
118:53	50.1, 147.3
118:106	181.2
118:139	78.1
118:158	23.1
118:163	18.1, 117.2,
	149.Q,3,
	150.3
131:4-5	55.3
132:1-2	3.36,37
139:5	140.4, 190.4
140:5	25.2
142:10	12.4

Proverbs

1:7	2.70
2:6	168.Q
13:8	118.Q
13:13	17.2
13:24	17.6, 25.1
17:11	70.2
19:10	8.5
20:13	43.1
22:24	2.95, 42.4
24:30-31	195.7
26:11	20.2
26:25	20.1

Ecclesiastes

2:2	8.28
4:9	174.7
4:10	3.7, 174.8
7:6	8.28

Song of Songs

2:5	2.17

Wisdom

2:20	134.8

Sirach (Ecclesiasticus)

19:1	17.2
21:23	8.29

Isaiah

1:2-3	152.3
1:3	2.33-34
1:18	117.5
5:2	195.9
5:4	195.9
5:21	203.1
7:9	167.4
53:4	177.1
53:4-5, 11	2.51

Jeremiah

2:21	195.10
9:23-24	167.1
48:10	5.3, 100.2,
	113.2

Ezekiel

18:4, 20	52.2
18:23	123.9
33:8	119.5
33:11	21.1

Daniel

1:6-16; 3:24-28	
	8.14

Amos

5:13	136.1

Malachi

4:2	12.5

Matthew

3:4	8.15, 11.32
3:6	21.6
3:8	19.Q, 21.2,
	26.3
3:10	21.3, 26.3
4:2	8.15
4:3	195.3
4:21-22	4.11
5:3	125.Q,3
5:4	52.Q, 155.3
5:5	47.Q
5:6	90.1
5:8	148.Q
5:9	160.Q
5:11-12	39.8-9,
	156.11
5:16	56.2
5:18	17.1
5:21	157.2
5:22	145.Q
5:23-24	72.5
5:25	180.Q,1,2

5:29	26.4-5, 76.2	15:24	185.4	26:15	195.4
5:29-30	175.4	15:26	185.5	26:51-52	172.2
5:39	158.1	15:26-27	98.1		
5:40	180.2	16:24	2.100,103,	*Mark*	
5:41	12.16		104,	8:35	83.2
5:42	185.Q,1		4.1,17, 69.1	9:34	64.1
5:44	156.Q	18:3	161.Q, 163.Q	9:35	3.35, 11.3,5
5:45	187.5	18:8-9	175.4	10:14	7.1
6:3	58.Q	18:15	5.7	10:29-30	5.5
6:5	166.5	18:15-16	191.3	12:30	14.3
6:8	126.2	18:15-17	16.1-3,		
6:11	173.Q,3		122.2-4	*Luke*	
6:13	179.Q,1	18:17	28.1, 73.1,	1:51	61.Q
6:25	128.Q, 173.1		175.2	1:79	12.5
6:31	91.1, 125.2,	18:25	188.Q	3:11	11.40
	127.Q	18:31	74.1	5:32	178.3
6:31-33	127.2	18:34	74.2	6:21	8.33
6:32	91.2	19:16-21	6.3	6:25	8.31, 53.Q,1
6:34	141.3	19:17	2.14	6:32	39.6
7:5	77.11	19:21	5.1, 8.23,	6:37	77.Q,1
7:6	171.Q		125.3	6:45	135.2
7:7	Prol.13	19:27	118.2	7:47	115.1
7:13	139.Q	19:29	118.3	8:20	32.1
7:14	140.Q	20:15	116.2	9:61-62	33.2
7:22-23	187.2	20:26	12.13, 39.Q,	10:4	172.Q
9:9	4.12		64.1	10:7	95.2, 173.2
10:9	11.36	20:26-27	46.3	10:16	70.3
10:10	99.Q, 129.2	20:28	64.2	12:15	141.Q
10:16	162.Q,1,2	21:28-29	70.Q	12:20-21	141.4
10:22	179.2	22:17, 19-21	196.1-2	12:23	5.1
10:23	158.2	22:36	1.1-3, 39.3	12:29	91.1
11:28	6.1	22:39	2.60, 39.3	12:29-30	127.2
11:29	62.2	22:40	2.2	12:33	185.3
12:35	45.3, 135.Q,1	23:5	187.1	12:40	67.1
12:36	17.1, 40.Q,1,	23:6	10.Q	12:47-48	Prol.16,
	174.3	23:12	62.2		119.Q
12:48, 50	32.2	24:42	Prol.19	12:48	182.1
13:20-21	202.4-5	25:15	114.3	12:57	185.5
13:22	54.Q,1, 126.2	25:18-25	3.18	14:8-10	10.2
13:23	114.2	25:35	2.65, 3.8	14:11	164.Q
13:42	175.4	25:35-36	127.4	14:26	4.8,16, 5.5
14:13, 15	9.14	25:36	3.8	14:33	4.2
14:15	153.1	25:40	2.66, 36.1,	15:6	27.1
15:16-17	168.Q		127.9	16:15	80.2
15:19	195.5	25:42	113.1	16:19-25	125.4

16:20-21	92.1	13:35	2.64	7:17	123.8
16:25	8.7	14:10	184.2	7:24	123.12
17:2	26.1	14:15	2.68,80, 153.1	8:15	4.7
17:10	82.4	14:15-17	124.1	8:32	134.7
19:13	114.3	14:26	125.2	8:35	14.6
19:18	18.3	14:27	160.2	8:35-37	2.104
22:19	134.2	15:10	2.81	11:20	164.Q
22:23	2.104	15:12	2.68	12:5	3.9
22:36	172.Q,3	15:13	29.3,4	12:6	3.13
22:37	172.1	15:12-13	15.4, 38.1	12:7	Prol.1
22:42	81.2	15:19	124.2	12:15	3.12
		15:22	119.2	12:19	158.Q
John		16:13	2.72, 12.1,4,	13:7	63.1
1:14	134.3		29.3	13:13	22.5
3:36	39.1, 122.5	18:10	172.2	13:14	8.6
4:34	84.4, 127.4	19:11	121.1	14:10, 13	77.3
5:14	128.3	20:28	15.4	14:15	72.3
5:19	12.1			15:1	177.Q, 200.4
5:30	111.1, 184.1	*Acts of the Apostles*		15:2	68.1
5:44	63.2	2:37	21.6	15:3	68.2
6:9	9.15	2:44	3.39		
6:27	127.Q	4:32	29.2, 89.2	*1 Corinthians*	
6:37	87.1	4:35	31.5, 91.3,	1:31	166.Q
6:38	12.15, 181.1,		94.3, 111.2	2:9	2.54
	184.2	5:29	13.8	3:1-2	2.71
6:63	125.1	6:4	Prol.3	3:8	66.2
7:24	77.1	12:8	11.34	3:18	203.Q
7:28	80.1	15:26	83.Q	4:1	15.1, 21.4
8:24	53.2	20:35	127.5	4:5	77.8
8:34	120.1	21:11	11.35	4:15	4.7
8:44	120.1			5:2	122.14, 164.2
9:28	41.2	*Romans*		5:3-5	77.5-6
10:5	13.9	1:13	202.7	5:6	30.1
12:25	154.1	1:30	42.Q	5:11	41.Q,1, 147.2
12:35	12.5	2:4	187.5	5:13	30.1
12:44	130.4	2:7	63.Q	5:14-15	134.9
12:48	Prol.15	2:22	5.7	6:1	5.8
12:49	12.2	2:23	17.3, 52.2,	6:7	5.9
12:50	39.2, 83.1,		53.2, 171.1	7:20	98.3, 101.4,
	84.2, 150.4	5:1	160.1		186.2
13:5	3.34	5:8	156.6	7:33	4.8
13:6-9	37.1	6:16	120.3	7:35	60.1
13:8	6.2, 184.6	7:14-15	123.7	9:12	198.1
13:9	184.7	7:15	123.11	9:14	82.7
13:34	30.1, 39.4			9:16	Prol.14

9:25	8.3	10:5	13.5	*Philippians*	
10:10	93.1	11:17	166.Q	1:15	187.6
10:13	179.2	11:27	8.3, 90.2	1:18	187.7
10:23	12.11	11:29	46.5, 191.2	2:2	164.4
10:29	198.1	12:11	166.Q	2:3	46.2, 62.Q,1
10:31	2.92, 56.Q,	12:14	118.5	2:5	65.1
	57.Q, 174.4	12:20	112.Q, 132.1	2:6-7	2.50
11:16	112.2, 133.2	12:21	52.3, 189.Q	2:6-8	134.4-5
11:22	11.7, 31.3			2:8	65.1, 69.1,
11:29	134.1				83.1, 126.1,
12:8	3.15, 168.Q	*Galatians*			131.3, 156.5
12:26	155.4, 191.1	1:10	59.Q, 60.Q,	2:14	71.1
13:2-3	187.Q		63.3, 144.1	3:1	51.Q
13:4	3.5, 142.Q,	1:18	13.11	3:13	151.1
	144.2, 164.Q	2:4-5	87.2,5	3:13-14	82.6
13:4-8	86.4-6	3:1	168.Q	3:19	9.10
13:5	165.Q	3:13	2.52	4:3	166.3
14:26	174.4	5:9	175.5		
14:30	136.3, 137.3	5:13	64.2	*Colossians*	
14:34	136.3	5:17	81.1	1:10	19.1
14:40	10.7, 197.1	5:22	8.Q, 9.Q	1:12	85.2
15:15	15.2	5:22-23	8.1	3:5	2.104
15:31	126.	5:26	146.Q,1	4:6	136.6
15:56	17.4	6:2	178.Q,2		
		6:14	4.8, 82.5	*1 Thessalonians*	
2 Corinthians				2:7	15.3
1:9	126.3	*Ephesians*		2:8	15.3
2:6	3.24, 16.3,	2:3	88.4	2:18	202.Q
	175.2	3:16	2.71	5:20	13.4
3:4-5	203.3	4:2	13.7		
3:5	184.1	4:13	2.72	*2 Thessalonians*	
5:14-15	134.9	4:26	157.Q	3:6	28.1
5:20	160.1	4:28	127.6, 173.1	3:8-9	82.8
6:3	8.2	4:29	40.4, 136.4	3:13	162.2
6:4-6	8.2	4:30	40.5	3:14	16.5, 42.4
6:7-8	59.3	4:31	130.Q,2,3,5,		
6:9	126.5		157.Q,3,	*1 Timothy*	
6:17	2.96		159.Q,1	1:10	183.Q
7:1	147.Q	5:1-2	156.7	2:4	168.1
7:9	72.1	5:17	167.2	2:8	108.3
7:10	50.Q,2, 52.1,	5:19	107.2	2:9	11.27, 143.Q
	72.1	5:21	12.13, 13.7,	3:2	11.27,
7:11	18.1-2,		64.Q		154.Q,2
	122.7, 147.4	6:4	7.1	3:6	100.2
8:21	45.5	6:6	146.Q,2	3:7	123.10

4:3	88.2	3:3	8.9	10:27	12.10, 138.Q,2		
4:6	Prol.1	3:15	7.1	10:28-29	122.16		
5:6	8.6	3:17	Prol.6	12:2	169.1		
5:21	112.1	4:2	16.4, 191.4	12:26	8.10		
5:23	9.17	4:14	42.5				
5:47	115.2						
6:4	164.6	*Titus*		*James*			
6:8	11.9	1:8	170.Q	1:5	167.Q		
				4:6	61.1		
2 Timothy				4:11	43.Q		
2:5	190.4	*Hebrews*					
2:21	11.37	5:12	2.71	*2 Peter*			
3:1-2	8.9	6:4	124.Q	1:4	2.53		
3:2	154.Q, 164.Q	10:23	89.3				

Bibliography

Original Sources

Basil. *Correspondence.* 2d ed. 3 vols. Edited and translated by Yves Courtonne. Paris: Les Belles Lettres, 2003.

Simonetti, Manlius. "Tyrannii Rufini Prologus in Regulam Sancti Basilii, cura et studio M. Simontetti." In idem, ed., *Tyrannii Rufini Opera*, CCSL 20, 239–41. Turnhout: Brepols, 1961.

Zelzer, Klaus, ed. *Basili Regula A Rufino Latine Versa.* CSEL 86. Vienna: Hölder-Pichler-Tempsky, 1986.

Studies

Bamberger, John Eudes. "ΜΝΗΜΝ-ΔΙΑΘΕΣΙΣ The Psychic Dynamisms in the Ascetic Theology of Saint Basil." *Orientalia Christiana Periodica* 34 (1968): 233–51.

Baudry, P. Étienne. "Apports syriaques de la tradition manuscrite du *Petit Ascéticon*. Pour une meilleure connaissance d l'histoire du texte de l'*Ascéticon* de s. Basile le Grand." *Studia Monastica* 50 (2008): 1, 41–68.

Baudry, P. Étienne (conception d'ensemble, choix et présentation des textes). *Petit Recueil Ascétique: inventer une vie en fraternités, selon l'Évangile.* Les 203 *Questions Ascétiques* avec *Lettres* 1, 2 et 14, *Les Regles Morales* 1 à 22 et des textes sur la Prière. Translated and annotated by Marie Ricard and Jean-Marie Baguenard. Spiritualité Orientale 91 (Bégrolles en Mauges: Abbaye de Bellefontaine, 2013).

Brooks, E. C. "The Translation Techniques of Rufinus of Aquileia (343–411)." In Elizabeth A. Livingstone, ed., *Studia Patristica* 18, Book 1, *Historica, Theologica, Gnostica, Biblica, Critica*, 357–64. Oxford: Pergamon Press, 1982.

Chadwick, Henry. *The Early Church.* Rev. ed. London: Penguin, 1993.

Clarke, W. K. Lowther. *The Ascetic Works of Saint Basil.* London: SPCK, 1925.

———. *St. Basil the Great; a Study in Monasticism.* Cambridge: Cambridge University Press, 1913.

Daniélou, Jean, and Henri Irénée. Marrou. *The Christian Centuries: The First Six Hundred Years.* London: Darton Longman and Todd, 1964.

Deferrari, Roy J., trans. *Saint Basil—The Letters.* 4 vols. LCL. Cambridge, MA: Harvard University Press, 1934.

Deseille, Placide. "Eastern Christian Sources of the Rule of St. Benedict." *Monastic Studies* 11 (1975): 73–122.

De Vogüé, Adalbert. "Les Grandes Règles de saint Basile. Un Survol." *Collectanea Cisterciensia* 41 (1979): 201–26.

———. "The Greater Rules of Saint Basil: A Survey." In *In Honor of St. Basil the Great 379,* Word and Spirit 1, 49–85. Still River, MA: St. Bede's Publications, 1979.

———. "Twenty-five Years of Benedictine Hermeneutics—an Examination of Conscience." *American Benedictine Review* 36 (1985): 402–52.

Elm, Susannah. *"Virgins of God." The Making of Asceticism in Late Antiquity.* Oxford: Oxford University Press, 1994.

Fedwick, Paul J. *Bibliotheca Basiliana Universalis III: Ascetica.* Turnhout: Brepols, 1997. See esp. "iii. The Latin Version by Rufinus: *Ask 1r,*" 4–43, and "A Comparative Table Between *Ask 1r, Ask 1s and Ask 4,*" 9–15.

———. "A Chronology of the Life and Works of Basil of Caesarea." In *Basil of Caesarea, Christian, Humanist, Ascetic: A Sixteen-Hundredth Anniversary Symposium,* edited by Paul J. Fedwick. 2 vols. Toronto: Pontifical Institute of Medieval Studies, 1980.

Fry, Timothy, ed. *RB 1980: The Rule of St. Benedict in Latin and English with Notes.* Collegeville, MN: Liturgical Press, 1980.

Gain, Benôit. *L' Église de Cappadoce au IVe Siècle d'après la correspondence de Basile de Césarée 330–379.* Orientalia Christiana Analecta 225. Rome: Pontifical Oriental Institute, 1985.

Gribomont, Jean. "The Commentaries of Adalbert de Vogüé and the Great Monastic Tradition." *American Benedictine Review* 36 (1985): 229–262. Translation of "Les Commentaires d'Adalbert de Voguë et la Grande Tradition Monastique." *Studia Anselmiana* 84 (1982): 109ff.

———. "Obedience and the Gospel: St Basil." *Hallel* 12 (1984): 3–30. Translation of "Obéissance et Évangile selon Saint Basile le Grand," *Supplément de la Vie Spirituelle* 21 (1952): 192–215.

———. "Sed et regula sancti patris nostri Basilii." *Benedictina* 27 (1980): 27–40.

———. "La version Latine de Rufin." In idem, *Histoire du Texte des Ascétiques de Saint Basile*, 95–107. Louvain: Muséon, 1953.

Keating, Thomas. "The Two Streams of Cenobitic Tradition in the Rule of Saint Benedict." *Cistercian Studies* 11 (1976): 257–68.

Kopecek, Thomas A. *A History of Neo-Arianism*. Cambridge, MA: Harvard University Press, 1979.

Laun, Ferdinand. "Die beiden Regeln des Basilius, ihre Echtheit und Entstehung." *Zeitschrift für Kirchengeschichte* 44 (1925): 1–61.

Ledoyen, Henri. "Saint Basile dans la tradition monastique occidentale." *Irenikon* 53 (1980): 30–45.

Lienhard, Joseph T. "Index of Reported Patristic and Classical Citations, Allusions and Parallels in the *Regula Benedicti*." *Revue Bénédictine* 84 (1979): 230–70.

———. "St. Basil's 'Asceticon Parvum' and the *Regula Benedicti*." *Studia Monastica* 22 (1980): 231–42.

———. "The Study of the Sources of the *Regula Benedicti*: History and Method." *American Benedictine Review* 31 (1980): 20–38.

Lundström, Sven. *Die Überlieferung der lateinischen Basiliusregel*. Uppsala: Academia Upsaliensis, 1989.

———. Review of Zelzer, ed., *Basili Regula A Rufino Latine Versa*. *Gnomon* 60 (Munich, 1988): 587–90.

Maran, Prudent, and Julien Garnier, eds. *Opera Omnia Sancti Patris Basili* (originally published Paris: Coignard, 1721–1730); 1839 imprint (Paris: Gaume fr.) republished by J.-P. Migne (Paris, 1857) as *Patrologia Graeca* (PG) vols. 29–32; *Regulae Fusius Tractatae*, vol. 31, 889–1052; *Regulae Brevius Tractatae*, vol. 31, 1051–1305. This version essentially represents a late editing of the Pontic recension of the *Great Asketikon*—what Gribomont calls the "Vulgate" recensions and Fedwick designates as "Asketikon 4." According to Fedwick 1997, the manuscript i303, the "Regius tertius," formerly Regius codex 2895, Paris, Bib. Nat. fonds grec 964, 11th c., used by Garnier as the basis of his edition, represents the best text family of "Asketikon 4"; see also Gribomont, "La version Latine de Rufin," 16.

Maraval, Pierre, ed. and trans. *Grégoire de Nysse: La Vie de Sainte Macrine*. SC 178. Paris: Cerf, 1971.

McCauley, Leo P., et al., trans. *Funeral Orations by Saint Gregory Nazianzen and Saint Ambrose*. FC 22. New York: Fathers of the Church, 1953. Reprint Washington, DC: Catholic University of America Press, 1968. See especially "On St. Basil the Great," 27–99.

Moffat, Ann. "The Occasion of St. Basil's *Address to Young Men.*" *Antichthon: Journal of the Australian Society for Classical Studies* 6 (1972): 74–86.

Murphy, Francis X. "Moral and Ascetical Doctrine in St. Basil." In Elizabeth A. Livingstone, ed., *Studia Patristica* 9, 320–26. Berlin: Akademie Verlag, 1976.

———. *Rufinus of Aquileia (345–411): His Life and Works.* Washington, DC: Catholic University of America Press, 1945.

Peifer, Claude J. "The Origins of Benedictine Monasticism: State of the Question." *American Benedictine Review* 51 (2000): 293–315.

Pouchet, Jean-Robert. "Basile et la tradition monastique." *Collectanea Cisterciensia* 60 (1998): 126–48.

Rousseau, Philip. *Basil of Caesarea.* Berkeley: University of California Press, 1994.

Saint-Laurent, George E. "St. Basil of Caesarea and the Rule of St. Benedict." *Diakonia* 11 (1981): 71–79.

Silvas, Anna M. *The Asketikon of Basil the Great.* Oxford: Oxford University Press, 2005.

———. "Edessa to Casino: the passage of Basil's *Asketikon* to the West." *Vigiliae Christianae* 56 (2002): 247–59.

———. "In Quest of Basil's Retreat: An Expedition to Ancient Pontus," *Antichthon* 41 (2007): 73–95.

———. *Macrina the Younger, Philosopher of God.* Turnhout: Brepols, 2008.

———. "Rufinus' Translation Techniques in the Regula Basili." *Antichthon: Journal of the Australian Society for Classical Studies* 37 (2003): 71–93.

Taylor, David O. K. "Basil of Caesarea's Contacts with Syriac-speaking Christians." In Elizabeth A. Livingstone, ed., *Studia Patristica* 32, 213–19. Leuven: Peeters, 1997.

———. "Les Pères cappadociens dans la tradition syriaque." In Andreas B. Schmidt and Dominique Gonnet, eds., *Les Pères grecs dans la tradition syriaque,* Études Syriaques 4:43–61. Paris: Geuther, 2007.

Voicu, Sever J. "P. Antin. 111, un testimone ignorato delle *Eratopokriseis brevius tractatatae* di Basilio." In Paul J. Fedwick, ed., *Basil of Caesarea: Christian, Humanist, Ascetic,* 565–70. Toronto: Pontifical Institute of Medieval Studies, 1981.

Wathen, Ambrose. "Methodological Consideration of the Sources of the *Regula Benedicti* as Instruments of Historical Interpretations." *Regulae Benedicti Studia* 5 (1977): 101–17.

Zelzer, Klaus., ed. "Zur Überlieferung der Lateinischen Fassung der Basiliusregel." In Franz Paschke, ed., *Überlieferungsgeschichtliche Untersuchungen,* 625–35. Berlin: Akademie Verlag, 1981.